# WHERE
# GIANTS TROD

# MONTY BROWN

# WHERE GIANTS TROD

## The saga of Kenya's desert lake

*Foreword by*
**Sir Vivian Fuchs**

**Quiller Press**

# DEDICATION

*With deep gratitude to my parents who fostered in me a love for wild and lonely places.*

Distributed in the USA by

SAFARI PRESS
A division of The Woodbine Co.
P.O. Box 3095
Long Beach, California 90803 USA

First published 1989
by Quiller Press Ltd, 46 Lillie Road, London SW6 1TN

ISBN 1 870948 25 4

Initial design concept by Peter Moore

Maps drawn by David Cox

Designed by Jim Reader

Design and production in association with Book Production Consultants, Cambridge

Typeset by Cambridge Photosetting Services

Origination by Anglia Graphics, Bedford

Printed and bound in Singapore by Kyodo-Shing Loong

*The land, through which we have gone to search it, is a land that eateth up the inhabitants thereof; and all the people that we saw in it are men of great stature. And there we saw the giants, the sons of Anak, which come of the giants: and we were in our own sight as grasshoppers, and so we were in their sight.*

Numbers 13 v. 32–33.

# CONTENTS

## STRIDING ONWARDS

# FOREWORD

FOR one who first visited Lake Rudolf nearly sixty years ago, and knew its joint discoverer, Lieutenant von Höhnel, it has been a long wait for a full history of exploration in the area. Indeed the harsh desert region of northern Kenya has been curiously neglected in the literature, bar the few books of the explorers themselves. In this work Monty Brown tells a wide ranging story of events during the latter part of the nineteenth century.

The book opens with a discussion of the surviving tribal beliefs that a race of giants once ranged the area—hence the title. Turning to factual matters there are useful descriptions of the nomadic peoples, which prepare the scene for the arrival of the white man. First came Count Teleki and von Höhnel in 1888, whose discovery led many others to venture into the harsh new lands. For most it seems to have been the excitement of big-game hunting that was the draw. Even so, the majority contributed to knowledge by plotting their routes, and specimen collections. Many approached the area from Somaliland or Ethiopia so the story covers a wide region to the north and east of Lake Rudolf itself.

As each traveller enters the story there is a brief biography giving the background leading up to his African venture. But it is not all explorers; noted administrators, the first traders and the beginning of the King's African Rifles are all discussed in some detail.

Altogether this is a comprehensive account, carefully researched and including unpublished material. For me, as I am sure it will be for others knowledgeable about the area, it has been an eye-opener. I certainly congratulate the author on a splendid work which has long been needed.

*Vivian Fuchs*

Sir Vivian Fuchs
May 1988

# AUTHOR'S NOTE

THE theme of this book is giants—the men who lived and travelled in a land of giant proportions. As defined in the *Concise Oxford Dictionary* a giant is a 'being of human form but superhuman stature; person of extraordinary ability, courage, strength, etc.' The pages to follow are full of giants. They came from differing races, differing cultures and ambitions, and there are even some mythical ones for good measure. In the rugged land of northern Kenya seventy years and more ago, only men of such calibre could survive and make a success of life.

Over the last thirty-five years, extensive wanderings in the lonely district in a variety of capacities have provided me with ample opportunity to make an intensive study of that marvellous land, but the inspiration to write about it did not arrive until recently. The catalyst was Baroness Marietheres Waldbott Bassenheim. The daughter of Count Wickenburg—the extraordinary Austrian explorer of many continents—she was instrumental in encouraging my thinking towards the little known exploration of Lake Rudolf.

The original concept was to produce a story of early days in northern Kenya that would have a popular appeal, while at the same time keeping a strict accuracy in all its details. The end result maintains that aim, and is a compendium of subjects, each an entity in itself, but all part of the whole and held together by a common bond—the historical metamorphosis of the region.

In this work I have inadvertently composed a salute to men of many diverse races. They all played their part. From the beginning my intention was to give the account a strong biographical accent. Part of the fascination of history is the assemblage of characters who make it by shaping its course. In the formative years herein described, many outstanding men were involved, and several of them, as I learnt during my research, had never before been portrayed. The eagerness to subject themselves to hardships—sickness, hunger (sometimes to the point of starvation), and loneliness, to name but some—was a test a few hardy individuals appeared willing to undergo. It seemed immaterial whether it was for the honour of their country, or to hunt wild animals in untrodden gamefields, or to trade with the indigenous inhabitants, so long as there was a challenge to confront.

To keep strictly within the context of the times recorded I have employed certain names no longer in use today. Abyssinia takes the place of Ethiopia, and East Africa stands for present-day Kenya (east Africa, incidentally, covers Ethiopia, Kenya, Somalia, Tanzania and Uganda). The two principal features, Lakes Rudolf and Stefanie, are now named Turkana and Chew Bahir respectively.

While the core of the tale is in the region of Lake Rudolf, the very extent of exploration takes one outside the boundaries of East Africa and into Abyssinia, Somaliland, Sudan and Uganda. East Africa's story, in its complexity, is inextricably bound up with those near neighbours, and hence the repeated mention of their politics and intentions. By understanding them one can better appreciate the problems facing the administrators of the British East Africa Protectorate.

Compiling this account has been a fascinating task, in many ways a revelation of what is little known about or appreciated today of the region's history. At all times it was highly entertaining. In support of my efforts to depict the atmosphere of those distant days I must add a few words from Stewart Edward White's *The Land of Footprints*, a charming account of the famous American writer's trip to East Africa in 1911: 'To set down the formulation of an ideal is one thing: to fulfil it is another. In the following pages I cannot claim a fulfilment, but only an attempt.' This then, is *my* attempt.

Monty Brown
Naro Moru 1989

# ACKNOWLEDGEMENTS

I N five years of research and writing I have enjoyed the assistance of many individuals and the facilities of institutions around the world. Most of these have been mentioned in the Text Notes at the end of the book. There were, however, others, and to them I wish to express appreciation for their co-operation in the face of endless requests and questions, and for so ably helping in my often difficult quests.

Foremost were the staff members of the Royal Geographical Society: Mrs Christine Kelly, the Archivist, a friend and fellow sleuth who helped me run to ground several elusive characters; David Wileman, the Librarian, who was always patient and considerate; Francis Herbert and John Finch of the Map Room, who produced a succession of maps for my inspection; and Nigel Winser, the Expedition Officer, who exhibited a steadfast enthusiasm for my project right from the start. These and others in the Society encouraged me with their friendliness and interest.

In my searches in Rhodes House Library, Oxford, I was given every assistance by the Librarian, Mr Alan Bell, and also Mr Lodge. Working in the up-to-date efficiency of the Public Records Office at Kew was always a pleasure, and at its equivalent in Nairobi, the National Archives of Kenya, I met with courteous and willing assistance. Lesley Forbes of the Oriental Library in Durham University always seemed to find the material I wanted. Others who came up with answers to my questions were the staffs of the Archives Nationales, Section Outre-Mer, Paris; Bibliothèque Nationale, Paris; Bodleian Library (Photo Section), Oxford; the British Institute, Nairobi; London Library; McMillan Memorial Library, Nairobi; Royal Air Force Museum, Hendon; Royal Automobile Club; Royal Commission on Historical Manuscripts; Royal Commonwealth Society; Royal Greenjackets Museum; Royal Scottish Museum, Edinburgh; Society for Psychical Research; The Orders and Medals Research Society; and the Whitehall Library (Ministry of Defence), London. Across the Atlantic my work took me to New York, where I visited the American Geographical Society, the Butler Library at Columbia University, the New York Historical Society, and the Public Library. In California I spent time in the Los Angeles County Museum Library, the Munger Library at the California Institute of Technology, and the University Library (U.C.L.A.). Important material also came from the South African National Museum of Military History.

My thanks go to trusting friends—Edwin Bristow, Fergus McCartney, Ray Mayers, Patricia Powys, Michael Prettejohn and Ken Smith—who kindly lent me books.

Three vital components in the creation of this story receive my gratitude for their able assistance, tolerance and encouragement. One of them, Anthony Lambert, my editor, entered the race at a late but important stage. His sympathetic treatment of the text gave me great relief. The other two, Dr Paul Robinson and my wife Barbara, joined at the very beginning. Paul was a steady generous staff on which to lean; Barbara shared my enthusiasm, at times with considerable forbearance, and was a discerning critic of the text in draft form. In the end she was the long-suffering typist who, with great patience, prepared the final script.

There were many others round the world who proffered ideas, words of advice and above all enthusiastic support. In the final say they were the stimulus that kept me going.

# PROLOGUE

*'On such occasions it would seem to me in
my simplicity that no continent could be
more beautiful, more admirable, than Africa.'*

Llewelyn Powys, *Black Laughter*

KENYA'S remote northern lands are hot, arid and intensely thirsty. Infrequent exceptions are few isolated mountain ranges, on whose aloof summits cool evergreen forests flourish, fitfully nurtured by the life-giving moisture gained from high-flying clouds soaring inland from the distant Indian Ocean. It is a country of barren and immense aspects, twisted and rended by the cataclysmic convulsions of a long-ago past. Within it lies a unique landscape in which there may be found the only true desert of large extent in East Africa, and the far-reaching stretch of water that was once named after a tragic European prince by the first white men to bring it to the notice of the outside world. Both these geographical curiosities are fringed by a seemingly endless turmoil of bleak lava ridges and desolate plains, where the surface of the earth is studded with boulders of many shapes and sizes; it brings to one's mind the stark prospect of a giant battlefield grimly littered with cannon shot. There, too, are countless acres of stunted acacia bushes, heavily armed with vicious thorns that pierce with the finesse of the stiletto or tear with the ruthlessness of the cat's claw. At times relentless buffeting winds pour across these wastelands, billowing clouds of dust and dirt as they pursue their fruitless chase over the desert land. And always the sun burns down, desiccating and browning the land. The air is dry, pitilessly withdrawing moisture from plant and beast alike, palpitating in the heat of day like a live thing bent on distorting the inherent beauty of this alluring and strangely lonesome corner of the earth. In this unforgiving land life's battle for existence continues as it always has, nature on occasion still holding the upper hand.

The eye may detect in this primitive place a constant blend of the ancient and the *'a country of barren* modern; the oldest rocks on earth, in the shape of mighty granite masses, rise with *and immense* dramatic power, often in sharply angled slopes and sheer escarps to reach their summit *aspects'* peaks thousands of feet above the plains shimmering in the heat haze far below, while

near neighbours of these silent reminders of an ancient era are the black scoriaceous lava fields, some erupted within recent times, stark and sterile to everything but a few struggling fragments of sparse vegetation. In between these limits of the time scale come the residues of erosion, heat-fractured and wind-blasted: sands from the granite rocks—red and clear grains of silica—alternate with the heavy loams and clays of lava flow disintegration. It is amongst these soils that many hardy plants proliferate, greening and blossoming with the rain seasons, withering and browning in the dry periods, demonstrating a continuous miracle of survival, in which the excitingly beautiful cycle of regeneration after the fall of rains is complemented by the starkness of grim drought.

Humans and wild beasts have lived in this land since time immemorial, witnessing years of plenty when the land was lush, the climate damper and kinder. The faltering early footsteps of man took place in those conditions, his eyes registering scenes quite different from those of today, when strange creatures of the wild shared his territory and provided him with food and raiment. Most are gone now. Over the millenia, as climatic changes altered the tableau, both facets of life—plant and animal—were influenced by the gradual drying up of their environment. Ancient peoples adjusted their ways of life to bend with the dictates of nature, endlessly manoeuvring in their need to maintain survival on a quietly dying land. Jostling, marching, fighting and mingling, they used their territories as best they could, ever seeking better horizons and weaker neighbours to oppress and destroy. In the process

*'acacia bushes, heavily armed with vicious thorns, contrast with black scoriaceous lava fields. . .'*

*'many hardy plants
proliferate,
demonstrating a
continuous miracle
of survival and
regeneration. . .'*

they enriched themselves, often for only a short space of time before in turn some stronger group arrived to exercise its power and establish a new domination.

Into this remote backwater of Africa—one of the last unexplored areas of the Dark Continent—the first white men slowly filtered during the final decade of the nineteenth century. With the discovery of a great lake, named at the time Lake Rudolf, an enticing new Mecca for prospective explorers was revealed. An irresistible attraction drew travellers to the lake; it was, in fact, the last major expanse of captive water on the continent to release its mysteries to geographers. Wanderers of many nations

turned their thoughts and footsteps towards that dramatic place. Who could tell what exotic discoveries still awaited on the trails to the sparkling lake, lying imprisoned in a land of such desolation.

Screened from the outside world by the mighty Abyssinian mountains to the north, the flat, arid and seemingly endless wastes to the east, the unhealthy horrors of the Nile lowlands in the west, and the refreshing highlands to the south, the beckoning sheet of water lay in its bed of no escape. Whipped by lashing winds and burnt by the intensity of the relentless equatorial sun, it is always reliant on the caprices of the tropical rainy season for replenishment.

And so the curious came in their numbers: sportsmen, naturalists, aristocrats and soldiers, approaching from all quarters of the compass. They came to satisfy their interests, some to tarry and study in detail, others to pass hurriedly on in their ardent pursuit of further new adventures and geographical quests. One of East Africa's best-renowned old-time ivory hunters trod countless miles in these parts following the lure of his game; another, a naturalist, trudged the endless wastelands making observations of remarkable accuracy which proved invaluable to those who followed; and yet another walked through on his way to the highlands of the south, where he finally dedicated his fortune, and his life, towards the development of that unique and wondrous equatorial land.

During the opening years of the twentieth century, an epicentre of human drama thrived in this obscure and isolated corner of the continent, far removed from the more apparent arenas of the outside world's labours. In its own small way it was a magnificent stage, on which acts and scenes ranging from full comedy to heavy tragedy were played. A few of the characters, through feats of arms or administrative ability in the course of their service, started their upward climb to positions of great repute, while others paid the untimely and ultimate price, and were laid to rest in lonely, unmarked and now long-forgotten spots.

*'a new Mecca for prospective explorers'*

ABOVE: *'the plains shimmering in the heat haze far below'*

RIGHT: *'a giant battlefield grimly littered with cannon shot'*

This derelict land was the focal point for a hotch-potch of conflicting forces. The wide variety of neighbouring peoples residing there, together with their contentious ambitions, produced tribal frictions and strife in many forms of deviousness and brutality. Border disagreements arose over the disputed boundary separating the British East Africa Protectorate from Abyssinia, in itself an artificial line which split tribal units and disrupted the passage of peoples within their ancestral lands. To these were added the pressures arising from Menelik's influence in Abyssinia, with his desire for territorial expansion ever southwards, and deep incursions of sizeable, well-armed bands of Abyssinian elephant hunters and stock rustlers which necessitated continuous counter operations by the authorities. As a result, the region came to be likened to a constantly stoked-up witch's cauldron, the fires sometimes sinking low as periods of good rainfall gave prosperity and peace of mind to the pastoral residents, boundary disputes were temporarily resolved following negotiations between Britain and Abyssinia, and disciplinary expeditions managed to gain the upper hand over the raiders from the north, when law and order would again prevail. These moments were never permanent, and in a harsh and bitter land where life is an eternal struggle with the elements and one's neighbours, the fire's flames often leapt up with renewed vigour, sometimes in unexpected and unusual circumstances, more often than not in predictable situations.

The turbulent character of Kenya's Northern Frontier District, as it once was entitled, has persisted into present times, albeit in a modified and updated form. To this day the endless swaying and striving of combatants continues, in an unceasing battle for survival and dominance in a land of great age, beauty and harshness; where, as always, there is little compromise between man and nature, and weaklings of body and mind do not survive for long.

# THE MYTHICAL GIANTS

*'There were giants on the earth in those days . . . the same became mighty men . . . men of renown.'*

Genesis 6 v. 4

THE hunter was a two-footed giant! He towered a gargantuan ten feet above the ground, his arms the thickness of doum palm trunks, his legs proportionately larger; he was a man of superhuman dimensions, in appearance a small giant, but all the same, just a human. His intended victim was a true giant too, but differed, being four-footed and simply a blundering rhinoceros, over a ton in weight, short of sight, and minding its own business in a fiercely hot land. Stealthily the hunter approached, carrying his weapon, a heavy volcanic boulder three feet in diameter, with ease, and ready for the final assault. The rhinoceros chewed contentedly at some herbage, contemplating a shady place in which to escape the torrid heat of midday. With silent steps the giant stalked from the rear of the unsuspecting pachyderm, poised the rock above his head, and dashed it down on the victim's neck. The rhinoceros collapsed without a sigh. A knife flashed, the recumbent's head was severed, raised on high, and the gouting blood was swiftly drained by the victor.

This tale was related in an equally evocative style by a Turkana tribesman, his

*A fine example of cairn grave situated at the foot of the Hurri Hills in northern Kenya.*

contribution to an entertaining set of camp-fire stories that told of thrilling feats performed by the mighty men of legend who spread over most of Kenya's northern lands in centuries past.

Who were those mythical giants of tribal lore? Their story is still an unsolved mystery which has long attracted attention from archaeologists and ethnographers. They have questioned the indigenous peoples of the region, pondered, and more recently initiated excavations of the ubiquitous burial cairns found throughout that barren country. The people who formerly lived there left nothing to indicate who they were, apart from their mute skeletons and a paucity of artifacts, giving no clues as to their point of origin or reasons for their disappearance.

Myths in Africa often die hard, especially among the nomadic peoples who live in distant parts and lack modern entertainment facilities. Within the pastoral groups of Kenya's far north, old tribal tales and traditional histories still play a significant part in the passing of leisure time, alongside discussions on the weather, their livestock and the state of grazing lands. The familiar fables tell of a legendary race of giants who were by repute capable of Herculean acts of strength, diggers of immense wells and herders of cattle, who allegedly lie buried beneath the stone cairns found dotted over their former territory, stretching from Mandera in the east to Turkanaland in the west. Very few of the present-day nomads living in the giants' former haunts have access to the learned papers written on the undecided question of their existence, and with far more vital matters to occupy their minds, they allow the mysterious people to live on in hereditary folklore.

Tantalisingly, there is still much that remains unknown about them, and many questions stand unanswered. For instance, how far did those men of myth spread their influence over the land? In part answer, evidence in the shape of burial cairns may be seen all over northern Kenya, some even being found far to the south on the lowest of Mt Kenya's slopes, clear signs of a long-departed race. Did these same far-ranging giants belong to a single ethnic group? Most nations have their giants of fable, and the various tribes living in the remote deserts of Kenya are certainly no exception: the Turkana with their rhinoceros-killing Nyam Nyams; the diminutive Sanya group with their Gojamas, who were legendary men of great size, likened to tailless apes, shy and rarely seen, but endowed with prodigious strength; the Gabbra, Samburu and Rendille with their lofty Wardai pastoralists; or the Borana and Somalis with their mighty well-digging Madanle. All these people have giants looming large in their hereditary folk-tales, awesome legends which impress on the listener the gigantic size and immense physical powers ascribed to their heroes. Whether in fact all these beings originally belonged to one great family group is a question that still evades a sure answer.

Over the years in which white men explored and administered Kenya's frontier region, many among them took a keen interest in the visual and oral evidence that pointed to the former existence there of a long-departed race of people. The information they assiduously garnered told of an ancient race who undertook formidable tasks, such as the construction of extensive well systems and the fabrication of complex burial cairns. Both feats called for considerable physical effort, and in their very immensity they helped to create the impression of giant men's handiwork. Some of these early investigators' findings contained tantalising ideas, which have since been revised and modified to accord with conclusions reached by more recent discoveries. Others are simply speculative, implanting in the reader's mind a feeling for the mystery attached to the people of lore. They have all helped to create a mystical atmosphere, adding another dimension to the attraction of this tiny corner of a continent already rich in ethnic, geographical and political interest.

Whoever the ancient people were, with their multiplicity of titles, it is improbable that their full story will ever truly be known. Were they, in all the huge expanse of territory they appeared to live in, simply one race, loosely bound by necessity in local units made up from confederations of herders, farmers and hunters? Did they have iron, and consequently ironsmiths, for no iron artifacts have been found so far in their graves or elsewhere? What language did they speak? The Somalis claim their giants spoke a Somali language, or variation of it, whereas the Borana claim theirs spoke a Borana-type language. Historic evidence can prove that neither side has a clear legitimate claim: the Somali culture only evolved in the northern section of Somalia in the fourteenth century; and until the sixteenth century the Borana language was used only in a very small area of Abyssinia. The problem of determining what language was used is complex, especially for a race which has no written history. Maybe they conversed in a language common to the whole region, with different dialects among the geographically separated groups, or alternatively, within the classes of cattle herders, cultivators and hunters. The latter system in a tribal group was quite possible: it exists amongst the Ajuran and Garre Somali today.

Historically, contact between the Somali people and the white man occurred long before a similar association began with the inland tribes, so one can safely assume that the earliest notes on the ancient wells and cairns were written following the interrogation of Somalis. Although their country is strictly speaking outside the borders of this book, their opinions are taken into consideration, for it is of value to compare what is held about the mythical people of both the eastern and western sections of northern Kenya, both through the medium of tribal tales and the conjectures of white men.

The mysterious ancients are known to the Somalis by the name Madanle. Several spelling variations of this title have been used in literature on the subject, resulting from the aural whims of alien interrogators down the years*. The names Madhinleh, Madanleh, Medenli, Madanli, Mathanli and Maanthinle are but some of those encountered in print, all bearing the same ring to the ear, but creating a confusing medley in the written word. The title Madanle is made up of two Somali words: Madan being a type of grass growing in the area, and -le meaning 'the people of'. Does this appellation suggest a pastoral race?

Early commentators on the Madanle's legendary achievements—well digging and cairn building—have much to say on the subject, and some of their revealing comments are well worth considering, if for no other reason than to give a background to later, more sophisticated reasonings.

In 1911, Lieutenant Leycester Aylmer, who was soon to meet his untimely end in the district, wrote a paper for the Royal Geographical Society describing an expedition he made from the Juba river across to Lake Rudolf. On reaching Wajir he was so

---

*The confusion was created by the polyglot procession of explorers who passed through the region between 1888 and 1909: Americans, Austrians, Britons, Frenchmen and Italians each publicised their interpretation of place- and tribal-name spellings.

impressed with the large number of wells he found there, all bored down through layers of hard limestone rock, that he took careful measurements of their dimensions. He made a note that most of them were circular and averaged three feet in diameter at the mouth, the water level resting between 22 and 28 feet (6.75 and 8.5 metres) below the surface of the ground. On making local enquiries into the identity of the well diggers he was given two different answers: some of his informants asserted that a tribe of Galla origin had done the work, while others insisted they were excavated by the 'Mathanli' people who had long since disappeared without trace. Aylmer also mentioned seeing many 'curious piles of igneous rocks' in the same area. His simple explanation for these 'piles' was that an early race had tidied up the ground adjacent to the watering points, and in the course of their industry they had stacked the rocks into mounds. This was just one of the many pioneer observations that excited closer scrutiny by later investigators, resulting in a mixed assortment of intriguing theories on the wells and their constructors. For the most part the ancient excavations and stone works in the Somali districts were attributed to the mysterious Madanle of the remote and hazy past.

In 1913, two years after Aylmer, came I.N. Dracopoli, an enthusiastic member of the sportsman-wanderer brigade who combined his passion for hunting with seeking untrod country to explore. In his account describing the first crossing of Jubaland to the Lorian Swamp he made a brief mention of the Madanle: 'the Maathinle, that mysterious tribe known by hearsay to all the dwellers in the horn of Africa, but which have now completely disappeared, leaving no trace except their name, and a few cairns of stone'. His informants produced an unusual little folk-tale about the 'race of giants' who had, apart from building cairns, cut many pools into the rocks of northern Jubaland. The tale went thus: 'it was believed that these people had done evil and had ceased to sacrifice to their god, at which the latter was so displeased that he sent a plague of bees which killed some and drove the rest out of the country'.

John Llewellin, in 1914, was one the earliest British administrators stationed at Wajir. In his time he was regarded as a local authority on the customs of the Somali people. One of his early notes told of a group of 'half Somalis named the Rahanwein' who existed in the Wajir area prior to the early part of the nineteenth century and were reputed to be 'very good at digging for water'. The supposition expressed by a section of his informants was that the Rahanwein were responsible for digging the Wajir wells some two hundred years before the arrival of the white man. But the majority of Somalis living in the area disputed this and were adamant that the deep wells were 'dug by a race of giants'. Could they have meant any but the Madanle?

During 1927, a man named Watson wrote an article in which he presented some plain facts on the construction of the wells and cairns found in the north-eastern corner of Kenya. He also came to a few conclusions about the people who made them. Although now outdated, his ideas reflect the thinking of the day, so they are worth recounting. The first point he brought to notice was the existence of two schools of thought on the subject, which confirms that these creations had aroused curiosity in many enquiring minds. Curiosity, indeed, which prompted diverse theories. One channel of thinking even attributed the Wajir cairns to volcanic origin; a somewhat strange idea in an area of strictly sedimentary formations comprised mainly of stratified limestone. That naive idea was obviously born of a mind untrained in the science of geology, and did not survive for long.

Those holding the opposite view, as Watson stated, 'believe in an ancient civilisation of a people who have left behind them no trace save their feats as water engineers and cairns that yield no bones, implements or records of any kind. This tribe has been called "the Medenli" '. Watson's paper almost persuades one to believe in a mystery race. It was a romantic piece of writing in many ways, if the word romantic may be permitted in describing an article from a solid ethnographic publication. Nevertheless, it did excite some interesting questions on the ancient people. Based on statistics in his paper, Watson postulated that the 'Medenli' occupied a land that was once far better watered and hospitable to humans and their stock, and he also computed that they must have been 'immensely numerous and wealthy'; a fact he substantiated by his 1927 count of four hundred wells in an area of two square miles around Wajir. In that year, he remarked, only two wells were needed to give an adequate water supply for the community of three hundred people who lived in the vicinity. He asked: 'Who then could these people have been who have required this immense water supply obtained by such laborious feats of engineering?' Furthermore, he suggested that the 'Medenli' were 'clever water diviners' and 'cunning engineers'.

With ancient wells and water supplies the overriding theme, this is a convenient point at which to digress a little and look at the hydrological conditions which have existed in east Africa over the last 10,000 years, bearing in mind that Watson, and later, Parkinson, both suggested that the Madanle may have lived in climatically more hospitable times. Long before the appearance of these people, the Pluvial Periods took place; they were significant times in east Africa's climatic history, when exceptionally wet conditions prevailed over the country for thousands of years, filling lakes of greater size than those extant today, and forming substantial rivers. One result of the abnormal wetness was the prevalence of generally cooler and lusher conditions. Following the last major Pluvial Period, which ended about 10,000 years ago, came two post-pluvial wet phases, the final one occurring around 1,000 years b.c. The Stone Age men who occupied east Africa in pluvial days were hunter-gatherers, but around 5,000 years ago, concomitant with the gradual drying up of the climate and the resultant recession of the lakes and rivers, a new lifestyle and economy for the early peoples appeared in the shape of pastoralism. As desiccation progressed, pastoralism became more widespread. In comparison to the present day there were almost certainly better water resources, both above and below ground. With water readily available, it is thought that the pastoralists led a much more static and settled life than they do in present times. In turn that led to the establishment of group communities larger than those found today; this is substantiated to a certain degree by visible concentrations of archaic burial cairns clustered around present-day waterholes, wells and springs, all of which undoubtedly produced ample supplies of vitally needed water in the days when the ancients lived there. With the increasingly drier climate that came in the wake of the last Pluvial Period, surface water supplies steadily diminished, some even disappearing underground and being obtainable only by the digging of wells. The reduction of water stocks also took place below ground level, with a dropping water-table gradually forcing the pastoralists to extend their wells ever downwards in the hunt for supplies adequate for their herds.

Returning to Watson's idea that the 'Medenli' had a special aptitude for water divining, it is doubtful whether in reality they had an unusual gift in this art. There are many people living in Kenya's desert lands today who are perfectly able to find well sites without the aid of modern instruments. The success of the 'Medenli' at water divination may be accounted for by the fact that underground water was not far beneath the surface, with the result that for a people instinctively able to detect the presence of water in familiar terrain it was not particularly hard to locate. A titillating fantasy recorded in the late 1920s by Pease, then an administrative officer at Mandera, recounts a quaint and rather frivolous Somali tradition that endowed the Madanle with the possession of unusually long noses, giving them the power to smell out water far underground. The peculiarity, it was also said, led to them being recognised as superbeings, compared with other races.

Complementary to the locating of ground water is the storing of the element, and it would be appropriate at this point to consider the methods the ancients may have used in the construction of their famous wells. No one knows what types of implements they had at hand, or whether they possessed instruments of iron to tackle the hardest formations. The material through which they bored in their quest for water was of many textures and scales of hardness, from soft and friable river-bed conglomerates to hard seams of limestone. In the softer formations digging sticks would undoubtedly have sufficed, and in a land of hard stemmed acacia trees the availability of these would have presented no problem. With a sharpened wooden point tempered by fire an excellent tool was at hand for jabbing away at soft rocks. The problem of harder rocks such as limestone no doubt presented greater difficulties, and would have entailed a long drawn-out process involving the initial cracking of the material by a series of fires on the site of excavation. If iron tools were available, many difficulties would have been eased, and it is just possible that iron may have been known to the ancients, although none has been found archaeologically. The Iron Age commenced about 3,000 years ago, and it could reasonably be assumed that at least some iron found its way to east Africa's coast within the last thousand years or so. Excavated graves have, however, held only artifacts of obsidian and chert, so one can well appreciate that iron, even if it did exist in the community, was of too much value to bury forever underground. It may never be known with what instruments the enormous well excavations at El Wak, Le and Gof were made, but none the less one can only admire the ancient race's extraordinary accomplishments, made with the assistance of limited and primitive tools.

Despite all Watson's statistics and postulations, he was unable to arrive at any definite conclusions, and he finalised his writing with the ever-recurring question: who built the wells? His earlier paragraphs, however, put forward the notion of a race which had disappeared into thin air, possibly the giants of classical folk-tales.

In 1927, the same year Watson was making his observations, another investigator, A.T. Curle, assisted the District Commissioner in his excavation of a large burial cairn of stone at Mandera, in the far north-eastern corner of Kenya. Later that year he repeated the operation on another, even larger, cairn at Wajir. Both cairns were carefully measured before operations commenced, and each important find was clearly described in an article that he wrote for publication six years afterwards. In it he explained that when the stones forming the Mandera cairn had been moved aside he found fragments of an earthenware bowl. After piecing them together, a vessel of unusual shape and design was revealed, unlike anything used by the people living in that region at the time of excavation. He commented that 'it's [sic] fragility would render it unsuited to the requirements of a nomadic race'. This remark suggests a race of people of habits different from the 'nomadic Gurreh' who inhabited the Mandera district during the time of Curle's excavation, and who, incidentally still live there. Adjacent to the bowl fragments Curle found pieces of clearly identifiable human bones, all in a very fragile state. From the position of the bones it appeared that the body had been buried at ground level in a sitting position and then covered by a chamber of wood, which had long since deteriorated and collapsed. Curle's excavation of the Wajir cairn revealed no bones, but here again he found fragments of a bowl 'exactly similar' to the Mandera bowl, implying that the people who lived in this area were of the same race as those at Mandera. On being questioned by Curle about the identity of the cairn builders, the local Somalis came up with a variety of replies. The following sample quite pointedly referred to the legendary giants: 'Somali tradition in Kenya ascribe them [the cairns] to the "Madanleh", who they maintain were supermen of great stature, who dug the wells which are still in use today at Wajir, and whose descendants were driven out to the Lake Rudolf area by the Galla'. These claims could hardly be more emphatic.

In 1935, John Parkinson, a geologist, very briefly summarised the comments made by Watson, Curle and other pioneer investigators. On the whole they tallied with his own findings at Wajir, where he in turn had made a careful examination of a cairn and found under it human bones and pottery. Again, the bones were found in a fragile state and placed at ground level, confirming earlier observations that no effort had been made to dig graves in the hard limestone. While Parkinson made no attempt to identify those buried beneath the cairns, he suggested that the unknown people had in all probability lived in the area during more hospitable times, and that with the onset of drier conditions they had been forced to dig for their water. The wells, he assumed, gradually had to be deepened as the water-table dropped, a situation which must have been universal throughout the country where the Madanle and their western relations lived. As conditions became even more critical, Watson's 'immensely numerous' Madanle and their huge herds of stock may have perished, or more likely, emigrated. Alternatively, they may have been driven out by a race of people better suited to living in arid conditions.

Based on information derived from tribal lore, investigators have arrived at tentative conclusions on the Madanle's possible occupations. Pease recorded a Garre tradition which declared they were farmers, while a more recent expert asserts they may have been cattle herders with associated classes of hunters, cultivators and possibly ironsmiths. Whichever activity occupied their lives, it is generally accepted that they were the engineers who were responsible for the rash of well-digging in the region, and who, most probably, lie buried beneath at least some of the cairns, although possibly not the oldest.

Before closing this short appraisal of the Somali's ancient Madanle, and the element of mystery surrounding them and their engineering successes, it should be mentioned that in opposition to Watson's early comment about the 'Medenli' being an ancient civilisation which had left behind no trace, some argued that the Madanle were an identifiable group which occupied a definite place in the history of northern Kenya. In the thinking of present-day anthropologists, which is naturally a development of earlier ideas, there is a view that the probable origin of the giants was from somewhere north of present-day Kenya. This is obviously a simplification of an involved and historically early movement of races, which concerted research in recent decades has not been altogether successful in clarifying. In fact, far from becoming clearer, the story in some ways has become even more complex.

While it is quite possible the original Madanle were overrun by more aggressive newcomers and assimilated into their ranks, or even totally evicted from their homelands, it is not the purpose of these pages to delve deeply into the involved debates of those attempting to unravel the mysteries of the past, nor is it intended to create more confusion by attempting further speculation. Suffice it to say that evidence continues to turn up which sharpens the diffuse picture of the early peoples' migrations.

Leaving the lands of the Somali people and their legends and moving further west, there is a store of evidence relating to an ancient race which once lived in Boranaland. Geographically situated between the Somalis in the east and the nomadic peoples of the Chalbi Desert and the Lake Rudolf basin to the west, the Boranas' traditional lore forms a link between the Madanle of the Somalis and the Wardai of the Chalbi Desert dwellers.

Whether the Madanle and the Wardai were one and the same people is not certain, but one thing is sure: they are both credited with having the same legendary characteristic of unusually large size. In their building efforts, too, they seem to have accomplished comparable feats, wells and cairns appearing regularly all the way westwards to the shores of the lake. Early travellers passing through Borana country noticed this evidence of a former race's labours, and descriptions in their chronicles draw attention to the remarkable nature of the wells in the area, including detailed reports of their depths and design. Of particular note was the similarity in their construction to those further east in Somali country. The following comments from these old records illustrate the point.

Dr Donaldson Smith, an American explorer who will be met again in later pages, was in 1895 one of the first white men to travel through Borana country. In the course of his expedition he visited the wells at Le and Gof in the south of Abyssinia. The first he described as 'curious' and accurately recorded its dimensions and peculiarities in his matter-of-fact manner: 'These wells, which lie in a broad meadow, are very remarkable, being approached by a winding passage, a hundred yards [92 metres] long, which descends gradually to the bottom of a large round chamber, fifty feet [15 metres] deep, and opening straight to the top. The passage-way and the chamber itself have both been cut through solid rock. In the latter are a series of basins for receiving water as it is drawn up from a narrow opening dug another forty feet [12 metres] below the bottom of the chamber. Rough ladders made of sticks, and whipped together by leather thongs, lead down to the water'. Failing to find any marks by which he might have identified the builders, he assumed by the fashion of their construction that the work must have been done by Egyptians, described by him as 'ancient colonists'. Donaldson Smith made no reference to any interrogation of the local Borana on the identity of the engineers, so his assumption of their origin was certainly fresh thinking, a break from the usual claims for Madanle handiwork. The wells he examined at Gof were even deeper and more extensive than those at Le, but again no questioning of the locals ensued. This was quite understandable, as on that occasion they were exhibiting distinctly antagonistic attitudes towards him and doubtless he was more preoccupied with avoiding conflict than with ethnic matters.

Following shortly after Donaldson Smith came Lord Delamere's party, their route

traversing much the same country as the former's expedition had done a few years before. Delamere also visited the famous wells at Le, and was as impressed as Donaldson Smith had been, noting in his photograph album: 'Every time one looks at these wells one is astonished at the extraordinary perseverance of a people who made such enormous excavations with the tools they would be likely to have'. On discussing the construction of these remarkable wells with the local Borana, he further noted that: 'The Boran say that these wells, which are numerous all over this bit of country were dug by some people called Madanle, Mussulmans who were conquered by the Boran and retreated westwards where they are now'. Delamere had heard yet another scrap of hazy evidence indicating the movements of the builders of the magnificent well systems in Boranaland.

Six years after Lord Delamere's visit to the region, Captain Philip Maud, a member of the first major boundary survey expedition to work on the disputed border region between Abyssinia and the British East Africa Protectorate, made extensive notes on the Borana people and their customs. From these came another early reference to the construction of wells in the area, notably those at Tullu Sullun and Gaddaduma. Maud was told by the Borana that a race called the 'Wurrda', driven out in the long-distant past by the Borana themselves, had constructed the wells throughout the country. On further questioning he was unable to find out anything more about the exiled race, but based on the merit of their extraordinary well-digging feats he ascribed to them the virtues of a 'far more civilised and energetic race than their conquerors'.

In 1915, Arnold Hodson, the newly appointed British Consul to Southern Abyssinia, visited the wells in Borana country adjacent to the Protectorate border, and several years later wrote briefly about them. His description of the wells indicated a construction similar in all respects to those detailed almost twenty years previously by Donaldson Smith and Delamere. Hodson regarded the wells as very substantial

*Rock etchings are a feature of Kenya's desert land, but found usually in 'galleries' close by the waterholes. These ones are all scratched into hard volcanic basalt rocks.*

engineering feats for a primitive people to have undertaken. So, can one again credit the ancient well-diggers with these concerted efforts, and were they the same people as those described by Curle as 'supermen of great stature whose descendants were driven out to the Lake Rudolf area'? It is just possible they were.

Having given fair consideration to the Somali and Borana views on who was responsible for digging the extensive well complexes and cairns in northern Kenya, this account finally enters the geographical confines of the Gabbra, Rendille and Samburu peoples. In that region there are two distinct physiographical features—Lake Rudolf and the Chalbi Desert. There, in the country lying between them, a sizeable community of Wardai may have lived, if one is to believe not only the oral accounts and folklore of today's resident tribal groups but also the visible evidence: more wells, great numbers of cairns and, in association, many sites rich in rock art, where graphic designs have been etched into flint-hard basalt boulders. With the crude tools available to the early artists, these must have been a labour of love, for considerable patient effort would have been required to etch the simple drawings of giraffes, antelopes and camels into the heat-blasted surfaces bordering the desert edge.

The Gabbra people, related ethnically to the Borana and the Somalis, live on the eastern edge of the Chalbi Desert and extend northwards to the Abyssinian border; it is a harsh forbidding district on the whole, excepting the grasslands of the Hurri Hills, the plains of the Golbo* along the Kenya/Ethiopian border and the forested upper slopes of Marsabit mountain. The Gabbra are geared to leading the lives of nomads, a lifestyle that may be very similar to the pattern once followed by the Wardai of their fablest. It is in Gabbraland the concentrations of cairns clustered in groups around the periphery of the desert, and associated with perennial water supplies from wells and springs, indicate where ancient communities would have lived. The Gabbra know the giants of legend as the Wardai, and one of their traditions refers to them in these words: 'The Wardai used to move in this area a long time ago. Now these stones and all these piles of stones, are said to be the graves of the Wardai ... They had dug wells, even in this Badha Hurri. The Wardai used to move in this area, and from all this area they were chased by war'. The Samburu and Rendille also use the name Wardai to identify that romantic race which was reputed to have been tall and warriorlike, and users of iron weapons. They also claim the Wardai were hunter-gatherers and cattle owners, some tales even contending they herded white beasts only. What became of the Wardai whose relatives lie buried under the cairns in the area remains a partial mystery. It is generally accepted that they were overrun and forced out of the district in a south-easterly direction by a more powerful force from the north, the Gabbra claiming the Wardai told them as they were departing that they had left 'their markings' on the rocks and would return to these places for it was 'their water, their grass and their land'.

With climatic change the Wardai were forced to search for vital supplies of water. A Gabbra folk-tale tells how the Wardai divined sources of this element: 'A heifer was tethered and denied water to drink. As time went by the animal became increasingly thirsty, until it was desperate. Only then was she released in the area where water was required by the people. She wandered at will, free to go where she wished, and if fortune was good and she smelled water underground, there the Wardai would dig'. A simple tale, but backed by fact, for animals do locate water in dry areas by smell. The Gabbra say all the deep wells in their country were dug by the Wardai, for were they not giants of men, 'so big they were able to pick up a fully grown cow by the tail and after a few swings send it hurtling at their enemy'? Boring down through the hard volcanic conglomerates in which the Balessa wells near North Horr are found would

---

*The Golbo is the hot low-lying plain below the Megado (Goro) escarpment which separates it from the high, healthy country of the Borana people.

†The story of the Wardai is a mixed one. Although the name has been used in the context of this work to denote a long bygone race, there is a present-day group with the name Wardai. They are a Somali-speaking people living along, but mostly north of the Tana river. The present-day Orma people, grouped on the lower reaches of the river, claim to be the remnants of, and hence related to, the Wardai race, which was squeezed out of its northern homeland by the Borana and Somalis during the early part of the nineteenth century.

have presented no difficulties to those powerful men, or so the Gabbra say.

The Samburu and Rendille, who live adjacent to the Gabbra, have their own tales of the giants, mostly variations of the constant theme extolling their great size and strength, a few adding that they possessed enormous herds of cattle. Two authentic contemporary incidents illustrate convincingly how the Wardai are established in the peoples' minds with these unusual qualities. Early one morning at Koroli springs in the Chalbi Desert, a small group of travellers stood contemplating the sight of a vast concourse of camels being watered by their Rendille owners. Whilst viewing the marvellous scene a disturbance attracted the attention of a male member in the party, who, on investigation, found that an adult she-camel had foundered in the mud, and was there to stay judging by the futile efforts of the herders to release her. An appeal for his assistance was made, and after a short struggle, the animal was re-established on dry land amidst loud exclamations of wonderment from the Rendille ranks. The rescuer was over six feet [1.8 metres] tall and powerfully built, so word quickly went round that here indeed was a true Wardai. Another incident saw a well-muscled man lift a 300 pound (136 kilogram) anvil single-handed, whereupon the watching Gabbra exclaimed in amazement, 'Wardai!'

Having examined the case of the ancient giants through the medium of old tribal tales, and from the writings of a few early observers, it is time to consider evidence recently produced in the hot and dusty scene of contemporary archaeological excavations. Most of the work has been undertaken on the fringes of the Chalbi Desert and along the eastern edge of Lake Rudolf, where some impressive concentrations of burial cairns and stone circles are located—veritable lodes of archaeological gold. Here the sites are easily accessible, a situation which has been exploited by investigators involved in research programmes relating to both the ancient and the contemporary cultures of the region.

An interesting feature of the excavation work on the burial cairns was the lack of interference or protest from the resident populace. This was also the case when Watson did his work several decades before. He even went as far as to mention that stones removed from cairns were used, presumably by government agencies, for building purposes*. The same applies today. Indeed, the inhabitants do not seem to lay any claim to the ancient tombs, a fact affirmed by extensive questioning across the country in which they are found. Generally speaking, the present-day residents of former Wardai territory do not appear to consider the excavation of ancient burial cairns as sacrilegious. The implication of this is obvious: there would appear to be no direct relationship between those buried under the cairns and the present-day people. In other words, the interred are from such a far-off age that the living do not make any proprietary claim, nor do they regard them with any particular sanctity.

A brief description of the three recognised models of burial cairn examined by the archaeologists in their searches will give an idea of their construction, and an understanding of the work entailed during exploratory excavations.

The materials used in the construction of all types of funerary monument naturally depend on the type of stone available in the vicinity. On the fringe of the Chalbi Desert there are unlimited quantities of fragmented lava rock, and that was the obvious

---

*One good example of this is to be found at the military fort near Mouwoligiteng springs close to Loiengalani, where the rocks from an immense cairn were used in 1911 in the construction of the fort's outer wall.

This unusual assemblage of grave types occurs close by Koroli springs on the fringe of the Chalbi Desert. Evident are cairns, one ring and a platform.

*It is rare today, except in isolated places, to find headstones on graves. This excellent example occurs close by the shores of Lake Rudolf.*

material for the ancients to use, whereas by Lake Rudolf, near Koobi Fora, flat sandstone fragments were laid on one another to form neatly built edifices.

Undoubtedly the more numerous, and most commonly seen by the casual traveller, is the mound cairn, a structure that varies considerably in size. Generally circular at the base, they are cone shaped. On occasion a headstone may be found perched on the apex, marked with an etched figure, of which the most usual on the east of Lake Rudolf is the circle mark. These signs were obviously of significance to the people who constructed the cairns, but the meanings have been lost, and it remains to be seen whether their message will ever be discovered*. Today these headstones are rarely found in position, most having long since fallen or been removed. The burial spot was centrally situated and underground, unlike the surface burials of eastern Kenya. The bottom of the grave lay between one and three feet (one metre) below the surface. The base diameters of the cairns vary greatly, some being a paltry few feet, while the largest yet seen measured an impressive 80 feet (24 metres) across. The cairns have in many cases suffered from the wear and tear of the centuries, and many have lost their original stature. As found today they stand anything up to 10 feet (3 metres) tall, a remarkable endurance when one considers that they may have stood exposed to the harshest elements for up to three thousand years and more. Some

*The cairns were most probably the burial places of local leaders. A plausible suggestion for the circle sign is that it indicated the head of the family group, the circle representing the enclosure in which his village stood.

vestigial remains are hardly noticeable, so small and decayed have they become, whereas others are magnificent monuments standing tall and compact as if they had just been built. A common architectural feature of these mounds is the ring of stones forming their base perimeter. Often larger than the average size used in creating the main body of the mound, the stones have been placed carefully, giving a trim and finished appearance to the better preserved graves.

The next most commonly seen structure associated with burial grounds is the stone circle, or ring grave. As with the mound cairn there is no set size, rings averaging from 10 to 20 feet (3 to 6 metres) in diameter. In the centre of the ring lies the burial point, usually marked by a flat oval bed of smaller stones, occasionally with two or more standing headstones positioned at both ends of the oval. A narrow path of small stones may sometimes be found connecting the oval grave with the wall of the ring. As with the mound cairns there is very often a neat row of large, carefully placed rocks defining the outside perimeter.

*In few localities concentrations of ring graves are found, many in excellent condition. This one, nearby the wells at Gus, clearly shows the central burial point.*

Pease made an interesting remark when he stated that the myth of a giant people was enhanced by the distance separating the grave headstones. On the Madanle ring graves they stood on average about 10 feet (3 metres) apart, and popular belief suggested a stature of that dimension. Recent excavations have disproved the idea, but it clearly shows how exaggerated legends were engendered.

The third model of burial cairn found in the desert is the platform variety. This type is infrequently seen, but in some respects it is the most interesting structure of the three. While each type of cairn represents a substantial physical effort on the part of the original builders, the sheer volume of rock moved in the construction of the platforms

must have required the greatest output of hard labour. They are found in squarish forms, the outside measurement averaging 15 to 20 (4.5 to 6 metres) feet, very often with the cardinal axes—north, south, east and west—roughly orientated with the corner buttresses, and built of rocks piled up to form a solid platform two or more feet above the surface of the ground. Excavation has proved that the burial was made in the centre of the platform, and as with the others it took place in a shallow hole underground.

The first serious attempt to examine a selection of these cairns was made in the Chalbi Desert area in 1979, when two professional archaeologists worked over an especially rich site near the beautiful springs of Kalacha Goda. There, it appeared, a large community must have lived centuries before. Using a slight rise in the near neighbourhood of the springs as a burial ground, the ancients left for posterity a small city of mound, ring and platform cairns where dramatic finds were made. Six cairns were studied and an overall appraisal of the three types was gained by systematic digging. For a work of this nature, six was a very modest number, but it did represent a big step forward in the archaeological search for answers to the fascinating mystery of the giants.

Most satisfying to the researchers was the discovery of human skeletons in all six cairns, proving beyond doubt that these edifices were burial sites, and not, as in the case of certain rings near Lake Rudolf, enclosures used by humans to house themselves and their stock. A few small stone artifacts were found with the bones, mostly in the

*Graves are found in a variety of situations.* LEFT: *high on the slopes of Mt Kulal,* RIGHT: *on the footslopes of Mt Ngiro,* RIGHT LOWER: *on the Chalbi Desert.*

*The graphic detail on a headstone, etched untold centuries ago.*

shape of obsidian, chert and quartz flakes. Significantly, no pottery was found, a notable distinction between them and the contents of the Wajir and Mandera cairns. Moreover, all the skeletons were found lying on their sides in a contracted position, contrasting with the style of burial in the Wajir area, where the skeletons were found in a sitting position. One may guess from these differing body positions and grave artifacts that the people who once lived in the Wajir area either were a different race from the Chalbi Desert dwellers, or, if from the same stock, the Wajir section may have experienced outside influence which had not penetrated to the interior.

But were they the skeletons of the long dead giants? Out of five complete skeletons unearthed at Kalacha one was six foot two inches (1.9 metres) tall, and three were six foot four inches (1.95 metres). Even allowing for a small shrinkage of the bones as a result of dehydration, and the effect of a flesh covering on the skeletons when alive, it may be assumed that none of those people could have been much over six foot five inches (1.97 metres) in stature. But that was no mean height when compared with the comparatively short present-day dweller of northern Kenya. Furthermore, had those ancient men possessed a physique matching their stature, they would most certainly have appeared as an impressively large people to outsiders of smaller size.

One last question arose: how old were the skeletons? On the bones being subjected to the process of radio-carbon dating, the tests, as hoped, disclosed valuable new facts. Of particular interest was the establishment of a series of age groups for the three types of cairns. The ring cairns were proved to be the youngest, two of them dating from five hundred years before, followed by the platform cairns aged at nearly one thousand years, and the oldest, the mound cairn, placed at three and a half thousand years old. It is not altogether satisfactory to draw conclusions from such scant evidence; but the indisputable fact is that all the cairns are of considerable age, and only further research will prove whether all mound cairns are of the same vintage as the single specimen examined, and therefore the oldest by far, or whether the ring cairns are really the youngest. Whatever the findings of future investigations, one thing is clear: the giants of lore, assuming they were those people buried under the cairns, were indeed of ancient stock.

And so, despite all the evidence accumulated over nearly a century of observations and scientific investigation, an element of uncertainty still hangs over the true nature of the mythical giants of tribal tales. That they once existed there is no doubt, for the cairns have produced their bones, and though they were not giants in the real sense, they were considerably larger than the present dwellers in their former lands. The evidence proves, however, that they did live many hundreds, even thousands of years ago.

Although many erudite observers and scholars have considered how the giants may have originated, from which direction they arrived, and to where they ultimately departed, one thing remains clear: there is still a mystery surrounding the long-gone people of the north, which may never be resolved to everyone's satisfaction. No one as yet has been able to state emphatically who the ancient Madanle and their ilk may have been, and in so failing have allowed the fantasies of tribal lore to live on.

# THE NOMADS

*'The stories I have given you, some were from before I was born ... what I am giving you is what I have heard ... what I have heard is much.'*

A Rendille remark to Neal Sobania (1975)

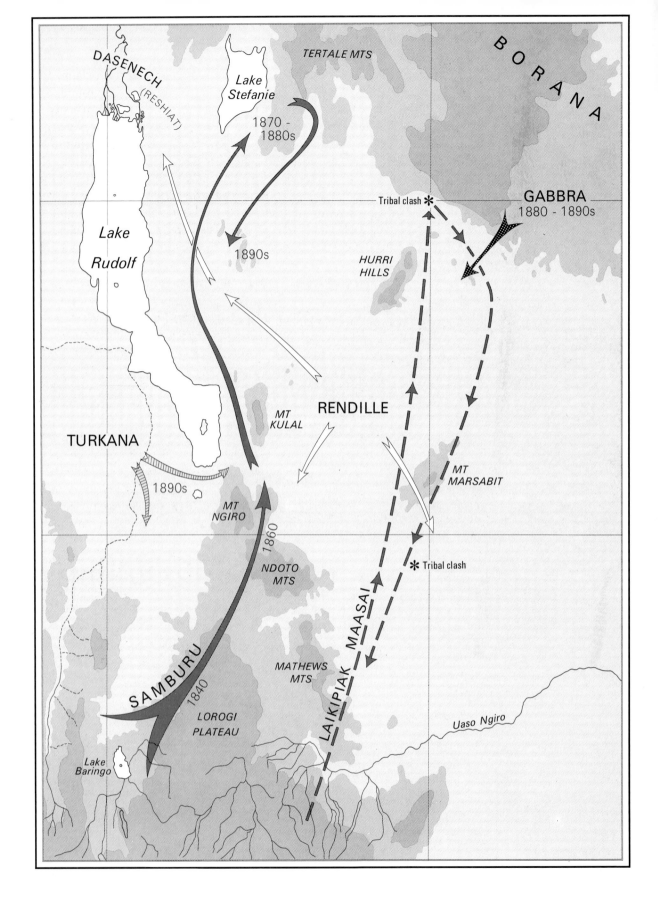

DASENECH
(RESHIAT)

BORANA

TERTALE MTS

Lake
Stefanie

1870 -
1880s

Lake
Rudolf

1890s

Tribal clash ✳

GABBRA
1880 - 1890s

HURRI
HILLS

RENDILLE

MT
KULAL

TURKANA

1890s

MT
NGIRO

1860

MT
MARSABIT

NDOTO
MTS

✳ Tribal clash

SAMBURU

1840

MATHEWS
MTS

LAIKIPIAK MAASAI

Uaso Ngiro

LOROGI
PLATEAU

Lake
Baringo

OVER the last five millenia Kenya's northern territory has been claimed by countless wandering stock herders as their exclusive stamping ground. This fearsome tract, embracing an environment filled with pitiless adversity for the stockman, is a place where animal and plant life compete in an endless exhausting struggle for survival, in much the same way as life in any other desert region of the world. Unpredictable, and at times precarious to the verge of disaster, it is on rare occasions relatively generous to the inhabitants who battle for a continuance of their life, the only one they know. Today there are opportunities and facilities for the tribesmen of the north to travel, trade and seek security away from the difficulties of their ancestral lands, but in the late nineteenth and early twentieth centuries these did not exist. It is the nomadic people of those times who are of most importance to this tale and whose lives and actions must be regarded closely.

The sole residents for untold years in that grim zone of turmoil were the large pastoralist groups, the Borana, Gabbra, Laikipiak, Rendille and Samburu, the tiny enclaves of the Elmolo fishermen and the Dasenech agriculturalists. Into their midst came the disturbing influence of the inordinately curious white man with his territorial aspirations. The newcomers initiated changes to the conservative tribal routines, but they did not entirely disrupt or destroy the structure of the nomads' age-old customs and traditions. Many of these tribal disciplines live on to the present day, preserving unique systems developed patiently over the years for the maintenance of life in the desolate lands of northern Kenya.

For many decades ethnographers have scrutinised the tribal customs and traditions of these people; many dedicated researchers have, with the collaboration and assistance of tribal members, old and young, gained a deep understanding and knowledge of the means by which the hardy nomadic tribes survived the bitter conflict between themselves and the unpredictable forces of nature. The results of these investigations give a clear picture of the *modus operandi* of the complex tribal systems which have held these rugged people in their tightly knit societies.

Since their beginnings the tribes of this area have shifted, fought one another, mingled, been ejected or even adopted by dominating enemies. Tracing the evolution and development of individual tribes by way of traditional histories can be a perplexing business, a specialist's task that often requires the detective's powers of reasoning. Oral information from different informers may give contrasting renditions of the same story, appearing to bear no relationship to one another. Often however, these differing tales have a common thread, which binds them together and so establishes a historical fact. The diligence and persistence of researchers has ensured for posterity a fascinating record of tribal histories, lore and customs.

Changes and improvements have come to the pastoralists' lives with the passing years. Modern science and medicine have given the people and their animals a modicum of relief from the fear of devastation by the epidemics of sickness and destroying diseases so common a feature of their troubled past. Transport facilities have added an element of ease in times of difficulty. But nothing can be done to control the vagaries of the climate, and in this region the seven lean years occur as frequently as the seven fat years, if not more often. As a consequence, the desert dwellers' survival mentality—a combination of stoicism and fatalism—has been hammered into those living in that inhospitable but starkly beautiful country.

The nineteenth century was a period of restless activity and turbulence among the

*General tribal movements in the nineteenth century east of Lake Rudolf.*

tribal groups of northern Kenya; invasions and the inexorable pressures of more powerful units driving weaker ones from their ancestral lands, often fragmenting tribes into splinter groups whose only options were flight to other lands, adjustments to the ways of new masters or ultimate destruction. The first course inevitably resulted in further confrontations as the fugitives met, and were in turn resisted by the residents of the territory into which they had escaped, starting another chain of events from which the strongest would emerge the victor.

In the last two decades of the century the pastoral peoples' precarious existence was further aggravated by a series of exceptionally erosive and immense disasters, when blasting droughts desolated the land, pernicious diseases decimated the humans, and cattle died in huge numbers due to an unprecedented outbreak of rinderpest* in the 1890s. The overall picture of tragedy was further exacerbated by increasing inter-tribal stresses that promoted further social upheavals.

Following these terrible periods of drought and disease it became imperative for those with surviving stock to find the means of sustaining their remaining wealth. Grazing had to be found, often at the cost of conflict as territorial rights were infringed. For those with few remaining animals additional stock had to be secured, and with raiding the traditional means of achieving this end, the stronger groups soon took advantage of weaker ones to supplement their herds. Both situations involved the employment of all the strategies known to the combatants for aggression, and more important, defence. Lifestyles also had to change, for many who were formerly owners of substantial herds found themselves denuded of their wealth and their food supply. In consequence they were forced into agricultural means of subsistence, or became humble fishermen if living by Lake Rudolf's shores, or even resorted to the ways of the hunter-gatherer until such time as more favourable conditions enabled them to regenerate their herds of domestic beasts. Some of those, through desire or force of circumstance, never resumed their former pastoral lives, preferring to continue with their new found occupations. Even more extreme measures were resorted to by the Gabbra and Borana, who in their dire distress found that ivory proved to be a prime form of currency for the purchase of cattle from the Somalis. They became hunters of elephants although they never killed them in any number. Yet another and even more desperate expedient undertaken in the search for food was the barter of their children to the Somalis—one sack of sustenance for one child being the recognised rate during those trying days.

During the last decade of the nineteenth century and the early part of the twentieth, two alien forces of imperialism arrived in the region to add to the disruption. They came in the shape of Emperor Menelik's marauders from Abyssinia in the north, and the hotch-potch of white explorers from all directions. The explorers first, and the early British administrators later, faithfully recorded the stances of the hardy resident nomads. Some were peaceful, co-operative and even welcoming; others were antagonistic, belligerent and uncompromising. The latter approach was understandable in the light of past history, when more often than not the appearance of strangers had represented a threat to their lives, their stock, and worse, to their lands. A deep inherent mistrust of strangers existed in the minds of the indigenous peoples

---

*Rinderpest is a highly contagious disease affecting cattle, sheep, goats and several species of wild beasts. Caused by a virus, it spreads quickly and is a swift killer, death coming in three to twelve days.

in those disturbing days. Understandably, it automatically induced a defensive posture and in the Africa of that time defence often went hand in hand with aggression.

The year 1888 was historically significant in the Lake Rudolf region: it marked the arrival of the first European explorers and presaged the white man's interest in the wild country where the nomadic tribes roamed. There, the foreign travellers found a multifarious collection of cultures, languages and economic systems, mostly based on pastoralism. Alongside the major tribal groups lived smaller entities: the tiny community of Elmolo fishermen who lived on the south-eastern shores of the lake, eking out an existence from whatever fish and hippopotamus they could trap or spear; the Dasenech, called Reshiat by the earliest travellers, a diminutive race of agriculturists who tilled the rich alluvium on the banks of the River Omo at the lake's northern tip; the Ariaals with their blend of Samburu and Rendille cultures, who lived further south towards the Ndoto Mountains, tending their mixed herds of camels and cattle; and the Laikipiaks, the once powerful section of the Maasai tribe who lived along the banks of the Uaso Ngiro river. With the exception of the Elmolo and the Dasenech, all the tribes in the region were wandering nomads, incessantly competing and skirmishing with one another, and when not involved in their internecine warfare and raids, struggling to cope with the interminable problems of survival in their testing environment.

The first explorers to arrive in the area were Count Teleki and his companion Lieutenant von Höhnel, trudging steadily northwards in 1888 on their quest for the mysterious lake which had been reported lying somewhere in the last blank space on the map of east Africa. From the lowlands around Lake Baringo they struggled up the rugged eastern wall of the Rift Valley, finally arriving on the cool and pleasing downs of the Lorogi plateau, with its revitalising chill winds and bracing climate. Only after they had crossed these rolling plains and reached the fringing range of the Lorogi Mountains did they encounter the first sign of human activity in the area, a fire ravaged forest which they assumed the peripatetic 'Wandorobbo hunters' had started. Little did they know that the Lorogi plains had once been part of the ancestral grazing grounds of the fearsome Laikipiak Maasai, the same people who had so tenaciously and effectively obstructed the Scottish explorer Joseph Thomson's trail-blazing march to Mount Kenya only five years before. Teleki and his huge caravan did not, however, experience the same scale of interference from the Laikipiaks which had earlier plagued Thomson on his travels. From what he observed, von Höhnel dutifully entered on his map that the north bank of the Uaso Ngiro river seemed to mark the northerly limit of the Laikipiaks, an interesting note illustrating the point these people had reached in their retreat from the extensive ranges they formerly occupied in the north.

*This photograph of a Maasai warrior was taken by A. C. Hollis in 1900.*

# LAIKIPIAK MAASAI

A FEW hundred years ago a race of stock-herding people living in the country to the west of Lake Rudolf commenced a steady exodus southwards, down the Rift Valley, and onwards into present-day Tanzania. From accounts preserved in tribal history this movement is recognised as the first appearance of the pastoral Maasai as a distinct people, a race that spoke the Maa language, a language now defined in technical jargon as belonging to the Eastern Nilotic branch of the Eastern Sudanic languages of Africa. The protracted exodus from their ancestral territory was forced on them by the relentless advance of drier and less hospitable climatic conditions, disrupting their purely pastoral existence.

As the main migrating body of this tribe made its way south small splinter groups broke away to the flanks. Force of circumstances then compelled some of them to seek alternative methods of survival in environments unsuitable for entirely pastoral activities. These separatists gradually organised their own variations of the Maasai culture, some becoming semi-pastoralists, others taking up the agriculturists' life, while a minority gravitated to the occupation of hunters and honey gatherers. One of the new sections formed in this process was a group which lived in the Maasai's northern range. They practised a semi-pastoral life and were known as the Laikipiak Maasai.

The Laikipiak were once a force to fear and respect. A scourge to the Samburu and Rendille, and a trial to trading caravans and travellers, their territory originally extended from the south end of the Ndoto Mountains down to Lake Naivasha, embraced the vast plains country from the Lorogi plateau across to the forest outskirts of Meruland in the east, and included an extensive portion of the beautiful valley between Mt Kenya and the Aberdare range. It was a magnificent pastoral area, where the powerful clan roamed in numbers, tending their huge herds of cattle and sheep.

A few years prior to Thomson's arrival in 1883 their power had started to wane. With this came a gradual retirement to the southern corners of their former range. This left the northern sections empty and unused, the state in which Teleki found them in 1888. The beginning of the Laikipiak's decline came in the mid-1870s, several years before the first travellers passed through, when numerous crushing blows were dealt to them by an alliance of their southern kinsmen, the Kisongo and the Purko Maasai. One defeat after another followed at the hands of those formidable foes, finally precipitating the flight of the Laikipiak leader, the Laibon Koikot ole Tunai, who disappeared into the west and over the Mara river forever, leaving behind a splintered, demoralised and ruined people. Never again were the Laikipiak considered an overwhelming force, and the story of the surviving remnants—those who were not assimilated into the conquerors' ranks—was a chequered one entailing a period of adjustment to new ways of life and other means of subsisting. Those no longer in a position to continue with pastoral activities drifted into the ways of the Wandorobo, stockless wanderers of the bush and forest whose occupations were hunting and honey collecting. Though demeaning in the eyes of the pastoralist, they were suitable alternatives to adopt in times of hardship. Remote groups of Laikipiaks, who through isolated location had not experienced the depredations of the Purko, continued their customary aggressive raiding and pastoral existence. Their power was broken, but their spirit was not, and in a desperate attempt to continue their traditional life as stock owners a significant number moved back to their old stamping grounds between the Uaso Ngiro river and Laisamis.

Thomson, in the course of his nerve-racking journey through the land of the Laikipiaks, observed the results of a destructive cattle disease which had swept through their herds; it was a disease that became responsible for the death of uncountable beasts, creating appalling scenes of animal misery, heightened by the numbers of decomposing carcasses lying everywhere. He noted: 'On our way we were greatly astonished to observe the dried carcasses of numerous cattle which dotted the entire district ... We came to the conclusion that some disease must be raging in the land'. Shortly after, he further commented: 'Round about the kraals the scene was simply fearful—hundreds of animals dying and in all stages of decomposition ... The consequence was that a fearful stench prevailed, and the people were in helpless distress'. Undoubtedly Thomson had been an eyewitness of the lethal outbreak of contagious bovine pleuro-pneumonia, a cattle affliction that was spreading over a wide front in east Africa, devastating the pastoralists' herds but leaving the wild buffalo and large antelopes unmolested. Ominously, it was only the first of the disastrous epizootics that depopulated whole areas of east Africa's pastoral country of its cattle herds, and later remained lurking as endemic killers.

Hardly had the Laikipiaks recovered from that problem than another and even more potent agent of death appeared on the northern horizon. In the late 1890s the most notorious rinderpest outbreak of the century swept through from Abyssinia and down to the Cape in southern Africa, spreading its tentacles of destruction across the continent to Senegambia on the Atlantic Ocean. The disease finally died out in the late 1890s after obliterating more than 90 per cent of the domestic cattle and wild bovines living in the affected areas. These devastating blows caused immense suffering to the Laikipiaks, and raised the spectre of starvation. Dire necessity drove them to make good their losses of stock by raiding the Samburu and Rendille to the north, an occupation they actively pursued as far afield as Marsabit Mountain and beyond, until the end of the nineteenth century. Even the fringes of Dasenech territory in the distant north west, and the southern parts of Borana territory in Abyssinia did not escape their ravages.

The denudation of the Laikipiaks did not end with cattle diseases; a killer of human beings now arrived from the south in the deadly shape of smallpox, a malady for which they had no cure. It had already killed a large number of people in east Africa, and was creeping northwards into Abyssinia. The Laikipiaks suffered damaging losses to their population, leaving the country even more bare and deserted; Richard Meinertzhagen, an officer in the King's African Rifles, observed in his account of a survey expedition he led over the rolling open downs on the northern slopes of the Aberdare range in 1903 that there was a total absence of human life in the district, except for a few signs of Wandorobo activity. It was in this same stretch of country, exactly twenty years before to the month, that Thomson had been continually harassed by obstructive Laikipiak warriors. Meinertzhagen's record provided further proof of the sorry decline of the once-powerful clan.

Following defeats by the Borana, Gabbra and Rendille, and later, the white man's control over their lands, the depredations of the Laikipiak were finally halted. By then they were a spent force living in pockets throughout their old territory, the subject of passing references in the chronicles of traders and hunters during the early years of the century. Their final demise came in 1912 when they were forcibly removed by the agencies of the British government to an area in the south of Kenya, where they were assimilated into the ranks of their former foes, the powerful Purko Maasai. The country adjacent to the Uaso Ngiro river was one of their last strongholds, and formed a common border with the Samburu tribe which was advancing steadily southwards, exploiting the decline of their former persecutors. To this day a few remnants of the once-dominant race are to be found living there, proudly claiming their kinsmanship with the long-departed Laikipiak Maasai.

*A fine example of the 'samburr' – the leather bag from which the Samburu (Lokob) tribe may have derived its name.*

# SAMBURU

A RECENT researcher has stated emphatically that the Samburu people have no true myths relating to their origin. Be that as it may, the Samburu believe that in distant times they were a minor branch of the Laikipiak Maasai, an idea strongly substantiated by the almost identical form of their languages, suggesting that Samburu is a dialect of Maasai. This clearly hints of an ancient tribal relationship. Although the name, Samburu, possibly derived from the leather bag (samburr) they frequently carried, has always been the generally accepted name for this people, among themselves they prefer the name Lokob (variously interpreted by foreigners in their writings as Laigop, Logop, Loikop, Lokkob, Lokub, Lygop).

In the context of the story of their origin, mention must be made of the researches done by an early administrator—K.R. Dundas. While stationed in the Baringo district during the first decade of this century, he made a point of studying the tribal traditions of the peoples living in the region. From the histories derived from these tales Dundas concluded that the disassociated groups of early people, the proto-Sams, who eventually amalgamated to form the Maa-speaking Samburu tribe, arrived from somewhere east of Lake Baringo. It is open to conjecture whether the movement started out from the Lorogi plateau, the Elbarta Plains or the area to the north in the vicinity of the Suguta valley and the western side of Lake Rudolf, but a recent ethnographer has recorded that Samburu tribal lore describes a great defeat in the early part of the nineteenth century at the hands of the eastward-advancing Turkana. The Samburu claim this reverse resulted in a retreat from their former lands to the west of Lake Rudolf.

Dundas made no surmises about the reason for these migrations to new lands around Baringo; whether it was nature's pressures, or human oppression and eviction. He assumed that the fusing together of small unattached groups to form a new identifiable race was accomplished in the Baringo area, which resulted in the founding of the Samburu people as a viable entity, capable of all the acts of defence, aggression and territorial claims associated with their new-found unity and power.

From Dundas's 1910 writings it was clear that a definite period had been fixed in tribal tradition for the appearance of the Samburu as a distinct race. He concluded from his researches that the population movements which triggered the formation took place during the first forty years of the nineteenth century, a deduction that corresponds very neatly with the results of many recent investigations into Samburu history. The salient factor in the establishment of a definite date is the evidence which points recurringly to a consolidated Samburu migration commencing during the time when the Kipeko age-set* were in their warriorhood, an historical period which is estimated to have occurred during the years 1837–51. Indelibly printed in the traditional history of the Samburu are the Kipeko, who are remembered to this day as

---

*Most east African pastoralist groups have a system of age-sets. They represent the period, usually 13 to 14 years, when the young men (moran) serve out their warriorhood. At the close they become junior elders, and a new age-set is initiated to its duties. Each age-set is given a specific name, a factor useful to ethnologists when dating events in tribal history.

the stalwart and enterprising young men who led their immature tribe out of the Baringo basin and into new territories. It was a protracted operation that gradually moved them north-eastwards towards the magnificent, well-watered mountain masses of Ngiro (sometimes spelt Nyiru) and Kulal, and the pasture lands lying in the valley between. Inevitably their troubles were not over, for they did not find an empty promised land, but a country with established tenants herding their animals and conversing in an alien language, a hindrance to their progress which had to be driven out, or eliminated. There is still uncertainty who these people were. Some informants contend they were Borana, while others describe them as a Borana-speaking race. Curiously the present-day Borana do not claim any knowledge of them, although they do admit they may have been part of a group described as the Wardai Galla whom their Borana forefathers had driven out of southern Abyssinia many years before. Without the strength to resist the aggressive Samburu newcomers, those relic Borana people were eventually driven from the area, an event that required only the short period of one age-set of fourteen years to complete. Borana (or Wardai) burial mounds may be seen to the present day on the lower slopes of Ngiro, Ol Doinyo Mara and Kulal mountains, silent reminders of the former residents in this present-day centre of Samburu culture.

The eviction of the Borana did not constitute the total elimination of a people, for many were captured, spared and eventually assimilated into the Samburu tribe. The integration was enough for several clans to trace their roots to the vanquished Borana. This is particularly noticeable within the powerful Masula clan, which claims many connections with Borana customs, including the exclusive ownership of Mt Ngiro—an exceptional proprietorship in a tribe amongst which communal ownership of land is the custom. The Masula, who today comprise almost three-quarters of the northern Samburu, also exert an ancestral ownership over the southern half of Mt Kulal.

The Samburu had only been in their newly acquired territory a few years before they realised that the grazing would not sustain an increase in their herds, and they would have to expand into further new pastures. But there were inhibiting factors: to the east lay the Koroli and Chalbi deserts, a poor and desiccated country for cattlemen; to the north were even more desert and stony wastelands; to the south, on the hospitable tableland of the Lorogi plateau, the firmly entrenched Laikipiaks were in control, ready to plunder and persecute any wandering Samburu who dared to encroach on their grazing grounds. For the hard-pressed Samburu there was only one option left: to follow the route along the eastern shores of Lake Rudolf, north to the extensive pasture lands situated towards the smaller Lake Stefanie in the east. This, they decided, was the road they should follow to the highly desirable country which they knew of, and still remember, by the traditional name of Uoto—'the far away place'—which stretched from Lake Rudolf to Lake Stefanie. There, at last, they arrived in a welcoming empty tract of open rolling hills and grasslands. In the middle of the nineteenth century, when the first Samburu moved there, it was well watered, free from population pressure and hospitable. Their Garden of Eden embraced two lakes and the Tertale Mountains (known to them as Dharrar), a powerful range of hills rising abruptly 5,000 feet (1,540 metres) above the eastern shore of Lake Stefanie, its treeless lower slopes cloaked in rich waving grasslands and topped with beautiful juniper forests. Lying to the west across the lake was the less conspicuous Hamar range, another excellent grazing area onto which the Samburu encroached, with their

*From this drawing it will be evident that the Samburu warrior of ninety years ago did not sport the ornate decoration of today's young men.*

superior strength of arms dominating and oppressing the tiny Hamar Koke tribe.

The land of Uoto marked the northernmost limit of the Samburu wanderings in search of more rewarding surroundings, and for a few decades they reigned supreme, instilling fear and respect amongst their weaker neighbours to the north, and steadily growing wealthy in cattle and other stock. At the height of their power, the Samburu herds fed over an immense part of northern Kenya; they encompassed the lands northwards from the grassy footslopes, forests and glades of Mt Ngiro, up the shores of Lake Stefanie and its lonely mountain environs, eastwards to Marsabit Mountain where they maintained a relatively peaceful status quo with their camel-herding neighbours, the Rendille, and down to the northern end of the Ndoto Mountains where they blended with the Rendille to form the small group of Ariaals. But it was in the Uoto region that the majority of the tribe and their stock resided in the decades following the final move in the middle of the century, a land of prosperity and relative peace, in which strife with neighbours was minimal.

In the manner of Africa this happy state of affairs did not last: in the 1880s came disaster. The Samburu herds were decimated by the overwhelming scourges that were destroying the animals elsewhere in east Africa, and intertribal raiding increased. Soon, once-powerful groups were defeated and dispersed, retreating to securer areas, and abandoning the lands they had previously so contentedly possessed.

During that violent period the Samburu suffered with the others, but to add to their problems nibbling raids by the remaining Laikipiaks on the fringes of their territory around the mountain retreats of Ngiro and Marsabit, were coupled with the arrival of voracious Turkana warrior bands. These swept up the east shores of Lake Rudolf, ruthlessly pillaging on their way. So rampant and unsparing were the marauders that the hard-pressed Samburu, by now in sparse occupation of the Uoto region, found it politic on occasion to combine forces with their Rendille and Dasenech neighbours in attempts to keep the intruders at bay. It was, however, in vain, and slowly the Rendille and Samburu were in retreat, the latter retiring to their old territories in the south where they could more easily hold their own in the mountain fastnesses they knew so well.

Only a small section of the population was left behind to guard the remnants of their rinderpest-ruined herds in the mountains of Dharrar. It was not long before even these survivors were squeezed out by Turkana pressure and driven forever from their northern outposts, joining their hard-pressed fellow-men in the south. There the bulwarks of Samburu survival, Ngiro and Kulal, were ready to shelter and resuscitate the mauled people and their pathetic herds.

By good fortune, their long association with Mt Ngiro and its forests initiated new interests through their contacts with the resident Wandorobo, a population said to have been an offshoot of the Borana people who formerly resided in the area. Comparatively safe in their mountain surroundings, but forced by necessity to practice survival occupations, they acquired from their Wandorobo neighbours the arts of the apiarian and the hunter. These linked the lives of the pastoralists and the hunter-gatherer, an unusual combination amongst the nomadic peoples of northern Kenya.

Trudging wearily across the Elbarta plains in the heat of February 1888, Count Teleki's party finally reached the southern footslopes of Mt Ngiro. In claiming to be the first white men to reach Samburu territory they made history. They soon met up with a few timid members of the people the Laikipiak referred to as the Burkeneji— 'those of white goats'. The Burkeneji, as von Höhnel also called them in his expedition account, were in fact the Samburu. At last Teleki could claim to have reached Samburu country, a land that stretched far before them, northwards to Lake Stefanie. Von Höhnel recorded with satisfaction: 'This flat stretch of country we were told was that Samburu to which we had eagerly looked forward for so long'. While camped at the foot of Mt Ngiro they were visited by a small number of Burkeneji, which von Höhnel recorded: 'Our visitors were Burkeneji, and were the southern representatives of the tribe of that name dwelling chiefly in the northern portion of Samburu'. For the rest of their time in Samburu country the two explorers encountered few people, and when finally Teleki and von Höhnel reached the lake they named Stefanie, their Burkeneji guide found, to his great disappointment, no trace of his people, the Samburu of Uoto. The survivors of his tribe were in fact not far off, sheltering in the Dharrar Mountains from the depredations of the Turkana.

Following in Teleki's footsteps came the elephant hunter Arthur Neumann, who travelled extensively through Samburu country in the 1890s. His hunting expeditions took him up the broad valley separating the Mathews and Lorogi mountain ranges, and on to the same camping ground under Mt Ngiro that Teleki had used six years before. There he met a few Samburu, who had come down from the top of the cloud-capped mountain that loomed over his base. Neumann's account tells how at first they were reluctant to approach his party: 'We failed to get into communication with the natives (Sambur) living in the mountain, as they were suspicious and did nothing but run away from us with their cattle, up into the fortresses'. This initial timidity on their part was reversed on his next trip in the region, when he noted: 'On this visit I succeeded in getting in touch with the natives inhabiting the mountain, and got some of them to come to my camp. They call themselves the Sambur tribe. They live entirely in the mountains'.

In the two decades following Neumann's visits to the area, the Samburu were re-establishing themselves and rebuilding their herds. While they had not suffered such a severe loss of human life from the ravages of smallpox as their neighbours the camel-herding Rendille, difficult times were upon them, and with new enemies hard on their heels life continued to be precarious and unsettled. They gradually fragmented and drifted for shelter towards neighbouring tribal communities, where they were accepted on terms dictated by their tolerant hosts.

The Dasenech, a tribe practising riverine agriculture and pastoralism in the vicinity of the River Omo at the north end of Lake Rudolf, were quite amenable to the incursion of Samburu refugees from the Uoto area. Many were assimilated into their tribe, and permitted to absorb the Dasenech culture. They joined in tribal activities to such a degree that they even developed a Samburu group within their host's tribal system—the Kuro section—which still exists today.

The advantages for the Dasenech were many. In return for their hospitality they received a new labour force to assist with work in the fields and stock herding, a reinforcement of spears with which to aid them in countering Turkana encroachment, and even a source of new women. These were welcome additions to the small and relatively weak tribe.

In their state of desperation the starving, destitute Samburu also appealed to the Elmolo for succour. There again they were accepted into a neighbour's tribal life, joining in the fishing and hunting activities of that minuscule group. It was purely a stopgap convenience for the Samburu, until such time as the foundations of new herds were laid. As a result of their superiority in numbers, the Samburu culture influenced Elmolo customs, affecting dress style, language and introducing the livelihood of the stockman to the fisherman community.

Other Samburu were conveniently absorbed into the Rendille tribe, which, heavily depleted in numbers as a result of the smallpox disaster, was incapable of tending and protecting its great herds of camels. Unlike the vulnerable cattle of the Samburu, these animals had not succumbed to the rinderpest outbreak of the 1890s.

A few remnants of the Samburu tribe took up life with the forest-dwelling Wandorobo, absorbing their vocation, and becoming honey collectors and hunters of wild animals for food. These were the people Neumann encountered during his early wanderings in the country between the Lorogi and Mathews mountain ranges. His comments on the Wandorobo were revealing, and not altogether complimentary. They rather belittled the image of the Wandorobo as daring and skilful hunters, capable of enjoying a life of plenty from their hunting. Neumann wrote: 'The Ndorobo . . . are a kind of degraded Masai, living on game, honey, etc., in the bush, something after the style of the South African Bushman, the grand object of their desires being elephants. They live a more or less nomadic life in small communities scattered over a wide extent of East Equatorial Africa, where no settled inhabitants are. The wild region here northwards to Lake Rudolf is left entirely to them'. He went on to add: 'Before I went among these people I had always supposed, from what I heard and read about them, that they were all skilful hunters, living solely on game. I have found, however, that this is by no means the case, at least in the region I am writing. The majority of them depend almost solely on honey and wild fruit, roots, berries, etc., for their existence; and, as may be supposed in a country to which nature has been by no means bountiful in edible products, they are usually in a state of semi-starvation; indeed it is a puzzle to me how they manage to live at all'. Of their hunting skill he observed: 'There are only a few among their number having any skill at hunting, and even these are not what I should call expert hunters. They kill now and then an elephant or two or a rhinoceros . . . Game of other kinds they seem hardly ever able to kill at all'.

By the turn of the century the Samburus' situation appeared to have improved, with herds steadily building up again and members of the tribe moving towards the desirable cattle country vacated by the Laikipiaks in their southerly retreat. Disturbingly, however, a new upset had arrived in which the Samburu, in their mountain retreats of Ngiro and Kulal, experienced an entirely different type of enemy, one armed with the first rifles they had seen in quantity. This was the time of the Sidam raiders from Abyssinia, whose principle targets were elephants, rhinoceros and giraffe. They stole Samburu cattle, and also donkeys to help in the transport of their ivory haul. The Sidam hunting excursions took them past Kulal, through the elephant-rich South Horr Valley, and on to the ivory reservoirs of the Ndoto Mountains. Their advance caused disturbance and loss of life to the Samburu populace, who were forced to vacate the area and join their fellow-tribesmen on the high plains of the Lorogi plateau. Their flight resulted in yet more pressure on those rangelands. In due course a resident population of such substance became established there it claimed the former Laikipiak country for its own.

In 1909, with the start of the British East Africa Protectorate's rule in the region, a protective influence, albeit a scant one, made itself felt in Samburuland. The new force was responsible for a steady decline in the incidence of Sidam raiding parties, although sporadic incursions continued for many decades. The British administration gave a feeling of security to the Samburu, and they started to drift back to their mountain homes and grazing lands in the north.

One perennial threat remained—the Turkana. Their aggressiveness had brought them into contact with the Samburu many years earlier, when they encroached up the eastern side of Lake Rudolf into Samburu- and Rendille-held territory. Their mobile forces were also striking right across the Chalbi Desert and into the Hurri Hills, causing terror and loss of life wherever they marched. Another Turkana spearhead thrusting into the Samburu flank came up from the Hades-like depths of the Suguta valley and confronted the Samburu at Baragoi on the Elbarta Plains. Over the rolling grasslands the two contestants battled back and forth during the first two decades of the present century. At times the Samburu were driven clear out of the area, and at one point the Turkana even managed to reach the Uaso Ngiro river before being turned back. Stock, not land, was the initial reason for these conflicts; the Turkana needed to increase their rinderpest-diminished numbers of cattle and found the weakly tended Samburu herds too tempting a target to resist.

During that troublesome time a well-renowned traveller passed through the strife-ridden zone, later making notes on the conflict. Captain Chauncey Stigand, well known for his keen study of nature and ethnic matters, crossed the Lorogi Mountains in 1909, a few miles to the south of Teleki's route of twenty years before, and arrived in the cul-de-sac valley of Operoi. There he found the Samburu well established. On continuing his march across Samburu country towards the base of Mt Ngiro, he encountered a group of Turkana residing at Baragoi in a state of uneasy peace with their Samburu neighbours: 'The Turkana and Samburr at Baragoi, it appeared, had fallen out over grazing grounds, and war between them was imminent ... As I passed the Samburr kraals on my way to Baragoi some old men turned out ... They poured out their troubles to me. It appeared from their accounts that the Turkana wished to oust them from their grazing ground, and from the well-grassed plain of Em Barta, threatening to fight them if they did not go. They said they were not strong enough to fight with the Turkana, and they could not move, for they had nowhere else to go'. Stigand mediated as best he could, and shortly after left for the north in his search for the Rendille. Earlier he had discovered that the Samburu did not extend in any numbers north of Mt Ngiro and the Ndoto range. Stigand left Samburuland with a high regard for its people, who he esteemed for their peaceful and intelligent demeanour.

When reviewed from the standpoint of their tribal lore, and also from the white man's experiences and records, the story of the Samburu from the days of their genesis as a tribe up to the year 1920, is one of endless movement and migrations to better lands, ensuing battles with neighbours, brief and all too infrequent periods of peace and plenty, times of deprivation as a consequence of drought and pestilence, and integration with outside tribal groups. The period culminated with the influence of the British government's new and alien policies for the pacification of the land under its control. All these manoeuvrings and adjustments involved the Samburu in a constant jostling for position over an enormous territory, creating in the process a tribe with many facets to its character. No longer were they a purely pastoral people. They had adopted the habits of other tribes: the hunters, becoming killers and eaters of wild animals; the gatherers, which trained them to appreciate the vegetable foods of the bush; the fishermen and agriculturists, who taught them the usefulness of their activities; and the Rendille, herders of camels, from whom they came to learn the value of such beasts. Despite their turbulent history, the Samburu's primordial instinct to survive enabled them to adjust and come through a complete, if battered people.

# RENDILLE

STIGAND marched out of Samburuland and into Rendille country with the immediate intention of obtaining a train of camels with which to supplement his transport for the long desert march lying ahead of him. Although he spent some time with the Rendille, successfully purchasing camels and establishing good relations with them, he was far from being the first white man to meet this interesting tribe. Teleki had achieved this in 1888 when he located a few 'Randile' in Reshiat country at the northern tip of Lake Rudolf. It was William Chanler, however, the ambitious young American explorer, who could claim to have made the first serious attempt to establish contact with the Rendille. This he did while on his ill-fated expedition in 1893.

All these travellers remarked on the similarity between the Rendille and Somali languages, and from this they deduced that the Rendille people must have originated in the east. Later, as their westerly migration progressed, it was assumed they gradually adopted the practices of the nomadic peoples with whom they came in contact, and in the course of time lost their Muslim faith and customs. Subsequent curiosity about the origin of the Rendille has focused on the blend of an essentially Somali mode of camel-based economy and strong language likeness, with the Samburu-like appearance of their warriors and similar customs.

The Rendille are no exceptions in possessing a store of tribal traditions about their origins. Some hint at the commencement of a tribal core in the basin surrounding the Chalbi Desert, with Marsabit Mountain forming a focal point; others indicate an origin in the region to the west of Lake Rudolf; and yet others tell of beginnings in such remote areas as Sakuye country to the east of Marsabit. One recent researcher, after careful analysis of documented evidence on population movements in the eastern part of Kenya's northern territory, has suggested that the Rendille and Gabbra peoples, amongst other allied types, originally stemmed from units of the Somali Garre group who had steadily migrated northwards from their stamping grounds on the coast. On looking at all these ideas collectively, a picture of sorts was formed. The Rendille were thought to be an amalgam of small splinter groups who rallied round one dominant nucleus, formed from a strong band of immigrants from the east who spoke in a Somali-type tongue. One may safely assume that each group contributed at least a few of their customs and habits to the whole, resulting in the Rendille culture, a curious blend of tribal influences from both the east and west of northern Kenya.

Amazingly, for a hardship area peopled by pastoralists who are by nature sensitive during times of rigorous conditions, the Samburu and Rendille enjoyed a close alliance, a fact clearly substantiated in tribal traditions. In spite of a definite language difference, their unusual relationship survived many ups and downs during testing times. They banded together to resist invaders, intermarried, assisted one another in adversity, and even displayed similar customs in their respective social structures. There were, of course, some major contrasts between these two peoples, the principal one being their mode of livelihood. The Samburu were almost entirely cattlemen, excepting their sheep and goats; the Rendille were by tradition camel herders. Their languages differed greatly, the Samburu being Maa speakers, quite at variance with the Somali influenced communication of the Rendille. Although their customs bore some resemblance, there were definite distinctions that set their tribal individuality apart. All in all, though, the relationship between the Samburu and the Rendille was a remarkable example of collaboration between two groups of essentially different ethnic origins; remarkable on a continent where petty jealousies often led to serious tribal frictions and conflicts. A traditional tale illustrating this relates how in far-off times a Samburu family named Logol settled near an encampment of Rendille warriors who, in need of a bull to slaughter for one of their rituals, begged one from the family. After performing their ceremony, they returned and married the daughters of Logol. Although only a simple folk-tale, the actual practice of requesting a bull from the Logol family by Rendille youths about to undergo the age-set ritual continues to the present day.

The hazy picture of the Rendille people's past begins to clear towards the middle of the nineteenth century when traditions indicate a movement of the tribe from an area immediately south of Lake Rudolf, eastwards towards the environs of Marsabit. At approximately the same time, it will be recalled, the Samburu had commenced their breakout from Ngiro and Kulal in a northerly direction. The Rendille, being camel men, did not require the rich pasturelands sought after by the Samburu, so they contentedly settled in the less hospitable country between the mountains of Marsabit and Kulal, spreading north west and south from this area in the years that followed.

The north-westerly movement took them into the arid country south of Samburu-held Uoto, and into contact with the Dasenech on the shores of the lake. In that harsh land, bounding on the southern limits of Abyssinia, their camels found ample forage. Relations with the Dasenech remained on the whole friendly, neither party competing with the other for a living. The years during the 1880s and early '90s, prior to the arrival of ravaging diseases and Turkana raids, were times of plenty for the Rendille, when they and the Samburu dominated the lands adjacent to the eastern shores of Lake Rudolf.

The Rendille's age-old enemies, the Laikipiaks, were, however, a continued source of irritation, especially with their northerly advance in 1879, and their attacks on the camel-herding people to the east of Marsabit and in the region of Laisamis. Driven out of these areas by fear of further raids the Rendille struck west, unwittingly towards another enemy, the arrogant Turkana, whose scouts were beginning to probe the area along the eastern shore of Lake Rudolf. The good times were ended for another two decades. A retreat was made, and with the only sanctuary available lying in the lands between Kulal and Marsabit, the harassed tribesmen established themselves in this harsh desert area.

The Rendille were not permitted peace for long. To add to the strife with the Turkana and Laikipiak marauders came the threat ever present in that arid land— drought. With enemies all around—for the Somalis were also attacking them from the east—and their camels dying from starvation, another problem arose to burden them. Their old allies, the Samburu, were clamouring for help in *their* time of need.

Providentially, the year 1890 marked a turning point in the Rendille's history, for it was then they finally gained the upper hand over the Laikipiaks. In a classic battle on the Merille river, a combination of Rendille spears, arrows and clubs and a resolve born of desperation managed to vanquish the Laikipiaks who were armed with heavy spears and shields. From the time of that historic fight the Rendille never again looked on them as a serious threat.

In the same year, after two years of almost no rain, the drought finally broke. But already many of their camels had died, and in a supreme effort to save the remainder of their beasts the northern Rendille left their homeland, and migrated north to the proximity of Borana territory. There they settled on the plains of the Golbo.

Their encounters with the Borana were of a mixed nature, peaceful periods alternating with skirmishes and raids, when the Rendille had to cope with attackers mounted on horses, a new type of warfare which they found difficult to handle at first. Later they found the answer to the problem: immobilise the enemy's horses with arrow wounds, so forcing them to march and fight on foot. The Borana's customary lightening tactics were immediately restricted. They learned their lesson and thereafter tethered their horses before going into battle. In victory the Borana were ruthless, invariably butchering or enslaving their enemies and driving all captured small stock and camels back to their highland fastness in Abyssinia.

The Gabbra people, who also frequented parts of the Golbo, lived in a permanent state of armed neutrality with their Rendille neighbours; occasional conflicts between them at waterholes on the desert alternated with times of peaceful coexistence, when a certain degree of intermarriage even took place.

When the fatal rinderpest scourge of the 1890s reduced the Samburu to an impoverished state, the Rendille willingly provided them with support and food. Employed by the Rendille as camel herders, many of the distressed Samburu were assimilated into their host's ranks, so reinforcing the bond which had allied these desperate people for so long, and affording them a breathing space in which to re-establish their sorely depleted herds of cattle. Seeing the healthy unaffected herds of camels inevitably raised a feeling of desire in Samburu minds, causing a marked increase in the theft and slaughter of Rendille camels to appease their hunger. Chanler's expedition account clearly recorded the unique relationship existing between the two types of Samburu he found living in the Kom area in association with the Rendille—the camel-herding slaves, and the thieving 'Dthombons', who also hunted wild animals for subsistence.

Relief from drought, their camels' immunity to rinderpest, and the retreat of their Laikipiak enemies did not mean, however, that better times were ahead for the Rendille. The ominous arrival of an epidemic of smallpox in the mid-1890s ravaged their settlements for several years. It was yet another affliction, and with serious consequences for their security. With their population heavily depleted, the Rendille, ironically, had to ask the Samburu for assistance in defence, in addition to their herding duties. The Samburu, chiefly through the partial immunity gained from an outbreak of smallpox in the Lake Stefanie area some years before, had survived this new manifestation of the disease better than the Rendille, and so were able to assist their distressed allies.

The symbiotic reliance carried through into the early years of the twentieth century. In those days the Rendille possessed huge herds of camels, but only a small number of able people were left alive to care for them. On the other hand the Samburu had very little stock, and in relation a surplus population. Regrettably, it led to a period of further raiding and strife between these old friends, with the Samburu warriors out of desperation and necessity once again filching camels, sheep and goats. It was a parlous state for both parties, but as Neal Sobania wrote many years later: 'Their [Rendille] misfortune, however, was the salvation of those they adopted, and their lost and stolen animals sustained others in the region, from the Samburu and Boran in the plains to those living as Ndorobo in the mountains or at the lake'.

The Rendille's next hurdle was the arrival of the British government's administration in 1909. Hampered by shortage of staff, and with remote, isolated stations at Archer's Post, Marsabit and Moyale, it was not in a strong position to implement its new measures. By then Borana encroachments on the Marsabit grazing grounds were forcing the Rendille people southwards, and into the area between Kulal and Laisamis. This last aggravation was not helped by the incipient administration's lack of a clear-cut policy, apart from their intention to counter the increasing Abyssinian incursions from the north.

More upsetting to the Rendille were the repugnant requirements of the government station at Marsabit: the demand of an annual tribute of 500 camels from the Rendille caused their immediate flight from the vicinity of the Marsabit to Archer's Post road, in an effort to evade the new affliction. It had the desired effect on the authorities, who cancelled the order but put into effect an alternative arrangement: the Rendille were ordered to lease their camels on a monthly basis. The new scheme met with more resistance, as camels were often returned at the end of their service worn out and in poor condition. Even more galling to the Rendille was the realisation that only they were encumbered with this obligation to the government. Later, the Samburu were included in the system, only to be relieved of the burden shortly after, in compensation for the losses they had suffered from Turkana raids. Once again the Rendille were the sole contributors, a situation that led, understandably, to further dissension between them and the administration.

More confining moves followed as government plans for the district were implemented, and distinct areas delineated for the containment of tribal groups. To aggravate the situation even further, the Borana in their flight from the Abyssinians had virtually overrun the Rendille grazing grounds on Marsabit, and the Sidam and Dasenech had made the area in the vicinity of Lake Rudolf unsafe. In 1919 came the final blow: the administration established an exclusively Rendille area which enclosed them in a tract bounded by Mt Kulal, the foot of Mt Marsabit, and Laisamis. While this was designed with the good intention of creating a sense of order and discipline in the region, its establishment was clearly the death-knell of any far-reaching future movements for the Rendille. So it came about that this interesting nomadic people finally reached a halt, depleted in human numbers, but wealthy in stock.

To this day the Rendille are found living in the same stretch of country, moving their camels wherever there is sufficient food and using their ancestral waterholes on the Chalbi Desert. They retain many of their customs, consort with their old allies the Samburu, and continue to converse in their distinctive language—so remaining a true and highly individual people of semi-desert lands.

*The quiet dignity of the Gabbra is clearly seen in this study of Yatani Sorale, an elder of his tribe.*

# GABBRA

TO the north of Rendille territory an immense arid area stretches towards the Abyssinian border, a land few other places in Kenya can equal for barren, unwatered grimness. There are, of course, parts of it that do not entirely match up to this description: for example, the exquisite Hurri Hills, a normally verdant island in the midst of desert, and the great plains of the Golbo stretching round the foot of towering Mt Foroli and on to the barrier ramparts of the distant Megado escarpment. These hills and plains are, however, more often than not waterless, only capable of accommodating large numbers of stock for an all too brief period after rains. It is a land of magnificent views, harsh desert flats, grass-covered hills, rough stony wastes, and wells. It is also a land of many colours, but strikingly dominant are the blacks, greys, and a multiplicity of browns. It is not a space to rest one's eyes on soothing green fields, for they are rarely found in this great, empty expanse.

This place is the land of the Gabbra, a race of gentle stockmen. Ethnically they are related to their neighbours the Rendille, but between them there is a marked contrast in looks, dress and culture. In one obvious respect they do have a bond—their common interest in camel herding. Their culture has strong overtones of outside influences, affecting the rules of their tribal structure, their language and their dress, but in common with other nomads in the region, they have developed their own strategies for survival.

The Gabbra people's background and culture has given them a remarkable ability to keep their history in a clear, precise manner. This has been made possible through the exceptional diligence of the community elders, who, with meticulous attention have maintained their myths and the accuracy of their history-keeping traditions over the years. A preoccupation with early events has always been a refined pursuit for the older men, and it is this very dedication to the past that has been invaluable to contemporary researchers. The Gabbra recognise two main channels in their story. One takes care of the traditions of their origins, lineages and important events. It is the pure history of the tribe and its ancient past, which, coupled with the stories of more recent developments, is of value in helping to establish rules of seniority and tribal discipline. This is of particular value to a people who live widely separated, but all held within the boundaries of an extensive region. The second form of their history is based on the chronological recurrence of climatic cycles, a phenomenon to which the Gabbra have wisely paid much attention. This is of great practical value, providing them with forecasts of coming seasons' prospects—an asset that helps the clan and family group leaders to plan their future strategies with a certain degree of reliability.

Influenced by Somali and Arabic methods, the Gabbra have developed a meticulous calendar based on seven-day weeks and lunar months. Confusingly, the Gabbra lunar calendar is not used in calculating their year. This is reckoned by working on a system using the cyclical recurrence of seasons, a method which brings their new year's day celebrations back every 365 days. The system gives the Gabbra a cycle of seven years known as the week-cycle, whereby each year within a seven-year cycle bears the name of a weekday. On the eighth year the week-cycle starts again. In addition to the weekday name given to each year may be added the name of a particularly important event which occurred during the course of the year. The custom of giving years specific names is of considerable value to the contemporary historian in relating events to particular periods in Gabbra history. By the applied use of their calendar, the Gabbra are able to fix dates with precision, their exact recollections stretching back eighty years, and, in exceptional cases, even further. Armed with this well-developed ability to recall the past in a reasoned manner, it has been possible for recent researchers to correlate the tales recounting Gabbra origins with a modicum of accuracy. Beyond that, reliance on traditions once more becomes the rule, and as with the myths of the Samburu and Rendille, an element of haziness then arises, leading to a variety of ideas and a certain amount of contradiction.

In the same way that the other people of northern Kenya were involved in turbulent movements during recent centuries, the Gabbra's migrations have also been bound up with the influences of more powerful outside groups encroaching on their territory. All these ethnic contortions have led to yet another amalgam of cultures and alliances, out of which developed the Gabbra race, a loosely bound unit made up of six principal sections, each with its own traditions on the subject of the Gabbra tribe's origins. It is known that during the eighteenth century—a period of fateful harassments and movements amongst the populations of eastern Africa—a section of the Somali people, the Garre, were squeezed out of their coastal homelands between the Tana and Juba rivers by a powerful incursion of Galla from the north. One recent scholar has postulated that a group of Garre prudently departed for the hinterland, heading first in the direction of the Lorian Swamp, later moving further northwards into the area of Marsabit, the Chalbi Desert and beyond. He further suggested that the Gabbra may have originated from part of the breakaway group. It is a plausible suggestion and tallies with certain Gabbra traditions telling of a branch of the Garre which joined up with the Borana in bygone times. Another capable author has quoted more traditions declaring the common origins of one Gabbra section, and some Rendille clans, to be from the Somalis. While a third expert has stated that in the distant past a population of Borana-speaking people lived to the west of Lake Rudolf, in common occupation of that remote territory with Rendille, early Samburu and others. All these groups, he learned from tribal traditions, were finally driven out by the Turkana invasion from the west.

Understandably, these conclusions are confusing, especially as they do not entirely correspond with one another. In attempting to clarify these disparate views, it should be recalled that the Gabbra entity is composed of six completely autonomous sections, each one totally independent of the other for their internal administration and leadership, but all of them maintaining a strong common loyalty and interdependency to a Gabbra unity on matters affecting the tribe as a whole. The Gabbra are recognised as an eastern Cushitic people speaking a Galla language, in this case Borana.

Paul Robinson, a leading authority on the Gabbra people, has discussed their origins in a perceptive dissertation: 'Gabbra ... maintain historical ties with the Borana homeland of Liban and Dirre in southern Ethiopia ... Whether these are in fact homelands for the Gabbra ... or whether their identification with Dirre and Liban is more predicated on political grounds of a need to identify with the Borana, is open to speculation. Indeed some Gabbra traditions do point to Dirre and Liban as homelands'. He goes on to add: 'Equally strong traditions indicate firm linkages with the Rendille, Somali and even Dasenech'. This latter remark accords with earlier suggestions about the common lineage of the Gabbra and Rendille, and is substantiated by recent traditions that tell of Rendille joining and being accommodatingly accepted into Gabbra communities. Conversely, traditions indicate the origin of one Gabbra section in the south from the Rendille. The complex nature of Gabbra origins is exacerbated by the traditional claims of the Galbo section, which asserts quite emphatically that they originated from the Wata people. The latter were a hunter-gatherer race which lived in the region long before the Gabbra arrived, and it is certainly possible that many Wata were assimilated into the groups of recently arrived camel herders that were seeking new lands in which to live. The historical tie was later to prove of inestimable value when the Gabbra were provided with refuge from drought and starvation in Wata country.

The extensive Gabbra traditions covering the subject of their origins have generated a perplexing variety of options on their ancestry, but in the main they all lead up to the same conclusion—that they arrived from the east and in all likelihood were once a part of the Garre Somali. In the course of their protracted travels they came into contact with a Galla people, the Borana, forming close associations with them, and undoubtedly even cohabiting with them in the highlands of southern Abyssinia. They brought camel herds with them, but finding Boranaland's cold and lush country unsuitable for their beasts, they were only too glad to move with the southerly migrating Borana into the warmer lowland Golbo country below the Megado escarpment, an area eminently suitable for a camel society. Another quote from Robinson succinctly defines the embryonic Gabbra's development during this period of association with the Borana: 'Increasing physical distance between these Garre/Gara and their homeland, as well as an intermediary Borana population, both led to an increasing identification of these individuals with Borana culture, language and religion and ultimately their abandonment of Garre culture and Islam'. Significantly, one part of Garre life the Gabbra retained was their mainstay of camel herding.

Out of all these convolutions, both real and mythical, emerged the Gabbra as a distinct race, their ancestral cultures forgotten, and a new and close affiliation firmly established with the Borana. During the nineteenth century the Gabbra were to be found in the region of the Golbo, along the southern fringe of which were the perennial waterholes of the Chalbi Desert. Included in their new-found territory were the beautiful Hurri Hills (the Badha Hurri—'forest mists'—of the Gabbra). For a period these hills were jointly occupied with the Rendille, a situation that inevitably led to conflict in the beginning. After years of intermittent skirmishing over their rights, the contestants finally came to an amicable understanding and shared the benefits of the hills. In time the Rendille left and retired southwards.

In the 1870s the Gabbra consolidated their position in their adopted homeland, peacefully moving their herds of camels and cattle between feeding grounds as the impositions of changing and variable seasons dictated. But it was only a time of relative quiet before the storm. The first disaster was the arrival of the marauding Laikipiaks on their northerly advance. Triumphant and confident after routing the Rendille, these newcomers were a resolute force, implacably driving the fearful Gabbra ahead of them up to the looming mass of the Megado escarpment. Even this formidable barrier failed to stop the Laikipiak's advance north to Mega and into Boranaland. At this critical point the Borana stepped in to assist their Gabbra allies and, opportunely, themselves. They had a novel weapon, never before experienced by the Laikipiak warrior—armed cavalry. It proved remarkably effective when deployed against the spear-throwing Laikipiaks. With the aid of Wata bowmen the Borana and Gabbra horsemen attacked, battles ensuing all along the chain of hills below the escarpment. A succession of decisive defeats was remorselessly handed out to the demoralised enemy, whereupon they were compelled to retreat ever southwards, driven by the concerted efforts of the defending cavalrymen into the hands of the Rendille. After the Laikipiak remnants were finally beaten by the Rendille in the classic battle already mentioned, the land enjoyed a few years of relative peace.

The respite did not last, for the infamous decade of tragedies which was shattering the livelihood and lives of the region did not bypass the Gabbra. First, like wildfire, came rinderpest in 1887, sweeping down from the northern parts of Abyssinia and relentlessly destroying the bulk of their cattle. It was a critical but not total disaster, for only a quarter of the Gabbra were cattle owners. The fortunate ones had camels. Their cattle almost eliminated, starvation soon took a terrible toll of human lives. The survivors wisely adopted the camel economy of their fellow-tribesmen, travelling down to the Golbo to join them in the country where camels could subsist and even thrive.

The Gabbra had hardly recovered from the horrors of their immense cattle losses when heavy rains fell in 1890. Normally a blessing, paradoxically it now brought a human blight in the form of an extensive and lethal plague of malaria. Mortality was severe amongst the people, and as if that affliction was not enough, an almost Biblical infliction arrived in 1891 with the advent of smallpox. It was the Gabbra's first encounter with this alien disease. Many of those who had survived starvation and malaria now succumbed to the new malignancy, leaving the weakened survivors to struggle as best they could through the remaining years of that appalling decade.

Contributing to the Gabbra's dire state during this trying period were the chronic drought conditions that prevailed through the last ten years of the nineteenth century, provoking further strife as stock-hungry neighbours became increasingly embattled with one another in their efforts to build up diminished herds of animals. The situation was further aggravated by the encroachment of Menelik's Abyssinians, bent on the same activity themselves. In those tense and grasping years everyone outside the Gabbra tribe was a potential enemy to them, raiding and counter-raiding being quite the order of the day for all.

Not everything, however, was gained by warlike methods, for a certain amount of peaceful trading took place in the region. Moreover, the Gabbra, in the same way that the Samburu did with the Wandorobo and Elmolo, adopted the life-styles of their nearby neighbours, the Konso agriculturists, and the hunter-gatherer Wata; the Gabbra lived with them until such time as conditions permitted the resumption of their old pattern of life. Among the Gabbra sections a keen spirit of brotherhood came into play, those with surviving stock assisting their less fortunate fellow-tribesmen. The true cohesion of the tribe was thus demonstrated in times so desperate that the Gabbra, as well as the Borana, were driven to eating their horses and donkeys in order to escape starvation. A direct result of this was a decline in the cavalry force and thus their military effectiveness.

Trading for new stock was a vital business, and undertaken amicably with the Somalis, who fortunately were in the position to spare a few animals from their surviving herds of cattle. Camels, ivory, rhino horn, goats and sheep were the Gabbra's main trade goods. Although not traders by inclination, necessity compelled them to seek out the Somalis and barter with them for cattle. Ivory was a particularly valuable currency in those hard days, so the Gabbra quickly learned to become elephant hunters. The elephants served their purpose, and to this day individual cattle have names associated with aspects of elephant life, indicating their origin from a beast once purchased by means of ivory. The very last resort employed by the Borana and Gabbra to stave off starvation was to sell their children as slaves to the Somalis. They fatalistically reasoned that if they themselves survived they could always reproduce more offspring. Happily, on many occasions the children were adopted by their purchasers and accepted into the family circle.

During the nineteenth century's closing years the effects of yet another new aggressor made itself felt: Menelik's Abyssinian Sidam arrived armed with guns—the first the Gabbra had ever come against. They were no more capable of resisting this new enemy than were the nearby Samburu, and their only hope lay in flight towards the Chalbi Desert and Lake Rudolf areas in the south west. Those Gabbra who failed to escape found themselves in the clutches of harsh and demanding new masters.

The arrival of the Sidam was not the final blow, for the new century started on yet another bad note: the Turkana arrived to take their toll. Caught unawares around their waterholes on the fringe of the desert, the Gabbra were butchered unmercifully by the Turkana raiders. A rout ensued and the fleeing Gabbra once more decamped, reluctantly retreating northwards. The demoralised Gabbra had only two alternatives: either death at the hands of the Turkana, or back into the bondage of the waiting Sidam. Their choice was obvious, and once more they became shackled by Menelik's men.

Onto this stage marched the first white man to traverse Gabbra country. Lord Delamere, while on his expedition through east Africa in 1897, regrettably did not keep a diary of his activities, and his only recorded comments were the brief annotations in his photograph album. This was a pity, for his interest in the country and the people was now superseding his earlier passion for hunting, and one feels that his enthusiasm as an amateur ethnographer might have produced much of value to add to the Gabbra story. His remarks were, however, terse and not overly informative.

The next to arrive on the scene was the noble-born Count Eduard Wickenburg, a precise Austrian cavalry officer. While tramping through the district in 1901 he noted the absence of Gabbra along the desert edge, although a note on his map infers that he saw evidence of their previous occupancy of these lands: 'fruher teilweise v.d. Gabra bewohnt' (formerly partly inhabited by the Gabbra). It was not until he reached the country lying below the Megado escarpment that he finally encountered a 'Gabra dorfer' (village), clear proof of the Gabbras' presence in more northerly haunts and undoubtedly enforced by the Turkana attacks of the previous year.

Encouragingly, the first decade of the century was one in which the Gabbra enjoyed a period of growth amongst their stock. Following the painful experience of rinderpest attacks, their policy had become one of changeover from cattle to a predominantly camel-based economy, and that in turn meant an intensification in their occupation of the hot and arid Golbo lands adjacent to the Chalbi Desert and its environs. Most probably this was the beginning of their acceptance of a distinct homeland in the region. Yet their troubles were far from over, for it was during those years, just prior to the arrival of the British administration, that internecine struggles and stock raids amongst the tribes were rife, no one being exceptional in their attempts by any means to enhance herd size at their neighbour's expense. It was a time of ferment, before the establishment of a formal boundary between Abyssinia and the British East Africa Protectorate, and before the imposition of stricter discipline by the latter's authorities. It was also a time of wandering, when good rains made fruitful lands; at one stage a few Gabbra were even found as far south as the Uaso Ngiro river and the Lorian Swamp.

With the second decade and tighter British control in the area came a feeling of security, encouraging emigration from Abyssinia to escape the scourge of tiresome taxation in a politically unsettled country. The Gabbra steadily increased in the district, moving towards and onto the northern slopes of Marsabit Mountain, in turn creating further problems for the new and understaffed administration. Despite the token security, not all was peace and plenty in those years, for yet another enemy appeared from the north west—the Gelubba (or Dasenech)—now armed with guns and seemingly aided and abetted by the Abyssinians. A widespread series of appalling raids were experienced by Gabbra settlements, stretching from the wells of Dukana to those of Maikona. Many died, but the tragedies had the effect of prodding the authorities based on Marsabit into establishing outposts in remote and strategic places, hoping they would deter the audacious incursions of Gelubba raiders. This move met with partial success, for although smaller raids continued for many years, never again did they extend so deeply into Gabbra territory or over such a general area.

For the Gabbra the first two decades of the twentieth century were a period of mixed fortunes. On the one hand improved climatic conditions had assisted the regeneration of their herds, but on the other the resurgence of anthrax, minor rinderpest outbreaks and drought caused heavy mortalities amongst their cattle and camels. Persecutions of their people by the Abyssinians from the north and the newly armed Gelubba from the west, were compensated for by the advantages of living under the protection of the British administration, which, although cramping in some respects, in others was distinctly well intentioned. From bitter experience the Gabbra were now firmly decided on the value of camels as the core of their economy; concomittantly, they were established in a distinct region, one with which they could hope to continue with their traditional lives, practising their well-organised cultures. In their utilisation of a particularly harsh environment they filled a niche of great importance in the life of northern Kenya.

# DASENECH

LAKE Rudolf's principal source of water is the perennial River Omo, a supply reliant on the seasonal rainfall in the Abyssinian mountains to the north. For the river's last miles of listless flow before spilling into the lake, it meanders over hot flatlands, winding steadily between banks cloaked with lush tropical forest and bush. During times of flood it may overflow these banks depositing rich alluvial soils from upcountry and creating healthy acres of nutritious agricultural land.

In this isolated corner of productivity live the Dasenech people, a small tribe which speaks an eastern Cushitic language, tills grain fields and herds stock. These were Teleki's Reshiat, with whom he enjoyed excellent relations. They are a curious little relic group whose language suggests origins far to the east, but whose traditions tell of a genesis on the western side of the lake. Von Höhnel, who was the first white man to write about the Reshiat, mentioned that they appeared to be a race of mixed cultures and customs, displaying 'Semitic' characteristics and features on the one hand, while showing distinct evidence of contacts with the Turkana, Samburu and Rendille on the other. In the decade following the discovery of this remote tribe, several more white explorers visited the Reshiat, benefiting from their agricultural labours and their peaceful demeanour.

Dasenech traditions are clear on their point of origin: everyone agrees they initially came from the western side of Lake Rudolf, from a country called Nyupe. They knew of themselves as the Nyupe people, just one of the groups living in Nyupeland that were forced to leave by the Turkana invasion from the west. Turkana traditions agree emphatically, adding that their advances towards the close of the eighteenth century split the Nyupe into two, the northern section fleeing northwards towards the corner in which they now live.

The Dasenech were a small pastoralist group when all this happened, but force of circumstances dictated a change in life-style, for their Canaan was a riverine, crop-growing country. Furthermore, it was not devoid of owners, for many small resident groups were engaged in a variety of activities in the hot, lush valley of the Omo. Agriculturists, hunters, fishermen and yet more stock herders were firmly entrenched. Conflicts between them and the overpowering Dasenech were inevitable. The conquering newcomers gained both land and new people to swell their ranks, a system of acquisition that continued as they consolidated their position in the region. From their alliances, whether by conquest or co-operation, the original core of Nyupe gradually coalesced the diverse groups living along the northern shore of Lake Rudolf, blending with the vanquished to form a composite tribe who were first known to the white man as the Reshiat, and later as the Gelubba, Shangilla, Merille or Dasenech.

As a consequence of this amalgamation of heterogeneous people, the Dasenech developed an economy of great diversification, an advantage that saved them from the horrendous losses that struck their purely pastoral neighbours in the tragic years to come. The most stable aspect of their lives was their cultivating activity on the rich flood beds left by the seasonally retreating River Omo. These fields supplied the staple necessities to feed themselves, and even starving friends, through many times of drought and pestilence. During the rinderpest devastation the Dasenech lost their cattle as other tribes had done, but millet and beans from their carefully tended gardens were their lifeline. Even the Samburu, Rendille and passing white men found succour from this vital source of food. The story of the Dasenech friendship and resulting kinship with the Samburu and Rendille has already been told; it was a relationship which is recalled to the present day in tribal traditions. Equally, many instances of Dasenech hospitality are recounted in several nineteenth-century white explorers' travel tales.

The Dasenech possessed a generous country where there was more arable land available than there were people to work it, a factor that helped to make outsiders welcome. Refugees were soon recruited to join the agricultural workers in the seasonal fields. The crops of millet, beans and tobacco were invaluable, not only for the tribe's sustenance, but as important barter goods. Traders came from as far away as the southern highlands of Abyssinia to exchange these for their products: iron, cloth, clay pots and coffee. The Dasenech wisely did not travel with their goods, most of which were headed for the land of their dreaded enemies, the Borana. The intermediary transport and trading was done by the Arbore, a diminutive tribe living at the north end of Lake Stefanie. They were true middlemen in the sense that they enjoyed ancestral, as well as friendly, relationships with both the Dasenech and the Borana, a convenient affinity benefiting all parties. The Konso, who were the agriculturist friends of the Gabbra, also filled a key place in the trading circuit as vital manufacturers of iron goods and cloth.

Hidden in their nook by the edge of the lake didn't mean the Dasenech were exempt from the effects of Menelik's southerly advance in the closing years of the century. The first true Abyssinians they met were hunters by profession and armed with lethal rifles. Significantly, they were not in search of land or stock, so the Dasenech soon put aside their fear and distrust. However, the initial friendship and co-operation was destroyed shortly after by the arrival of Menelik's Abyssinian army on its trail of conquest and acquisition. Its raids into Dasenechland were brief and brutal, purely in the quest of riches and taxes. The hot, unhealthy Omo delta did not suit the highland Abyssinians, and history records that in the beginning they only embarked on intermittent raids. Later, permanent army posts were established to ensure the regular extortion of taxes from the local people. During this troublesome period a Machiavellian character appeared on the scene—Count Leontieff, a nobleman employed by the Russian government to further their interests with Menelik and Abyssinia. A superb opportunist, almost totally self-centred and with a greedy readiness to serve his own ends, he was given command of a heavily armed force of Abyssinians and detailed to explore the south-western sector of Abyssinian territory. Leontieff, who was described as unreliable, dishonest in money matters and highly unscrupulous, pillaged and burned as he went, indiscriminately killing the people he met. His destination was Dasenechland, and there he established a temporary base from which to devastate and discipline the primitively armed residents.

In later years relations with the Abyssinians became more amicable and peaceful, following the Dasenech's reluctant acceptance of Abyssinian dominance and rule. The next step in the relationship between Dasenech and Abyssinian was collaboration. The partnership was menacing, and resulted in a joint participation in the latter's nefarious occupations of raiding and elephant hunting. Disturbingly, the alliance led to the riverine people acquiring firearms in ever increasing number. Gradually they developed their new-found strength into a force to be feared, giving rise to the infamous reputation of the Dasenech, or Gelubba. The last name struck terror into the hearts of primitively armed tribesmen down the eastern shore of Lake Rudolf for many years thereafter. In their early days they regularly joined forces with the Abyssinians in predatory forays against the Samburu, Rendille and elephants. Their pernicious raids against the Gabbra have already been described. Well armed with superior weapons, they also took the opportunity of settling old scores, hunting down their age-old and primitively armed Turkana enemies. The uneven match was only squared when the Turkana themselves acquired rifles. By then the Dasenech were no longer simply a peace-loving tribe of riverine gardeners. They had added raiding to their activities, and become a scourge to neighbours and wildlife, and a threat to the agencies of order, an invidious enemy that continued its needling raids for many decades.

*The face of Lokok Elanabir, an Elmolo 'aitat' (master spear-fisherman) exhibits definite Cushitic features.*

# ELMOLO

NESTLED closely together in a sheltered bay on the bleak and arid south-eastern shores of Lake Rudolf, Teleki found three barren little islands*. Viewed from the shoreline they appear rocky, wasted and totally devoid of any hospitable aspect. A derelict and hostile place, its rich shades of black, brown, red and yellow contrast strikingly with the restful green tones of the lake and the matching blue of the sky. From a cursory glance nothing appears to inhabit these rough craggy islands, but closer examination will reveal small clusters of human habitations, much the same in appearance today as they were when von Höhnel first described them in 1888 as 'primitive hayrick-shaped huts made of stones and grass'. Ever since von Höhnel's visit these islands have been known as the Elmolo Islands, a name that was derived from the curious little group of people who lived in isolated contentment on the shores of those jagged lava projections.

Since 1888 the Elmolo have been studied with considerable curiosity. As this tiny and out-of-the-way community was at one time estimated to number less that one hundred, it was believed to be dying out. Tucked away in their lakeside fastness they lived an Ndorobo-like existence, their lives centred on fishing and killing hippopotamus for a living, possessing no stock and never straying far from their base. Their traditions tell of many alliances down the years, but their origins appear to be tied closely with those of the Dasenech and Arbore people in the north. Furthermore, Dasenech traditions commenting on their close affiliation are emphatic in declaring their unwillingness to fight one another in any circumstances. A delightful Dasenech myth illustrates the close link: in ancient times a party of people went down to drink water at a pool; while they drank a frog started its raucous croak; on hearing this fearful noise the drinkers became so terrified they split up and fled, one group going north and forming the Dasenech, the rest leaving to start a section of the Elmolo. Whatever the true story of their origin, one fact is indisputable: they have coexisted peacefully with their neighbours for countless years. It is a most unusual record in a land of turmoil and warfare.

Changes came into the uneventful and simple lives of the tiny Elmolo community during the last decade of the nineteenth century, when the disasters already described forced Samburu to seek refuge amongst them. During that hard time the gradual adoption of Samburu language, customs and economies overrode their own. In consequence their ancient language was almost lost, their Elmolo cultures were eroded and altered to blend with Samburu rules, and a livestock economy became more evident. The Samburu relationship inevitably came to an end as they re-established their herds and dispersed to better grazing grounds, but the impact of the virile race had had its effect, causing changes that remained deeply engrained in the Elmolo way of life.

The opening of a British military station at Loiengalani in 1910 created a new influence on the Elmolo. They soon became conscious of the advantages of trade and

---

*With the severe drought conditions of recent years the lake has receded far from its 1888 level, and today there is only one island.

protection under the paternal white man's rule. A friendly eye was kept on these remote people long after the post was abandoned a few years later. This interest manifested itself in 1921 when a regrettable raid by a band of Samburu warriors killed eight Elmolo by mistake; the government stepped in and confiscated some thousands of sheep and goats from the Samburu as blood money payment to the tiny tribe.

The compensation was another step forward in the Elmolo involvement in pastoralism. It represented another step away from their strictly Ndorobo way of life. By then their numbers were increasing, but only at the pathetically slow rate a hard climate and mainly fish-based diet permitted. Many years passed before better conditions improved their chance of survival, but despite these changes they clung to their fishing activities and their Elmolo name.

# TURKANA AND BORANA

NTERWOVEN among the tribal chronicles of the foregoing pages are the influences of two ethnically opposite people—the Turkana and the Borana. While their homelands are beyond the borders of the territory being examined, their impact on the resident Samburu, Rendille and Gabbra makes it essential to discuss them briefly. The Turkana and Borana are poles apart in almost all respects, even their geographic origins. The Turkana were a true Nilotic people which invaded the western part of Kenya from the Uganda region and settled in the arid country west of Lake Rudolf; the Borana are part of the Galla race which was established once throughout the general area of southern Abyssinia. Likewise, their language, customs, dress and physical appearance are strikingly dissimilar. The only characteristic they seem to have in common is their pastoral existence.

By the nineteenth century the Turkana were becoming a formidable and aggressive force dedicated to territorial consolidation. Tall, powerful, dark-skinned men, their hard ruthless nature had been tempered by the austere country in which they lived. Woe betide those who stood in the way of their intransigent warrior bands. Swinging round the southern end of the lake they fanned out eastwards, causing strife and abundant bloodshed wherever they roamed. An immensely disturbing influence on the region, their attacks extended far from their home ranges and deep into alien territories. Plunder and murder rather than settlement seemed to be their objective, keeping them moving from place to place, and leaving in their wake a fearful reputation for savagery.

The depredations of the Turkana were comparable in extensiveness to those of the Laikipiaks in their final days. Their raids took them to the Uaso Ngiro river in the south and to the Hurri Hills on the borders of Abyssinia. Turkana penetrations can be viewed as one more feature of the disquieting state of affairs existing in the region prior to the arrival of the white man's administration, a period in which there were tribulations enough for the people to combat without the added presence of the Turkana raiders. The newly arrived administration soon became aware of the problem and set itself the difficult task of curbing their activities. The exercise proved immensely frustrating. Although the frequency of raids was reduced, Turkana infiltrations into neighbouring lands were never stopped.

The Borana are a group of the once-powerful Galla race which for centuries dominated a huge tract of country in southern Abyssinia and northern Kenya. A pastoral tribe herding camels, cattle, sheep and goats, they were also—through their ownership of horses—accomplished horsemen. The advantage played a major part in maintaining their position of power in the region. Although the story of their involvements with small neighbouring units of Somali people is outside the scope of this work, their sway over one such group, the Gabbra, is relevant. In their close association with the Gabbra they shared many problems, one of which was the Abyssinian invasion that forced many of them southwards from their highland homes in Dirre to the Golbo and on to the mountain slopes of Marsabit, an area with which they have remained connected.

When Dr Donaldson Smith marched through Boranaland in 1895 on his way to

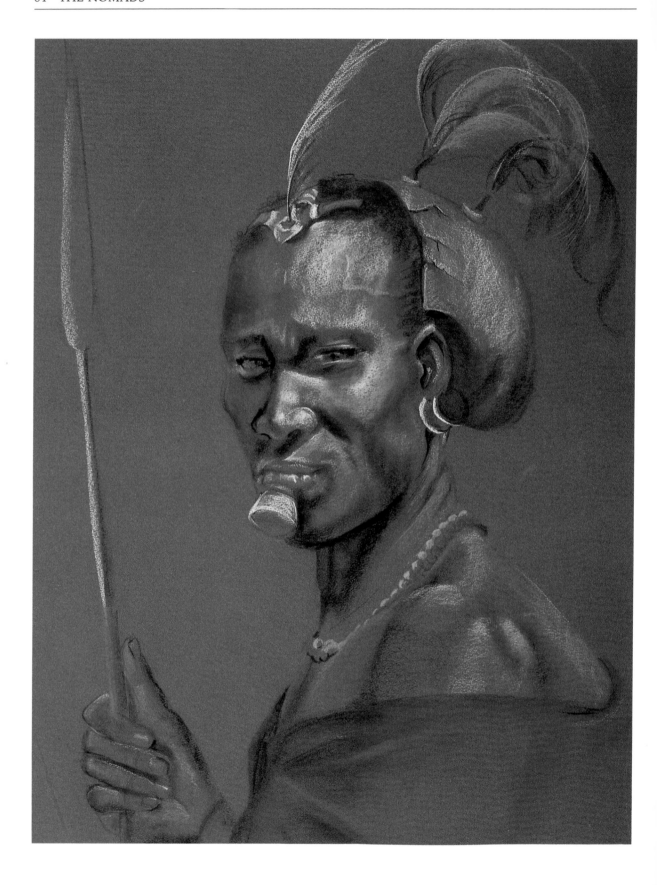

LEFT: *This study of a Turkana in yesteryear's headgear reveals some of the ferocity of these people's nature.*

RIGHT: *In the pose of Molu Galgalo, an elderly Borana of considerable means, some of the philosophic acceptance of a hard life is evident.*

Lake Rudolf, he experienced a warlike confrontation with the Borana. His meeting with their cavalry was a demonstration of their supremacy in the region at the time. Shortly after, however, the arrival of Menelik's hordes on their southward advance signalled an end to the Borana dominance in southern Abyssinia. Within a few years they were forced either to retreat southwards, or accept subjugation by the well-armed Amharic invasion.

In the early years of the twentieth century the Borana's waning influence made itself felt in far-reaching raids into Rendille-and Samburu-held territory. With their highly mobile horsemen, they travelled far and wide, watering at the desert wells and

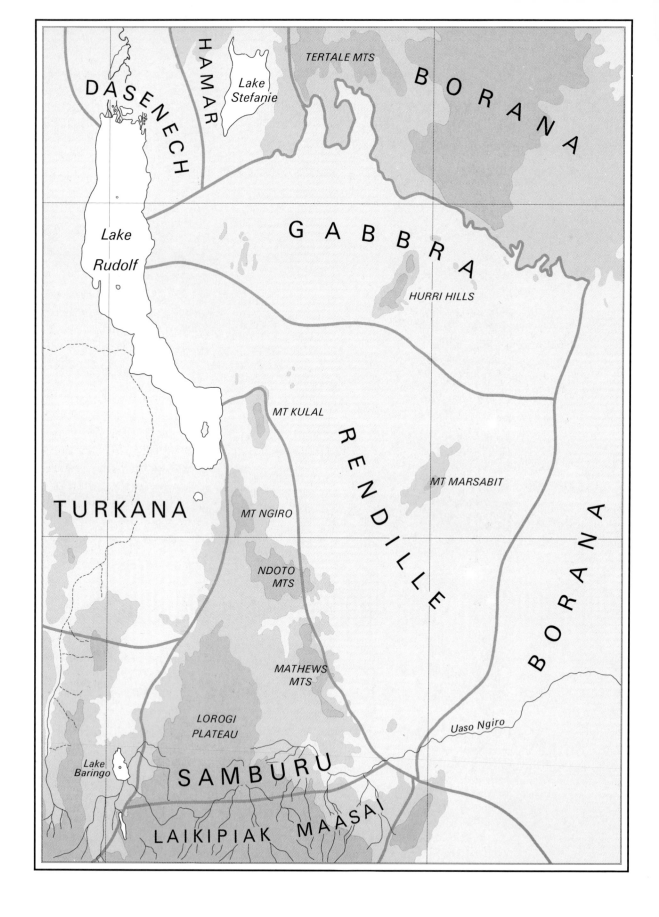

*The approximate distribution of the desert tribes in 1900.*

springs, and striking at the ill-prepared pastoralists with their swiftly moving cavalry. It was a dying effort, but effective, and traditions still tell of the callousness of those stock rustlers with their whirlwind tactics and uninhibited brutality. On the establishment of British administration the possession of horses was severely curbed in an effort to stop this activity. With this dictate the military might of the Borana finally came to an end. Thereafter they followed the lives of peaceful pastoralists, continuing to use their traditional grazing lands on both sides of the border between Abyssinia and Kenya.

\*　　\*　　\*

In the preceding pages much has been written concerning the human vicissitudes in northern Kenya during the nineteenth and early twentieth centuries. In attempting to analyse that time of metamorphosis, one must recognise the special importance of the period in the historical evolution of the people living in the region. Its early years marked a beginning, the later years an ending. Even allowing for the weaknesses of unwritten history, most of the old tribal legends indicate that a distinct gelling process took place within the various embryonic groups during those vital years. In other words, from incohesive little sections they grew to become recognisable tribal entities. This was clearly their beginning in the eyes of present-day historians. The intervening period was filled with leisurely migrations, skirmishings, sickness and, for one destroying decade, a crushing and quite unprecedented series of losses, the likes of which have never recurred. They were the free, formative years before the inhibiting influences of the twentieth century came to hamper the old ways of existence, binding the people with strange laws and containing them within declared boundaries. It brought an end to their wild drifting lives, when they could follow the caprices of the seasons and the dominance of their powerful warriors. It was a precarious system which suited its time, but could not have survived the inexorable advance of human development. The arrival of an alien government signalled the end of the period, before the fresh influence helped to alter the ancient pattern of life.

The effects of an alien administration were both good and bad in the eyes of the wandering pastoralists. They were bad for the simple reason that the imposition of control over their age-old habits was against their nomadic practices; it curbed their traditional instincts and strategies, and prevented them from following their whims and desires. The new rule was good in that their lives, previously insecure through the depredations of unfriendly neighbours, were now reasonably safeguarded by forces of law and order. It is impossible to judge whether the bad effects outweighed the good ones, or vice versa. The nomadic peoples' cold-blooded assessment would probably have decided in favour of the former. Whichever the case, the people of those desert lands now became part of the outside world's grand scheme. It was a scheme that happily did not alter their lifestyle at too great a pace, wisely permitting them to continue with their long-established customs, and, in effect, allowing them to carry on their tenacious battle with the vagaries of the fearsome country in which they struggled for existence.

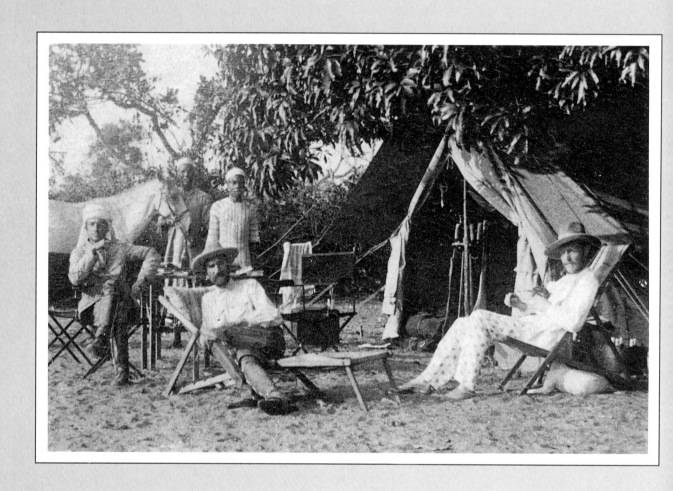

# THOSE INTREPID SOULS

'Many unknown little patches and corners
still exist in the dark continent for the would
be explorer who wishes to break new
ground. It has long been one of my favourite
recreations to sit with the map of Africa
before me and plan out exploring and
hunting expeditions.'

C. H. Stigand, *To Abyssinia through an Unknown Land*

IN June 1900 a meeting of considerable importance took place at the headquarters of the Royal Geographical Society in London. Attended by a large crowd of enthusiastic members, the gathering heard the reading of a paper by Captain Montague Wellby, describing his momentous journey through Abyssinia to the Nile the year before. When Sir Clements Markham, the President of the Society, stood at the end to speak, he included these pertinent words in his vote of thanks to the young explorer: 'The region which has so recently been travelled by Captain Wellby is one to which our attention has been turned for the last six or seven years, and is one of the most interesting of the unknown parts of Africa'. A vital portion of the 'most interesting' region negotiated in Wellby's epic trek lay in the intriguing land to the south of Abyssinia, a patch of little-known Africa embracing the bleak and enticing Lake Rudolf. During the last dozen years of the nineteenth century—a century which had been one of prime geographical revelations for explorers in Africa—this special corner proved to have an irresistible attraction for the white man. In the year Sir Clement's speech was made, an era of industrious exploration had just come to a close, most of the continent's main secrets had been laid bare, and all that remained was to fill in the few blank spaces left on the map. A major chapter in the world's history was over; it was one in which a motley series of resolute and persevering men had been involved, most of them afflicted with an identical wanderlust fever, but each driven by a different motivation.

In the early 1880's the determined young Scottish explorer Joseph Thomson became the first white man to penetrate and successfully traverse the land of the erstwhile fearsome Maasai, a feat which in itself brought him and his small caravan great acclaim. During the course of his extensive journey through East Africa he had occasion to tarry at Njemps, a hospitable agricultural area in the vicinity of Lake Baringo, well recognised in those days by Arab trading caravans as a dependable revictualling post. But for white men, northwards of that haven, *terra incognita* stretched for hundreds of miles.

While he was camped at Njemps, Thomson acquired a titbit of very tempting geographical information from some itinerant 'Wa-kwafi'*. They spoke of an immense salt lake that lay in a valley away to the north—'the great Lake Samburu't. The 'Wa-Kwafi' had obviously visited the mysterious lake, for they were able to furnish him with some tantalising physiographic particulars, convincing enough for him to mark its position vaguely on the map he later produced detailing his travels. He ascertained from his informants that the lake was 'twenty to thirty miles [32–48 kilometres] broad; but its length they knew not, as they had never seen the northern end'. Moreover, they described its mighty mountain surrounds, its salt water, fish, crocodiles and hippopotami. Armed with that nebulous data he speculatively drew the outline of a salt lake on his map, named it 'Samburu', and described it as a 'large salt lake about 100 miles [160 kilometres] in length'. In 1885 his book *Through Masai Land*

---

* A.C. Hollis, an early authority on the Maasai, in 1905 defined the name 'Wa-kwafi' in his book *The Masai* as follows: 'In olden days the coast people termed them [the Maasai] without discrimination Wa-Masai or Wa-Kwavi ... The meaning of Kwavi (or Kwafi) in Masai is countries or somewhere'.

† Probably the first white man to record the presence of a lake in the region was the German missionary, Dr Ludwig Krapf. His two-volume book, *Reisen in Ost—Afrika*, published in 1858, clearly indicated a lake—from hearsay information—which was named Lake Zamburu.

was published, a classic tale of high adventure, audacity and bravery, all recounted in ornate Victorian prose. Thomson's journey was hailed as a magnificent achievement. For him personally it was an immensely satisfying and fulfilling triumph. But does one detect in his words describing the unknown regions surrounding 'Lake Samburu' a distinct yearning to be there, exploring that mysterious and uncharted terrain? 'Clearly there is a region of great interest and importance here, the exploration of which will be a rich reward to the adventurous traveller; and I can only say I shall envy the man who is first in the field'. Thomson never returned to continue his quests, but his written words were the spark which lit a fire, for within two years of his book being published in English, French and German, an expedition in the grand manner was being prepared to look for the hazy 'Lake Samburu'.

Far to the east, in Somaliland, the white man's probings had been in progress for many years prior to Thomson's arrival at Lake Baringo. Fringing the easternmost of the ancient Indian Ocean sea lanes, that country, barren though it was, had long attracted the attention of eager wanderers, their forays in pursuit of sport and adventure leading them up the Juba river, and inland along the well-travelled Somali trade routes to Boranaland. Those early expeditions did not, however, attempt the crossing of the vast dreary waste lands stretching in their flat monotony westwards from the Indian Ocean. That bleak, waterless and unwelcoming barrier remained a guardian of the hinterland for many years, forbidding any extensive movement. Only in the early years of the twentieth century did venturesome travellers finally manage to break through and gain access to the unknown territory in the interior.

To the north of the mystical, and as yet unproven 'Lake Samburu', reared a mountain barrier sheltering a land of unique qualities in the annals of African history. A fiercely independent country, its people claimed an ancient association with Biblical events, followed a form of Christian worship, and were capable—uniquely in Africa—of tracing their sovereigns back several millenia, when the earliest of their kings was said to have commenced ruling. It was a land of the most convoluted internal power struggles, in which were interwoven external influences that over the years involved, amongst others, Arabs, Greeks, Jews and Portuguese. In 1855, under the rule of Emperor Theodore—the extraordinary man who could rightfully claim the distinction of starting on the foundations of present-day Ethiopia—it became a unified country. Eventually, however, his moral decay caused the decline of his empire and defeat by a disciplinary British force in 1868, followed by his suicide. Rising up at that stage through the ranks of minor leaders was a young man—at one time King of Shoa—who bided his time, played his cards correctly, and eventually, in 1889, was triumphantly crowned Emperor of Abyssinia. Negus Menelik II, King of Kings, was a remarkable individual, the man who finally succeeded in consolidating his kingdom. Besides that achievement were his territorial ambitions and expansions to the south, complemented by enlightened plans to update his backward country through the utilisation of European concepts. The final proof of his ability to lead the country came at the fateful Battle of Adowa (present-day Adwa) in 1896, when his overwhelming force of 110,000 men roundly defeated a well armed but poorly led Italian army of 16,000 men. That victory clearly established Abyssinia in the eyes of the outside world. Increasingly, Menelik proved to be an enterprising, able and strong ruler, for whom the European powers had considerable respect; their legations sprang up in Addis Ababa at this time, a tangible indication of foreign recognition of Abyssinia as a fully fledged state. The years of Menelik's rule were remarkable for their enlightened advances, and increasing numbers of foreign travellers were allowed to pass through his domain on their way to explore and hunt in the little-known regions to the south. In those days, the southern parts of Abyssinia were only vaguely understood, some districts having just been acquired by Menelik in his imperial claims. The first incursions of Abyssinians into the Lake Rudolf area only took place in the last few years of the century, hard on the heels of the earlier white explorers, so geographical ignorance of the zone was equally shared by both parties.

The routes to 'Lake Samburu' from the western side of the country were not popular. They didn't have logistically preferable starting points for one thing, and for another the southern part of Sudan was dominated by the hostile Mahdist forces between the years 1885 and 1898, effectively closing it to outsiders. During the last decade of the century the well-known routes inland to the lake from the north, south and east had the added advantage of seaboard facilities, where expedition supplies could be conveniently shipped. The west had nothing but the miasmic swamps of the upper Nile, and the isolated Uganda forts. Furthermore, Somaliland was in a position to supply experienced guides and men, camels and donkeys, essentials for travellers heading to the Lake Rudolf region. The west was unsophisticated in such matters. Nevertheless, at least one expedition from Uganda and another from Omdurman on the Nile, did start out from that quarter. The western approach could never, however, claim to have been popular.

The location of Lake Rudolf in 1888 by Count Teleki and von Höhnel attracted a veritable hive of explorers. Encompassed by exotic scenes, strange peoples and countless wild animals, it was a paradise which held an almost Mecca-like lure for the restless nineteenth-century European in search of sport and adventure. Of fascination, too, was its unique position in a barren and excessively hostile terrain; it contrasted dramatically with the positions of other great lakes in Africa, lying in their verdant hollows and surrounded by indigenous populations thriving on the agreeable nature of the adjacent countryside. Lake Rudolf had none of that. A few tiny groups of people lived on its verges, eking out a fragile living from whatever they could garner in the waters and by the shore. The lake's environs were unbelievably harsh and sterile; bleak wastes of sand and endless acres of volcanic rubble stretched away into the distance, providing infrequent and ephemeral sustenance for the scant herds of stock occasionally living along the fringe of the water. The very horror of that scene of desolation impinged itself on von Höhnel's mind, compelling him to describe it as 'a revelation to us; and like some threatening spectre rose up before our minds the full significance of the utterly barren, dreary nature of the lake district. Into what a desert had we been betrayed! . . . No living creature shared the gloomy solitude with us; and as far as our glass could reach there was nothing to be seen but desert—desert everwhere'. But in that very desolation there was a fascinating beauty. An allure that has continued through the years to attract adventuresome travellers seeking isolation and wildness, a view of primitive and unspoilt places, where the mind can contemplate how the world might have looked before man-made creations desecrated the intrinsic exquisiteness of the Almighty's creation. The early explorers may not have regarded those scenes with quite the same equanimity, struggling as they were with the problems of survival, but nevertheless it would have taken a hard heart not to have observed some of the exotic qualities of that terrible country. Disappointingly,

*Menelik II, Negus Negasti, King of Kings, Emperor of Ethiopia (Abyssinia) – sketched on the occasion of Prince Henri d'Orleans' visit to Abyssinia in 1898.*

few of them were artists of the pen, their accounts often being sternly dry, crammed with geographical and ethnic facts, and constantly peppered with tales of gripping battles with ferocious beasts of the wild.

As news of the 'most interesting' region filtered back to Europe, a new prospect for the ambitious wanderer was opened up. Focusing their sights on Lake Rudolf, many doughty men soon found the attractions of that obscure land irresistible: magnificent mountains beckoned from distant horizons, and far-reaching plains studded with jagged hills were intersected by tree-fringed river beds wandering at random to nowhere. A land full of exciting 'little patches and corners', all waiting to be explored and exposed to the curious outside world, it was never a place to be meddled with. Nonetheless, its rewards to the diligent hunter, naturalist and geographer, were bountiful, the results of their efforts enhancing scientific collections and knowledge in many an esteemed European and American institution. In a wistful appraisal of that unique part of Africa, Archibald Butter—a young Scotsman who travelled extensively there at the turn of the century—once wrote: 'When I go home I always dream of Lake Rudolf as a Mecca ... This very name conjures up in my mind visions of all that is mystical and savage and delightful. A hunter's and a naturalist's paradise untouched by the civilising hand of the white man, and as remote as anything one could imagine from the bustle and stress of the 20th century with its railways, and motors, and artificiality'. Those heartfelt words were written in 1903. The days of the explorer in that country were as good as over, and all too soon the tentacles of civilisation crept over that lonely but thrilling land.

# TELEKI EXPEDITION
## 1886–8

SOMETIME during the long, bleak wintry night of 29 January 1889, two lonely shots rang out in the secluded hunting lodge of Mayerling, romantically hidden away in the beautiful forest-clad hills of Lower Austria. Tragically, they signalled the end of two young lives and an intense one-sided love affair between the indifferent thirty-one-year-old Crown Prince Rudolf of Austria—Emperor Francis Joseph's only son—and Marie Vetsera, the seventeen-year-old baroness who craved his affection. Prince Rudolf had been a remarkable young man, an aristocrat of liberal and progressive thinking, holding attitudes not customary in the royal court at that time. His enlightened and rebellious ideas all too soon brought him into conflict with his more orthodox father, the long reigning head of state who had established the Dual Monarchy of Austria and Hungary many years before. To the Hungarians, who four decades earlier had struggled without success to break free from the shackles of Austrian rule, Rudolf was a friend. He was moreover, a scholar, and had joined in the co-authorship of an extensive historical work on the Monarchy. His intellectual involvements, however, extended much deeper than simply recording his family's historical manoeuvres, for he also displayed a keen interest in the advancement of geography and the natural sciences, becoming at an early age a patron, and later, Protector of the Austrian and Hungarian Geographical Societies. He was a prolific author, writing many books and articles on geographical, political and natural history subjects.

Accounts of exploration were of particular fascination to Rudolf, living as he did during the period when the great powers of Europe were frantically engaged in attempts to grasp chunks of newly opened-up Africa. It was therefore possible that the enthusiasm of the moment may have coloured the Prince's thinking on the occasion when a Hungarian aristocrat friend discussed his plans for a hunting expedition in the equatorial land of east Africa. It might have been more than geographical interest that suffused the royal mind; maybe the idea of territorial gains played a minor part in the events which were to follow.

The year was 1886. Anchored close by the island of Lacroma, on the shimmering blue waters along the Dalmation coast, was the Emperor's sumptuous paddle-wheel yacht *Grief*. On shore, the Crown Prince and his consort, Princess Stefanie, were entertaining their old friend Count Samuel Teleki, a jovial Hungarian aristocrat of immense wealth and their popular companion of many European tours. Undoubtedly their conversation must have ranged over a variety of topics of mutual interest, for Teleki was an adventurous person, a fine sportsman and game shot, an excellent mountaineer despite his somewhat stout build and a tireless traveller. On this portentous occasion, Teleki, then forty-one years old, was full of enthusiastic plans for his approaching hunting trip to Lake Tanganyika in the company of his friend Baron Arz. Ambitiously, he also aimed to reach the summit of the unconquered Mt Kilimanjaro. One can imagine the keen discussion which must have taken place between the Prince and the Count, as plans and ideas were mulled over. Behind the

*Crown Prince Rudolf of Austria and his wife Princess Stefanie, who was a Belgian.*

scenes the young Austrian naval lieutenant Ludwig von Höhnel—the royal yacht's navigation officer—had heard word of the Count's projected disappearance into the heart of Africa. A person of impecunious background, von Höhnel had from early youth craved the life of a sailor and explorer, avidly reading every book on African travel he could find. Besides geography, natural history had also captured his interest, so it is not surprising that von Höhnel should harbour an intense desire to join Teleki's expedition. While it was fortunate for von Höhnel personally that the Prince's powerful entreaties on his behalf were successful in persuading Teleki to take him in Arz's place, geography was to benefit too. Having been included on the trip, von Höhnel directed his efforts to altering the objective of Teleki's plans. Using all his persuasive powers, doubtless supported by the Crown Prince's enthusiastic preoccupation with geographical affairs, von Höhnel managed to convince the Count that a journey of exploration would be far more valuable to science than a somewhat unambitious hunting trip in an already familiar territory. Considering von Höhnel's youth—he was only twenty-nine years old—and modest station, prevailing on the highly ranked aristocrat was another triumph, and an indication of the diplomatic but forceful spirit which would manifest itself in the years to come.

Everything was now set, and the two members of the cast were agreed on their goal; all that remained was to commence the massive preparations for a 'journey of several years through uncivilised districts'. But before plunging into the uncertainties of the expedition, one must take a look at the principals more closely. It is important to know something of their backgrounds, the nature of their personalities, their aspirations and—most important for the smooth functioning of the enterprise—their mental compatibility.

\*     \*     \*

Count Samuel Teleki von Szék, or 'Samu' (pronounced 'Shamoo') as he was familiarly known, came of an outstanding family in the realm of Hungarian patriots. Of noble line, he was able to trace his forebears back to the influential old family which, in the course of their relentless amassing of wealth in the fifteenth century, had bought an immense estate in Transylvania named Teleki\*. The transaction contributed yet more to their already substantial holdings, but a strange twist of fate was about to alter the scheme of things for the Telekis. By one of those quirks of genetics, which no end of material possessions could rectify, another old Hungarian family, the Garázdas, was almost to disappear through lack of male progeny; this state of affairs was fortunately resolved by an auspicious marriage in 1605, when Mihály Teleki wedded Anna Garázda de Szék. Happily, that union produced male offspring, thereby breaking the streak of ill fortune which had threatened the family's continuity. Some ten years after that event, Mihály was appointed Captain of Bodyguards, a rank of high authority and great prestige in Hungary, and an appropriate honour for a member of the prominent old Hungarian family. Significantly, Mihály was also responsible for another turning point in the family's story: by combining the Teleki with his wife's family title he founded the house of Teleki de Szék. Impressive as those achievements had been, his star was outshone later in the century by his grandson, Mihály II, who gained even more fame for the family. His brilliant and dignified career in the post of Chancellor to the Prince of Transylvania, reaped him the award of an earldom in 1685. After his death four years later, and in solemn recognition of the high esteem his diplomatic achievements had earned him, the honour of earldom was bestowed in perpetuity on all members of the Teleki family born after 1685. The Teleki family circle was an exceptional one indeed. Since the middle of the seventeenth century it had furnished Transylvania with many outstanding politicians, statesmen, scientists, scholars and soldiers. Hungary, and Europe too, benefited from the versatile abilities of this talented family.

Count Samuel Teleki of Africa fame was born in 1845, just three years before the abortive Hungarian uprising against their Austrian overlords. The Teleki family, being true nationalists, were seriously involved in the thick of the action. Three prominent members played parts in the cause, which resulted in one of them, the authoress Blanka Teleki, being incarcerated in prison for a term, while the politician Lázló Teleki and Sándor Teleki, a colonel in the Hungarian army, were both sentenced to death *in absentia*, although the order was never carried out. The independent spirit of this remarkable family even extended into their religious feelings, the allegiance of the Count's branch being towards the Calvinist-Protestants, at variance with the religion practised by his monarch, the Catholic Habsburg, Francis Joseph of Austria.

Samuel Teleki was no exception to the family rule. His early aspirations were inclined towards an army career, but first came eleven years of study in Göttingen and

---

\*'Telek' in Hungarian means a plot of land.

Berlin universities, where he received a good grounding in the natural sciences and astronomy. After that rather drawn out academic stint, his earlier wish was satisfied and he joined the army as a hussar officer for a few years. On the completion of his military duty, he was involved in politics, his noble breeding and great wealth standing him in good stead. After his election to local government, Teleki settled down to the comfortable, but at times grey and humdrum existence of the rich landed gentleman. His life had slipped into a round of social occasions, shooting parties, estate management, travel and the drudgery of government meetings for which he had no heart. But being a member of Parliament raised him from near anonymity and introduced him to a new circle of influential persons. Among them was Prince Rudolf. Very quickly the two men developed a warm friendship, which lasted until the end of the pathetic Prince's life.

Teleki's great social success can be attributed partly to his gregarious and good-natured personality. A confirmed bachelor to the end of his days, the affluent aristocrat was a most generous friend*, an excellent companion, both indoors and in the hunting field, and entranced guests with his easy, gracious manners and gift of witty conversation. From all available accounts one forms the opinion that he must have been a *bon vivant* of a most genial temperament, always calm and collected, and possessed of a wry sense of humour. A fellow passenger on the ship from Aden to Zanzibar writes of him as 'a most agreeable travelling companion' with 'many amusing anecdotes' to tell. Frederick Jackson—himself soon to gain fame in east Africa—described him as 'very amusing and outspoken, and good company generally. Some of his ideas were quaint, if not actually jarring'.

In Africa, Teleki threw all court formalities to the wind, revelling in the relaxed atmosphere of the wilds. He always wore his shirt open wide, shaved his already nearly bald head and to start with, wore a 'kofia'—the coast African's cloth cap. At Taveta, to the possible horror of the staid and etiquette-bound Englishmen camped nearby, he never wore a coat to dinner, and constantly smoked his long-stemmed German pipe. Nevertheless, he was a social success, a straightforward man who spoke his mind, as Jackson soon discovered. While discussing the inaccuracies and exaggerations of earlier Africa explorers, he had these tongue-in-cheek words to say: 'My dear Mr. Jackson, all African travellers are liars, and' (with a slight bow, and patting his bare, brick red chest) 'I am going to be a liar. If I do not discover a lake I shall say I did; if I do not discover a mountain I shall say I did; and who will disprove it, until long after I have received the credit?' His viewpoints and actions in terms of present-day thinking could be termed callous, but as was customary in the Africa of those days, he regarded everything with a harsh practicality. He enjoyed the spirit of the hunt, and fearlessly shot his share of wild animals, large and small, but all for good purpose: meat to supply his caravan, and elephants, from the sale of whose ivory he hoped to recoup some of his expenses. He expressed a dislike for black men, fighting them when they resisted him on his journey, but none the less, he pitied his porters when they died from the stresses of travel. Count Teleki, or 'Bwana Tumbo' (Mr Belly) as he was fittingly named by the men on his Africa expedition, was, at the outset of his travels, of generous dimensions. The arduousness of his journeying, however, rapidly reduced the portly aspect of this sobriquet, and Jackson was told, on meeting him at

---

*Teleki could easily afford to be generous. On his death in 1916 he left a 20 million florin fortune, apart from his estates and other assets.

*The man who was instrumental in exposing Lake Rudolf to the outside world, the genial
aristocrat and sportsman Count Samuel Teleki de Szék.*

Taveta, that within a few months of the Count's departure from his starting point he proudly claimed to have lost 'something between four and five stone'. Single-mindedly resolute and constitutionally very tough—he rarely succumbed to sickness during the entire trip—Teleki was well qualified to lead his caravan in the course of its gruelling march to Lake Rudolf and back to Mombasa.

*     *     *

Sometime about 1750, during the stirring years of Maria Theresa's autocratic reign over Austria, one of Ludwig von Höhnel's ancestors emigrated from Prussia to Vienna. His father, Dr Gottfried von Höhnel, followed the humble path of a civil servant, his employment with the Tax Department being important but hardly adventurous work, which entailed repeated moves from one city to another. He must have been an earnest and hard-working man, for his diligence finally earned him the Regional Directorship of the Tax Department in Trieste (then part of Austria-Hungary). In the last year of his life the long span of conscientious service to his country earned for him the honour of a knighthood. He died in 1868, leaving four sons, two of whom were in turn to leave their individual stamp on the professions they chose to follow. The four boys grew up in the seaport of Trieste, a fact which later influenced the thinking of one of them at least. Both Franz and Ludwig, the youngest child, became noted naturalists and geographers in their time. Well-travelled, their contributions to the sciences of nature and geography were of international repute, winning fame for them in later years. Franz, a brilliant scientist, ultimately held the chair of Professor of Botany at the University of Vienna, a post in which he excelled; his specialisation in the field of mycology led him all over the globe in his detailed studies of fungi, a subject in which he was recognised as a world authority.

His younger brother, Ludwig, also became keenly absorbed in nature and travel. But before that, at the early age of eight, he fostered an intense ambition to go to sea, a desire which was eventually fulfilled in 1876, when, after displaying exceptional ability as a student, he graduated from the Naval Academy at Fiume as a Naval Cadet. In characteristic von Höhnel fashion, Ludwig must have applied himself to his calling; his appearance as the navigating officer on the Royal Yacht in 1886 being full proof of a thorough application to his duties. For his full naval life of thirty-three years, von Höhnel served with honour in his monarch's navy, retiring in 1909 after a varied and illustrious career. His work took him to many lands, but the most important years to him were his earliest, when he accompanied Teleki on his journey to seek Lake Rudolf, and later with the young American explorer Chanler, when he suffered severe injury from a rhinoceros attack. On both these trips he displayed a remarkable ability to observe and record what he saw with exemplary accuracy and precision, despite frequent debilitating setbacks from disease and hunger.

For several years after his return from the second African expedition, von Höhnel served ashore, working firstly in the naval section of the War Ministry and later in a division of the technical committee. In 1899, with his elevation to the rank of corvette captain, he was assigned the court duties of Wing Adjutant (aide de camp) to the Emperor, a four-year task to which he committed himself competently, earning as his reward a promotion to Frigate Captain in 1903. Two years later his grand tour of the east commenced, during which his torpedo cruiser *Panther* steamed down the Red Sea to its first stop, the port of Jibouti. From here he marched overland to Addis Ababa with a large retinue of men and mules, plus an escort of sailors from his ship. In the

*Lieutenant Ritter Ludwig von Höhnel. In his lifetime he became a high ranking naval officer in the Austrian Navy, an intrepid explorer in Africa, and a scholar in natural history and geography.*

capital he was enthusiastically welcomed by Menelik, with whom he successfully discussed friendship and future trade relations between Abyssinia and Austria. Having fruitfully completed that task, von Höhnel proceeded on his travels to Ceylon, Indonesia, Australia and New Zealand, where he was instrumental in introducing the chamois he had brought with him from the Emperor's private hunting grounds in Austria. For the few remaining years of his naval service promotion was rapid, and following a protracted visit to New York, he came to the end of his naval career at a shore base in his homeland with the rank of Rear Admiral. As a result of a clash of personalities with the Port Admiral, von Höhnel prematurely, and most regretfully, resigned from the navy. By doing so he missed out on the opportunity of seeing action in the First World War. A faultless naval officer to the end, von Höhnel became an ardent admirer of the British Navy, whose activities he traced with the greatest interest, an enthusiastic follower of exploration and travel in Africa, and an admirable naturalist.

The final years of his life, although steeped in financial hardship, were spent in scientific studies, his efforts in this field adding further to the international acclaim he had already earned from his contributions to geographical knowledge. Honours poured in from many countries, and on his death in 1942 at the age of eighty-four the

3.)

to know, he, when coming on board, related that a Hungarian Count had arrived to take leave from the Highnesses before starting on an Africa Expedition. Hearing this, I said: "I must go with him" "Really, you would like to go to Africa?" "Yes, by all means; it is my hearts desire". "Well, as the Count is leaving tomorrow night, I'll go on shore early in the morning, and see him".

On his return at noon, he told me, that the Count at first flatly rejected any such thought, that he consented to go on board and see me only on the insistance of the Highnesses, who both knew me well and were in favour of my demand.

The Count Samuel Teleki came on board at 3 o'cl. with Schweinfurth's famous book: "In the heart of Africa" in hand. The Captain introduced me, led us to the saloon and let us there discreetly alone. With a mien not very friendly he opened the book, spread the maps, pointed to a route drawn by him in pencil, and said: "It is this route that I intend to take". All the while he had hardly deigned to look at me. As it did not matter to me where he intended to go, so long as it was in Africa, I merely glanced on the map and said: "Yes, that can be done". The pencilled route ran from Bagamoyo to the Lake Tanganyika and from there, right into the arm of the Mahdi in northeasterly direction. He seemed to be in a hurry, named a village in Transylvania as his address, said he would see me in May world lost a self-effacing but imposing man of whom Sir Vivian Fuchs, a past President of the Royal Geographical Society and a well-known explorer in his own right, once wrote: 'With the death of Admiral Ritter Ludwig von Höhnel a link with the past was broken, for there were few who could still claim to have travelled in the Africa of Livingstone and Stanley, at a time when the white man was still unknown to a majority of the native peoples'.

*　　*　　*

When Teleki and von Höhnel first met at Lacroma in 1886, it was at Prince Rudolf's request. The initial meeting was very brief: five or six minutes of curt conversation sufficed between Teleki and the naval lieutenant before each went his own way. One can but sympathise with Teleki at that stage. His private arrangements had been thrown askew by the Crown Prince's interference, and instead of the pleasant and proven companionship of a trusty old friend and partner from previous hunting trips, he had been encumbered with an upstart young naval officer. Von Höhnel was a man he knew nothing about, and who was trying to divert him from his original plan and take him into unknown country. Teleki's abrupt manner was quite understandable in the circumstances, but he had no choice but to accept the imposition for the Prince's wish was as good as a command.

With marked lack of enthusiasm Teleki agreed to change his plans for Tanganyika and reluctantly dropped his friend, Baron Arz, in favour of von Höhnel. For this reason the Count adopted a cool off-hand manner towards the young officer throughout the expedition. It was an unfortunate but forgivable attitude which was not to change until von Höhnel's two volume account of the trip wrote complimentarily of Teleki, his leader. Only then did a friendship develop between the two men. None the less, during the journey Teleki was fully aware of von Höhnel's qualities and abilities, and in a letter to Prince Rudolf, written from Africa, he spoke praisingly: 'Höhnel is a very knowledgeable man, a good fellow, we never clash over anything; moreover he is clever and brave. Should fate make it impossible for me to recommend this in person to Your Imperial Royal Highness, I will do so now in writing, convinced after a year's experience that this clever and useful man will be able to render great services to the Navy'.

On his part, the tall, slim and very correct von Höhnel clearly considered himself the right man for the Teleki expedition; his own words written late in life give a lucid, if boastful categorisation of his wide talents: 'I think I may say that science had benefited by my choice, because it may be surmised with more than probability that Arz in many ways was less qualified for scientific work of this kind, not conversant with the history of exploration in Africa and the geography, surely not trained for astronomical observations, mapmaking, ecc.ecc. I spoke fluently six European languages and very soon also Kisuahely. I was an untireable pedestrian, stood the heat like an nigger, was a remarkable good shot and had splendid nerves, which never gave way'. Von Höhnel did not let Teleki down.

Preparations for the expedition kept Teleki and von Höhnel busy for some months. They had agreed to meet in Zanzibar at the end of October 1886, but in the meantime they had their allotted tasks to discharge. To raise the substantial funds needed, Teleki sold a hunting estate and a diamond of great historic value which had once belonged to his illustrious ancestor, Mihály Teleki II. The sales raised 130,000 gold crowns, equivalent in weight to forty kilograms of gold. No expenses were spared for the success of the trip; Teleki even had a complete battery of rifles built by the prestigious gun makers, Holland & Holland of London.

When all was ready von Höhnel set sail for Zanzibar accompanied by the basic stores which amounted to one hundred and forty bulky cases and bales of the equipment, supplies and barter goods so essential for African expeditions of the time. Teleki was delayed by a month, an interval put to industrious use by the enthusiastic von Höhnel who sorted out the small mountain of stores and, vitally important, established contact with personages who might be of value to the expedition. He also took advantage of the time to continue with the Swahili lessons he had started on board ship. Finding himself in the exciting position of seeing the very sights he had read so much about in travel books, he was entranced by the exotic scenes all around him. Thomson's book must have been close at hand, for von Höhnel also evinced a desire to meet the personalities—Martin, Kimemeta and others—who had accompanied that explorer on his travels. In some respects he met with disappointment: 'Alas! I must confess that the somewhat romantic ideas I had conceived in my study of books on Africa received a very severe shock, for they were altogether different from what I had expected'. It was not the last rude shock von Höhnel was to experience in the course of the next two years. Despite the distractions of Zanzibar, he had made satisfying progress with most of his labours by the time Teleki arrived towards the end of November. One worthwhile achievement had been the hiring of the well-known Arab trader, Jumbe Kimemeta, to act as a guide. Apart from a wide knowledge of the hinterland gained from his own journeys, Kimemeta had travelled with Thomson on his famous expedition in 1883. On that last journey he had reached Baringo, which was of importance to Teleki who intended stopping there to replenish his caravan's food stocks. Kimemeta's agreement to travel with him turned out to be a fortunate liaison in the days to come. On Teleki's arrival in Zanzibar activity accelerated. With the aid of General Lloyd Mathews, the British naval officer who commanded the Sultan's embryonic and somewhat ragtag army, their preparations were soon completed. Porters and guides were engaged, their loads packed in 'five and a half stone' (77 pound, 35 kilogram) bundles and Kimemeta despatched to the mainland to arrange for more porters and the purchase of a mob of donkeys.

Their caravan had to be large enough to carry goods for at least two years. Teleki had listened carefully to the seasoned advice of Sir Richard Burton, the inimitable nineteenth-century traveller, and hired seven Somalis in Aden; one of them was Qualla Idris, the unusual young man whose experiences had included visits to America and Europe, plus six years of toilsome expedition work with Stanley on the Congo. The small unit of Somalis became the solid core of the whole rambling entourage, invaluable to Teleki in his hunting forays and indispensable as a disciplinary force. It is not clear from von Höhnel's account how many porters actually left in the pay of Teleki's caravan. Mention was made at one point of two hundred Zanzibaris being selected, the rest to be recruited on the mainland. Two pages later von Höhnel stated: 'Two hundred Zanzibaris, nine Askari, and the nine guides were in readiness to start, as well as 450 porters'. Later, after their arrival on the mainland on 24 January 1887, Teleki and von Höhnel were described trying to recruit

ABOVE: *Experienced in east African travel, Jumbe Kimemeta was the Arab trader and caravan leader who accompanied Teleki's expedition.*

ABOVE RIGHT: *Qualla Idris, following his participation in Stanley's Congo venture, led Teleki's armed Somali escort.*

porters at Pangani, only seventy-two being signed on after one week's effort. For the precise student of the expedition's well-known story, further confusing figures arose, as von Höhnel declared they departed for their first camp on 28 January, only *four* days after their arrival in Pangani. At that camp he declared they had '283 porters and 25 grey donkeys, to attend upon which another seven fellows were engaged'. Presumably they still had their two hundred Zanzibaris, guides and askaris, since they had an inventoried 470 loads to carry. Allowing for the apparent inconsistencies in von Höhnel's statements, it was nevertheless a substantial body of men which headed off into the hinterland of east Africa. His account of the problems they experienced with this motley bunch of men—the desertions and the losses of essential equipment and stores, including the case containing their valuable scientific books—is a graphic tale of frustration and distress. Persistence, plus some stiff discipline, ultimately won the day. Only then, minus many loads, did they gradually wind their way inland and away from the problem of desertions.

At the end of March the expedition trudged into the well-used haven at Taveta, on the eastern foothills of Mt Kilimanjaro. Here they tarried for three and a half months, during which time Teleki and von Höhnel paid a quick visit to Mt Meru and followed it by an assault on Kilimanjaro. Teleki, full of enthusiastic energy, climbed to an estimated altitude of 17,387 feet (5350 metres) before turning back to join his failing companion. It was while they were at Taveta that they met the last white men they were to see for a year and a half: three English sportsmen whose company they enjoyed for a brief spell.

Six and a half months after leaving Taveta they had fought their way successfully

*'The open space between our tent and the warehouse was particularly popular, and was always full of women and children offering their wares for sale'. (von Höhnel) – Teleki's camp at Taveta, 1887.*

through Kikuyuland, thereby becoming the first white men to traverse that forbidding territory from south to north, climbed to an altitude of 15,355 feet (4,725 metres) on Mt Kenya—the highest point yet reached by a white man—again accomplished by the stalwart Teleki, and crossed the notorious land of the Laikipiak people, in whose hands Thomson had been so impertinently treated five years before. Von Höhnel and his leader then marched into Njemps, on the edge of Lake Baringo. There, they sojourned and gathered food supplies sufficient for the next stage of their journey in search of Thomson's mysterious 'Lake Samburu'.

Persistent interrogation of the natives of Njemps produced no definite facts: 'Days were consumed in talking the matter over with Jumbe Kimemeta and the natives, but we could get no certain intelligence whatever. No one really knew whether there were two lakes or one in the north, or even how far off was the nearest lake if two there were. We had answers in plenty to our questions, but they were all either vague or manifestly false'. In the course of questioning Teleki did, however, ascertain one important detail: starting from Lake Baringo there were, confusingly, three possible routes to the lake. Moreover, using the verbal information they had received, von Höhnel drew up an 'imaginary map of the district' lying to the north of Lake Baringo. How Thomson would have envied those two travel-hardened men as they made their final preparations to march north from Njemps. Food sufficient for thirty-five days had been gathered, and two local guides recruited who knew the country on their route. Thus prepared, they left Njemps on 10 February 1888, tramping with anticipation at

*'Imaginary map of the district north of our camp at Njemps'. Map drawn by von Höhnel based on information from Wa-kwafi.*

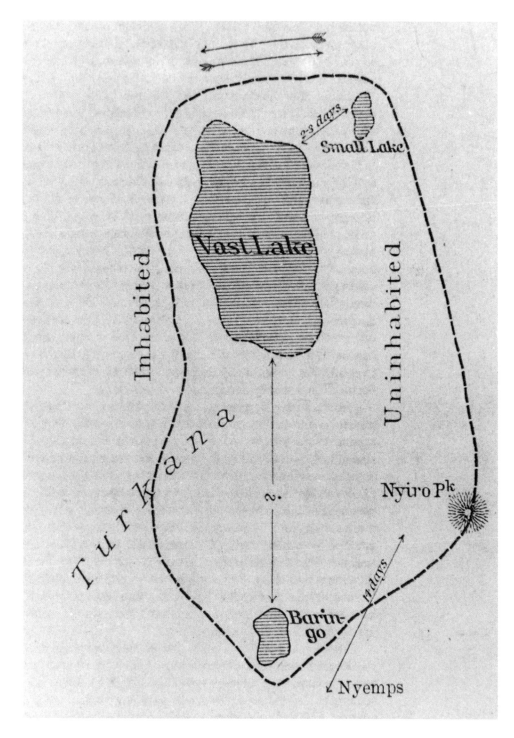

the head of a very much reduced procession comprised of 197 porters, 8 Somalis, 14 Askaris, 6 guides and 3 Swahilis, assisted by 19 hardy little 'grey donkeys'. Nine invalids and one Askari were left to guard their stores at Njemps; the remainder, 228 in all, marched—'a brave and determined-looking little troop'. At the tail of the column rode von Höhnel, 'though I was still a mere skeleton, I mounted my grey steed to bring up the rear'. Needless to say, Teleki, although no longer as portly as the day he had started out, led the way with his customary gusto. From now on they would have to rely on stern discipline, the ability of their formidable battery of Holland & Holland rifles to feed and defend them and, more than anything else, good fortune.

Under the direction of their Njemps guide, Sokoni, a well-travelled and experienced caravan man, Teleki's group clambered steadily up the eastern wall of the Rift Valley, finally arriving on 'the edge of a far-stretching tableland'—the Lorogi plateau. Two days of comfortable marching in the cool of the highlands brought them to the edge of the 'Loroghi [sic] chain' overlooking 'a vast landscape altogether new to us'. This magnificent viewpoint exposed a vista as yet unseen by any other white man, and the explorers' eyes now feasted on the distant procession of lofty mountain ranges running in crenellated sequence from north to south. One particularly impressive series of heights—called Lengiyu by their guide—they decided to name the 'General Matthews [sic] chain, in honour of our friend General Lloyd Matthews [sic], who has done so much to help us'. Proudly they claimed this as their first geographical discovery, one of several they were to make as their footsteps took them northwards through 'unknown' lands. Dropping down from the cool freshness of the hills, the caravan once more felt the parching torments of thirst as their guide led them further into the desiccated bushlands of Barsaloi. Late at night, after hopes of finding water had faded, fortune smiled when a tiny supply was located by frantic digging in a dry river bed. But it was hardly enough to satisfy everyone's needs, and in Teleki's mind Barsaloi was certainly not a place to stop for long.

After a three-day respite, badly needed to revive their strength and spirits, the porters once more hoisted their hefty loads and started the long march to Mt Ngiro, an appalling 50 mile (80 kilometre) trudge across the hot waterless Elbarta Plains. That bleak stretch took its toll, and by the time Teleki's caravan reached the foot of the looming mountain four men had died. On the southern flanks of the massif a welcoming valley, filled with high shady acacia trees, evergreen bush and best of all a tiny stream of fresh water, greeted the exhausted group. Today, the little brook—the Uaso Rongai—flows much as it did on 27 February 1888 when Teleki staggered in with his men; it remains a paradise for thirsty men and beasts. Teleki was well content with their successful traverse of that awesome tract of country, for they had 'broken through the barrier dividing the inhabited from the uninhabited districts', and in doing so achieved one of 'the most difficult' of their aims. The hunting here was splendid, and Teleki soon put his rifles to profitable use, nine elephants falling to his bullets before the expedition left the foothills of the mountain.

After five days of rest, Teleki and his men continued northwards, skirting along the western footslopes of Ngiro Mountain. Von Höhnel later described the awful terrain in tersely descriptive words: 'The scenery became more and more dreary as we advanced. The barren ground was strewn with gleaming, chiefly red and green, volcanic debris, pumice-stone, huge blocks of blistered lava, and here and there pieces of petrified wood. There was no regular path, and we had to pick our way carefully amongst the scoriae, some of which was as sharp as knives'. Encouragingly, a solitary 'Burkeneji' whom they met on their path assured them of the lake's close proximity. Bolstered by this hopeful information, and with the vision of a hospitable land of plenty ahead, they 'happily resumed' their march. But the hidden lake did not give up its secrets readily, for 'with every step the scenery grew more and more dreary and deserted looking'. Continuing his graphic description of the country in the vicinity of the lake, von Höhnel went on to say: 'Steep rocky slopes alternated with ravines strewn with debris, which gave one the impression of being still glowing hot and of having but recently been flung forth from some huge forge. And this glaring monotony continued till about two o'clock. The good spirits with which the thought that we were nearing the end of our long tramp had filled us in the morning had long since dissipated ... when all of a sudden, as we were climbing a gentle slope, such a grand, beautiful and far reaching scene was spread out before us, that at first we felt we must be under some delusion and were disposed to think the whole thing a mere phantasmagoria ... We hurried as fast as we could to the top of our ridge, the scene gradually developing itself as we advanced until an entirely new world was spread out before our astonished eyes. The void down in the depths ... appeared to be closing up from every side to form a fitting frame for the dark-blue gleaming surface of the lake stretching away beyond as far as the eye could reach'.

At long last this hidden geographical gem had been exposed to the eyes of the world, closing a major chapter in the history of Africa's exploration, and at the same time opening an exciting new one for countless later travellers anxious to see for themselves the attractions of Teleki's unique discovery: 'For a long time we gazed in speechless delight, spell-bound by the beauty of the scene before us ... at the sight of the glittering expanse of the great lake, which melted on the horizon into the blue of the sky. At that moment all our danger, all our fatigues were forgotten in the joy of finding our exploring expedition crowned with success at last'.

Teleki's and von Höhnel's great 'moment' came at two o'clock on a broiling March afternoon—the hottest time of the year in that region. The date was 5 March 1888, an important day for the two lonely white men, who for thirteen months had suffered the anguish and enjoyed the pleasures of travel in the obscure and desolate hinterland of east Africa. The euphoria which followed from the stunning success of their ambition filled both of them with a deep sense of indebtedness to the man who had so graciously encouraged them in their plans. One can well imagine the solemnity of the moment as the aristocrat and the young naval officer stood contemplating the scene they would remember as one of the greatest moments in their lives, far from the plaudits of their fellow-countrymen and from the security and comforts of their respective homelands. Sobering, but intensely thrilling, the final formality was dispensed by Teleki, von Höhnel's staid words describing the scene: 'Full of enthusiasm and gratefully remembering the gracious interest taken in our plans from the first by his Royal and Imperial Highness, Prince Rudolf of Austria, Count Teleki named the sheet of water, set like a pearl of great price in the wonderful landscape beneath us, Lake Rudolf'.

The thoughtful moment passed, for Teleki and his party had yet to reach the lake. In 'capital spirits' the final march was made. They didn't however, reach the water's edge until the following day, so appalling were the remaining miles. Von Höhnel's anguished words aptly described their walk: 'The mountain district between us and the lake was, in fact, a veritable hell ... When the sun rose higher, its rays were reflected from the smooth brownish-black surface of the rock, causing an almost intolerable glare, whilst a burning wind from the south whirled the sand in our faces, and almost blew the loads off the heads of the men'. Despite the horror of those final miles their morale was high; ahead lay 'the one bit of brightness in a gloomy scene ...

*'a fitting frame for the dark-blue gleaming surface of the lake stretching away beyond as far as the eye could reach'. (von Höhnel)*

we felt our spirits rise once more as we stood upon the beach at last, and saw the beautiful water, clear as crystal, stretching away from us'. Their joy was not to last, for the 'water was brackish' and almost undrinkable. What a despondent anti-climactic scene it must have been; blasted by the sun's heat radiating from boundless jagged rocks, and buffeted by the howling 'sand-laden' wind, the exhausted body of men stood disconsolately on the edge of a vast supply of seemingly unusable water. Slowly the sombre realisation of the situation's seriousness dawned on them. With at least fifteen days travel through a virtually uninhabited region before they would reach the hospitable Reshiat country at the north end of the lake, and only ten days' food supply remaining, their position was grim. That day two more men died.

The following morning saw the caravan hastening away from 'this valley of death as quickly as possible', stumbling northwards along the stark rock-infested lake shore, where neither firewood nor grazing for its stock was to be found. Desperate to augment his food supplies, Teleki abandoned the monotonous wilderness of the lake shore on the third day, and aimed for 'the broad pyramidal' Mt Kulal in the hopes of finding people and stores of grain. It was an abortive effort, yet not a total loss, for at midday they reached 'a little streamlet which issued from the base of a perpendicular rock'. Those minimally descriptive words of von Höhnel's portray one of the gems of Kenya's northern district, a haven of exquisite beauty in striking contrast to the barrenness of the immediately surrounding terrain. Hidden in the depths of a remote cliff-edged valley, and fed by the sudden upwelling of an underground flow from nearby Mt Kulal, are the lovely springs known as Mouwoligiteng, meaning in the Samburu language 'the cow's horns'. Unchanged from the day when Teleki first stumbled on them, one can well appreciate the scene as the disheartened explorers first arrived at the top of the cliff and looked down on the tree-lined green sward through which the crystal clear 'streamlet' wandered. Here they found a group of zebras and oryx grazing, of which Teleki's skilful marksmanship soon took its toll—a welcome addition to their sorely pressed food stores. Changing their minds about finding supplies on Kulal, and rested after a night in that lovely place, the caravan proceeded on its way. Within a few hours, gratifyingly, they reached another oasis, 'Ngare Dabash' (Lare Dabach), quite different in feature from the previous one, but equally welcoming and hospitable. Here a delightful series of springs nurtured a sheltering grove of doum palms and acacias, providing fresh water and shade for the travel-weary party. A halt was called, and for a day Teleki's men rested, ravenously feeding off a rhinoceros their leader had slain near to camp.

Recovered after a sustaining day in such pleasing surroundings, Teleki ordered a return to the lake-side, which was only a short march away. At the point where the caravan struck the lake were three small islands, which their guides assured them were inhabited. This information was borne out shortly after by the appearance of a few timid Elmolo, the first signs of human life they had encountered on the lake. After ascertaining that 'there are about 200 or 300 Elmolo altogether', followed by the Count's success in 'bringing down two hippopotami' in the bay for welcome sustenance, the expedition strode on to camp nearby, on 'a dried-up and rubbish-encumbered channel of a stream'.

For the next four days, according to von Höhnel's account, they trudged along the lake shore, food supplies dwindling ominously in spite of meat from the occasional rhinoceros killed by Teleki. It was at this critical stage that the last of their small herd of 'we reached at mid-day a little streamlet which issued from the base of a perpendicular wall of rock'. (von Höhnel) – Mouwoligiteng spring.

'we camped by the source of a swampy little brook . . . Our pool of water was bordered by fresh green rushes and grass'. (von Höhnel) – Lare Dabach spring.

cattle, weakened by the lack of forage, was slaughtered on Teleki's order. Even the flesh of a leopard shot by Teleki was devoured with relish. The effect of long hard days of ration-short marching was beginning to make itself felt on the caravan, and 'it became more and more apparent that the men were getting weaker'. By the time they reached the prominent lake shore landmark, Mt Longendoti, one more porter had died, followed by yet another the day after. The situation was worsening rapidly; four men were so exhausted they had to ride donkeys, and on the demise of one rhinceros and one large bull elephant to Teleki's rifles, the need for sustenance was so great that von Höhnel could not resist describing the desperate scene: 'The number of those who could eat elephant-meat was now considerably increased, and a very few hours later there was nothing left but the skin and bones of the huge beast, whilst cooking and eating went on day and night'. Unbeknown to them, they were on the verge of an even more desperate stretch. Mt Longendoti's lake-side slope tumbled steeply into the water, affording no passage for man or beast. The only alternative was to proceed inland and round the range, through uncharted terrain, hoping they would discover water on the way.

The gruelling march that followed, although of no great distance, required all the

*'A double onslaught . . . the Count found himself in the uncomfortable dilemma of having to choose between the trunk of an elephant and the horn of a rhinoceros. It was a critical moment'.*
*(von Höhnel)*

will-power and force of discipline that the expedition leaders could muster. Their men, exhausted by weeks of incessant hard trekking, were in dire need of a prolonged rest. Nor could they survive on meat alone, and the reported grain supplies of the Reshiat were still days away. With all that in mind, one can well understand the urgency with which Teleki ordered his men on through the arid heat-baked wastes. Regularly men fell by the wayside, totally exhausted and unable to continue. Von Höhnel, advancing up the line from his position in the rear found this depressing scene: 'Half the men were lying about staring vacantly before them; loads and animals were in the most hopeless confusion; donkeys and sheep wandering aimlessly about, the former either without their saddles or with those saddles under their bellies or round their necks . . . All discipline was at an end, and the men were utterly demoralised'. Further on he found the Count in a narrow ravine walled in by towering columns of basalt. A scene of chaos prevailed, men and animals jostling and pushing round a tiny supply of water at the base of a cliff. The struggle to find sufficient water reached frantic porportions, finally requiring the use of Somali whips and Teleki's personal efforts to control the shouting mob and ensure a fair share for everyone. The whole dreary night was spent this way, searching for and watering the stragglers. Early next morning the caravan staggered the remaining few miles to the lake. Tragically, the death toll continued— four more men had died.

Despite all the trials an important milestone in Teleki's journey had been reached; Alia Bay, where the caravan was camped, marked the beginning of better travelling conditions. Not only was the going easier for the men, but to his delight the Count now found himself in a rich and extensive gamefield, and every day the thunder of his firearms signalled scenes of excitement and action. For the caravan there was no lack of meat, as elephants, rhinoceros, buffalo, zebra, oryx and gazelle abounded. The week spent in the area was very rewarding for Teleki. A group of Elmolo living there produced a small amount of grain, a few sheep and some fish, but more important was news of the proximity of Reshiat country, from where the welcome grain had come. The Count also has a heyday in his pursuit of ivory, shooting seven elephants with tusks weighing a total of 887 pounds (403 kilograms), and purchasing a further four teeth weighing 384 pounds (175 kilograms). Huge tuskers abounded in the district, many with teeth weighing over 100 pounds (45 kilograms) each, and had it not been vital to hurry on to the Reshiat, doubtless the energetic Teleki would have accumulated an even bigger hoard of ivory. The sojourn at Alia finally came to an end, but not before another two men had died. Despite the tons of elephant flesh available, 'our people do not seem able to recover their health', and with two hundred men to feed, all thoughts were now turned towards finding the renowned Reshiat food stores. From that point to the northern extremity of the lake took a further nine days of short fatiguing marches. The slowness of their progress was partly due to the weak state of the porters, but was also brought about by the indefatigable Teleki in his enthusiastic chase after elephants and his purchase deals for ivory; a further 545 pounds (248 kilograms) of the valuable commodity was added to his collection before the expedition eventually arrived at the top end of the lake on 4 April 1888.

Teleki and von Höhnel were the first white men ever to lay eyes on the Reshiat, and the latter claimed: 'This was perhaps the most interesting day of our whole journey, for we were now for the first time face to face with a perfectly unknown people'. The lack of any aggressive spirit on the part of the Reshiat astonished the

'in its furthest corner [we] came upon the van of the caravan, all huddled together and jostling each other about a shallow pit at the base of a wall of rock'. (von Höhnel)

travel-hardened explorers, who were grateful for the cordiality of relations with that contented race. A camp was soon constructed and brisk trading started. Food was plentiful, and 'our men got such good rations now that they were able to eat their fill without any trouble'. Of Reshiat behaviour in camp von Höhnel was complimentary: 'They did not beg or attempt to steal, they were neither importunate nor shy, and they maintained this satisfactory behaviour from first to last'. Ten days of pleasant camp life were spent amongst the Reshiat, everyone's spirits and health improving with the protracted rest and ample nutritious food.

The contented period of inaction finally came to an end, as Teleki and von Höhnel 'were once more seized with a longing for new discoveries and fresh experiences'. Having ascertained that the second lake they were looking for was not far off, they cached their excess stores and hoard of ivory, and struck away eastwards towards a nearby range of hills. It was their good fortune that the rainy season had just started, as the pools of water they found enabled them to cross an otherwise impassable stretch of land. A week of travel brought the explorers to their next discovery, found after crossing a 'flat country stretching away on the south of the Basso Ebor'*. Little

---

*Basso Ebor was the Samburu name for Lake Stefanie.

enthusiasm seems to have been evinced by them at that point, and von Höhnel's words strike one as being, if anything, somewhat disenchanted: 'As far as we could make out, the immediate neighbourhood of the lake was very disappointing, and as there was nothing to tempt us down to the beach, we camped near a good-sized pool of rainwater'. Their disappointment at failing to find any inhabitants in the area was compensated for by a successful elephant hunt in which the Count bagged three more of the beasts. Finally, the party reached the shores of the lake, and von Höhnel's later description told of a sheet of shallow water, very brackish, and teeming with dead and dying fish, crocodiles and birds. He suggested that the lake 'is evidently rapidly receding', and had it not been for the 'rainpools it would have been impossible to remain' there. It was not a particularly exhilirating discovery, but Teleki nevertheless went through his ritual and 'named the newly discovered sheet of water Lake Stefanie … in honour of her Imperial Highness the Archduchess Stefanie'.

Teleki's job was now done, and a celebration of sorts was called for. It appears that was the only time the redoubtable pair really let their hair down during their two years in the depths of Africa, and 'we brewed ourselves a bowl of foaming liquor'. A powerful concoction it was indeed; honey, water, tartaric and carbonic acid were tossed in to make a brew 'which tasted delicious', and with which they toasted 'the royal pair with whose names it is our proud privilege to associate all the geographical results of our arduous undertaking'. Singing, dancing and volleys of gunfire followed in the celebration of their momentous achievements, and it was with a light-hearted sense of relief that the caravan retraced its steps to the base camp on Lake Rudolf. Everyone was revived by the thought of the homeward journey.

Originally, the plan had been to return by way of the western shore of Lake Rudolf, a scheme that met with immediate and positive resistance from the Reshiat. No amount of persuasion or supplication would change their determined opposition; no guides were obtainable, food supplies were denied, and while not actively hostile, the Reshiat were totally intransigent in their attitude. A further complication then arose with the setting in of the heavy rains. For days on end rain fell, and with the rising Omo river flooding the low-lying land it soon became apparent that a crossing without the aid of boats would be impossible. Finally, and with the greatest reluctance, they were forced to retrace their steps, von Höhnel mournfully writing: 'Day by day the terrible fact became clear that we should have, after all, to return by the east coast'. Food and ammunition were running low, and it was only through von Höhnel's energetic forays that two tons of precious grain were successfully purchased. Preparations for the journey were hurriedly made, loads of staggering size being put together, for 'our men were expected to make such efforts as nothing but a case so desperate as ours would have justified'. No one was expected to carry less than 110 pounds (50 kilograms); the heaviest load weighed 148 pounds (67 kilograms). What men they must have been to hump such back-breaking burdens in the withering heat of the lake's desolate shore. Spirits were understandably low when they set forth on 14 May, their destination and fortunes uncertain to say the least. Of that time von Höhnel wrote: 'Many of our poor fellows tottering beneath their heavy loads, thought that we should all perish'. To add to the leaders' worries, Teleki felt the effects of approaching fever, a rare occurrence for the rugged man. Despite that, he and his caravan doggedly tramped down the shore finding a country greatly altered in appearance after the beneficial rains, with not an elephant to be seen. Indeed it had been their good fortune the northward journey was undertaken during the dry season, when the wild beasts were concentrated by the lake waters. Desperation lent wings to the men's feet; they reached their original camp at the south end of the lake in sixteen days, only half the time it had taken them to do the outward journey.

At that critical stage a decision had to be made on which way to go—south, back along their old track, or west through Turkanaland. They decided in favour of new territory, fortunately known to their well-travelled guide, the staunch Lembasso. The fact that they might conflict with the reputedly fearsome Turkana did not deter them: 'we had neither time or desire for diplomacy, absolutely no device was open to us; go through Turkana we must and would!'

Von Höhnel now made his own little discovery. Trailing at the rear of the caravan, he decided to investigate the volcano they had passed on their outward march. The whole area appeared to be quietly active, but black clouds of smoke, poisonous sulphur and chlorine vapours, and raw flows of lava attracted his attention. Deciding to do a little exploration on his own account, he wandered over this ruined ground, but was soon halted by an impassable stretch of perilous-looking lava in which 'crevices began to occur more frequently, most of them being covered with a treacherous crust of earth. Finally a fissure . . . put an end to further progress'. Von Höhnel very wisely decided to desist from his lonely investigation; the marching caravan was well ahead and not waiting for him anyway, so he quietly 'ventured to give the volcano the name of "Teleki", in honour of the leader of our Expedition, as for him it was reserved to bring home the news of this still existing centre of volcanic activity in the Dark Continent'. That was the last day they spent on the great lake they had suffered so much to find. Neither Teleki nor von Höhnel ever returned to the shores of Lake Rudolf, but their names were assured a permanent place in the annals of African exploration, stalwart heroes of an epic two-year hike.

Some five months after leaving the lake's shore, the sadly depleted expedition staggered into Mombasa, laden with bales of rare and valuable specimens for the Imperial Natural History Museum in Vienna. Within the collection was material which kept botanists, zoologists and geologists busy for months, as they worked their way through the thousands of specimens diligently preserved by von Höhnel and his little band of assistants. Rewardingly, many of the plants and insects were new to science, the names Teleki and Höhnel as their specific titles giving them scientific posterity.

Teleki's expedition was remarkable not just for its extensiveness or the importance of its discoveries, but for the rapport the two explorers appeared to have with one another. Nowhere in von Höhnel's lengthy account can one detect any signs of disagreement or discord. Unlike Burton and Speke who had fallen out bitterly during their journey in Africa years before, Teleki and von Höhnel seemed to enjoy a harmonious accord throughout the two stressful years of their march. This was all the more amazing in view of the somewhat unpromising first meeting between the two men, but it was a reflection on the calibre of the two men's personalities. Count Teleki, the aristocrat and the elder by twelve years, was the sponsor of the expedition and obviously in command. Ritter von Höhnel, holding a lesser title inherited from his father, was the technical expert. Teleki's pleasure was hunting, von Höhnel's was in his scientific and geographical surveys. So one can only surmise that these men's complementary activities managed to sustain a satisfactory accord in the workings of their huge expedition.

One sour note, regrettably, has filtered through. The natural history specimens were presented to the Vienna museum, the ethnographical collection went to the Hungarian National Museum. That dispersion was undoubtedly agreed on by prior arrangement, and it appeared a satisfactory division of the spoils. When it came to the important matter of declaring the expedition's results to the world, for some reason it was the junior member, von Höhnel, rather than the leader, Teleki, who rose to deliver the first spoken account, to the Austrian Geographical Society*. Was it because Teleki did not have the ability or desire, or was it more correct for an Austrian to address his national organisation? Remembering that Teleki was a patriotic Hungarian, do the partisan words of John Xantus, Vice President of the General Assembly of the Hungarian Geographical Society, spoken at a meeting in 1890, insinuate some half-hidden feelings: 'It is very regrettable that Teleki's scientific results were not introduced into the learned world by the Hungarian Geographical Society'?

Teleki's apparent inaction in preparing a story of his exploration cannot be put down to intellectual ineptitude. Far from it, for he was a scholar and a gifted correspondent if his letters to his close friend Rudolf and others are any indication†. Hilariously descriptive, they give the scenes they describe a warm true-to-life quality, quite the opposite of von Höhnel's dry matter-of-fact style. It is as well to remember that Teleki's expedition diaries were used extensively by von Höhnel while he was compiling the voluminous account of their long trek. The reason for Teleki's failure to write anything extensive about his travels, was, most probably, simply aristocratic indolence. He was a pleasure-loving man, not overly ambitious or hardworking, and the prospect of months of intense desk work did not appeal to him. How much easier to hand it all over to the diligent von Höhnel, the junior officer, who obviously enjoyed that type of challenge. Whatever may have been the case, one thing is true today: the geographical and scientific results of Teleki's expedition rank with the highest in the story of exploration in Africa, and von Höhnel's classic two-volume account of their arduous travels will forever make exciting reading.

---

*The world first received Teleki's own written account of his triumph by way of a letter written by him to *The Times* of London, printed on 26 December 1888. The next report came from Antonio Cecchi, the Italian Consul in Aden, who wrote a brief letter to the Secretary of La Società Geografica on 30 January 1889. Those two notices, strangely, preceded any written reports to Austria or Hungary.

† An example of Teleki's writing style may be found in Appendix 1.

*William Astor Chanler in his early twenties.*

# CHANLER EXPEDITION 1892–4

EARLY in 1891, a little more than two years after his return from the African expedition which had established him as one of the eminent explorers of the times, von Höhnel received a brief letter from a complete stranger, an American called William Chanler. Writing from his home in New York, Chanler wanted to know whether he might be interested in joining his next expedition to east Africa. For von Höhnel, Chanler's offer was just another of many similar invitations received by him since his return to Austria after the successful Teleki trip. The other offers had held no appeal for him and had been rejected out of hand, but the latest one aroused his curiosity and prompted him to mail an equally terse reply expressing his interest in the idea. In due course a meeting in Vienna took place between the two men to thrash out the proposal. Unbeknown to von Höhnel at the time, their rendezvous was for him the beginning of an experience and a friendship strikingly dissimilar to those of three years before.

*       *       *

Twenty-four years prior to von Höhnel receiving the American's communication, William Astor Chanler was born in New York City. The son of a wealthy lawyer and Congressman, the child grew up in the magnificent old family home called Rokeby sited on a rise overlooking the tranquil peace of the Hudson River. There, surrounded by all the comforts and ease that riches could provide, young Willie lived happily with his three brothers and three sisters. Tragically, when the boy was only ten years old, his mother died suddenly; about a year later his father followed suit. In spite of their unexpected deprivation, life for the orphans continued as comfortably as before, except that a body of guardians took over the responsibility of their well-being, and the organisation of their lives. The Chanler children were an extraordinary little group, and early showed signs of the energetic self-reliance which characterised their later lives. Willie was no exception in his possession of that attribute. If anything, it was even more highly developed in him than the others, his restless aggressive spirit continually driving him in pursuits which required violent physical action and dangerous excitement. Academic activities certainly didn't appeal to him, and at eighteen the allure of hunting in the Florida Everglades attracted him far more than the tedium of a cramming college in Newport. Nevertheless, in the autumn of 1886 he somehow managed to pass his entrance examination to Harvard. Shortly after, he arrived at college with a generous allowance, and accompanied by the fourteen-year-old son of a local gardener. George Galvin, as Chanler's young factotum was named, faithfully accompanied his master around the world through thick and thin, war and peace, for many years thereafter. At Harvard Chanler proved a lackadaisical student, preferring to take life lightly and indulge his passion for horses—polo was his craze. With barely suppressed impatience he waited for his twenty-first birthday to arrive, when he would then be free to choose his own course in life. Promptly on that day he left Harvard, and some months later sailed for England in a zestful and uninhibited search for adventure.

That Chanler was an extraordinary man there can be no doubt. One sees in portraits of him a boundless self-assurance staring back from his handsome open face, the firm set of his jaw clearly indicating a determined and tough personality. Loquacious and argumentative, he also possessed a spirit of defiant independence, which at times broke out into a display of aggressiveness verging on pugnacity*. A driving personality who thrived on the thrill of genuine danger, he was a dynamic product of his race. But despite his impetuous and hot-headed ways, Chanler was a popular member of his set. He had a big heart, one that always favoured the underdog, and he was gentlemanly, his cultured background and urbane upbringing allowing him to face the world with an easy polished manner, giving him an ability to make friends at any level of society. Chanler once described himself as 'too medieval a person'. Fortunately for him, during his youth there were still a few situations in which he could practise that idiosyncrasy. Chanler's own words to von Höhnel, his respected companion in Africa, sum up in an unusual display of humbleness a candid self-appreciation: 'Your influence has been all for the good and I must tell you that I feel to be a better person since I have known you. I fear many & many times I have caused you pain & now I ask your pardon. I have a bad—really bad—temper and on looking back I wonder at the kindliness with which you often met my roughness'. How many times the self-controlled and rock-steady von Höhnel must have had to repress his indignant feelings when Chanler's impetuous temper and rash acts came to the fore.

For nine carefree months after leaving Harvard the wealthy young Chanler gadded about Europe, often in the company of his equally spirited sisters. But his sights were already set on a scene of robust action far from the well-trodden European tour, a place which would challenge even his enthusiasm for action and adventure—east Africa. So in March 1889 he was to be found in Zanzibar, just three months after Teleki and von Höhnel had departed. Accompanying Chanler was the dependable George Galvin, then barely sixteen years of age. Deciding to hunt in the Kilimanjaro area, Chanler left Mombasa at the head of 120 Zanzibari porters, and for some months he daringly roamed the country between Tsavo and Taveta, pitting his energies against all manner of wild and ferocious animals. In that way he satisfied his desire for violent and often punishing action. But the excursion merely whetted his unappeasable appetite for more episodes of a similar nature, and almost immediately on returning home plans were being turned over in his restless mind for an extensive expedition through the unexplored parts of British East Africa, in the neighbourhood of Mt Kenya. The trip materialised, and from mid-1892 to early 1894, Chanler was engaged in his ambitious African sortie with von Höhnel; one which tested every fibre of his obdurate nature and physique in the hardest and most disappointing ways. Despite the professional abilities of his companion, the expedition did not prove to be a success. Sickness, injury and wholesale desertions finally defeated even Chanler's formidable enthusiasm.

On Chanler's return to the United States his exploring feats and discoveries crowned him with glory; his old friend Theodore Roosevelt exhorted him to write a book on his African travels, and one of his sisters even tried to persuade von Höhnel to

---

* At one point in his life Chanler was joint owner of a 'stable of fighters' in New York, and enjoyed working off thwarted energies by sparring with his employees in the boxing ring.

*Chanler's faithful factotum, George Galvin, a companion in many escapades and journeys.*

return to Africa with Willie and another of their irrepressible brothers.

A new challenge, however, had seized Chanler's attention and distracted him for the time being from further global travels—politics. Once again his fiercely independent spirit revealed itself: his loyalty to the Democrats' cause led him into total opposition with family loyalties and those of his great friend Roosevelt, involving him in the rough and tumble of political imbroglio. Success was his reward, and in 1897 he was elected to the New York state legislature.

Shortly after, with ominous war clouds building up over Cuba, Chanler's increasing sympathy with the anti-Spanish faction fighting their guerilla campaign enticed him to shelve his political career temporarily, in favour of the excitements of running contraband war materials to his friends on the island. It was a hazardous task, undertaken at his own expense and risk, and boosted by his intense desire—in this case supported by his Republican friend Roosevelt—to drive all European powers out of the American arena.

Following that adventurous interlude, Chanler returned home to the more sober world of state legislature, for which he had very little heart. Mercifully for him that tedious spell did not last too long as the possibility of American involvement in the war against Spain in Cuba was rapidly escalating, and Chanler, together with faithful George Galvin, could not resist the call to arms. Hardly was the United States committed to the fight than Chanler was recruiting his own unit to take to the battlefields of Cuba, again at his own expense. It was with a sense of deep frustration that he had to abandon the ambitious project and opt for a lesser alternative—the recruitment of a tiny band of ten mercenaries to be used for the same purpose. Disappointingly for Chanler that project was also knocked on the head, this time by the American President, who arranged for him to become a staff officer instead of a combatant. From then on things fell into place; honour and glory came Chanler's way when first he administered and later managed his transfer to the front line, where he fought with indomitable energy through the war, gaining mentions for bravery in many of the leading actions, and most important for him, providing an outlet for his driving urge to be where the action was hottest.

Chanler ended the war an honoured hero with the rank of captain. He once more took up his political career with his customary vigour. His astounding success in roundly defeating a well-established Republican opponent gained him a seat in Congress, and yet more salutes. He served his term unspectacularly, finding the sedentary life of a congressman irksome, and for his ebullient nature, oppressive. Politics, in fact, frustrated him joining the South African Boers in their fight against the British at the turn of the century. Not to be outdone, he equipped and paid a fellow-countryman to do his fighting for him. By doing that he felt he could strike a surrogate blow against the British, for whom he had developed a deep-rooted antagonism since his legal wrangle in Zanzibar at the close of his second African expedition.

At the end of his congressional term he retired from politics for ever, leaving active public life to follow another course. Chanler's inclinations were tied up with the world of intrigue and the underdog, and for the rest of his life he found time, concurrently with the running of his business interests, to assist energetically in a variety of filibustering exploits. Some fighting in Venezuela with his small army of American adventurers in 1905 was followed by a period in the Libyan desert in 1910, when he lived the life of a Taureg, smuggling in arms from Turkey and assisting Senussi tribesmen in their strivings against the Italians. Immediately that was over he was off to Somaliland to assist the Mad Mullah in his fruitless rising against the Italian and British forces. During those hectic years robust action was his unmitigated craving, and in its pursuit he was lucky enough to find many opportunities to burn up his seemingly unlimited supply of driving energy. In 1914 he lost a leg, and from that time his health started to deteriorate. After the First World War he spent most of his time in Europe, with business interests ranging from America to France, from horse breeding to marble and ochre mining. Behind them all his tangled life continued: the shadowy world of espionage preoccupied him until his demise in 1934, when his body, worn out by the excesses of a tempestuous life, could no longer stand the pace.

Chanler was given a final resting place in the family vault in Trinity Cemetery,

Manhattan, overlooking the serene breadth of the Hudson River. The graveyard peace of this green corner is crudely destroyed by the tearing traffic on adjacent Broadway, with its unending roar, a situation of which Chanler's turbulent spirit would undoubtedly approve, reflecting at the last the man's mortal enjoyment of both the tranquility of the great outdoors, and the aggressive struggle of metropolitan life.

*     *     *

Having once exposed himself to the potential in African travel, with its dangers, thrills, and unorthodox challenges, it was impossible for Chanler to resist a second try. Wilful, idle and hedonistic though he may have been at home, his boisterous enthusiasm overrode obstacles that would have deterred many another man, and he now applied it to the planning of his second visit to the African continent. The thoroughness of his preparations was based on his previous experience of east Africa, combined with what he had learned from the written accounts of other expeditions in the same field. Everything was done in a quiet authoritative manner and nothing was omitted—Galvin was even trained by a professional magician to perform an inventory of devious tricks, and Chanler took several pairs of flesh coloured rubber gloves with which to hoodwink simple tribesmen into believing that he was skinning himself, a subterfuge that would have hugely impressed the necromancing Joseph Thomson himself. The photographic equipment taken to record the expedition's highlights was no exception. Armed with two of the latest cameras—one of which was capable of using the new-fangled telephoto lens—and nine hundred photographic plates in sealed tins, Chanler was prepared to return with a feast of valuable pictorial material. He aimed to be away for at least two years and, if all went well, to travel at least 3,000 miles (4,800 kilometres), much of it in previously unexplored territory. Money was no object to him and everything was meticulously prepared, even to the selection of a suitable companion to join him on his extensive journey. The first choice was the Austrian von Höhnel, the person who had accomplished so much with Teleki, transcribing his observations into exquisite maps, and returning with countless specimens of nature to enhance the world's reservoirs of knowledge. With that idea foremost in his mind, he sat down and wrote von Höhnel a letter.

The Austrian considered the contents of the letter, then consulted his senior, Admiral Baron von Sterneck, commander of the Austrian navy. They agreed that before any decision could be made, a meeting between the three men should take place. A date was arranged, and in due course von Höhnel met Chanler at his hotel in Vienna. Von Höhnel was duly impressed with the young man's appearance and manner; direct brown eyes looked out of a resolute and even arrogant face, giving the older naval officer—there was a ten-year difference in their ages—the definite impression that he was dealing with a determined and forceful personality. On listening to Chanler's frank, convincing words describing the aims of his expedition, von Höhnel realised that here was a man worthy of his companionship in the wilderness of Africa. The next day they set out together to visit the Admiral. In his youth, von Sterneck had been, like Chanler, a vigorous man of action, so his reaction to the young man's courteous, but candidly emphatic manner was sympathetic. At the end of an hour's discussion, von Sterneck recognised that Chanler was indeed an exceptional individual, and with whole-hearted approval granted his junior officer indefinite leave to join the American's venture. Immediately after the crucial meeting the two adventurers went their separate ways; by agreement Chanler was to arrange for the purchase of equipment and supplies in England, von Höhnel was to attend to the matters of scientific and military gear in Austria.

In June 1892, the busy pair joined forces in Port Said, and Chanler wrote home the news that his naval companion had brought: 'among other things for convincing the natives that I am a "dear sweet boy", 4 savage Illyrian dogs [retrievers], 200 rifles, and 35,000 cartridges'. Later in the same letter he dauntlessly wrote: 'If I have luck two years will see me more or less famous as an explorer and then I can settle down and tackle life at home . . . If I fail in Africa I shall not be utterly cast down . . . If I die, I die in a decent cause'. Naturally the faithful George Galvin, now nineteen ears of age, was following on with the trading goods and supplies. Von Höhnel stopped off at Aden to search for a string of camels and engage a few Somali camel-men, plus a dozen Sudanese soldiers—a tedious chore which Chanler's impetuous spirit would not tolerate. It was at that early juncture that things started to go seriously wrong. With forethought, von Höhnel had obtained permission in advance from the German Colonial Government to recruit Wanyamwezi porters from the mainland of German East Africa—'men used to travel, trained to hardships, used to carry 100 pound (45 kilogram) loads like nothing, who moreover never thought of deserting'. Chanler, who preceded the others to Zanzibar, disregarded von Höhnel's sound advice, and recruited a band of local porters. Unfortunately, a large caravan had only recently left Zanzibar, taking the best men with it. On seeing Chanler's crew von Höhnel exclaimed: 'I, to my disgust found that 90 percent were a rabble of unfit, inexperienced young men, unfit to carry a heavy load'. The group of pathetic creatures recruited by his leader appeared to him far from able to face the hardships and labour of the miles ahead. His protests were in vain, and Chanler's impatient dictates won the day. It was a move he lived to regret as the months went by. Having gathered their 130 'mere youths and men of inferior physique', Chanler and von Höhnel embarked for Lamu, where they found the ever reliable Galvin patiently waiting at the nearby village of Mkonumbi. This marked von Höhnel's first meeting with Galvin, and he was duly impressed with the cool-headed competence of the stocky and powerfully built youth who possessed the additional gift of being an excellent handler of men, a practical asset that was to prove of great value. Base camp at Mkonumbi was a hive of activity as the three men arranged the packing of the porters' loads, drilled the somewhat undisciplined Sudanese, instructed everyone in elementary musketry, and completed the multitude of jobs associated with preparation for a lengthy stay in the hinterland. At last everything was completed, and their final plan detailed: they would ascend the Tana river to the vicinity of Mt Kenya, then strike north to Lake Rudolf, across to Lake Stefanie, back eastwards to the Juba river, and thence down to the port of Kismayu. With this programme in their minds they marched from their base on 18 September 1892, Chanler wearing an Arab turban and riding at the head of a procession of 160 men, 15 camels, a pack of donkeys, and a group oxen, sheep and goats. Von Höhnel once again took his customary place at the rear, which allowed him to do his survey work at his own pace.

Chanler, in a parting letter to one of his sisters, had these exuberant words to say: 'If we are only moderately successful this journey should be attended with such valuable scientific results that it will make us famous. We have plates for more than

*Chanler with his escort on the Tana river, wearing the turban he used in the early stages of the expedition. (From the Rokeby collection)*

one thousand photographs, scientific instruments of all kinds and last but not least von Höhnel knows how to use them all'. That he relied on von Höhnel's able experience there was no doubt: 'Lieut. von Höhnel is a wonderful fellow & will do much to make my journey pleasant as well as successful'. It was just as well Chanler had the stable and precise Austrian with him, for the inconsistencies which occur in his own published account of the expedition, and in the papers he wrote to the Royal Geographical Society during the journey, hardly reveal him as a dependable and accurate recorder of names and events.

Chanler's simply written chronicle of his march up the Tana river was yet more evidence of the endless attrition that characterised travel in those days. The same old problems of porter desertions, deaths of load-carrying animals and worst of all, human mortality from disease, contributed to a wearisome trek along the jungle-covered and fever-infested river banks. To add to their woes, two of the 'savage Illyrian dogs' died of thirst, one porter was shot dead while abandoning the expedition, and Chanler himself had his first attack of fever and dysentery—one of the many he would experience before his travels were over. Many years later von Höhnel wrote these regretful words on their choice of the Tana river route: 'it turned out that the Tana route which we took, was the worst route we could have chosen for penetrating into the interior; full of hardships, and offering no resources whatever; it was a mistake I had made'. It was a sombre confession, but he could not be entirely blamed, for Piggot, Dundas and others had used the river before them with success.

In early December the struggling caravan reached the abandoned post of Hameye*, positioned at the furthest navigable point of the river. Here, a halt was called, and because of the need to send back to the coast for more porters, Chanler revised his plans. With the coastwards-returning canoes went their letters, scientific specimens and exposed photographic plates. To put the weeks of waiting to good use, Chanler and von Höhnel decided to take a side trip and do some exploring.

On 5 December, leaving Hameye camp in the charge of Galvin, they set out once again, heading northwards to search for the elusive 'Lake Lorian' von Höhnel had failed to reach in 1887. With them went eighty men, and although they fully expected to be away for at least five weeks, they took sufficient food for only thirty days, trusting in their battery of Holland & Holland expresses, and the lethal new 8mm Mannlicher carbines—both had been von Höhnel's recommendations—and Chanler's Winchester rifles to supplement their stores; this trust was soon put to useful purpose as they entered the rich game fields on the eastern footslopes of the Nyambeni Hills. Their path took them to the confluence of the Mackenzie river, shown on today's maps as the Rojewerot. Here they abandoned the Tana, and following the course of the smaller stream soon found themselves in country new to white men's eyes. Chanler's trail then took the party to a close inspection of two sights as yet undescribed to the outside world—the 'Jombeni' range and the 'Embe' people‡. Among the latter they were fortunate in finding a guide, but not without first experiencing moments of apprehension as hundreds of demonstrating warriors put up a vociferous protest to the caravan's sudden arrival in their midst. Motio, their new recruit, had travelled extensively and spoke Swahili fluently; in addition he was well acquainted with the local geography, and during the ensuing year of travel with Chanler's expedition he proved his value countless times over. Continuing its northerly direction, the expedition crested the north end of the Nyambeni Hills and dropped down to camp on the slopes of the extraordinary crater of 'Ngome', well known for its valued supply of magnesium-sulphate salt§.

On 24 December 1892 Chanler and von Höhnel arrived on the bank of the Uaso Ngiro river, about 75 miles (120 kilometres) downstream from the extreme point reached by von Höhnel in his 1887 travels. Two more questions were now clearly answered: the Mackenzie river did not drain 'Lake Lorian', and nor did the Uaso Ngiro river flow into the Tana river. Two old speculations were thus disproved, and with great delight the explorers celebrated their arrival at the river by opening one of their two remaining pints of champagne. Next day was Christmas, and although far from their homes they 'received what providence had given us with a thankful spirit. The rushing river assisted our minds in reverting to home and our people.' The day was spent in a sheltered and palm tree-shaded camp, the ever industrious von Höhnel religiously attending to his map-making, while Chanler passed an hour or two questioning Motio about the neighbouring countries and peoples.

---

*Hameye was a station on the Tana river built by the Imperial British East Africa Company in early 1890.
†This river was discovered by Piggot in April 1890, and named after George S. Mackenzie, then a director and also the first administrator of the Imperial British East Africa Company.
‡The Nyambeni Hills and Meru people of today.
§Chanler's 'Ngome'—he also spelt it 'Ngombe'—appears on today's maps as Magado or Kombe, but the Meru people also know it as Eombe, meaning salt-rich ground.

*The expedition leaders camped under a mango tree near Mkonumbi, at the start of their venture (l. to r.) Chanler, von Höhnel and Galvin. (From the Rokeby collection)*

The following day the rested body of men trudged on downstream. About noon a faint roaring sound attracted their attention. Soon the cause was revealed: the river thundered over a sheer cliff of black columnar lava, some 60 feet (18 metres) thick; then, resembling a miniature Niagara, it flowed on through a vertically walled gorge which the water's erosive action had cut over aeons of time. A stark scene in a stark countryside, it had a spectacular handsomeness all of its own, and for Chanler it was a bonus, earning his expressive words: 'Below the falls these two streams again met, and forced their way between two precipitous walls of black lava; foam was churned and thrown high into the air, and the leaping, tumbling, frothing stream had a really wild and savage aspect'. Those falls, unbeknown to him, were to be one of the few major finds of his ill-fated expedition, but at that point the discovery was treated in an almost trivial way, so much more important in the explorers' minds were their main targets. Chanler, in a letter home, only just remembered to mention the fall's discovery: 'I forgot to say that on the Guaso Nyiro River I discovered a most beautiful waterfall which I have called "Chanler Falls". So the family name will be handed down to history after all'.

They hurried on their way, for the reliable Motio had told them of a viewpoint from whence 'the vast expanse of Lake Lorian could be seen ... the hopes of both Lieutenant von Höhnel and myself rose to a high pitch, and we felt that we were about to make a great geographical discovery'. They soon reached the summit of the flat-topped lava plateau of Merti, which rose steeply 500 feet (155 metres) above the river valley. From there Chanler and von Höhnel peered eagerly eastwards across the 'boundless desert', their eyes following the tree-fringed Uaso Ngiro river's meanderings over the flat featureless country and into the distance, where 'in the northeast our eyes were greeted by the sight of what appeared to be an enormous sheet of water, distant about thirty miles [48 kilometres]. Lieutentant von Höhnel and I turned silently to one another, and with deep feeling clasped hands, delighted to think that the stories of the size of the lake had not been exaggerated'. It was another dramatic moment in von Höhnel's African experiences, and for Chanler as well. Von Höhnel immediately took his bearings and announced the lake's estimated length—60 miles (96 kilometres). How elated the pair must have been; one more geographical question mark had been solved, and all that remained was to reach its distant shores and record its extent.

Eagerly setting out, Chanler's men continued downstream, stimulated by the expectation of soon reaching the elusive lake. From that time on, the struggling caravan would endure a vexatious succession of hardships and tragedies, which in the end foiled Chanler's plans and resulted in the abandonment of the expedition. But as they optimistically approached the anticipated sheet of water, there was certainly no thought of failure. Before long, conditions rapidly became worse; tall rank grass inhibited movement, violent and unexpected charges by rhinoceros caused confusion and chaos, and fever and dysentery from the 'dank, and noisome vapours . . . from the sluggish stream' created havoc with the men. Even Chanler and von Höhnel began to suffer from fever, and then porters started to die. The ground became soggier, and the grass became ranker, but still no lake appeared, and on they battled. In desperation, and with the party's morale at a pathetically low ebb, the harassed pair finally resorted to scaling a nearby tree, and from that elevated position they scanned in vain far and wide. A disastrous revelation prompted Chanler to write these despairing words a few years later: 'From this vantage point we took one long look, and then with half suppressed curses descended to the ground. There was no *Lake* Lorian! It is but a vast swamp, overgrown with papyrus and watergrass . . . The vast sheet of water we had seen from the top of the plateau had been a mirage. We felt that we had been tricked and duped by Nature at every turn. Our feelings of dejection were shared by every member of the caravan'. That night was hell on earth for everyone; the ravages of a myriad of mosquitoes dispelled all sleep, compounded the bitter disappointment of their discovery, and led to one frantic thought: 'how to get out as quickly as possible from this abode of pestilence and death'.

The story of Chanler's speedy retreat to Hameye was one of hard marches and death-defying fights, as his men raced homewards before their dwindling supplies of food came to an end. One saving feature of the country they trekked through was the vast concourse of wild animals living there, and the landscape reverberated to the crash of their ever-ready rifles, working hard to keep the food pots in use. Aiming to return over the centre of the Nyambeni Hills, the caravan first had to pass through the stronghold of the Wamsara tribe, from whom, Motio gave Chanler his assurance, the caravan would be able to purchase ample rations. Such optimism was soon shattered, for the warlike Wamsara determinedly resisted all access to, and passage through their country. Bodily weak from illness and shortage of food, and low on ammunition, the five days spent fighting their way over the heavily populated Nyambeni Hills gave the explorers much concern, and it was with great relief that they finally descended to the peace of the open Mackenzie river plains. Sixty-seven trial ridden days after leaving Hameye, Chanler's exhausted entourage staggered back into their base camp, only to find that all was not well. Certainly, Galvin had done his duty and kept the establishment in good order, but it had been outside his powers to save the animals from disease—all their transport oxen were dead, only five camels were left, and the donkeys were dying fast. It was a depressing return home, made more so by the death of ten men on the Lorian trip, and shortly after, accentuated by the desertion of a further ten porters. Chanler himself was a very sick man, fever and dysentery having taken its toll, and for two weeks he languished on his cot. His irrepressible spirit was, however, far from broken, and debilitated though he was, preparations for the grand northern march were soon being made.

Almost one month later the revitalised caravan was ready to move, but not happily, for Chanler 'beheld the looks of discontent upon most of their faces, and heard a low murmer run through my caravan'. On 8 March they set forth, Chanler's horse 'so ill that he was unable to carry me; so I hobbled along at the head of my men, supported by a stick'. For the next few days the unfit porters toiled and sweated under their loads. Many attempted to desert. Galvin manfully struggled with the problems of a reluctant caravan, organising loads, chasing runaways and generally applying his youthful vigour to maintaining a semblance of order. But their donkeys continued to die; reluctantly Chanler was forced to camp in the foothills of the Nyambeni Hills until such time as he was able to procure more. Galvin was duly dispatched into 'Embe' country with instructions to trade for food and donkeys, Chanler in the meanwhile holding a small deputation of 'Embes' as hostage in assurance of Galvin's well-being. To add to their problems the rainy season had commenced, with its attendant affliction of ill health affecting everyone; von Höhnel had fever, Chanler's liver complaint continued to debilitate him, and the men suffered continually, sick porters dying of 'pulmonary complaints'—probably pneumonia. As if these problems were not torment enough, a grass fire destroyed part of their camp, forcing them to build a more substantial one nearby. As it turned out, the new place at 'Daitcho' became their base for the rest of the expedition and would be in Galvin's care when the others disappeared yet again into the wilds.

Slowly but surely, Chanler and von Höhnel prepared plans for their next venture—a search for the 'Rendile'. Foodstuffs and donkeys were amassed, and a brotherhood treaty was made with the 'Embe', a politic move to ensure Galvin's safety from attack during his leader's absence. Finally, a letter of instructions was written for Galvin, in the event of the party failing to return by 1 January 1894.

Accompanied by sixty-five men and a pack of thirty-seven donkeys, the resolute pair confidently left base camp on 5 June. They had food for seventy-five days, and some livestock; for the rest they would rely on their marksmanship. With all that, Chanler felt confident he had adequate supplies in hand for a five-month trek in unknown country. There, he hoped to purchase a herd of camels sufficient in numbers to transport his caravan on the expedition's final stage—the march to Lake Rudolf and back to Kismayu. Heading in a northerly direction Chanler's group retraced its steps to 'Ngome' crater, and thence direct to the magnificent rock known as Mt Lolokwi, described by him as having 'steep sides and flat top giving it the appearance of a monstrous sepulchre'. In the neighbourhood of that prominent block they expected to

*Chanler Falls: 'The wall of lava, being higher in the middle than at the sides, divided the river into two streams'. (Chanler)*

find a community of 'Wanderobbo', who would be able to guide them to the 'Rendile', a tribe of camel herders notorious for their warlike behaviour to strangers. Travel problems in various forms—more donkeys died and guides were not forthcoming—delayed the expedition in its Lolokwi camp for a whole week, before its march resumed, led by a 'Burkeneji' whose pessimism about finding the 'Rendile' was not lessened by his forebodings on the terrors of the waterless desert they were aiming to cross.

Determination was needed, a quality Chanler possessed in plenty, and it now carried him across a piece of country he described as 'nearly as thorough a desert as Sahara. Without a guide a heavily laden caravan would soon perish from thirst in this dreary waste'. On that disagreeable stretch his donkeys continued to die, and the cattle then had to be pressed into load-carrying service. In such a forbidding terrain no one dared desert. Safely reaching the welcoming oasis of 'Seran', the party rested and the next move was planned: Chanler aimed to advance with a small body of men in an attempt to locate the 'Rendile', while von Höhnel would stand by and await orders. By a stroke of luck Chanler's little group did not have to travel far before they encountered a band of 'Rendile' by the Kom waterhole. It was a thrilling moment, as the occasion marked the earliest meeting of white man and 'Rendile' tribesmen—an historic first for both parties. The outcome did not turn out well for Chanler. The 'Rendile' refused to sell him any camels, and the caravan narrowly escaped attack by the hovering warriors. Despite the set-back, the 'Rendile' had finally been located, and Chanler was able, with certain reservation, to strike another item from his list of objectives: 'Our visit to the Rendile except for the purpose of discovery, and the interest which they had excited was anything but satisfactory'.

A more serious complication arose at this stage with the abscondment of one of the caravan's Zanzibari headmen, together with six porters. In order to forestall any false reports they might take back to Galvin, Chanler marched directly across country to 'Daitcho' taking three and a half days to cover 75 miles (120 kilometres)—a record-making march. Von Höhnel retraced his steps to their distant camp at Lolokwi to await his leader's return, the time being put to good use with continued surveys of the district. Finding all well at 'Daitcho', and the loyal Galvin in full control, Chanler immediately about turned, and with his band of reinforcements reached the Lolokwi camp in fifteen days of leisurely marching. Picking up the rest of his party he continued, reaching the 'Sayer' (Seya) river some days later. A brief rest on the pleasant riverside enabled him to recover from yet another bout of the ever-present fever, and gave von Höhnel an opportunity to scout the district for the 'Wanderobbo' they needed as guides for the onward march to Lake Rudolf.

One will never know quite why they needed guides at that stage, for the 'Sayer' is only a matter of 25 miles (40 kilometres) from Barsaloi, the starting point for von Höhnel's grim trek to Mt Ngiro with Teleki only six years before. It is inconceivable that von Höhnel, a skilled cartographer and experienced Africa traveller, would not have felt quite at home in the familiar valley between the Lorogi and Mathews mountains, the more so as he himself had been responsible for compiling the very first map of the area. It is a question that will never be answered, but indirectly it had serious consequences for the course of Chanler's problem-plagued expedition.

The 'Wanderobbo' were found, but they were in such dire straits from acute starvation—'the entire community seemed mere bags of skin and bones'—that they demanded to be fed before producing guides. For that, elephants had to be found. The two white men had no alternative but to comply, and in the rounds of their hunts successfully managed to shoot a few of the great beasts. It was while on their last foray into the rhino-infested Lorogi Mountain forests that disaster overtook them; von Höhnel was attacked and seriously injured by one of those unpredictable beasts.

Only then, far from his base at 'Daitcho' and many weeks away from a doctor, did Chanler come to realise how inept he was in medical matters—'my skill in surgery was very meagre'. This very lack of ability was also reflected in the ill-prepared state of his medical supplies, as 'most of our store of medicine was at Daitcho'. In retrospect one wonders at the loose thinking that permitted them to leave on an extended trip into such wild and savage country so poorly equipped. It was von Höhnel himself who coolly directed Chanler in the dressing of his wounds, and undoubtedly it was his tough and disciplined nature that assisted him to bear his sufferings with such calm fortitude, until he eventually reached a doctor many weeks later. Depressed by his companion's grave accident, Chanler recorded, a little selfishly maybe, the admission: 'My feelings of grief at Lieutenant von Höhnel's accident were accentuated by the fact that I was perfectly aware that from that time the expedition would be unable to profit from his skilled assistance'. Hurriedly they beat a retreat to 'Daitcho', von Höhnel being humped along in an improvised litter carried on the shoulders of toiling porters. It then appeared they were doomed to battle with the whole rhinoceros population, for innumerable confrontations with the pugnacious pachyderms later led to Chanler's vivid recollections: 'I can conjure up nothing but a nightmare of continuous horror and anxiety. The anxiety was occasioned by the sufferings of my friend; the horror was caused by the fact that during this entire march from Sayer until we reached Daitcho, all the rhinoceroses in East Africa seemed to have clustered about our pathway, and to have religiously devoted all their attentions and energies to charging us as frequently as possible'. On the same fearful trek one porter was killed by a charging rhinoceros, and on several occasions poor von Höhnel's anguish was not mitigated by his litter being precipitously dumped on the ground when his bearers fled from attack.

The hand of ill-fate had now descended heavily on the expedition, although Chanler's dogged nature stubbornly intended proceeding with his plans. On reaching their base at 'Daitcho', von Höhnel's weakening condition necessitated his speedy onward movement to the nearest doctor—at Kibwezi, six weeks distant. Galvin and twenty-five men were detailed to carry the ailing man there, and Chanler now settled down to relax, study the Maasai language, and consider how best he could salvage what was left of his crumbling ambitions. While waiting for Galvin's return, Chanler also hunted and explored the neighbourhood, pleasant occupations only interrupted by the arrival of newly recruited porters from Mombasa—a bunch of eighty unfit malcontents who were to cause him no end of frustration and trouble in the days ahead. Distressingly, his health now took a turn for the worse, and he 'grew thinner day by day'. To add to his trials, the rainy season set in, causing him anxiety about the possibility of Galvin's return being delayed by the flooding Tana river, an almost unfordable obstacle on such occasions. Stuck in 'Daitcho' camp with 150 men, and now too weak to go out hunting, Chanler was increasingly disturbed by the dwindling stocks of food.

While in that unenviable position two events of note took place: firstly, he made one final discovery when he shot a strange little antelope on the hill behind his camp—the previously unrecorded Chanler's reedbuck (*Cervicapra chanleri*); secondly,

*The only picture extant of the wounded von Höhnel being carried back to Daitcho by porters. (From the Rokeby collection)*

and most devastating for his plans, all the newly arrived porters walked out on him and left for home. Any hope of completing his onward march now relied entirely on Galvin returning with a fresh supply of donkeys. The doughty youth finally managed a crossing of the flooding Tana (the rains had been abormally heavy that year) bringing with him fifty donkeys, the survivors from the seventy-five he had purchased at Kibwezi. Galvin had had a hard struggle on the return journey, but his success boosted Chanler's hopes: 'At this time we thought our trials and tribulations were almost at an end, and hoped the New Year would find us well on our way'.

Two days later another heavy blow struck the luckless expedition. A complete walk out by all of the remaining porters left him with a crew of only twenty-five men. These included his few Somalis and the Sudanese soldiers. To put a final seal on Chanler's expectations, all but one of the Sudanese deserted four days later, leaving him with a token force of fifteen men and a scraggy herd of donkeys. Chanler's dispirited words described the situation: 'At this time our position was not one to fill me with good cheer. We were fairly safe where we were, but the expedition was utterly broken up, and there remained no thought, but how to get back to the coast'. It was a gloomy New Year prospect for him, and on 9 January, faced with no other alternative, he destroyed his wealth of stores—'trading-goods and the stores of food represented an expenditure exceeding $9,000 (U.S. money)'. On the morning of that dismal day a mighty bonfire was lit, which destroyed all their small-calibre ammunition and his 'pile of trading goods—food in tins, pickles, sauces, desiccated fruits, tea, coffee, soup, broadcloth, silk, plaid shawls, hundreds of yards of American sheeting, hundreds of pounds of beads and wire, and in fact, supplies sufficient for an expedition of 100 men journeying two years in the interior of Africa. In twenty minutes the result of a large expenditure of money and months of care and forethought had ceased to be'. The following day they left 'Daitcho' on the start of their long dreary march down to Mombasa. Thirty days later they arrived in the old sea port. Chanler had spent twenty trying months in the interior, and his words summing up the expedition's achievements during its time of hardships expressed his disappointment: 'nevertheless I could not bring myself to admit that they were commensurate with the idea which had induced us to undertake the journey, or the pains and suffering we had undergone in their accomplishment'.

One final blow awaited Chanler at Mombasa. A curt letter from the Prime Minister of Zanzibar, Sir Lloyd Mathews, instructed him not to return to Zanzibar as he would be unwelcome; furthermore, he was to arrange payment immediately for the porters who had deserted—some $8,000—and then leave Africa as speedily as possible. Rumours were rife that the deserters had returned to Zanzibar with gruesome tales of untold cruelties and hardships inflicted on them by Chanler, and worse, that the complaints had actually been accepted by the receptive ears of the authorities. These ridiculous claims riled Chanler into cabling Mathews in characteristically arrogant fashion: RENT ME VILLA. INTEND TO STAY IN ZANZIBAR TWO MONTHS.

It was an unpleasant two months for Chanler, battling against a prejudiced bureaucracy who stubbornly would not even consider his arguments, and adamantly refused to listen to the statements by his few loyal servants. The acrimony generated was furthered by his realisation that the perfidiousness of politics was then becoming increasingly obvious. The Imperial British East Africa Comany was innately suspicious of the American's intentions in a territory over which they claimed a trading monopoly, and government offices in London had been stirred into making enquiries about his activities. Chanler fought spiritedly within the letter of the law, but the guns aligned against him were too big, and finally he had to leave Zanzibar, refusing to pay the porters' wages and, unfortunately, having generated in his mind an intense hostility against the British and their *modus operandi*, an animosity that was to grow steadily as the years went by.

Chanler's expedition was undoubtedly hounded by ill luck. Others before him had experienced severe hardships in their roaming quests through Africa, but few had such persistent poor fortune. Wealth, youth and a brash determination were not enough to push his project through to its deserving end, and the bitterness of his experiences decided him never to return to East Africa again on a peaceful mission. In compensation for the partial failure of his persevering efforts came a lasting friendship with the fully recovered von Höhnel, honours from the Royal Geographical Society and the Austrian Geographical Society, and an honorary master of arts degree graciously conferred by Harvard University on its dilatory ex-student. Gratifyingly too, many scientific specimens were available for donation to the Smithsonian Institution, of which several were later identified as completely new species.

Last, but equally important, von Höhnel's beautiful maps described another corner of the little-known northern territory of the future British East Africa. So, in the final tally, and despite Chanler's lack of success in fulfilling all of his ambitions, the net results were of appreciable value to both geographers and scientists alike, conceding him a small claim for a place among the ranks of the famous. Disappointingly for him, his expedition was the only major one to the region which did not manage to reach its goal—Lake Rudolf. Regrettably, Chanler himself was mainly to blame, the old proverb—'More haste less speed', undoubtedly being the key to his lack of absolute success.

# NEUMANN EXPEDITIONS
# 1893–6

THROUGH the curtain of dense green bush the murmur of voices could clearly be heard, carrying from the vicinity of the tiny stream that babbled down the looming south flank of Mt Ngiro. Drawing slowly into sight up the winding footpath were two ambling figures: one, bent and worn with age, the whitened irises of blindness peering from his wrinkled old face; the other, a young moran (warrior) red-ochred in Samburu fashion, proudly bearing his spears but gently guiding his ancient relative along the dusty track. On meeting white strangers in their path they halted, greetings were exchanged and a simple question asked of the moran: 'Has the old man ever heard of Nyama Yangu?' A brief discussion between the two preceded the youth's reply: 'Yes, many, many years ago, my grandfather tells me, when he was a small child he lived with his people on top of the mountain. One day the cry went up: "Nyama Yangu has arrived at the bottom of the mountain, we must go and meet him". Then too small to accompany the others down the steep slope, he remembers well the excitement as the young men hurriedly left to descend the hill and meet their newly arrived visitor'. Enthralled, the questioner gazed on the ancient, a relic of a long-gone past, a man who had personally experienced a brief, albeit indirect, contact with the lonely little elephant hunter, Arthur Neumann, or Nyama Yangu as he was familiarly known to the natives of the country where he had hunted. After farewells, the pair plodded on, slowly disappearing into the bush, the venerable Samburu wondering, maybe, why a stranger should be so interested in a white man who had last visited them seventy years before.

\*     \*     \*

Halfway through the nineteenth century, on 12 June 1850, Arthur Henry Neumann came into this world, the second son of the Reverend J. S. Neumann who was then vicar in the tiny village of Hockliffe in Bedfordshire. The full story of Arthur Neumann's early years will never be known, but it is evident from his only published work that even as a child he had a retiring nature, much of his boyhood being spent in solitary amusements in secluded corners of the peaceful countryside around his home. For the rest of his life he was obsessed with seeking lonely, remote country.

The first definite record of his activities tells of his arrival in Natal, South Africa, in early 1869 as a young man eager for adventure in wild unknown lands. For a year he worked on a coffee plantation in the lush rolling northern hills of that province. With growing enthusiasm for the possibilities of his new life, he encouraged his elder brother, Charles, to join him from England, and together they rented a property on which to try their hand at growing cotton and tobacco. Apparently the venture did not meet with success, and Neumann next tried his luck in the Transvaal gold diggings. The enterprise failed, however, to satisfy his longing for out-of-the-way places, and he drifted back to his old stamping grounds in Natal. Several years of haphazard industry followed, when he travelled extensively, hunting and trading in Swaziland and the

*Arthur Henry
Neumann towards
the end of his career
– circa 1905.*

eastern Transvaal, steadily acquiring an intimate knowledge of the country and the Swazi language. In 1879 the uprising that developed into the Zulu War led him to join a Swazi contingent, with the rank of captain, when his extensive knowledge of the people and their language soon proved of great value to the British forces. In the same year he met a man who became a close and lifelong friend—Norman Magnus Macleod of Macleod, the government's political agent in Swaziland. Lately an officer in the 74th Highlanders, Macleod was the aristocratic head of his Scottish clan, and laird of Dunvegan Castle in Skye. He had served for many years in India, and latterly held legislative positions in Natal. He and Neumann were kindred spirits; in fact he himself had only recently returned from fifteen months' exploring and hunting in the interior, gleaning valuable experience of the wilds along the banks of the River Zambezi. Separated though they were in the social standing of the time, Neumann and Macleod had many interests in common. Bearing arms together as fellow officers, they campaigned against the formidable Zulu forces, and in later years Macleod was able to write these words of commendation about his comrade: 'Mr. Neumann speaks Zulu well, and has had long experience amongst the Kafirs. I always found him thoroughly trustworthy and reliable, full of energy and with plenty of common sense. He is a gentleman, a sportsman and a good companion. He never drinks. In my opinion it is not easy to find a man with so many qualifications for a position of trust'.

Shortly after the war was over, Neumann rejoined his brother who had by then become the owner of a farm called 'Desert', close to the little town of Pietermaritzburg. But the urge to wander did not allow him to sit still for long, and soon he was off again on another solitary excursion. For seven years he indulged his wish to live and hunt in unspoilt places, but even so his spirit yearned for country even more remote than his haunts in the Limpopo river region. He was next found in East Africa, a new land full of high promise for the sportsman and ivory hunter. Disappointingly for his plans, he discovered on arrival there that the costs of travel in the interior were far too high for his pocket. Instead, he took employment with the Imperial British East Africa Company in May 1890, and for a year he supervised labour gangs cutting tracks through the bush. Following that uninspiring interlude he worked and travelled with the original survey party for the proposed Uganda Railway. His senior officer then was Frederick Lugard, a man even more diminutive in size than himself, but a man endowed with immense drive, who later became a famous though controversial personality in the political field of east Africa.

Laconic and at times impatient, Lugard wrote in his diaries of Neumann's lack of qualifications for the job, his sometimes irrational preformances, and that he was 'extremely deliberate and slow'. There were redeeming features though, and Lugard later commented: 'I was delighted once more to talk to a sportsman'. From Lugard's writing a faint picture emerges of Neumann's make-up: one of shy reclusiveness, ponderous thought and unhurried movements, probably accompanied by a element of stubborness and single-mindedness.

Following his spell of survey work in East Africa, during which he was wounded in the arm by a spear thrust when his camp was attacked by Lumbwa warriors, Neumann returned to Zululand to take up the offer of a magistrate's post. It proved a task of such tedium to his restless mind that he finally decided to throw it up and return to the attractions of East Africa and the magnetic lure of the elephant hunter's life. In 1893 he arrived back in Mombasa, and for the next three years his energies were

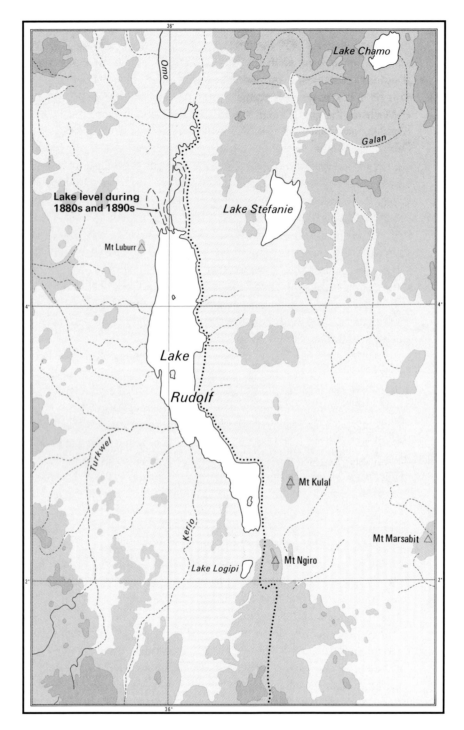

*The route of the Neumann Expeditions 1893–6.*

concentrated on elephant hunting in the far interior. On the completion of this second expedition, towards the close of 1896, he returned to Britain, where he buried himself in the quiet of his friend Macleod's castle home on the Isle of Skye. There he spent his time compiling the classic tale of his experiences on the ivory trail in East Africa. Highly acclaimed, it was his only published work and immediately earned him the reputation of being one of the continent's most skilled elephant hunters. It was a status reached only in his middle age, as he did not shoot his first elephant until he was at least forty years old.

While in England, Neumann had the good fortune to meet a brilliant man—the famous nature artist, John G. Millais—who was to become a steadfast and sympathetic friend, and who also shared a common love of the African veldt and its animals. Long after Neumann was dead the artist-sportsman remembered his lonely friend with these thoughtful words: 'He was a man of an extremely shy, hypersensitive nature, and subject to alternate fits of gaiety or depression, but when happy was of such a charming, lovable temperament to all who knew him intimately that his society was a continuous pleasure'. Almost seven decades after those words were written, Millais's son, Raoul, himself a brilliant artist of the wild, confirmed what his father said, recalling from his childhood memory that Neumann was 'a jolly little man, lots of fun, and very good with children'.

Neumann's sojourn in England was unpleasantly interrupted by the start of conflict in South Africa. In November 1899, barely a month after war had been declared, he was back in that troubled country, where he immediately volunteered for service with a newly formed colonial unit, the South African Light Horse. It was a regiment of mounted infantry that was soon to earn distinction in battle, and with which he served as a lieutenant for a good part of the war. Participating in the actions which led up to and included the infamously lethal Battle of Spion Kop in Natal, he had one close call when a Boer bullet pierced his hat and flicked through the hair of his head. Shortly after that occasion, Neumann rode with the triumphant cavalry brigade that was given the honour of leading the relieving column into the beleaguered town of Ladysmith. On the conclusion of hostilities in 1902, Neumann added another military campaign medal to the one he had already earned for his part in the Zulu war, and once again could justly claim to have 'done his bit' for Queen and country.

On leaving his regiment his thoughts turned once more to the chase of elephants, and shortly after he was back again in Mombasa, preparing for a return to his old hunting fields. Discouragingly for Neumann, much had changed since he had last been in the East Africa Protectorate. But there were some advantages, and a train could now rush him far inland, saving weeks of toilsome travel. So it was not long before he was back in his old haunts, hunting along the tree-fringed Uaso Ngiro river, on the stark shores of Lake Rudolf, in the dense, cool forests of Mt Marsabit, among the fever-ridden tracts of the Lorian Swamp, and further west, into Turkanaland. The four solitary years spent in those far wildernesses were productive for Neumann, but fatefully time was running out for him, his increasingly reclusive life being threatened by ill health. His morale too was being eroded by ever more cramping bureaucratic constraints, which were slowly restricting the old-time freedom of commercial ivory trading. The well-known young army officer, Richard Meinertzhagen, who met him briefly in early 1903, described him as 'a quiet, unassuming little man, with a faraway and rather sad outlook on life'. More and more he seemed to search for a life of isolation, far from civilisation, with his only company the simple native folk who had become so much part of his life. A crossing of swords with a senior government official at that time did not ease his state of mind, and only helped to further the deep-seated feeling of persecution from which he suffered. Paradoxically, his desire for solitariness did not prevent him from keeping up a lively correspondence with numerous friends, including Macleod and Millais. Unhappily, his last East African diary poignantly records recurring frustration and depression at the restrictions which were slowly curbing his career and an increasing debilitation from some unknown malaise; two facts he did not divulge in one of the last letters he cheerfully wrote to Millais from Mombasa in 1906. In October of that year he arrived in London with £4,500 worth of ivory, which he sold on arrival at a dockside sale. Neumann's last grand scheme was to return to East Africa, and with government sanction administer a huge area in the region of the Uaso Ngiro river, which he had recommended be kept as a reserve for the Samburu and Wandorobo people living there. His plan never materialised. On 29 May 1907, in the quiet of a house situated in an elegant little side street in the centre of London, Neumann shot himself with one of the rifles he so often used on his African hunts. That pitiable event marked the end of a life which clearly had outlived its times.

\*    \*    \*

'I hankered after the untouched wilds which I knew still existed in Equatorial Africa: where the elephant yet roamed as in primeval times; where one would never see the wheel-mark of a Boer's wagon nor hear the report of any gun but one's own'. Those words from Neumann's pen were eventually fulfilled on 23 December 1893, when he hurried inland and away from Mombasa before the Christmas festivities commenced among the tiny white community living there. Neumann didn't have the means of a Teleki or a Chanler, or their geographical ambitions, so his caravan was a small one: fifty men—all armed with Snider rifles—and a score of donkeys were enough for his simple needs on his first sally into the 'bara' (interior) of East Africa. The primary aim was to tread in unknown country if possible, but in the course of his wanderings elephants were to be the principal quest. His occupation as an ivory hunter should not be decried; there were many others of similar bent in those far-off times. While Neumann can barely be classed as a full-blooded explorer, he could claim a few geographical and zoological discoveries during his wanderings. Without doubt he was an enthusiastic and observant naturalist. His contributions to geography and science included much material of use to map makers and zoologists alike, his meanderings taking him into previously unvisited corners of the country, and his ever-ready butterfly net trapping the insect life of those selfsame places. Commendably, too, he managed to traverse the lands of many primitive peoples with minimum recourse to force of arms, making enduring friendships along the way, and earning from them the never to be forgotten title, 'Nyama Yangu', meaning in Swahili, 'my meat'.

While making his preparations in Mombasa, Neumann's plans were boosted by a marvellous stroke of luck. There he found the wounded von Höhnel patiently waiting for a ship to take him back to Trieste. What better advisor could Neumann have found than the celebrated Austrian traveller. Soon, with von Höhnel's recommendations to assist him, Neumann had finished his plans, and with the names 'Laiju' (Chanler's 'Daitcho'), 'Sayer' and Lake Rudolf in his mind, he was filled with hope for success: 'It had the special attraction for me that the country that way was least known, and I was not likely to be hampered by rival travellers, official or otherwise, there'. Travelling along the familar path in country through which he had laboriously hacked a track only three years before, he advanced up the Uganda road, through Kibwezi and into Ukambani. It was there that he unexpectedly crossed paths with Chanler, now on his retreat homewards, and a few hours of pleasant discussion provided Neumann with 'much useful information', plus the gift of Chanler's little terrier—a friend who kept him 'charming' and spirited company for many months thereafter. Two months after leaving the comforts of Mombasa, Neumann reached Chanler's derelict base camp at 'Laiju', a section of which he promptly rebuilt to suit the small size of his caravan.

It was not long before he was on friendly terms with the natives of the district, a factor for which he 'felt grateful to my predecessor', the unfortunate Chanler. From his camp at 'Laiju', Neumann made several short visits to the surrounding country in the vicinity of the Nyambeni Hills and the eastern slopes of Mt Kenya, always with an eye and an ear open for elephants. As a result of the restraint he exercised during the four months he spent in the area, there was only one dispute with the residents, which, unlike Chanler's strife with the 'Wamsara' some time before, luckily ended without bloodshed. Even the warriors of the 'Embe' and 'Wamsara' had learnt their lesson from Chanler's tough tactics, and eagerly extended the hand of friendship and co-operation, a welcome gesture which enabled Neumann to travel freely and extensively within the district. While wandering in the forests of Mt Kenya and in the 'Laiju' area he found a wealth of butterflies, many of which he collected and preserved for future identification. Rewardingly, three of them proved to be new species, and one was later named after him.

Having established that there were few elephants living in the neighbourhood, Neumann decided on a move towards the lands of the 'Ndorobos', which lay to the north of the Uaso Ngiro river. Relying on the information he had recently received from Chanler, he was confident that the prospects for accumulating a store of ivory were promising in the valley between the Lorogi and Mathews mountain ranges. So, leaving his well-fortified camp at 'Laiju' in the care of six men—a clear proof of the amicable relations he enjoyed with the natives of the district—he trekked north. For the next four months he wandered at will, spending his time hunting and familiarising himself with the people and the territory between 'Laiju' and the southern foot of Mt Ngiro.

Partially successful with his hunting, and eager to continue his journeyings to the elephant-rich country on Lake Rudolf's shore, Neumann decided to return to the coast and sell his stock of ivory, then re-equip himself for a longer sojourn in the distant wilds.

On reaching 'Laiju' he had news of another white man in the vicinity, a Dr Kolb, who was exploring the district around Mt Kenya. The lonely German was welcomed in camp, as Neumann recorded: 'I, on the other hand, should be glad of his comradeship . . . a white man being, under such circumstances, a host in himself in Central Africa'. For a while they joined company and hunted, collected and explored in the proximity of 'Laiju'. Eventually, after three months, in which he failed to obtain much ivory, Neumann headed back to Mombasa with his caravan. On arrival there he could claim that his first expedition—fourteen months of contented life in the bush—had been a complete success. With that he settled down to enjoy the comforts of civilisation for a short spell.

*Some samples from Neumann's collection. Keen on nature, he kept his butterfly net busy on his travels.*

Fig. 1.

Fig. 1a.

Fig. 2a.

Fig. 2.

Fig. 3.

Fig. 3a.

Fig. 4a.

Fig. 5.

Fig. 4.

♂ *Mylothris neumanni, Fig.* 1, 1*a.*
♀     ,,        ,,       ,,   2, 2*a.*
*Catochrysops cuprescens, n. sp., Fig.* 3, 3*a.*
♂ *Mycalesis dentata, n. sp., Fig.* 4, 4*a.*
♀     ,,        ,,       ,,     ,,   5.

*Bale & Danielsson, Chromo*

Profiting from the experience acquired on his first trip, Neumann then, in typical painstaking fashion, confidently made arrangements for his next expedition. The plan was for a more ambitious journey, into the Reshiat country so highly acclaimed by von Höhnel. For economy's sake he selected only thirty-five of his best porters for the job, a diminutive group compared with the hordes that the likes of Teleki customarily took with them on their travels. Eager for the march, Neumann's little cavalcade of porters and a score or so of donkeys once again struck inland, leaving Mombasa on 16 May 1895, following the now familiar route through Ukambani. Their advance, coming as it did immediately after the season of big rains, was beset with aggravating delays and hinderances: the Tana river was flooding heavily, and held them up for several days before a crossing could be effected by means of a canoe his men carved out of a baobab tree-trunk; the rank vegetation and long grass on the eastern slopes of the Nyambeni Hills impeded their progress; and worst of all, some of his donkeys started to die from the inevitable scourge of the tsetse fly bite. Philosophically, Neumann pressed on, following his old trail through 'Laiju', past the now familiar crater of Magado, on over the hot lava-strewn plains to the Uaso Ngiro river, into 'Ndorobo' country, and finally reaching his familiar camp by the tiny El Bogoi stream, which tumbled off the nearby Lorogi Mountains. It had taken him three months of hard trekking from Mombasa to reach his old base, and despite his indifferent health—an unrelenting low fever was on him—he immediately sallied out to hunt. In compensation for his set-backs, the next few weeks were an encouraging start. Setting out along the tranquil Seya river valley he penetrated a picturesque country as yet unseen by white man, a land lived in by wild animals alone and guarded by the mighty Mathews range towering in the east. In that new country he was rewarded with great success amongst the elephants, his party staggering back to its base at El Bogoi under a decidedly profitable load of tusks.

Productive as the Seya district had proved, Neumann was anxious to reach the ivory El Dorado of Lake Rudolf's northern shores. Ordering his reliable headman, Abdulla, to return and purchase fresh stocks of food and donkeys from the people on the Nyambeni Hills, Neumann decided to spend the time in hunting and exploring excursions in the vicinity of El Bogoi. Clambering over the Lorogi range he passed close to the spot where von Höhnel had been injured by a rhinoceros just two years before. Wandering over the high Lorogi Plains, Neumann next examined the soda-rich Lake Kisima—the first white man to do so—where he collected some antelope specimens for the British Museum. But, disappointingly, his elephant quarry proved elusive, forcing him to return to his base, where he champed to be on the move again to more productive fields. Abdulla had not yet returned from his second trip to purchase supplies from the 'Mthara' people, and Neumann was restlessly anxious to investigate the country round Mt Ngiro: 'I therefore determined, though rather reluctantly, to go on ahead as far as Mount Nyiro and wait for him there. I hoped to find elephants in that district now, and, at all events, it should be less monotonous than waiting longer at El Bogoi'. Leaving his camp and animals in the charge of two men, he departed on 30 October, and for one week trudged across the arid unpopulated country between El Bogoi and Mt Ngiro. Pitching camp in the already familiar valley of the Uaso Rongai streamlet, Neumann endured an unwanted and fruitless month of waiting, when his 'patience was nearly worn out'. This was an unusual admission for a man who appeared to enjoy a leisurely pace in his life. To add to the tedium the district was devoid of elephants, a group of Wakamba hunters having recently disturbed the animals in the course of their hunting activities.

When at long last Abdulla arrived with the supplies and animals Neumann had left behind at El Bogoi, everything was set for an advance to Lake Rudolf. Relying on information he had received from his scouts, aided by advice he had doubtlessly been given by von Höhnel, Neumann chose to negotiate the western flank of Mt Ngiro, a difficult route that duplicated Teleki's harsh experience of almost eight years before. Four days later his exhausted men reached the lake's shoreline. It had been a hard tramp, but they were now at an important milestone in their travels; it was immensely pleasing to Neumann, who commented: 'I had the satisfaction of drinking and bathing in the bitter water of Lake Rudolf. It was a desolate and forbidding land, but with a wild grandeur of its own which had great charm for me'. What a contrast are these simple but appreciative words, compared with the melancholy description of the same scene by von Höhnel. Neumann's compact entourage appeared to have contained more skilled fishermen than Teleki's, for they kept themselves comfortably fed thereafter on the bountiful harvest they landed from the lake's abundant stocks. As Teleki's party had done before them Neumann's men then experienced the misery of travel along Lake Rudolf's shore; the burning heat, howling winds and abominably rough ground forced him to 'confess I was feeling a little bit low-spirited'. However, with the welfare of only a small party to consider, and a good stock of food in hand, he continued to make steady progress; the only incident of interest occurred when they suddenly came upon evidence of a white man's camp, which from the signs had only

*Neumann hunted extensively in the bushland between the Lorogi and Mathews mountains.*

*Mt Lolokwi, a prominent landmark, was one of the centres of Wandorobo in existence in Neumann's day, and the country for miles around was one of his special hunting grounds.*

recently been vacated. Naturally Neumann did not know it at the time, but it was Dr Donaldson Smith's expedition on its southward journey, and for a brief instant the introverted hunter felt lonely: 'I wished I had been a little quicker coming up, so that I might have had the pleasure of meeting a European in this far and lonely desert'. They had missed one another by only four months. News of elephants up ahead soon dispelled the moment of lonesomeness, and with von Höhnel's map to guide them across the waterless stretch behind the forbidding Longondoti range, the small party arrived shortly after at Alia Bay. For the following ten days they trudged along the lake shore, encountering increasing numbers of wild animals, but still none of the elephant herds which Teleki had attacked so remorselessly on his momentous trek. Celebrating Christmas Day in that isolated place—they were now only a short day's march from the Reshiat—Neumann evinced a heartfelt sentiment somewhat at variance with his usual disposition: 'I had been feeling a shade low-spirited, the effect, perhaps, of the contrast the day suggested between my loneliness and the convivial associations usually considered appropriate to the season'. The following day they reached a Reshiat village and duly received the peaceful welcome which appeared to be customary from the people of that remote region. The caravan had, with relief, at last reached the land of plenty, reports of substantial elephant herds in the vicinity were reassuring, and they had enjoyed an easy journey. As Neumann's words admitted: 'All through this wide wilderness we had been able to travel quietly and comfortably without any hardships or privations worth speaking of'.

For the next four months Neumann and his men lived in the stretch of hot, mosquito-infested terrain which lay along the northern fringe of Lake Rudolf and up the jungle-covered banks of the 'Warr' (Omo) river. There were plenty of elephants with massive tusks and sufficient supplies of millet, and the local tribes proved hospitable and anxious to assist Neumann in his hunting. The time he spent in the region was punctuated by successes and disasters. Neumann's elephant score rose rapidly, but it was the superb quality of big tusks that was even more impressive, and his store of ivory steadily became of considerable potential value. It was to be one of the high spots in Neumann's short, but successful, career as an elephant hunter, and a munificent reward for his patient years of waiting. But tragedy followed. The first was the death of his faithful servant, Shebane, who, right in front of Neumann's eyes, was dragged into the swirling muddy depths of the Omo river by a monster crocodile. Inauspiciously, the fatal event took place on New Year's Day, 1896. Exactly eleven days later, another and almost equally disastrous episode took place: Neumann himself was caught and almost pulverised by an enraged cow elephant. Bush justice had nearly been meted out. Fortunately, the animal left him before dealing a fatal blow, but for two painful months he lay in his camp slowly recovering from the aches of broken ribs and the agony of suppurating wounds. Much later he recorded his narrow escape: 'I always knew that there was a probability of an accident happening some day. In fact, if one keeps on at it long enough, sooner or later he is bound to be caught ... Just retribution perhaps you will say; and for my part, I harboured no ill-will against the elephant for avenging its kith and kin. It was the fortune of war'. The kindly concern of his men, the availability of nutritious food, and his hard physical condition won the day for him, and gradually his strength returned, even allowing him to do some gentle pot hunting to augment the caravan's badly needed meat supply. The stark realisation that his food reserves were now only just adequate to sustain his party over the lengthy homeward lap to El Bogoi, with little chance of building them up further from Reshiat sources (it was the end of the dry season), led Neumann to the unavoidable decision that he would have to attempt the long southwards march forthwith.

Three months after his accident he started his retreat, determined to return one day to hunt in Lake Rudolf's enticing, ivory-rich sanctuary. Weak though he was from his enforced convalescence, he managed to keep up with the ponderously laden convoy of ivory-humping porters and donkeys, and even managed to do a little elephant hunting as his nerve and strength gradually returned. Some six weeks after leaving the Reshiat district the heavily burdened caravan—some porters were bearing on their shoulders tusks weighing in excess of 100 pounds (45 kilograms)—they reached camp at El Bogoi. Back in the comfort of the now familiar place, Neumann, with an insatiable enthusiasm, planned some more elephant hunting. It was a moment of greed, as his ivory cache was by then far in excess of the somewhat limited transport he had available to move his goods to the coast. Using a ferry system, whereby his porters carted the ivory to a store in Ukambani, then returned with food and mail, the bulk of ivory was satisfactorily moved. Only then, having had no further success with the elephants, did Neumann reluctantly decide to return to Mombasa, triumphantly marching into that town at the head of his heavily laden cavalcade on 1 October 1896.

Reviewing the results of Neumann's long excursion, the debit side showed that he had sadly lost two faithful servants in the bush, one to a crocodile, one to a lion, and he himself had only narrowly escaped death. On the credit side, he had procured by his skill and tenaciousness a good quantity of ivory, and for the scientific world he took back with him many zoological specimens. In addition he had made some minor geographical discoveries.

More will be heard of Neumann's later escapades, but the modestly written account he published describing his first expeditions filled an important niche in the story of early exploration work in Kenya's northern territory. It was a classic volume, the only book he ever wrote, and a fascinating narrative of the lonely man's success. Using the minimum of porter assistance and financial backing, he managed to traverse some of the harshest country in the whole of East Africa, leaving in his wake befriended people of many tribal groups; this trust was in itself a worthy achievement, the benefits of which later travellers would enjoy soon enough. Neumann did not return to East Africa for another five years, and when he did it was to find changes that did not suit his retiring nature; but the ground he broke, and the information he returned with from his first two treks earned him a worthy position in the ranks of pioneers in Kenya's desert north.

*Dr Arthur Donaldson Smith, M.D., in 1900, at the time of his second expedition to Lake Rudolf.*

# DONALDSON SMITH
# EXPEDITION 1894–5

'ALL this, I think, places Dr. Donaldson Smith in a very high position as an explorer of unknown countries, and I think that he deserves the highest praise that can be bestowed on him by geographers.' Those resounding words by Sir Clements Markham were a laudation well-deserved by the American explorer, following his success in resolving the uncertainties of travel through the lands of the Galla people. Donaldson Smith was no newcomer to the lecture room at the Royal Geographical Society's headquarters when Sir Clements proposed a 'very cordial vote of thanks' to him in late 1900. It was the second of such talks he had delivered to the Society describing his momentous expeditions from Berbera on the Gulf of Aden through Gallaland to Lake Rudolf and beyond. With the advantage of considerable private wealth, the young doctor from Philadelphia was well able to indulge his appetite for travel and sport, and when the opportunity arose he had not been tardy in seizing the chance to sample the attractions of big game hunting in Somaliland. His brief shooting trip to that country in 1893 was simply an appetiser for more challenging future excursions, as he later wrote: 'An exploring expedition offered me an opportunity for gratifying all my desires and ambitions'. Following that first enticing introduction to African travel, two more journeys were needed before Donaldson Smith's hankering for the unknown on the Dark Continent was finally satiated. Maps of amazing accuracy, a host of zoological specimens of previously unknown species, and fresh scenes of geographical value were all products of his arduous march, earning him an appropriate comment from Markham: 'He has not only explored a new region, but has done so with the greatest care'.

\*    \*    \*

Arthur Donaldson Smith's first right to geographical fame resulted from his arrival on the shores of Lake Rudolf in 1895, seven years after Count Teleki's great 'discovery'. Donaldson Smith's expedition was the second led by a white man to reach the lake's edge, and he might well have been beaten to it by his fellow-countryman, Chanler, had ill fortune and ultimate failure not attended the latter's path.

It was fortunate for Donaldson Smith that he had been born into a family of means. His father, being a wealthy resident of Philadelphia, allowed young Arthur to grow up in comfortable circumstances with access to such outdoor sports as riding, fishing and hunting. In the last two he excelled. Furthermore, from his early years he shared with his sister an absorbing interest in natural history, a subject in which his keen intellect maintained an abiding enthusiasm for most of his life.

At fifteen he was given a place in the University of Pennsylvania, where for four years he studied a broad variety of subjects ranging from the classics to the sciences. With a Bachelor of Arts degree to his name, his next step was to a science course at Johns Hopkins University which included biology and geology. One year later, with his voracious appetite for learning unassuaged, he enrolled at Harvard Medical School, where he remained for two years before moving on yet again, back to his original university and into the medical department. At that time it was regarded as one of the leading institutions in America for a doctor's training, and in May 1889 he graduated as a fully fledged physician and surgeon. Immediately that was behind him he departed for further studies at Heidelberg, the oldest of German universities. It was the final act in his pursuit of medical learning, and put the seal on his already exceptional academic record.

When Donaldson Smith returned home in 1890 he was twenty-four years of age, and his character had by then developed the qualities that would have made him a most successful practitioner. Physically he was good looking, with brown hair and blue eyes, and he stood slightly under average height—he was about five feet, seven inches (1.72 metres) tall. Soft spoken and considerate in manner, he also possessed an assertive and confident nature, endowments that qualified him well for the profession he had chosen.

In 1892 his father died, leaving three orphans. After the family assets had been divided up, Arthur, the youngest, suddenly found himself a man of substantial wealth. Young, inquisitive and with a passion for the great outdoors and its associated sports, the doctor decided to abandon medicine and roam the world before finally settling down. Trips to Mexico, Norway and Somaliland were followed by his first major expedition to Lake Rudolf in 1894. An extended journey through China in 1897 was capped by wanderings in India, where, for some of the time, he worked as a physician to the British army in the rugged Tirah campaign which drove the invading Afghans from the Khyber Pass in 1898. One wonders whether, during that hectic time, he ever came close to meeting Montague Wellby, the adjutant of the 18th Hussars, who was also fighting the Afghans and was very soon to become his competitor for the honour of being the first white man to cross the unknown territory between Lake Rudolf and the Nile. After considerable efforts indeed Donaldson Smith managed to achieve his ambition to cross the huge stretch of swamp lands between Lake Rudolf and the Nile. Although he was not the first man to make the traverse, the scientific value of his journey and the exactness of his maps, boosted his already impressive reputation as an explorer. It was, as it happened, his last trip to Africa.

On 20 May 1901 Donaldson Smith was presented with the Patron's Medal at a formal occasion in the Royal Geographical Society's rooms in London. Sir Clements Markham made complimentary remarks on his skill as an explorer and map maker, and concluded by honouring him with one of the last of the Society's medals to bear the image of Queen Victoria. It would have been hard for those attending that special occasion to believe that the travel-hardened explorer who received the coveted award was destined never to make another journey of exploration.

The remainder of Donaldson Smith's life was marred by his declining financial resources and an affinity for alcohol. In 1909 he was given a post in the United States Consular Service in Turkey by his old friend Theodore Roosevelt. Within a year he had been transferred to Greece, and then to Mexico. By 1912 he had left the Service and was back home in Philadelphia. During the First World War he served for a short time as an army doctor, before resuming his life as a general practitioner. In the early 1920s a setback in the stock market finally reduced him to penury. At that point he moved into the backwoods of Pennsylvania, to the little town of Roulette, where he remained for many years practising medicine as best he could. His periodic binges did not help, and nor did the depressed state of the remote little town after the collapse of the lumber boom. In February 1939 he died, aged seventy-two years. He was laid to rest in an unmarked grave in the family plot in a Philadelphia cemetery. For Donaldson Smith, the gentlemanly American, and one of the most remarkable of the nineteenth-century explorers to visit east Africa's uncharted corners, it was a sadly nondescript end.

*     *     *

The keen-minded and travel-eager young American viewed his short hunting trip to Somaliland in 1893 purely as a practice run. Only twenty-eight years old at the time, with an excellent medical training behind him, and funds more than adequate for extensive journeyings in hinterland Africa, Donaldson Smith made studious preparations for his ambitious scheme to succeed where others had failed. He planned to start in Somaliland, cross the formidable Galla people's territory, and penetrate to Lake Rudolf; a journey never yet completed by white man. His attitude was positive, as his account related: 'Money I must spend, and plenty of it; but as I am willing to risk my life ... to accomplish my purpose, I dare not shrink from any expense that may increase the chances of success'. Previous expeditions had been defeated by the vigorous and united resistance of the warlike Galla people, and this was a challenge that Donaldson Smith could not resist taking up. If at all possible, he hoped, he would be able to talk his way amicably round the Galla obstacle, rather than battle his way through, a predicament which had been forced on earlier travellers. He clearly recognised that the fame of the expedition would be geographically sensational if he succeeded, or even if all it achieved was a traverse of the *terra incognita* between Somaliland and Lake Rudolf. That alone would complete the important task of establishing a link-up between the eastern approach to the lake and Count Teleki's proven access from the south. But that was not the sole prize that would satisfy Donaldson Smith's full desires. Before he left for Africa he applied himself diligently to a short course in survey techniques, given to him by the Map Curator in the Royal Geographical Society, who also generously loaned him a complete set of surveying instruments. While he was in London he also took the opportunity to study at the British Museum the most up-to-date methods of collecting and preserving natural history specimens. And to make absolutely certain of success in this important task he employed a young English taxidermist by the name of Edward Dodson to accompany him. In Donaldson Smith's mind complete success would be represented by the traverse of Gallaland, accurate maps of the region and a comprehensive collection of natural history specimens.

On finishing his London preparations Donaldson Smith's arrangements were complete. He didn't lack encouragement from his friends at that stage, although much of it was tinged with downright scepticism, a feeling that might just have dissuaded him from his resolve had it not been for his determined nature. 'The expression of such opinions served, however, only to increase the zeal I felt in the enterprise'. The final touch to his painstaking groundwork was the inclusion of seventy rifles in his stores. It was a sound decision, taken just in case the Galla lived up to their fearsome reputation, and was to prove its worth before his journey was over.

On 1 July 1894, five months to the day after leaving Somaliland on the completion of his first trip, Donaldson Smith and his two companions—a friend named Gillett had also joined the party—arrived at Berbera, eager for their adventure. *En route* they had stopped at Aden, spending ten days engaging men and purchasing the trading goods he would need on his journey. With characteristic foresight, Donaldson Smith had warned the men he used on his first expedition that he would shortly need their services again. By doing so he saved much valuable time, which otherwise might have been wasted in recruiting a new body of men. Fifty-five seasoned Somalis, three mules and three ponies accompanied the three white men on the decrepit little coaster that ferried them across the gulf to Berbera. To his disappointment he found only seventy weakly camels waiting for him. Following the system customarily employed by caravans in Somaliland, Donaldson Smith aimed at using camels as his main form of transport. By his reckoning he needed a minimum of 110 to carry all his baggage and food. He managed to purchase another fourteen, but it was still a heavily overladen caravan that set out across the desert on 10 July, bearing food supplies, men's rations, and a hundred boxes containing scientific equipment and chemicals, specimen boxes, cases of ammunition, a Berthon collapsible boat and a generous supply of wines and spirits. Alongside the overburdened beasts tramped Donaldson Smith's party of eighty-two Somalis. His projected ten-month trek had started; little did he know that another six months on top of his estimate would be needed to complete the task he had set himself.

One month after leaving Berbera the caravan reached the country of Donaldson Smith's dreams, as yet unseen by white man, and full of rich reward to both naturalist and sportsman. There Donaldson Smith and Dodson found much to keep themselves occupied; their scientific work had already preserved over seventy bird specimens, including a new species of nightjar, the diminutive *Caprimulgus donaldsonii*. Needless to add, Donaldson Smith also kept himself busily occupied with his surveying exactitudes, which would earn him words of well-deserved praise in later years.

As they progressed, their routes took them steadily westwards and into Galla territory. When these people were encountered, they were not, fortunately, in the ferocious hordes the caravan had anticipated with such apprehension. Instead, only a few furtive stragglers were found, who complained bitterly of their persecution at the hands of the overlording Abyssinians with their ruthless demands for taxes and slaves. By then the Gallas were certainly in no position to hold up the progress of Donaldson Smith's march; instead they guided it westwards to a first encounter with the oppressive Abyssinians.

It was at this critical juncture the expedition's plans experienced two setbacks. The first came from the stubborn obstructiveness of the Abyssinians, who would not permit the caravan's onward march through their territory without written authority from their emperor, Menelik. Reluctantly, Donaldson Smith wrote his application to the king, who was at that time living in the distant capital Entoto. Halted for almost a month, he impatiently awaited a reply. It came, as he had pessimistically feared, in the negative. There remained no other course open but to retrace his steps eastwards. The party had not, in fact, wasted time kicking its heels around camp; local exploring trips and collecting work had added yet more material to their growing store of knowledge. During that discouraging period—the cold, wet weather had also depressed everyone—Donaldson Smith experienced the first signs of dissension amongst some members of his staff. They had had enough travelling, they grumbled, and wished to return home. It was fortunate that his two headmen remained loyal and discipline was maintained, but despondently he observed: 'I do not think the prospects of ultimate success of any expedition ever seemed gloomier than did mine for the next three months. It was one continual wrestle with the desires of most of my Somalis to return home'.

In spite of those frustrations, he was determined at all costs to reach Lake Rudolf, and as he retraced his steps a new idea arose in his mind. Why not continue his eastward march until he was out of range of the Abyssinians, then head south for a stretch, after which he could strike in a westerly direction again, hoping by that manoeuvre to outflank the Abyssinians and leave them to the north of his path? It was a simple plan, audacious and born of desperation. His meandering circuit had already cost him three and a half months of precious time and supplies, but with his new scheme his morale was high again, and most important, his animals were fit for the long trek ahead. Stores were, however, ominously low in some departments, so Donaldson Smith decided to despatch his best headman, Salan, back to Berbera with orders to purchase fresh trade goods and new camels. It entailed a 900-mile (1,440 kilometre) round trip and Salan was only allowed forty-five days to complete the journey. Time was valuable, prompting Donaldson Smith to write gloomily on New Year's Day 1895: 'I have had a most serious set-back ... Starting out with the expectation of finishing my work in ten months, I now find myself back in Somaliland, without having accomplished the one thing I set out to do,—and six months gone out of the ten I had anticipated'. In the meantime his caravan proceeded to a point on the Shebeli river where it could rest and await the return of the stores party from Berbera. It was to reside in the riverside camp for over two weeks, the time being profitably spent, as always, in hunting and specimen collecting. Bad news came down from Berbera in Salan's hands: Gillett's father had died, and family affairs required his return home. Taking advantage of the opportunity, Donaldson Smith despatched eight boxes of specimens, his mail and some reports for the Royal Geographical Society with the homeward-bound party. The expedition's fortunes and progress took a turn for the better after that, when it aimed once more in the direction of Lake Rudolf, marching westwards through the arid wastes of Somali territory.

For three weeks Donaldson Smith's party trudged along in a more or less westerly direction, passing through the lands of the Aulihan and Degodia Somalis. The latter people he found cowed and intensely distrusting of his caravan, a fear he claimed had resulted from the high-handed methods applied to them by the aristocratic Italian sportsman, Prince Ruspoli, and later by the explorer, Captain Bottego, who had only recently passed through the region*. Both those expeditions had been forcible in the acquisition of food supplies and animals from the resident Degodia, employing strong-arm methods whenever they met with resistance. As a consequence it took time and diplomacy before Donaldson Smith could make the people understand he did not intend to use the same oppressive methods. His policy reaped a satisfying reward when the Degodia finally agreed to sell a few camels to the caravan.

On 19 February a significant milestone was reached—the junction of the Daua and Juba rivers. Having safely herded his whole caravan over the latter river and established them on the south bank of the Daua, Donaldson Smith was able to heave a

---

*It was unfortunate for Donaldson Smith that he left Europe before Bottego had published the account, together with maps, of his first expedition in the region.

sigh of relief with the realisation that at long last he was out of the Abyssinians' range and could pursue an unimpeded course to Lake Rudolf. With a sense of release he wrote: 'Once across the Jub, I felt that the strain I had been under for three months, to keep the caravan together, was removed; there was no more fear now of the Abyssinians, as they had never got so far south, and my men . . . were too far away to think any more of their homes'. With that load off his mind a new enthusiasm returned, for they had arrived in the land of the 'Gere Gallas'—Garre Somali. Everyone struck along the bank of the Daua river in high spirits: 'We had all settled down contentedly . . . my boys singing merrily as they worked'. For several days they cheerfully followed the river's broad valley westwards, finding rich collecting grounds in the bush and forests along the river banks.

Forced to abandon the valley when it disappeared northwards into rugged and impassable hill country, the caravan experienced a dreary four days of waterless march across a terrain that was 'very mountainous, and covered with dense, bushy jungles'. On that distressing stretch Donaldson Smith lost several of his valuable camels, a loss sadly compounded by the enforced abandonment of five boxes of stores 'containing wine and tinned fruit'. The reduction in his civilised luxuries must have hurt him considerably; he regarded it as 'a heart-rending thing to do'. Despite the set-back the party survived the thirsty stretch and reached the western borders of Garre country without further loss. There they met their first Borana, and for ten days they rested in comfort, trading in a friendly manner with both the Garre and the Borana. When they departed from that hospitable spot* Donaldson Smith could satisfyingly 'count seventy-eight good camels' in his caravan. He and Dodson had also enjoyed good sport amongst the numerous rhinoceros and elephants living in the vicinity.

Climbing steadily into the mountains of Boranaland the expedition then experienced the cold, damp discomfort of the rainy season, with daily storms flooding the countryside and hampering the camels' progress. In spite of the inclement weather new sights came into view to intrigue them as they trudged through the highland region. Donaldson Smith recorded meeting a few Gabbra people, described by him as 'low-caste Boran'. They also climbed down into the giant wells of Le and Gof. In the course of a hunt Donaldson Smith made a curious and erroneous faunal identification, when he shot what he described as a 'Thompson's [sic] gazelle'. Mystifyingly, it is uncertain what he did collect as his usual meticulous observations were at variance on that occasion. While it was quite possible he had, in fact, encountered the northern variety of the Thomson's gazelle—the Mongalla gazelle, *G.t.albonotata*—in the area he was exploring, the body measurements of a specimen he collected definitely negate his identification, as they relate to an animal in the size group of the distinctly larger Grant's gazelle. It was one of the few zoological errors he made.

Deep into the land of the Borana Gallas, and comfortably past the Abyssinians, Donaldson Smith decided to keep to the high ground on his route around the lake. Swinging north west, his caravan plunged further into Borana territory, and there, at last, he encountered the famed Galla resistance about which he had so often been warned. It started with the discreet murder of one of his men, a crime that earned swift retribution when one of the Borana killers was gunned down. From that moment the situation deteriorated, and he grimly commented in his diary that: 'there is war in the

---

*Present day Banissa, in north-eastern Kenya.

air, and we are making all the preparations we can to resist the attack'. The following day the caravan proceeded another 13 miles (21 kilometres) along its path, and that evening wisely pitched camp in an open space, but not in peace, for there were 'Boran all around,—many mounted and many on foot! Large troops of cavalry were rushing about, and an attack seemed imminent ... There were between two and three thousand men in the field, with more than a thousand ponies ... There will be an attack tonight, very probably'. The caravan spent an uneasy night and the grey light of morning disclosed the worst, with 'great masses of savages scattered over valleys and hilltops!' Resolutely, but with considerable trepidation, the expedition group began its daily march. During the day two Borana came in peace to offer their services as escorts. In good faith Donaldson Smith accepted, and in doing so fell into a well-planned trap. The expedition was shown to a camping ground situated in a belt of thick bush, where it would be at a definite disadvantage. Sure enough, hardly had a thorn zariba been constructed than a full-blooded cavalry attack fell upon it, and Donaldson Smith's men were soon severely pressed. Volley after volley from their rifles took a terrible toll of the spear-armed enemy as they feverishly tried to force their way through the zariba, but at the last critical moment there was 'one more roll of musketry', and the spearmen's nerves failed. Precipitously they fled from the battlefield, leaving the bodies of their fallen comrades lying scattered around the zariba. The Borana had had enough, and the following day negotiations with their chiefs established peace. From then on the caravan enjoyed an undisturbed journey. For future white travellers it proved to have been an important victory, paving a peaceful road through Boranaland.

Donaldson Smith was on the eve of fulfilling his ambition to reach Lake Rudolf from the east, but before doing so he had one small task to complete. A lake named 'Aballa' had been tentatively sited 'on the maps of North-east Africa', and he was anxious to confirm its presence. A brief diversion took him through the lush highlands of the 'Amara' people, where the hospitable inhabitants enjoyed the riches gained from a fertile land. It was mountainous country, divided by wide valleys in which teemed countless herds of wild animals of many species, some familiar, others as yet unencountered in his travels. It was a region full of rewards for the naturalist collector, and the ten days they were forced to wait for a guide to Lake 'Aballa', were put to very good purpose, as Donaldson Smith commented: 'The work of collecting natural-history specimens was always a delight to me ... There were many birds and other natural-history specimens about the Galana that we had not seen before, so that Dodson and I employed our time to the best advantage in collecting'. At last, the 'Amara' porters arrived, and the party made its quick dash to the shores of Lake Abaya, the local name for Lake 'Aballa'. Triumphantly he stated: 'a happy man I was as I looked over the beautiful sheet of water and felt that I was the only white man who had stood on its shores'. A shortage of supplies prevented him from making further investigations, and because of that he then made a forgivable geographical error. His Lake Abaya was not, in fact, the true lake of that name, but was the smaller lake to its south, known as Lake Chamo. The two sheets of water are separated by a narrow strip of land, called by the natives of the region the 'Bridge of God', and for some reason—probably because they were anxious to return home—the 'Amara' guides never informed Donaldson Smith that the main, and far larger, lake lay to the north of the insignificant barrier. In fairness, it should be mentioned that he was not entirely wrong, as both lakes were formerly called Abaya, meaning 'great water' in the language of the local people. The name Chamo was used by the tiny Burji tribe, which lived at the southern end of the little lake. Donaldson Smith did not come across these people, so was unaware of the alternative, and now recognised, name for his Lake Abaya. With the new discovery securely recorded in his diary, and all his meticulous mapping work completed, he hurriedly tramped back to his base camp at the foot of the 'Amara' mountains.

There was one more feature to be surveyed before Donaldson Smith's link-up with the most northerly point reached by Teleki could be realised: Lake Stefanie. His route took him down the Galana (Sagan) river, which he was positive flowed out of Lake Abaya and into Lake Rudolf*, and over the northern ranges of the towering Tertale Mountains. On 1 June 1895, two weeks after starting, he camped close to the shores of Lake Stefanie, from where he could clearly see the Galana river flowing into the lake. His surprise was complete, as he confessed: 'And there was the Galana Amara surely emptying itself into this water. I was astonished, because I thought the Galana flowed into Lake Rudolf'. Foiled in his attempts to cross the river by heavy flood water, Donaldson Smith elected to walk clear round the lake, investigating the whole area thoroughly as he progressed. A red-letter day for the expedition came in mid-June, as Donaldson Smith happily wrote later: 'Two more marches now brought us to Count Teleki's camp (June 12). There was much rejoicing among us, as we had now accomplished one of the things we had long been striving for—to join Count Teleki's line of march, and so complete the circuit from Berbera to Zanzibar'.

At long last Gallaland had been crossed by a white man, and, into the bargain, it had been accomplished without due strife; it was a most satisfying result and full compensation for the frustrations experienced by the expedition in its early stages. Having managed to achieve his goal all that now remained was for Donaldson Smith to turn down Lake Rudolf and head for home. But his inquisitive mind was not prepared to do that, and nor did he particularly wish to follow along the beaten track down the lake shore. There were still a few little corners he wanted to look into on the way back to the coast.

It took eight days to walk the 120 miles (192 kilometres) round Lake Stefanie's uninhabited shore line. At the end of the march Donaldson Smith could rightfully claim to be the first white man to have completed the circuit. Arrived at the north west corner he discovered a long narrow arm of the lake extending 10 miles (16 kilometres) to the north, which, simply for lack of a local name, he called Lake Donaldson. At the tip of the creek he found people—the Arbore, a small tribe of agriculturists which had never seen a white man before. They proved hostile, despite his peaceful advances, but their primitive bows and arrows were no match in the ensuing conflict against the rifle-armed caravan, and soon they capitulated and begged for peace. A brisk trade for cattle and sheep followed, after which the expedition proceeded peacefully on its way, passing in the course of the next week through a land populated by a collection of small and distinctly separate tribes—the Burle, Dume, Kule and Bunno peoples.

Turning southwards, the caravan started its final march to Lake Rudolf, by a straight line only 60 miles (96 kilometres) away. The inhabitants of the region had made repeated warnings that there was no clear road to the lake, a fact soon borne out

---

*Donaldson Smith was partly correct in his contention. Lake Abaya had indeed been connected to Lake Rudolf at one time, and through it to the River Nile, but that was many thousands of years before.

when the party had to hack its way first through thick unyielding bush, and then wade barefoot down the bed of a flowing stream for several days. Under those testing conditions it took Donaldson Smith and his men ten arduous days to reach the lake's environs, but eventually, on 10 July 1895, they spotted the sight 'that appealed to the heart of every man in the caravan. It was Lake Rudolf'. Once again the matchless first sighting of the unique lake was to make an indelible impression on newcomers. For Donaldson Smith it was an intensely thrilling moment, which he expressed in these contented words: 'This journey had been the toughest allotment of work I had yet given myself . . . Yes, Rudolf was in sight, and I felt that I had attained in a measure the greatest ambition of my life,—that of being able to add a little drop to the sea of knowledge possessed by civilised mankind'. The expedition had been a year on the road, and his muted pride on attaining such a high personal ambition was justified, but a nostalgic note in his diary entry for that historic day frankly imparted his desire for the civilised world: 'I long to be part of it once more. I long to see my friends in America and England, even if I do not envy them the regular lives they lead'. Two days later the caravan was on the lake shore and among the Reshiat, then greatly impoverished after the rinderpest plague of the early 1890's, but still showing friendship towards foreign travellers.

There was one more digression Donaldson Smith wanted to make before starting his homeward march. He was curious to explore the river which flowed into the northern end of the lake—Teleki's Nianam. He planned to continue past the point von Höhnel had reached in his search for food supplies in 1888, studying on the way the numerous small tribes reported living along the river banks. Departing at the head of a small party of thirty men, he left Dodson at their base camp with instructions to explore the northern waters of the lake by boat, and determine whether the stream von Höhnel marked on his map to the west of the Nianam actually existed. For the next eleven days Donaldson Smith's little party struggled through the interminable swamps and mosquito-ridden jungles fringing the river, eventually reaching, with great relief, a low range of hills some hundred miles north of the lake. From his lonely vantage point he had a clear view of the mountainous country lying far to the north and west, of which he wrote: 'One splendid group of mountains thirty-five miles [56 kilometres] to the north of us and nine thousand feet [2,770 metres] high, I have named after myself'. The prominence he marked on his map as Mt Smith is today's Mt Mago. He noted later that from his elevated seat: 'I got a clear view of the country to the west nearly half-way to the White Nile. It was nothing but one great expanse of grassy desert, with only two low mountain chains visible'. While contemplating the scene, an idea became fixed in his mind—one day 'I must pursue the setting sun from Rudolf to the Nile'. One can easily imagine the solitary traveller's feelings as he gazed longingly from his hilltop view point over that grassy desert fading into the west, dreams of future marches through virgin country uppermost in his mind. The return to Reshiat was uneventful, and with their track already cleared the party made good time, reaching their base in five days of fast marching. There they learnt that Dodson's explorations had failed to find a second river flowing into the lake, thereby casting doubts on von Höhnel's claim. Anyway, with their river explorations completed, it was time to load up and move on again.

Three days later, on 8 August 1895, the caravan headed down the lake shore on the start of its homeward trek, 'everyone in the best of humour'. Two weeks of hot

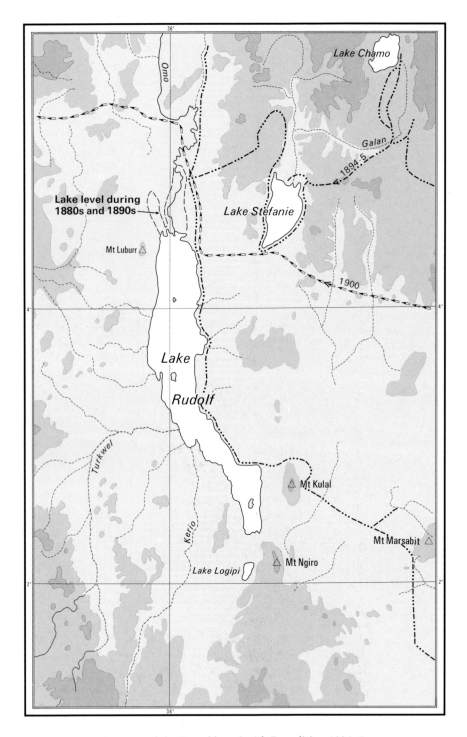

*The route of the Donaldson Smith Expedition 1894–5.*

uneventful tramping brought the expedition to Elmolo Bay where, for the second time in history, a white man's gun provided the Elmolo with mountains of hippopotamus meat. At that point Donaldson Smith decided to leave the lake and trek east, skirting the north slopes of Mt Kulal, and on into hitherto unexplored country. In front of them lay an arid volcanic landscape, in which, they were warned, no water would be found for at least two days after leaving the haven of Lare Dabach springs, where Teleki had camped in 1888. With no guides to lead the way through the 'parched and desolate' land, the party started 'on our most risky undertaking'. And indeed it was risky; for two days the sun's rays beat down on us with relentless fury' and on the third day they were obliged to 'march through such a fiery furnace' with only the dregs of their scant water supply left. The fourth day was agonising torment, but the caravan in desperation 'pushed on all day almost maddened by thirst', reaching at sunset 'the deep fissure that splits Mt Kulol in two'. And there, in the tranquility of the sequestered gorge, the desperate men found ample supplies of clear water. El Kajarta Gorge, as the extraordinary fissure in Mt Kulal is called, can justly claim to be one of the most singular physiographical formations in Kenya. Snaking tortuously into the very bowels of the mountain, its narrowly separated walls—in places barely twenty feet apart—reach countless hundreds of feet skywards in sheer vertical faces, shielding one from the outside world in a quiet isolation of monastic magnitude. The loneliness of the cloistered ravine is even more intensified by the distant sky far above, in places a mere sliver of blue light, filtering down to the shadowy recesses of the long winding passage. Inside the serene dell the only sounds to be heard are the solitary echoing cries of rock-dwelling baboons and hyrax, the mournful cooings of speckled pigeons and the burbling murmur of the pristine streamlet feeling its way between the rounded grey boulders which strew its bed. In that amazing place—rarely visited by white men even to this day—Donaldson Smith and his weary companions rested for three days, recovering their spirits and their strength.

On 4 September, with an ancient 'Burkenedji' from the mountain to guide them, the revived caravan set forth in an easterly direction, which took them into Rendille territory on the western footslopes of Marsabit Mountain. Remembering Chanler's account of his problems with the fearsome nomadic people, Donaldson Smith approached their villages with an understandable caution and trepidation. To his amazement he met with a friendly reception, and to add to his satisfaction the Rendille even showed a willingness to sell him a few camels. In the four days he spent amongst those well-inclined people he managed to replace many of his travel-worn beasts with a new lot of strong healthy animals, capable of seeing him through the final leg of his journey to the coast.

Looking up from the Rendille lowlands, Donaldson Smith could see the 'splendid mountain group called Marsabit' looming temptingly in the east, as yet unexplored by white man. A Rendille guide had offered to show him the road southwards to the Uaso Ngiro river, but he found it impossible to resist the temptation of a short diversion from his homeward path to add another geographical discovery to his register. Three days of rough, monotonous walking took the party up into the cool confines of the forest-capped range, and there a delightful hidden treasure was revealed to everyone's eyes—'a lake a mile square, clear and deep'. Closely surrounded by dense forest, it lay in one of the ubiquitous volcanic craters that pock-mark the slopes of the Marsabit

ABOVE: *'According to European ideas, nothing could be more charming than this Marsabit'.* (Donaldson Smith) *A view of his Crater Lake at dawn.*

LEFT: *'in the deep fissure that splits Mt. Kulol in two, we made our way . . . almost without hope for another day on earth'.* (Donaldson Smith)

chain, a tranquil sanctuary where for aeons wild beasts of many kinds have sheltered*. For two days the explorers camped by the Crater Lake, spending their time in the forest busily collecting 'many rare specimens of birds and mammals'. But all too soon the time came to leave the peaceful haven, and on 13 September they moved on once again.

Nine days of 'long and fast' southwards marching took the party through to the banks of the Uaso Ngiro river. They had crossed a pitiless region never before traversed by white man; it was almost waterless, and temperatures soared daily above 100°F (38°C). By the river, and close to the escarpment from which Chanler and von Höhnel had viewed the chimerical 'Lake Lorian' almost three and a half years before, the caravan tarried for an exciting eight days whilst the two men had a hunting spree amongst the numerous rhinoceros and elephants living in the neighbourhood.

On 1 October the expedition roused itself for one final long trek 'across an indescribably desolate and monotonous region'. Donaldson Smith's words aptly described the gloomy situation: 'there were no birds to relieve the death-like oppressiveness of the picture. There was no vulture even in the heavens, and no movement upon the baked, glaring earth in this land of despair. Only the fury of the sun was felt, casting its heartless rays upon the caravan as it wound its way in and out among the half-dead acacias, struggling onward with a determined energy engendered by the dread of death from thirst'. Despite the grimness of it all, their spirits were lifted

---

* Today the lovely spot is known as Lake Paradise, appropriately named three decades after its discovery by an American couple, the Martin Johnsons.

by thoughts of home, and on 7 October they reached the Tana river banks, close by Chanler's old base at Hameye. While they rested an astonishing scene suddenly projected itself: 'a canoe hove in sight just around a bend in the river,—and in that canoe sat a man holding a pink umbrella! Yes, true enough, a pink umbrella, and underneath a man in a white suit!' It was none other than the indefatigable missionary of Tana river fame, the Reverend Robert Ormerod, on his homeward journey to the coast. Eagerly joining forces with the cleric, Donaldson Smith's party took to canoes and paddled on down the river in comfort. The camels followed, lumbering steadily beside the river. Two weeks of leisurely travel brought the expedition safely to Mkonumbi, at which point Donaldson Smith could at long last say his arduous journey was over.

How differently the Donaldson Smith and Chanler expeditions had ended. The former's ebullient words summed up his sixteen-month trip: 'Dodson and I are little the worse for our four thousand miles [6,400 kilometres] of marching and all the labors we have undergone, and my good followers are happy and merry as can be. The thirty odd boxes containing the results of my expedition are safe and sound. Have I not every reason to rejoice?' He had every reason to exult on looking back over his brilliant achievements: superb mapping work was to provide the Royal Geographical Society's cartographer with immaculate material to work with; well over three thousand zoological specimens were collected, of which twenty-four birds and eleven reptiles were identified as new to science; over three hundred botanical and geological samples were catalogued; and, to top it all, a substantial collection of ethnographical objects had been gathered from nineteen tribal groups. Satisfied as he was with his achievements, and eager to see his friends and civilised things once more, Donaldson Smith's final thoughts were, if anything, distinctly wistful: 'But yet, as I pace to and fro, and see the shores of Africa receding gradually from view, I cannot shake off a slight feeling of sadness'. In those words can one detect a deep-seated longing, in his case not fully satisfied, for the vast empty spaces of that continent, 'with its glorious climate and freedom from cares and ambitions'? And in that ambivalent frame of mind he sailed for England and geographic fame.

# BOTTEGO EXPEDITION
## 1895–7

BETWEEN 1888, the historic year when Teleki first reached Lake Rudolf, and Neumann's exodus from the place in early 1896, only five white men had left their footprints on the sun-baked lake shore sands. However, news of the place was spreading fast, and others were busily preparing to investigate the lonely spot. One tantalising major question still remained. Where did its sustaining and apparently perennial river-borne water supply originate? Teleki's men had only advanced a short distance up the River Nianam from its point of debouchment into the lake. Neumann in his quest for elephants had continued a little further upstream. Donaldson Smith had pushed on considerably more, but even he did not arrive at a conclusion. Neither of the last two men were to produce any maps for a year or two after their return home, and in the meantime the baffling question of the Nianam's source remained unanswered—but not for long. Already an indomitable man, an Italian, was planning his second expedition of discovery to Africa. His primary aim was to follow the great River Omo, which, rising in the western highlands of Abyssinia, was conjectured by some geographers to flow westwards into the mighty Nile system, and by others to constitute the start of the eastward flowing River Juba. It was one of those taunting issues which challenged explorers of many nationalities to tackle the mysteries of eastern Africa in the last years of the nineteenth century. In October 1895, the same month that Donaldson Smith was contentedly preparing to depart from Lamu at the conclusion of his first expedition, Captain Vittorio Bottego commenced his long tramp into the hinterland of Somaliland in the company of four fellow-countrymen. Well-organised, led by an old hand in African travel, and brimming with eager confidence, the ill-fated party was on the eve of answering an important geographical riddle.

\*    \*    \*

Set high on the face of a drab olive-coloured building looking over the Via della Repubblica in the aged town of Parma in northern Italy are two conspicuous white marble wall plaques. They commemorate the births of two notable sons of the region. One of the tablets announces that Vittorio Bottego was born in the house at 93, Strada San Michele—as the street was then named—on 29 July 1860. Bottego arrived during tense times. The country was in a state of turmoil, and the Italians, with their illustrious leader Garibaldi in command, were in the throes of their war against the Austrians. Bottego's mother, Maria Acinelli, a Genoese woman, found in Parma both a sanctuary from political persecution and a husband—Dr Vaghi. Following his untimely death soon after, she married another doctor, Agostino Bottego. In due course they produced two sons and a daughter, and it seemed only fitting for them to name one of the sons Vittorio after Victor Emmanuel II, the first king of a newly united Italy.

During Vittorio Bottego's boyhood the family moved to a substantial country house on the outskirts of Parma. There, in a comfortable home in San Lazzaro

*Captain Vittorio
Bottego. (From
L'Omo)*

Parmense, Vittorio's love of the outdoors blossomed rapidly, developing a side of his nature that would find fulfilment in Africa in the years ahead. Today the house is incorporated in a large nunnery, hidden away in the middle of a heavily built-up residential area. A discreet marble wall plaque to the left of the front door reveals that Bottego formerly lived there.

Bottego early displayed all the spirit of one born under the sign of Leo. It was while in his late teens that some of the vital spark of his nature first displayed itself. Two notable examples of these will suffice. As a boy of seventeen he gallantly saved the life of a man drowning in the Torrente Parma, the ephemeral stream that sometimes rages through the centre of Parma during the winter and spring months. For his courageous act he received a medal from the Minister Secretary of State. That event occurred about the same time as he flagrantly disobeyed one of the strict rules in his college and fought with a schoolmate. For that major infraction he was expelled, a sentence that did not disturb him in the least, for his sights were already set on the military training centre in Modena. There he spent a year before moving on to the prestigious Military Institute at Torino, where he studied for three years.

By then Bottego was developing the physical and mental characteristics that were to mature with the passing years. In stature almost five feet, nine inches (1.8 metres), his lithe muscular figure encased a being with all the qualities which make a good leader and soldier: great moral and physical strength, immense courage, tough tenacity and an obstinacy that was legendary amongst his compatriots and friends. Despite those rugged properties there lurked behind his dark piercing eyes mitigating moods. To temper his proud and resolute character he had been given a gentle and generous nature. Moreover, he possessed a reserved and shy personality that disguised his keenly perceptive intellect. The combination of these qualities served him well in his hazardous African wanderings.

From early youth Bottego was a man who needed action to fulfil himself, and like many others of that bent he eagerly sought a cause to fight for, and yearned to be a hero. In his boyhood he dreamed longingly of Africa, and when only twenty years of age he wrote the words he was soon enough to practise: 'L'Africa è la terra meravigliosa dove un uomo ha l'esatta misura delle sue capacità e del suo coraggio' (Africa is a marvellous land where a man has the exact measure of his capacities and courage). Years later he was to express deep feelings of gratitude to the sponsors of the two major African expeditions he was entrusted with leading. Having been given their trust he proved himself in his driven desire to succeed despite bitter hardships. His determination was clearly supported by his personal dictum: 'Bello il morire in tali imprese, ma più bello il riuscire' (Admirable to die in such undertakings, but better to succeed). To the message of these words he held rigidly, and in the end he paid the full price.

The years of preparation at Torino were followed by a stint at the old-established cavalry school in Pinerolo. It rounded off his schooling in the soldier's arts, but even there he rebelled, this time against the out-of-date methods and strict rules under which the equestrians trained. His determined resistance to antiquated riding-school techniques won the day, prompting radical changes in the illustrious institution's teaching methods. It was another victory for the unusual man. In 1884 he was promoted to the rank of artillery lieutenant. Eventually, his longed for opportunity came, and in 1887 he pressed for inclusion in a special contingent of officers bound for Eritrea, where he was confident he would at last find the action he craved.

To Bottego's delight his request was granted, and in late 1887 he landed at Massawa, the seaport and capital of Eritrea. For the remaining ten years of his life Africa was to be his home and his great love. It did not take him long to discover the wonders of nature in the arid wastes, mountains and seas of that land, and soon numerous specimens of all types and sizes were busily being shipped back to the Natural History Museum in Parma—birds, mammals, fish, reptiles, insects, rocks, corals and plants. His absorption with the wonders of nature did not end with living creatures. Shortly, geography became a major interest, so it is not surprising to read that while dining with General Gandolfi, the Governor of Eritrea, he broached the subject of an expedition to explore the origins of the Juba river.

In 1891, with the backing of the Italian government and the support of La Società Geografica Italiana, Bottego was ready to leave on his first major journey. Unfortunately, home politics intervened, and the departure date was delayed. To his dismay, Bottego was ordered back to Italy. However, never one to waste a moment, and with a keen eye to the future, he spent his one year stay in Florence honing up his knowledge of botany, astronomy, mineralogy and photography, adding further skills to his already wide-ranging repertoire.

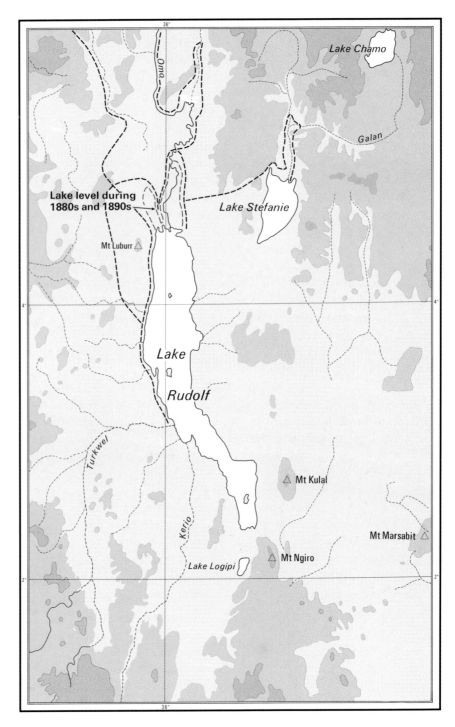

*The route of the Bottego Expedition 1895–7.*

In August 1892 Bottego and his wealthy friend Captain Grixoni, who was to be his sole white companion on the Juba expedition, landed back in Massawa. La Società Geografica had accepted responsibility for the expedition's arrangements, and for the ensuing thirteen months Bottego and his men marched, fought and explored across the north-eastern corner of Africa. The story of their tribulations, the disintegration of Bottego's friendship with the pampered Grixoni and its acrimonious aftermath, and the heavy mortality in men and transport animals, is outside the scope of this work; but for Bottego and his prime concern—the mapping of the Juba river from source to mouth—the expedition was a resounding success. He returned to Italy a proclaimed hero, received La Società's highest award, the prized gold medal, laudatory praises from many esteemed institutions, and wrote a voluminous book, *Il Giuba esplorato*, describing his gruelling experiences.

Shortly after his return home an upsetting episode occurred: he fell seriously in love. Soon he was affianced to a beautiful Florentine girl. The love match very nearly disrupted his single-minded attitude to the Dark Continent and its attractions. On carefully weighing up the pros and cons in his mind, Africa finally prevailed. Accordingly, Bottego broke off his engagement, and never again did he permit any emotional links to divert his aims: in undeviating words he declared: 'Il mio idealismo mi vieta di seguire un'altra via' (My ideals forbid me to follow another path).

That Bottego had triumphed in clearing up doubts on the Juba river's geography there was no doubt, for two other Europeans, a German, Baron Claus von der Decken, and an Italian, Prince Eugenio Ruspoli, had died in vain on the same quest. But there still remained one major question to be resolved—was the River Omo which rose in the western highlands of Abyssinia the same river that flowed into Lake Rudolf, or did it join the Nile? It was a challenge Bottego was eager to meet, for it entailed exploration work in the little-known mountains north of the lake. Soon, he proposed a plan to La Società, which, to his delight, was fully accepted. For an explorer and naturalist of Bottego's calibre, the new project must have appeared as a gift from heaven. Once again there was the prospect of facing the dangers and challenges of Africa—the life he cared for most of all.

*   *   *

Some seven months before starting on his second major expedition to eastern Africa, Captain Vittorio Bottego gave a lecture in the provincial library in Naples. During the course of his talk he quoted an old Arab proverb, which, he explained to his audience, he felt was eminently suited for the occasion. The wise words ran thus: 'L'uomo a cui nell'atto di partire sorrida un bel volto, non sarà colto dalla sventura' (the man on whom a pleasant face smiles when he is about to depart will not incur misadventure). Bottego followed these words by expressing the hope that his audience would wish him well by sharing the sentiment. There can be no doubt that he himself must have borne a smile on his face, for he knew that soon he would be treading once more the wastes of his beloved Africa, readily accepting the challenges put in his way.

In 1894 Bottego submitted his strategy to La Società for the solving of the River Omo mystery. The river's ultimate destination was a problem exciting the interest of contemporary geographers all over Europe, so it was with an alacrity born of fierce national fervour that his proposal was seized at La Società's headquarters in Rome. The project could hardly have been put in more capable hands. Already a seasoned African traveller, familiar with much of the region in the vicinity of his target, a keen observer of nature and meticulous diarist, Bottego was above all an intensely patriotic Italian, willing to serve his country to the bitter end if required. It was a foregone conclusion that he be entrusted with the responsibilities of the expedition's leadership.

In the year Bottego came forward with his suggestions on how the Omo puzzle might be answered, certain definite facts about the river were known. The region of the Omo's headwaters had been worked over by several industrious explorers in the preceding fifty years, and some speculative theories put forward on its terminal point. Borelli, a Frenchman who explored the headwaters of the Omo in the late 1880s, came closest to the mark when he deduced from local hearsay that the elusive river flowed into a lake he named 'lac Schambara'*. But ill-health prevented him following his lead to a conclusion. At almost the same time, Teleki was investigating his newly discovered Lake Rudolf, and pondering on where the river Nianam flowing into its north end originated. But neither Teleki nor Borelli were in a position to pursue their curiosity, and so the mystery remained unsolved. Donaldson Smith, on his epic first expedition in 1895, took the matter a stage further, but on following the Nianam upstream from its debouchment into the lake, he missed its sudden westerly turn in the thick riverine forest, and for a short distance unwittingly followed one of its minor tributaries instead.

The second Bottego mission was an important one, important enough to earn the blessings of both the Italian government and King Umberto himself. These two parties subscribed 60,000 and 40,000 lire respectively towards the expedition's funds, while La Società, for its part, assumed full responsibility for handling the onerous chore of making the arrangements for Bottego's long journey.

Bottego was allocated three main tasks. Firstly, he was to carry his geographical investigations onwards from the furthest point reached by his earlier exploration to the source of the Juba river, into the mountain regions to the west, and down into the Lake Rudolf basin. Those had been the unfortunate Prince Ruspoli's ambitions before he was killed by an elephant in the Sagan river valley a few years earlier. In the course of scouring the region Bottego aimed to follow the Omo river downstream from Borelli's lowest point to its eventual terminus, be it at the Nile or 'lac Schambara'. Secondly, Bottego had instructions to start a trading post at Lugh on the Juba river with a view to encouraging commerce with the Somali people. Thirdly, with the idea of establishing a political foot-in-the-door, he was ordered to leave a garrison at the Lugh trading post under the command of an Italian officer.

Concurrently with all these activities the expedition was to devote time to making a thorough scientific study wherever it travelled, and to assist Bottego in the formidable programme he was allocated three excellent men: naval lieutenant Lamberto Vanutelli to record all astronomical and geographical data; infantry lieutenant Carlo Citerni whose jobs were official diarist and photographer; and Dr Maurizio Sacchi to handle the scientific collections and meteorological observations. With the combination of powerful patronages, far-reaching assignments and the expertises of three qualified lieutenants, Bottego was all set to carry the heaviest burden yet of his successful career. Although he had no inkling of it on his departure

---

*Without doubt Thomson's 'Lake Samburu'.

*Members of the ill-fated, but successful Bottego expedition.*
TOP: *Dr M. Sacchi.*
BELOW LEFT: *Lt. C. Citerni.* BELOW RIGHT: *Lt. L. Vanutelli.*

from Italy, he was about to commence a journey which a few years later would be hailed by the Royal Geographical Society: 'The expedition . . . was . . . one of the most successful and fruitful in geographical results that have been accomplished within recent times'.

On 3 July 1895 the four Italians departed from Naples on the first leg of their journey, taking with them their scientific instruments and personal belongings only. It had been arranged for the field equipment and supplies to be obtained from government stores in Massawa, and the personnel were to be recruited from the local inhabitants. In the seaside capital of Eritrea a great welcome awaited the small party, and soon frantic preparations were in hand as loads were packed, arms checked and a motley band of 250 men assembled. The officers attached to the Italian garrison presented Bottego with their national flag and the Navy provided one of their vessels, the *Dogali*, to transport the expedition in its entirety to Brava on the southeast coast of Somaliland. Eighteen days after leaving Massawa the *Dogali* dropped anchor off Brava.

Ten days later, having gathered together an assortment of 120 camels, 30 mules, 10 donkeys, and a good-sized herd of cattle and goats, Bottego's caravan was finally ready for the road. On 12 October it marched out of the desolate town to a farewell salute of gunfire from the *Dogali*. The white men's hearts were full of high hopes for their successes: 'Il nostro entusiasmo è al colmo, piochè sembra sorriderci l'avenire' (Our enthusiasm is at its highest because the future seems to be smiling on us). With them travelled Captain Ugo Ferrandi, the man who had been given the task of establishing an Italian presence at Lugh.

Marching his huge caravan inland, Bottego followed a route well known to him from his 1893 journey, running some 30 miles (49 kilometres) parallel and east of the Juba river. While crossing the dreary wastes of Somaliland the expedition was attacked by hordes of 'Rahanuin' tribesmen. It was just another in a series of battles Bottego experienced in Africa, and for which he was castigated by later travellers. In the ensuing battle his party suffered its first casualties: Dr Sacchi was wounded in the shoulder by a spear thrust, and was for some time thereafter stretcher-bound; and one of their buglers had to have a hand amputated using the crudest of instruments, because much of the expedition's medical equipment had been lost when the stores were being ferried across the Shebeli river at an early stage in the journey. The tough break-in period ended on 18 November, when Bottego's entourage wound its weary way into Lugh, then the most important inland trading centre in southern Somaliland.

They found Lugh a smouldering ruin, corpses lying putrefying on the hot dusty ground and the place empty of people. Gradually refugees from the holocaust filtered back from their bolt-holes in the bush, and Bottego then learnt of the devastation caused by the Abyssinian marauders, a curse that pervaded the whole region at the time. Clearing up the town, such as it was, building a stockade and re-establishing the former rulers took Bottego's party several weeks, and when eventually they continued their march on 27 December, they left the well-fortified centre in the charge of Captain Ferrandi and forty-five soldiers. It was some months before the Captain saw another white man, and in the meantime he had to rely entirely on his own wits and slender resources.

On leaving Lugh, Bottego marched his men up the Juba river for four days to its junction with the Web Gestro, a minor tributary of the Ganale. He made a short diversion at that point, and followed the Gestro Valley northwards in the hopes of finding signs of the Arussi Galla people. In this he was successful, although they met him with a certain amount of antagonism in the beginning.

Bottego rejoined the Juba river, or Ganale as it was thereabouts named, at its junction with the Daua river. At that juncture he departed from territory familiar to him from his first expedition, and headed the caravan westwards along the old-established trading route leading to Boranaland and the Abyssinian lake district. For eight weeks he tramped along the highway, following in Donaldson Smith's footsteps for many miles, skirting the Daua river valley until a sharp northerly bend took it abruptly away from his course. By then the expedition was approaching the mountainous region of Sidam, and shortly after, on clambering out of the hot dank river valley, the party arrived amongst the Borana people, who, surprisingly, welcomed them in peace. With the attack of the 'Rahanuin', and the bellicosity of the Arussi still clear in his mind, it was a relief for Bottego to find the Borana so well disposed towards the expedition. While crossing the tranquil countryside he found much of interest. Several of the famous deep wells were examined, an important salt mine was investigated by Dr Sacchi, and the prominent trading town of 'Ascebo' (also known as Arero) came in for a quick inspection.

On 23 March 1896 the expedition reached the southern footslopes of the Amarr Mountains. Climbing into those hills Bottego arrived in the fertile food-rich land where the Burji people lived. They were friendly and hospitable to his caravan, and Guio, their chief, made the Italians feel welcome in his village. Close by, to their surprise, they found the carefully tended grave of their fellow-countryman, Prince Eugenio Ruspoli. Apart from the late Ruspoli and Donaldson Smith's brief visit of the previous year, no other white men had penetrated that far into the mountain district. With the Burji displaying open friendship it struck Bottego that he had reached a convenient place to take stock and prepare for the exploration work lying immediately ahead. Of geographical significance, too, was the stream that he had crossed in the nearby hills, which, from its flow westward, suggested an important watershed may have been reached. To verify this Vanutelli and Citerni, with an escort of thirty-five men, were ordered to drop down into the low-lying Sagan river valley below Burji and make a short reconnaissance of the river.

While they were on their errand, Bottego and Sacchi, who had remained in camp, organised the expedition for the next and most important stage. The four men were kept busy at their various occupations for a month. Camels would be of little use in the mountainous terrain ahead, so a mixed collection of equines was selected to take their place: 96 donkeys, 21 mules and 30 horses were to be accompanied by a small herd of 16 camels. Unlike many later travellers in those bitter highlands, Bottego had selected his transport wisely. Of the 250 men he had started out with from Brava, only 134 remained in service. The rest, discounting Captain Ferrandi's contingent at Lugh, had deserted on the road. One other person still travelled with the group: Batula, the faithful slave girl*. With all her family in bondage, she could find no reason to leave Bottego, her friend, so she too, marched out of Burji on 6 May with the revitalised expedition, at the start of the next step in its historic mission. In Burjiland Batula had an important part to play, for it was her home country and she was well qualified to act

---

*Batula was amongst a small group of Burji which had been enslaved by the Arussi Galla. Bottego, in his skirmishes with the latter people, had secured their freedom.

as interpreter and guide. She, in fact, had given Bottego the enticing information about a great lake that lay to the north—Lake Pagade, or Abaya—on whose waters no white man had as yet laid his eyes.

On 12 May 1896, two hundred days after their departure from Brava, the four explorers sighted the glinting sheet of water—the largest of the Abyssinian rift valley lakes. In the excitement of the moment all thoughts of their hardships vanished, and as a token of respect to their Queen they promptly named it Regina Margherita. Directly below them lay the smaller Lake Chamo, Dr Donaldson Smith's discovery of the year before, a fact of which they possibly had no knowledge. Hurrying on as fast as they could through the rain-soaked Badditu Mountains, it took them another four days to reach the lake's edge, and there disappointment awaited them. The thought had crossed Bottego's mind that the lake might have some association with the Omo river. The survey instruments soon proved otherwise: 'non c'e dubbio, queste acque non possono avere alcun rapporto con la corrente dell'Omo' (there is no doubt, it is impossible for this water to have any connection with the Omo river).

The day after Bottego's arrival on the lake's shore, his party's peace was rudely shattered by the arrival of a war fleet of seventy canoes filled with a remonstrating horde of spear-armed men. A brief struggle ensued in which his men prevailed, and after a short space of time good relations were established. The caravan then experienced no further trouble from the people living on the lake's islands, but a menacing note had been struck and it seemed a portent of worse to come.

Bottego's expedition spent twenty-five days in the lake district, during which time a complete survey of the lake's shore was undertaken and a brief visit made to Lake Chamo. For the sportsmen in the party, time was spent profitably hunting the numerous elephants that lived in the nearby swamps.

While at the north end of the main lake, Bottego experienced his first confrontation with the Abyssinians. It was only a verbal exchange, but it was rather ominous, and the message was quite clear: he could proceed no further north. If he attempted to do so the way would be violently contested. Bitterly disappointed, he realised he would have to alter his approach route to the Omo river. Instead of commencing his downstream march from the southernmost limit of Borelli's exploration, he was forced to plan a start from a point further down the river; to reach that place from his lakeside camp it would be necessary to find a direct road across the foreboding cloud-enshrouded mountain ranges looming above him in the west.

By early June Bottego and his companions had completed their extensive survey of Lake Margherita (Abaya), and preparations were put in hand for the next leg of the journey. One of the elephants they had shot provided them with the assistance in this matter. It had immense, 6 feet (2 metre) long tusks, and these valuable trade items were eagerly exchanged for 10 donkeys and 2 horses. Even with the extra animals Bottego was unable to move all his goods, and he was forced to cache a collection of elephant tusks and two boxes of specimens in a Burji friend's care. Finally on 10 June, everything was ready.

The following day the expedition started its long struggle up the steep mountain slopes. The weather was merciless in the high Abyssinian alps, and their anguish is expressed in these words: 'Veramente orribile una notte di pioggia a 3000 metri d'altezza! L'acqua, le nebbia, l'umidità, il vento, il freddo, penetrano fin sotto le tende' (Truly horrible is a night of rain at 3000 metres altitude! The water, the mist, the dampness, the wind, the cold, penetrate even through the tents). As if all that was not enough, the precipitous trails cost several baggage animals their lives; but even worse were the warlike demonstrations of the Abyssinians themselves. Brimming with confidence after their massive victory over the Italian army at the Battle of Adowa three months before, they did all they could to hinder Bottego's labouring caravan. It was a desperate march, needing every ounce of resolve the four white men could muster. 'La nostra posizione è molto grave, quasi scoraggiante' (Our position is extremely grave, almost discouraging). Their determination to reach the Omo river was rewarded on 29 June when, deeply fatigued but jubilant, they finally stood 'sulle rive del maestoso fiume' (on the banks of the majestic river). Bottego's patriotic heart must have been wild with joy at his new triumph in the name of Italy.

The Italians may have been exultant as they stood beside the Omo river and contemplated the roaring torrent, but their main task still lay ahead of them. Where was the elusive river's destination? And, challenging them, another question also remained unanswered. Was the river they stood by positively the Omo? They were confident it was, for the people of the region had assured them it was the 'Uma', or Omo. The Abyssinians had, however, forestalled definite scientific proof of that by denying them access to Borelli's terminal point upstream. They were, in fact, only about 31 miles (50 kilometres) down the river from the all-important place. Disappointment invested their observation: 'come potremmo provare scientificamente che il nostro Omo è proprio lo stesso lasciato da Borelli a 6° e 44'? Le supposizioni, le

*A placid stretch on the Omo River as it flows through the Abyssinian highlands.*

opinioni, le teorie non possono creare un fatto geografico positivo' (how was it possible to prove scientifically that our Omo was exactly the same left by Borelli at 6°44' Suppositions, opinions, theories cannot establish a positive geographical fact). The nagging doubt would have to await a positive answer by a later explorer, and in the meantime Bottego had more pressing problems to contend with.

Facing the expedition on the opposite bank of the river stood a formidable force of Abyssinians in battle array, under the command of a full-blooded Ras, 'Uoldo Ghirgis'. The river was in spate and the Ras was threatening, so Bottego had only one option, and he took it; desperately he hacked a path down the bush-clad river valley for three days before finally escaping from its claustrophobic clutches and clambering once again into the gloomy cloud-girt mountains. For several days he encouraged his men, guided his pack animals across the terrible terrain, and resisted the attacks of the pursuing Abyssinians, who snapped furiously at his caravan's heels like a pack of hunting dogs. Despite all these distractions Bottego kept the Omo river ever in sight, winding along its course in the valley far below. On 23 July the exhausted caravan abandoned its mountain trail, dropped down to the broad empty spaces of the riverine plain, and trudged wearily on towards the bank of the Omo river. Only then, and with unanimous relief, could the four men confess: 'Oh, come avevamo desiderato il deserto! È proprio vero che in Africa spesso è preferibile il viaggiare appunto nei deserti al passar per regioni molto popolate' (Oh, how we longed for the desert! It is very true that in Africa it is often preferable to travel across deserts than to pass through heavily populated regions).

Following the course of the slowly meandering river was a delight compared with the rigours and dangers of the Abyssinian highlands, and the party steadily advanced southwards on its quest, swung eastwards with the river's great bend, and then, unknowingly, fell into the same trap that Donaldson Smith had fallen into the year before. At that stage Bottego had arrived in a district of great swamps and riverine forest at the confluence of the river 'Usno' and the Omo. Unaware that he was not following the Omo, he led his men northwards along the fringes of the swamp, somewhat perplexed by the strange twist in the river's direction. It was not until two days later they reached its banks, and here, to their surprise, was found not the gently wandering Omo but a smaller rushing torrent in full spate. The expedition's onward march was delayed for a week while waiting for the stream to subside, and in the meantime Bottego climbed the same hill from which Donaldson Smith had gazed longingly westwards over the 'grassy desert'.

After making a successful crossing of the 'Usno' river, it took Bottego's men only six more days to reach Lake Rudolf's shore. Their arrival at the lonely spot came almost as an anticlimax. When the white men finally rested their eyes on the shimmering 'distesa argentea di acque' (silvery expanse of water) they had no guides to tell them where they were. It was not long, however, before their curiosity was satisfied. A passer-by gave them the name of the lake at their feet: Bass Narok. What jubilation the travel-weary men must have felt. Their long journey, filled as it had been with a multitude of trials and suffering, had proved worthwhile, and now Bottego could proudly proclaim: 'Da questo momento il gran problema della geografia moderna è risoluto, il nostro sogno avverato. L'Omo si getta nel Rodolfo!' (At this moment the great problem of present day geography is solved, our dream come true. The Omo flows into Rudolf!).

With his main objective accomplished, together with the chance finding of Lake Abaya (Margherita), Bottego had managed to satisfy a bit more of his insatiable appetite for exploration. In his characteristically determined manner he had executed the tasks entrusted to him by his country; with his rich results he could well have returned contentedly to Italy, where undoubtedly, he would have received further acclaim and honours. But destiny dictated otherwise, for the call of the unknown remained strong, and there were still some loose ends to be tied up.

First of all, Bottego, accompanied by Vanutelli, made a side excursion to Lake Stefanie. They were away from the main expedition, now established on Donaldson Smith's old campsite, for over three weeks. The time was spent in exploring the countryside along the Sagan river north of the lake, where they were rewarded with the presence of great herds of elephants. With an eye to both sport and commerce the two men promptly shot fourteen in the space of five days. While in the district they also had the good fortune to meet with a Somali trading caravan from Lugh. They were, luckily, people they had met earlier at 'Ascebo', and conveniently for Bottego they agreed to bear his ivory collection as far as Lugh.

On Bottego's return to Lake Rudolf, a new industry was promoted—ivory trading. On that errand Sacchi and Citerni set forth up the Omo river, and on their return eleven days later they carried with them a satisfying load of fifty-seven elephant tusks, purchased from the Murle people. Their profitable haul brought the expedition's store of ivory up to a grand total of 4,410 pounds (2,000 kilograms).

Obviously the great bulk could not possibly be transported by their own animals, so Bottego arranged for Dr Sacchi to escort their hoard back to Lugh, together with all their reports and the scientific specimens they had collected. Provided with an escort of twenty-three armed men, Sacchi joined the Somali caravan by Lake Stefanie. He never returned to Italy. On his way to collect the goods and ivory they had cached on Lake Abaya, he was attacked and killed by bandits, a tragedy about which Bottego himself never learnt. Fortunately for the waiting world of science, the doctor's specimens and papers eventually reached Lugh safely, and the later analysis of his meticulous records proved of great import.

With Sacchi's departure a major turning point in the expedition's programme and fortunes was reached. Bottego decided he should continue his journey with an investigation of the unexplored west shore of Lake Rudolf. On his march he hoped to satisfy two issues. Firstly, he intended to reach Teleki's northernmost point on the lake's western shore line, and so complete the mapping of the lake; and secondly, and more important, he wanted to resolve the question of whether an overflow from the lake into the Nile basin even existed.

On 5 November Bottego's men and animals were ferried across the Omo river. This date in effect marked the commencement of their homeward journey. The long path down to the Turkwel river and back to the north end of the lake took five weeks of hard tramping, but the establishment of one more definite geographical fact was their reward: Lake Rudolf without doubt lay in a land-locked basin, and was sustained almost entirely by the Omo river. Bottego's journey had satisfactorily solved the problems remaining to geographers, and Lake Rudolf no longer had any major mysteries left.

Bottego then made the decision that was to cost him his life. Rather than return home by way of Lugh, or even better, by British East Africa, he chose to extend his

*Samples of new species of animals collected on Bottego's journey.*

J.Green del.et lith.                                    Mintern Bros.imp.London.

*1.Chalcides bottegi.*
*2.Megalixalus gramineus.3.Hylambates vannutellii.*

exploring a stage further. His route took him north west of the lake and across the mountains to the Akobo river. Following the river for three trying weeks, the caravan at one stage struggled through interminable swamps, where for days there was no sign of human habitation. Weary of the exhausting drudgery Bottego changed direction northwards and headed instead for the Ghelo river. There he was once again trapped in vast swamps for several weeks, and when he finally extricated his caravan from the unpleasant morass he aimed northwards yet again. The year of 1897 had so far not brought him good fortune, but on 26 February the fatigued caravan arrived on the bank of a huge river, nearly 1,000 feet (300 metres) across. After all their hardships, it was understandable that the Italians exulted when they learnt that they were standing by the verge of the Sobat, the Nile's great tributary. The famed river was the last significant geographical feature Bottego's party laid their eyes on, and for five days they enjoyed its company as they marched upstream.

Abandoning the Sobat, the expedition climbed into the threatening Abyssinian mountains once more, and advanced into Menelik's territory. Bottego, perhaps foolishly in view of his recent disturbing experiences at the hands of the Abyssinians, decided he was going to finish his long journey in the country's capital, Addis Ababa. Accordingly, he wrote a letter in Italian to the nearest chief, requesting permission to proceed through his territory. For a few days all went well. The caravan was hospitably received, and hopes were high that soon their travails would be ended. But the Abyssinians had treacherous intentions and on 17 March they overwhelmed the caravan at Daga Roba. When the battle was over, Bottego lay dead, Citerni lay wounded and many of their faithful followers also lay scattered on the field. Of the Italians, Vanutelli alone was unharmed, but soon he and Citerni were shackled in irons. For the next ninety-eight days the unfortunate pair remained prisoners of the Abyssinians, and only on their arrival in Addis Ababa on 22 June were they finally freed.

Shortly after the expedition's distressing finale, Citerni and Vanutelli returned to Italy, where they set to and began the difficult task of compiling their report of Bottego's ill-fated journey. It was very fortunate that Citerni, the diarist, and Vanutelli, the mapmaker, had survived, because little of the material collected after leaving Lake Rudolf had been as lucky. It was most providential, too, that Dr Sacchi had left the expedition before the end, taking with him the specimens and reports accumulated between Brava and Lake Rudolf. Despite his demise they reached Lugh, and eventually Italy, in good condition. Although the loss of valuable material at Daga Roba was vexing, the collections examined by the experts in Italy and England contained a mass of material which proved of great interest to the world of science and geography. Many new species of animal life were described, and on the geographical side superb maps were produced detailing the country through which the expedition had travelled. When their volume was eventually published in 1899, the two survivors could well be proud of the acclaim it received. The labour which had gone into its production had tested them severely, for much of the information it contained had to be recalled from the depths of their memories.

There is a last troublesome note to the sad ending of Bottego's second expedition. While he was quite prepared to die in his country's service, his untimely end was a waste. It could well have been prevented by the intercession of a fellow European who sat exaltedly in Menelik's court. Years later an Italian diplomat divulged that Monsieur

*The memorial statue to Bottego as it stands opposite Parma railway station.*

Alfred Ilg, a Swiss engineer living in Abyssinia who had gained Menelik's confidence and subsequently became his right-hand man, might easily have prevented the disaster at Daga Roba. Ilg knew Bottego was leading an expedition with purely scientific aims and not a political one with territorial intentions against Abyssinia's sovereign rights. He alone might have saved Bottego from his fatal confrontation, but he did nothing to advise the Negus of the Italian's peaceful objectives. One may wonder whether the industrious explorer's life, and the scientific results of his arduous travels were sacrificed because of the personal aspirations of a man who may have been jealous and suspicious of Bottego's motives, and who, possibly, was eager to ingratiate himself with Menelik for his own ends. It is a question that probably never will be answered.

In Italy, Bottego became the hero of his time. Today, his memory has fittingly been maintained in his home town of Parma, where he stands, cast magnificently in bronze. Another sheltered monument, the Bottego Museum in the town's ancient university, contains an impressive assemblage of specimens, conscientiously collected by him during his travels in east Africa. He was also remembered in Africa: nine years after his death the name Bottego was given to a lonely snow-covered and windswept 15,000 feet (4,600 metres) high peak in the Ruwenzori Mountains by a renowned Italian mountaineer—the Duke of Abruzzi. And, at long last, on 28 April 1940, a magnificent obelisk was unveiled on Daga Roba hill. Constructed by the Italians to Bottego's memory, all that remains today is the crumbling masonry of the once-immaculate monument. Over the years many accounts have been written of Bottego's extraordinary life, and others are even now being composed—a clear indication of the stature he attained amongst the giants of Italian exploration epics.

# CAVENDISH EXPEDITION
## 1896–7

BY the time he was twenty years old, Henry Cavendish was already a seasoned traveller. Moreover, he had had the chance to familiarise himself with the exhilarating thrills—often mortally dangerous—attached to hunting the wild beasts of Africa. On his return to England in 1896 from two years of journeying in South Africa, where he had been agreeably occupied in 'shooting and sight-seeing' pleasures, the young man found everyone agog with word of the fabulous new playground for explorers—Somaliland and Lake Rudolf. His nationalistic fervour was immediately aroused: 'It occurred to me that somebody ought, as soon as possible, to explore the west coast of Lake Rudolf, and that, as no Englishman had yet attempted exploration in that part of Africa, it was high time for British travellers to bestir themselves in the matter'. So he did just that—and in a hurry! Within three months of his homecoming from South Africa he was prepared for the road again, and, moreover, inside one and half years he had read his report on the expedition's success to a meeting in the Royal Geographical Society's headquarters, receiving these magnanimous compliments from Africa-wise members of his critical audience: 'These . . . things show that Mr. Cavendish is an excellent traveller . . . Our friend here only reached his majority last year; he is probably the youngest man who has ever read a paper before this society . . . I am very glad of the opportunity to offer my very hearty congratulations to Mr. Cavendish on his plucky journey . . . I am sure you will be proud to hear that in all my experience we [the British Museum] have never had such a caravan full of things come into the Museum, as the result of one expedition'. Cavendish had indeed performed his duty in exemplary fashion, and astoundingly, all before he was even twenty-two.

\*    \*    \*

Henry Sheppard Hart Cavendish must have been an individual of exceptional energies. Born in 1876, he was the elder son of W.T. Cavendish of Thornton Hall, Buckinghamshire. Immediately after his four years' schooling at Eton he left England on his first adventure, to South Africa. Following his journey to Lake Rudolf in 1896, he was thwarted, as was Donaldson Smith, in his plans to travel across the country between the lake and the Nile. He made a scientific expedition to Patagonia instead. With the start of the Boer War he promptly volunteered for service with the South African Light Horse, in which he held the rank of captain. Fellow soldiers in the unit were the exuberant Winston Churchill, and the man who had also visited Lake Rudolf, Arthur Neumann. As soon as the war ended he was on the move again, to Australia and the Solomon Islands. In 1916 he was commissioned into the Royal Warwickshire Regiment, in which unit he was employed on the staff for a time. It is recorded that he may have served with the Royal Flying Corps for a year. In 1932 he inherited the title of 6th Baron Waterpark. Born with an unduly large share of wanderlust, Cavendish must have been in the enviable position, when he was young, of following whatever course

*Henry Sheppard Hart Cavendish at the age of twenty-one years.*

he may have set his sights on. Many were fruitful journeys for he brought back specimens for museums and material for the Royal Geographical Society's archives. He also remained a Fellow of the Society for fifty years.

\*   \*   \*

It was while leisurely cruising back to England from Cape Town that Cavendish first read about the wonders of travel in east Africa. By the time he reached home in June 1896, his mind was made up; he had decided to start for Lake Rudolf 'as soon as I could get an expedition ready'. That chore was dispensed with in a remarkably short time, the youthful adventurer having the valuable assistance of an influential friend, Lord George Hamilton\*, to ease his path through the preliminaries, and with his 'kind advice and help, I soon had everything ready'. Fired with a spirited eagerness for his

\*Hamilton was then the Secretary of State for India.

new enterprise, Cavendish embarked for Aden. It was then the end of August, and he had, with the zestful energy of youth, managed to activate in amazingly short time an ambitious project, the scale of which would have tested the mature planning ability of many an older and considerably more experienced man.

His problems began at Aden. Whether they can be blamed on sheer inexperience or simply the impetuousness of youth will never be known, but once he was in the clutches of the rascally Adenese the shenanigans commenced. The first mistake he made was signing on a headman with rather dubious talents, a man who had travelled with Count Teleki. Promptly offering his services to Cavendish, he recruited the eighty-four men needed for the expedition. That he did it successfully for his own account is patently obvious from Cavendish's words: 'Half of my troubles during the journey were due to the rascality of this head-man, through whose dishonesty I had to pay more than double the usual wages'. The next move was to purchase his trade goods, and once again the driving fervour of youth landed him in trouble, for he was then 'badly swindled over the transaction'. Regardless of these exasperations Cavendish soon had everything in order for a start. He even found a companion, a footloose young lieutenant, H. Andrew, who was on leave and kicking his heels around Aden.

Carefree he must have been and completely unequipped for such an excursion, but nevertheless Andrew quickly threw in his lot with Cavendish, and together the exuberant pair crossed the sea to Berbera with their caravan. At last they were in Africa and almost ready for the long arduous road ahead of them. Before they could move, however, transport animals had to be bought, and once again Cavendish had to dig deep into his pocket, 'though for several reasons I had to pay heavily for camels, and even then could not get good ones'. It had been an expensive start.

Finally Cavendish considered his caravan in a condition fit enough to commence marching, but for some unknown reason only half the party left Berbera on the first leg. Possibly impatience at the slowness of the camel marketing played its part, or maybe the lure of the hunting grounds ahead drew the two men away from the tedium of Berbera. Whatever the reason, the caravan rearguard did not catch up with the forward party for three weeks, by which time it was 150 miles (240 kilometres) from its starting point. Thereafter the whole group struck resolutely southwards, tramping over practically the same ground Donaldson Smith's party had traversed exactly two years before. Far to the south of Berbera, on the Shebeli river, Cavendish found depressing evidence of Abyssinian encroachment into Somali territory; it was significant and ominous proof of how the inexorable easterly advance of Menelik's well-armed hordes had engulfed yet more people and land since Donaldson Smith's visit. Continuing southwards and deeper into Somaliland, the caravan, apprehensive lest it should be forced into conflict with the nearby Abyssinians raiders, wisely decided to aim west towards the Juba river. There Cavendish found the isolated fort of Lugh, garrisoned by a beleaguered body of soldiers with Captain Ferrandi still in command, tenaciously holding their own against repeated attacks. At that point Cavendish elected to tarry for a week of rest and hunting.

Lugh, as it turned out, was a convenient point for Cavendish to swing his expedition westwards in the direction of Lake Rudolf. Trudging on, he reached the Daua river in early December, and in that unhealthy valley half his caravan was struck down by fever. Without the broad natural history and geographical interests of a von

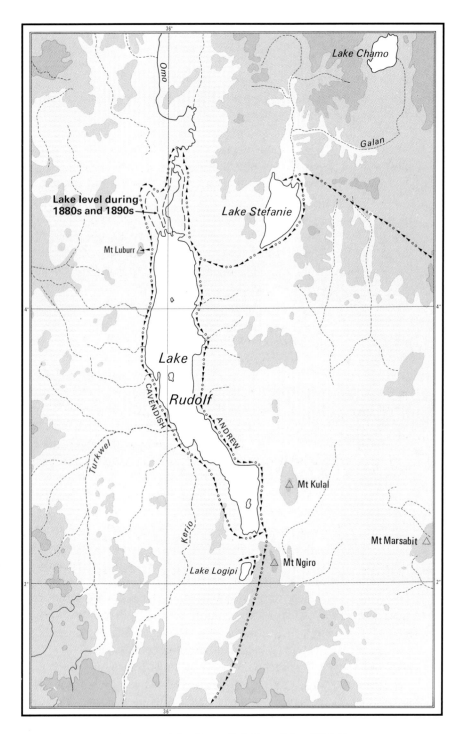

*The route of the Cavendish Expedition 1896–7.*

Höhnel or a Donaldson Smith, and with the burden of ailing men on his hands, Cavendish quickly moved on: 'We carried our sick on the camels, and immediately left the swampy neighbourhood of the Dau'. His route took the caravan further west and into the land of the 'Boran Gallas', the tribe which had previously given Donaldson Smith so much trouble. In sharp contrast to the latter's experience, travelling through the Borana country was a pleasure to Cavendish, his description of these people being wholly complimentary: 'They treated us in the most friendly manner ... in fact, looking back on our sojourn in the Boran Galla country, I would say it was the pleasantest time we spent among natives between Berbera and Mombasa'. Deep in Borana territory, he was in country already visited by Donaldson Smith and Bottego, and it was quite evident that the natives of the region had by then learnt that the white man was a harbinger of peace, as opposed to brutal exploitation. Cavendish undoubtedly benefited from the paths smoothed by the endeavours of the two previous expeditions, and he was 'sincerely sorry to leave' the Borana people. A bonus for the eager young hunters was the large number of elephants they encountered, and they had ample opportunity to try their hunting skills, 'bagging ten fine tuskers averaging 60 lbs. [27 kilograms] a tusk'. The pair had early on decided what they considered fair game amongst these beasts, Cavendish declaring that 'during the whole expedition we made a rule never to fire at an elephant whose tusks we calculated were under 80 lbs. [36 kilograms] a pair'. Those were golden days for the sportsman, before the wholesale slaughter of elephants by the Abyssinians had taken its toll.

In early February 1897, the expedition reached the north end of Lake Stefanie, and set up camp close by the Sagan river, near the spot where Bottego's party had stopped only three months previously. Clustered in this area were a group of people friendly towards the caravan, who 'cultivate crops and gather honey, but do not hunt or fish'. These, Cavendish named 'Wandorobo'. They were, in fact, the same 'Watu' that Donaldson Smith had met in the vicinity of the river twenty months before. Continuing on its way Cavendish's party reached the southern end of the lake in three days, and there he made a most extraordinary discovery in that essentially volcanic region—'coal, and coal in large quantities'. The find was marked on the map of his journey in bold type, and is one of the mysteries of his expedition. Geologically it was almost an impossibility for coal to exist there. It is uncertain what he did actually locate, or whether he even took specimens back to England for identification, but contiguous with this peculiar discovery came another, and far more exploitable one—elephants. The two young men decided to settle down in the district for an extended stay and enjoy some profitable sport, just as Bottego had done in the same spot only four months before. As it turned out the tables were turned and their stay became an enforced one. Cavendish, while hunting an elephant, wounded it, and then suffered a chastisement horrifyingly similar to the one Neumann had experienced near Lake Rudolf the year before. Fortunately, his wounds were not to keep him in bed for more than ten days, during which time a party of forty men were sent up the west of the lake to visit the Arbore and the Hamarkoke. The latter, a hill people, attacked the visitors on meeting them, but later made peace. The event marked the expedition's first warlike encounter with the peoples of the interior.

On Cavendish's recovery the caravan was able to proceed on the next leg of its march. Five days after leaving Lake Stefanie, the party arrived on the shores of Lake Rudolf. Having reached that landmark they felt they deserved a well-earned rest. It was well earned, for in six months of hard travelling they had crossed hundreds of miles of difficult country, and, commendably, had avoided serious conflict on the way. That the path had previously been prepared by earlier explorers and consequently the caravan's passage eased, there is no doubt. None the less, for a young man just on the eve of his majority, the expedition's accomplishments were a clear indication of his ability as a first-rate leader, well meriting the success that had come his way.

The expedition was far from over though, and the main objective was still ahead—to explore the hardly known western shore of the great lake, where the reputedly ferocious Turkana tribe lurked in wait. So, after eight days' rest, the caravan once more left camp, following the lake shore northwards to the mouth of the Omo river. The Reshiat were there to meet them, friendly as always, but still in the poor state that Donaldson Smith had found them in 1895. Disappointingly, they were in no position to assist Cavendish in his crossing of the Omo river, so he was faced with a major problem. As the stimulating prospect of achieving his aim was immediately in front of him, he was more determined than ever to complete the task he had set himself. Consequently 'I held a consultation with Andrew, the outcome of which was that we decided to separate; for, even though I should succeed in crossing the Omo with a few men, it would still be impossible to take the main caravan, with loads and camels, across. We therefore arranged to meet again at the south end of Lake Rudolf, Andrew taking the east coast, while I was to attempt the west'. It was a critical juncture in their travels. Just as they were about to enter the territory of the savage Turkana they were being forced to divide their expedition. They were, however, a resolute pair; furthermore, Cavendish had by good fortune found an excellent guide to show him the road round the north end of the lake. Although apprehensive of success, their hopes were high as they prepared to part company and follow their individual paths.

On 26 March 1897, Andrew and Cavendish split the caravan and went their separate ways: Andrew to follow the track familiar to only a handful of white men; Cavendish, unknowingly, to follow in Bottego's very recent tracks. Cavendish, with his party of forty-two men proceeded upstream in search of a convenient crossing point. Three days later they met with success, locating a suitable place and finding two dug-out canoes belonging to the 'Murle'. It then took a considerable measure of haggling before these suspicious people finally agreed to hire out their craft. But in the end all was well, the caravan was ferried across the Omo river, and Cavendish commenced his southward march. Cavendish, it will be recalled, had set his sights on being the first to travel down the lake's western shore, a hope now strengthened by the incorrect information he received from the local people, who gave him the news that Bottego had failed in this selfsame objective when he 'after five days incessant fighting had been obliged to retire'. Unaware that Bottego had in fact reached the Turkwel as planned, Cavendish was confident he was on the eve of achieving his goal. It was a daring feat he was about to attempt, but leading a diminutive body of men through the land of the formidable Turkana was a gamble the twenty-year-old Englishman was willing to take. Hugging the lake's shore-line Cavendish skilfully exposed only one flank open to attack, and thus proceeding he managed to travel a considerable distance down the lake, skirmishes occurring continually, both day and night. Using good tactics, he made a habit of situating his camps on sandspits, giving him an even shorter front to defend. During the anxious march Cavendish made only one brief diversion, when he climbed Mt Luburr, a prominent mountain rising steeply from the lake's northern shores. From the lofty viewpoint he gazed westward into the distance where mighty forest-capped mountains rose from the great desert plain. Resisting the temptation to visit them, he turned back to his task. It had been a short respite from the strife along the lake shore, and on descending he once more took up the fray.

The climax to the desperate trek along the sweltering sands came after ten days of almost continual fighting and skirmishing, in which several of his men were wounded. They managed to capture a hostage, and with her co-operation, communication with the Turkana was quickly opened. Thereafter all went well, assurance having been given that the intruders were merely passing through and had no intention of stealing Turkana stock. With the assistance of guides they managed to struggle over the last 50 miles (80 kilometres) to the south end of the lake, an appalling wasteland of waterless mountain ranges, crossed only once before by white men when Teleki and von Höhnel traversed them in 1888. Six weeks after separating, Cavendish and Andrew met up as planned on the lake's eastern shore.

Cavendish's expedition to Lake Rudolf was notable for two reasons. Not only was it the first occasion an expedition had explored the full length of the lake's western shore, but it was also the first time an expedition's combined efforts had circumambulated the lake. No longer did the lake's edge hold any secrets from the outside world. Moreover, Cavendish could proudly claim to have been the 'British traveller' who did in fact 'bestir' himself to do the job. With considerable personal satisfaction he could consider his main task done; all that remained was to lead the caravan safely back to Mombasa.

While climbing out of the inhospitable valley that sheltered the lake, Cavendish reached an important milestone in his life—his twenty-first birthday. One may wonder how the aristocratic youth celebrated the special occasion, far from the formal functions which would have been customary in the ancestral halls at home. Surely he was content where he was, his reward a worthwhile project accomplished.

Although then on their homeward march, the two explorers had not yet come to the end of their discoveries. Some dozen miles to the south of Lake Rudolf, and separated from it by a rugged barrier of volcanic debris, lay another lake, deep down in the torrid bottom of the Suguta valley. This was Lake Logipi, today far reduced in size from the extensive stretch of water Cavendish first visited in May 1897. The desiccated relic of an ancient lake exists in an environment of unsurpassed hostility, where temperatures soar daily to heights reached nowhere else in east Africa, and it was to those Hades-like depths that Cavendish's footsteps led. According to his account the two hardy young men 'paid many visits to it', noting that it was about 25 miles (40 kilometres) in length, had an arm 10 miles (16 kilometres) long and was 'fed by two rivers'. Exploring the valley floor on foot must have been extremely tiring work, for even the water in the lake was found to be 'exceedingly hot'. Near its northern shore they visited a smouldering cone which was named 'Andrew' volcano by the expedition leader. Commendably, it was the only alien name they bestowed on a geographical feature of their finding. Today the volcano is dormant, a few steam jets being the only sign of latent power, and the lake itself has shrunk to almost nothing, only regenerating very briefly on rare occasions after extensive rains.

Cavendish chose a hard road to Lake Baringo, his next port of call. Lurching and staggering southwards along the slopes of the Rift Valley his caravan was to find little water as it went; his guides were of dubious reliability, and the caravan men, tired of the adventure, became mutinous. Fortunately for them they crossed the pitiless stretch during the rainy season, when they were lucky to find 'a few puddles', otherwise 'we should never have got through this country'. Two incidents *en route* didn't help to ease their problems. On one occasion the camels ate a plant which poisoned them temporarily and left ten dead; on another Andrew was charged and knocked down by a rhinoceros. Surprisingly, he survived to tell the tale, but he was incapacitated for several weeks and could not walk a step. Despite these setbacks, the caravan eventually strode wearily into Baringo in early July. There they heard welcome news of the presence of other white men in the neighbourhood, one of whom was Teleki's old friend Frederick Jackson.

Cavendish's expedition was then on the fringe of white man's influence in East Africa, and from that stage it enjoyed the ease of marches along a well-cleared road, following its dusty endlessness to distant Mombasa. Towards the close of his long journey Cavendish found the probing advance guard of the latest travel facility in East Africa—the embryonic Uganda Railway. The whole party eagerly and gratefully boarded a train and rattled off along the brand-new track to Mombasa. The fortuitous connection, in effect, saved Cavendish's caravan from one final week of dreary tramping across the arid and waterless wastes of the Taru desert. So ended the expedition's year of rigorous but rewarding travel, led by an adventurous and singularly mature young Englishman. His efforts had well entitled him to the complimentary description—'an excellent traveller'.

Cavendish's far-reaching east African trek may have come to a close, but his mention of an unknown land to the west of Lake Rudolf, supported by intriguing photographs taken from the summit of Mt Luburr, fostered a deepening interest in yet another 'little corner' of unexplored Africa. Cavendish never did return to east Africa to continue his explorations; as with Neumann, a war was shortly to interrupt his plans. As both men fought in the same regiment it is hard to imagine that they did not meet up at some stage and swap notes on their travels as they campaigned in the far south of the continent they so respected.

# DELAMERE EXPEDITION
## 1896–8

ALMOST at the same time as Cavendish was saying farewell to his Italian friend Ferrandi at Lugh, another young English aristocrat was on the eve of leaving Berbera at the start of his latest African adventure. He, like Cavendish, was a seasoned traveller in Africa. A veteran of four earlier hunting jaunts in Somaliland, he was well qualified to break out of the by now familiar bounds and journey to new and more distant horizons. Hugh Cholmondeley, the third Baron Delamere, then a man of twenty-seven years of age, had read with keen interest the account of Teleki's journey which von Höhnel's pen had so ably composed. With no intention of curbing his desire for the attractions of the continent's lonely spaces, he eagerly made his plans for an extensive journey of exploration. By then his enthusiasm for hunting was beginning to wane. Only three months separated the departures of the Cavendish and Delamere expeditions from their common starting point, Berbera, and both followed approximately the same road for the early stages of their journeys. But a differing outlook and ambition separated the two men. Cavendish was driven by an energetic wanderlust that would not be assuaged for some years to come; Delamere, older by seven years, was already considering the idea of settling down. Significantly, his eyes had viewed Africa for some time as the most likely place to do just this. Little did he know that his fifth and most serious expedition would lead him ultimately to the land of his dreams.

*     *     *

On 28 April 1870 Hugh Cholmondeley was born into an old and well-established family of aristocrats, a family which had possessed land in the lovely vale of Delamere—once a royal sporting forest in Cheshire—for two hundred and fifty years. His parents' home was appropriately named Vale Royal after the magnificent Cistercian monastery that once dominated the grounds and had long before been razed in the destructive Dissolution of the Monasteries. Cholmondeley and his sister grew up in the comfortable years when Queen Victoria was sovereign of an expanding empire, when Englishmen around the world were either admired or feared, and sometimes both. At Eton, Cholmondeley did not excel. In much the same way as Chanler, his contemporary on the other side of the Atlantic, he disliked the schoolroom, but thrived on horse racing and hunting. And, like his American counterpart, he left school early to attend a cramming college. At that stage in his life his aim was to join the army, but when he was only seventeen his father died. Suddenly, all plans were changed. With the inherited title of third Baron Delamere he was instantly projected into the world of titled people. He became the owner of an estate, albeit a smallish one which was not too productive financially, found himself the owner of a very adequate hunting stable, and most important he was master of the family. With alacrity the young lord embarked on a period of indulgence which the mortgaged estate could ill afford.

Delamere was ginger haired and possessed a swift and violent temper. The latter trait made him difficult to control as a child. Even his mother's discipline failed on occasion to have any effect. After he succeeded to the title of baron his headstrong nature developed even more, and he quickly became a somewhat irresponsible character. His passions continued to be hunting, at which 'he was a courageous but sometimes a rash horseman', and racing, both money-consuming hobbies that ate avidly into the estate's dwindling coffers.

In his physique Delamere was short and lightly built. Despite this, he was strong, tough and durable—all characteristics that stood him in excellent stead for the rest of his life. Unfortunately, his constitution was never robust, a factor that contributed to his comparatively short life. In temperament he, like Chanler, could be arrogant, overbearing and intolerant, often the by-products of driven souls who felt curbed by the foibles of the society in which they lived. With shooting and hunting foremost in his mind (the social whirl appalled him) it was only natural that the African game fields should appeal to his sporting spirit. But his mother could dictate the course of his life until he was twenty-one, and she refused him her consent to go to Africa.

As a compromise Delamere paid a visit to Australia where he spent much of his time wandering in the sheep country. There he absorbed with interest and enjoyment the crafts of the sheep farmer, gaining an experience which served him well in later years when he became a pioneer farmer in Africa.

On reaching his majority in 1891, Delamere took his leave and hurriedly departed for Somaliland. For some unknown reason he and his two young companions elected to travel via the Cape to Zanzibar and Aden, an extended journey that must have exposed Delamere to the various political and commercial scenes along the east African coast. Undoubtedly a seed was sown in his mind on the voyage, one that would germinate and flourish.

Delamere's first hunting expedition in Somaliland, led by a European guide, lasted for three months, and at its end he did not return home with his prodigal companions. Despite pleas from his mother he prolonged his stay by another four months, satisfying his cravings for the wild excitements of the hunting fields.

From that time on Delamere was well hooked on sport in Africa, and for the next four years he regularly returned to chase lions, stick warthogs and track any other beast that showed itself. The escapades were not without incident, and a severe mauling by a lion left him with a lifelong limp, but the set-back did not deter him from planning future travels on the continent. By then Delamere had become totally addicted to the marvels of Africa, and with his hunting instinct largely satiated he planned his fifth and most important journey. It was designed to be an expedition with geographical and scientific aims, complete with a photographer, taxidermist and doctor.

This latest extensive expedition was not destined to be Delamere's final foray in east Africa. On his return home he married, and shortly after, taking his youthful bride with him, he travelled one more time to that alluring country. Intending to make full use of the visit, he again took an taxidermist, and in October 1899 the small party left Mombasa for the highlands of present-day Kenya. By then the famous Uganda Railway—the well-publicised man-eaters had made it so—had stretched far inland, the nucleus of a capital, Nairobi, had started its rickety rise, and the earliest murmurings of a country in the making were permeating back to England. A few months after their return to England in May 1900, a son was born to the Delameres, and

*A pig sticking party in Somaliland, 1896. (l. to r.) Sir Edmund Loder, Lord Delamere, Sir Alfred Pease, (seated) Lady Pease.*

they then settled down to enjoy the life of the landed gentry. But it was not to continue for long. Delamere's restless spirit stood the dull routine of estate owner and country gentleman for only two years before the call of East Africa beckoned him yet again for one last look. On reaching Nairobi he soon found himself embroiled in the complex problems which were confronting the white man in his early efforts to settle in the new frontier land. Gradually becoming more entrapped, Delamere was eventually fettered by a cause that his biographer, Elspeth Huxley, so clearly expressed: 'For himself he believed in the future of the highlands as a white man's country fervently and consistently from the beginning—probably from the time when he first came down from the north in 1897—until his death'. From the time of his return to East Africa in 1902 until his death in 1931, Lord Delamere devoted all his energies and most of his worldly wealth to the country which lay at the end of his exploring trail, becoming in his time a giant and a leader in the eyes and minds of the white community who so hopefully threw in their lot with the fortunes of British East Africa.

\*     \*     \*

During the years between 1891 and 1896 Delamere proved himself to be a tireless wanderer in the remote solitudes of Somaliland. Despite a weak constitution, his

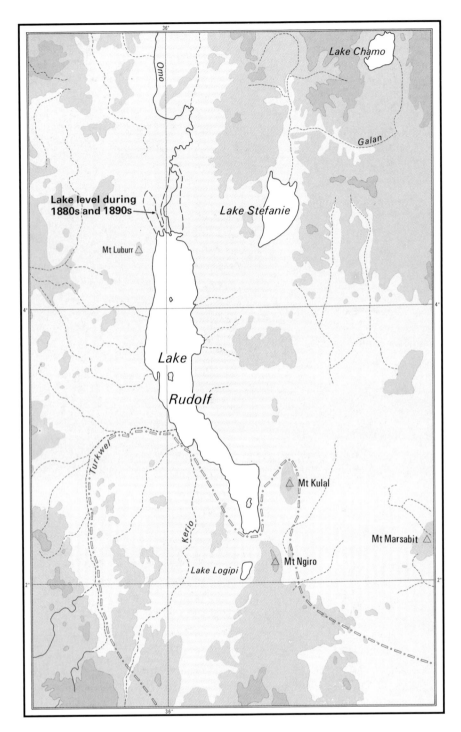

*The route of the Delamere Expedition 1896–8.*

*Dr Atkinson on Christmas Day 1897.*

resolute spirit and hardy physical stamina endowed him with an enthusiasm that was hard to best, a quality which carried him through four expeditions in that austere corner of Africa. There can be little doubt that he was one of the first white men to travel extensively in the arid wastes of the Ogaden. Others followed soon enough in his tracks, and notable amongst them was the American explorer, Donaldson Smith, who blazed a trail through this tract to Lake Rudolf in 1894. The latter's account of his history-making journey was not published until 1897, but his reports to geographical societies would certainly have been available to Delamere, and these, in addition to von Höhnel's classic two-volume tale of the 1888 discovery of Lake Rudolf, were probably amongst the principal motivators in planning a fifth journey—his most ambitious undertaking by far.

By 1896 Delamere had become a competent caravan leader, with well-established contacts in Aden to assist him with his outfitting requirements, so he had no difficulty in organising a further trip. But this time he intended travelling entirely on his own. Whether he liked it or not he did not have his way, for motherly apprehension insisted he take a companion, and it had to be a doctor. Strangely, it was Rowland Ward, the world-famous taxidermists and travel book publishers in London, who were instructed to find the right man, and find one they did, a person soon to earn a reputation of notoriety in East Africa. The selected man was Dr Atkinson, then twenty-six years old, and on the eve of completing his final examinations for a Fellowship of the Royal College of Surgeons. He willingly agreed to trade the scalpel for the rifle. And the rifle was to be Atkinson's tool of trade for some years to come, until he eventually fell foul of the authorities in East Africa for the reputed killing of some Rendille in a disagreement over the price of ivory.

Preparations for the great adventure were in full swing during 1895. Atkinson had consented to forego his examinations in place of Africa, and plans were accordingly made, but first Delamere's tiger hunt in India intervened, followed by an elk hunt in Norway. Then on the eve of making his final arrangements, Delamere suffered a violent fall from his horse, and for six months was prostrated in bed. Finally, however, Atkinson left for Aden in the summer of 1896, with Delamere following a few months later, accompanied by the two experts he had signed on for the trip—a taxidermist and a photographer. Experienced in the fickle ways of African natives, Delamere went prepared for the worst, taking along with him an armoury of one hundred rifles and a machine gun. As it turned out none of this equipment was ever needed on their two-year journey.

Delamere's starting point was the familiar town of Berbera. In December 1896 his massive and heavily laden caravan commenced its march southwards, following at first the well-trodden track to Hargeisa. The four white men rode at the head of an immense column of 200 pack camels, over twice as many as Donaldson Smith had left with on his journey. Arching eastwards in a long curve away from the latter's path, the caravan lurched slowly over the Haud and Ogaden, both waterless deathly places for the inexperienced traveller. But the curve eventually brought the column back to the hospitable Shebeli river, across it, and on to Lugh on the Juba river. The lonely Italian outpost at Lugh was fast becoming a crossroads for white travellers: Delamere's party arrived there in March, four months after Cavendish's group had enjoyed Captain Ferrandi's hospitality.

A complication cropped up at Lugh—Delamere found his trade goods were running low. It seems strange that this predicament should have arisen so early in his trip, when the caravan had been only three months or so on the road, and especially if one considers the immense carrying capacity of his large camel train. Possibly Delamere had been over generous with his gifts along the way. This could well have been the reason, as it was characteristic of his nature to pay excessively in barter deals, but it created an untimely problem for him. Anyway, Lugh was a convenient spot to arrange for Atkinson to travel down the river and catch a boat to Zanzibar, where he could buy replenishments for their stock of trade goods. In good time he purchased £1,000 worth of cloth and beads, and then hastened back to rendezvous with Delamere's caravan, now camped at Melka Erri, situated close to present-day Mandera. It was not a trouble free return journey for Atkinson; a succession of mishaps delayed him on the way, and he reached Delamere's camp only in May. Despite the irritating delays the mission had been successful and the caravan was once again ready for its onward trek.

In the year Cavendish and Delamere passed through Lugh the depredations of the Abyssinian raiders were beginning to have deleterious effects on the Galla people living in the region. Luckily both expeditions managed to evade the Abyssinian forces, who were, in any case, not operating at the time in the immediate vicinity; they were

*The Delamere camel train trekking through the wastes of Somaliland in 1897. Taken by Delamere's photographer Giles.*

too busy coping with the Italian invasion from the north. For Delamere's party the only pressing problem on this section of the journey was the state of the drought-parched land where water was worryingly scarce; marches were long and dusty nightmares of hardship, with the dreary miles marked by the skeletons of animals. Trudging along in Donaldson Smith's footsteps, the caravan reached and passed the familiar wells at Banissa and Derkali, climbed gently into the higher Borana country and visited the ancient wells of Le and Gof, previously described by the American explorer. Up to that point Delamere had followed the trails of former expeditions, so, apart from satisfying his personal curiosity, there was little he could claim to have added to the outside world's geographical knowledge.

On leaving the wells at Egder, Delamere suddenly changed direction. Leaving his predecessors' routes he dropped down from the highlands and aimed for Mt Foroli, the towering sentinel of the low-lying plains country of the Golbo. Magnificent in its lordly isolation, this superb mountain towers over the scattered neighbouring hills, rising steeply 4,000 feet (1,230 metres) from its base on the plain to the monumental red and grey granite rocks of its summit ridge, a quiet haven for the elusive kudu antelope sheltering in the bush-clad corries. Five feebly trickling and ephemeral springs are hidden away in deep crevices on the slopes of the solitary hill, a meagre water supply incapable, even at the best of times, of sustaining anything but the smallest population of human and animal life. Delamere's party could rightfully claim to be the first white men to walk by the remote mountain, and he used it as his next turning beacon. From there he struck directly southwards, leaving the rolling Hurri Hills on his right.

Sixteen days later, having trudged across a vast, empty, stony landscape with little water to be found, the caravan reached the springs at Koroli. Bubbling from the ground on the billiard table flatness of the Chalbi Desert's desolate floor, the springs are a serene oasis, providing an endless supply of crystal clear water; though brackish to human taste, it is highly palatable and nutritious for the animals which daily congregate to drink their fill. Delamere found some Rendille living nearby, who exactly as they had done two years previously with Donaldson Smith, agreed to trade him several replacement camels. On leaving Koroli the expedition once again met the earlier explorer's path, and toiled up the barren slopes to the cool tranquillity of Marsabit Mountain's forests. With gladness they camped by the forest edge on the northern slopes of the range, near a spring of water which for many years thereafter was popularly known as Delamere's 'Njoro' (spring). In this hospitable place the party rested for three pleasant weeks, every day Atkinson exercising himself in his favourite sport—elephant hunting. His score of twenty-one tuskers was clear proof of the large numbers of these beasts that then frequented the dense forests.

Departing from the haven of Marsabit the caravan dropped down the gentle mountain slopes and over the sweltering red-dust plains of the Kaisut Desert on its way to Laisamis. Reaching the well-known waterholes at Laisamis, Delamere again decided on a sudden departure from the beaten track, and headed west for Lake Rudolf, with the added intention of continuing up to Lake Stefanie. It was a strange manoeuvre, and compared with the routes taken by other explorers on their way to these lakes, it was much longer, but at least he could say that a part of the country he was tramping over had never before been seen by white man. When he finally rounded the rough northern foothills of Mt Kulal, and stumbled down the lava-ridden slopes to the lake's shore, Delamere was so exhausted and dispirited by the rigours of travel through such a desperate landscape that he decided to forego the journey to Lake Stefanie. Instead he walked south, his caravan picking its way through the jagged rocks at the end of Lake Rudolf, past Teleki's dormant volcano, and over the mountains to the Turkwel river.

Delamere's rambling route up to that stage appeared on the map as a sinuous directionless line, giving the impression that he may have had no definite aim in mind. Many years later this was verified in a statement made by Atkinson, who claimed that Delamere told him he had no real objective on his expedition except to visit country described by Teleki and Donaldson Smith. Delamere's apparently aimless track took another sharp swing when he reached the Turkwel river and turned his caravan south towards Lake Baringo's well-trodden shores.

At Baringo Delamere divided his caravan. He was not yet ready to return to what he regarded as the tedium of the English country squire's life, and anyway there was still much country left to be explored. Realising he no longer needed a vast concourse of animals and men to carry his baggage, he instructed Atkinson to return to Somaliland with half the force. This the doctor did, travelling directly down the well-worn trade route to Mombasa. Delamere in the meantime clambered eastwards up the steep slopes of the Rift Valley wall—a similar hike to the one Teleki had done only ten years before—and onto the open rolling plains of the Laikipia plateau. This was a paradise of freshness contrasting strikingly with the seemingly endless oppressiveness of the hot desert lands he had negotiated in the previous twelve gruelling months. Could it have been during the pleasant marches across this hospitable and well-watered country, in which nothing moved but the wind and drifting herds of wild beasts, that Delamere first realised the potential lying dormant there?

The remainder of Delamere's long trek took him across to the Uaso Ngiro river, past the point von Höhnel had reached in 1887, and down along its banks in its tumbling course into the lowland haunts of Chanler and Neumann. On rejoining Donaldson Smith's old southbound track near the eastern end of the prominent Merti plateau, Delamere made yet another of his mystifying turns and headed due north again, back towards Laisamis and Marsabit. It almost appeared as if he was spinning out the time before he had to face the stern realities of life in England once again, but there at Marsabit he temporarily ran out of enthusiasm for African adventure. Atkinson, who had in the meantime disposed of the excess camels, rendezvoused with Delamere on the lonely mountain, but only in time to join his leader in retracing their steps on the long homeward march by way of the familiar route to the Uaso Ngiro river. While crossing the rock-strewn and sun-baked plains in the vicinity of the river, the party witnessed the tragic death of Neumann's friend, Dr Kolb, from a wound inflicted by a charging rhinoceros. In spite of all his medical skills, there was nothing Dr Atkinson could do to stay the inevitable outcome, and the German was buried on the spot.

Delamere's homeward journey then took him through Meru country, at that time a luxuriant and forest-clad district, across the southern extremity of Kikuyuland, past the British fort at Machakos, and on to the railhead at the notorious ford on the Tsavo river where man-eating lions were avidly consuming the Indian coolies working on the railway construction. The two-year trek came to a close at Mombasa. Soon after, Delamere returned to his ancestral responsibilities at Vale Royal, with a view to settling down to his tasks as a landowner. That his intentions did not last is a well-known story; only eighteen months elapsed before the restless lord was once more found wandering in East Africa.

On careful analysis of Delamere's expedition certain significant features become apparent, which display to a marked degree its unusualness in the more conventional annals of exploration. Firstly, despite the fact that there were four Europeans in the party, there are no known daily records of the journey. This was quite extraordinary when one recalls that most explorers in Victorian times applied an exemplary diligence to the keeping of diaries, often rambling on for pages on even trivial subjects. Secondly, none of the participants ever published an account of their travels. Again this was amazing, as it was quite the fashion in those times to regale the reading public with tales of high adventure and gore, titillating the senses of armchair sportsmen and explorers in the process. By that means, too, there was always the hope of establishing oneself in African history for posterity. Thirdly, no learned papers were read before meetings of esteemed societies, and no scientific collections were carefully recorded and catalogued for the world's repositories. In fact it is disappointing to think that nothing except a photo album appeared to have been deposited in the security of any libraries or archives.

The problem of putting the tale of Delamere's expedition together originally rested with Elspeth Huxley, his biographer, who thirty-seven years after the event had to rely solely on two tenuous sources for the details: the lucid memories of the ageing Dr Atkinson, and one ancient annotated photograph album containing yellowing pictures of dead lions, camels, people and thorn-bush country. These were minimal materials to use in describing the long meandering trail that the footloose English lord followed in his quest for fulfilment. In the end he found his place—a home and a life in East Africa. There he was destined to lead a young community in a newly awakening country which he served with honour, and with the respect of those he spent the remainder of his life representing.

# WELLBY EXPEDITION
## 1898–9

'CAPTAIN M. S. Wellby, 18th Hussars: It is with great regret that we record the death, from wounds received in battle in South Africa, of Capt. M.S. Wellby, one of the most intrepid and successful of the younger generation of explorers and an officer of great promise in his profession'. These succinct words of appreciation, composed for the *Geographical Journal* in 1900, opened a stout-hearted man's obituary, appearing only a few months after his enthusiastically received paper had been read by his father at a meeting of the Royal Geographical Society. Wellby, like Cavendish, was an Englishman. Besides that he was a soldier, an officer from a crack British cavalry regiment. During the closing years of Queen Victoria's reign—the halcyon period when the imperial dream was at its peak and the patronising remark that the 'sun never sets on the British Empire' was boastfully proclaimed by Englishmen around the globe—there was ample scope for officers in faraway garrisons to satisfy their wants in wars, hunting escapades, or explorations. The eager officer in pursuit of sport and travel needed only adequate funds and a generous leave from his duties. For many the first commodity was readily available, and for most the second appeared, in those leisurely days, to be equally attainable. The dimension of time held a value very different from the frenetic chase and turmoil of present-day existence. It was then, during the final decade of that stirring century, that Wellby, like a passing comet, flashed brightly across the explorers' heavens. Patently a born wanderer, he managed to achieve unusual success in the short life he was given to enjoy. In one three-year period he concluded two sensational journeys of discovery on what many travellers of the day might well have described as shoe-string budgets. Almost six decades after his untimely death a fellow soldier had these words to add: 'Wellby . . . was a young soldier-adventurer who, before he was killed, had already won a place in that long line of imperial explorers that began, perhaps, with Sir Walter Raleigh—and surely has not ended'. Appropriate words for a young man capable of reaching heights never to be attained, but who none the less left his mark in one of Africa's many engrossing chapters.

\* \* \*

Montague Sinclair Wellby's forebears may well have first arrived on English soil amongst William the Conqueror's men, so it is fitting that to this day the Wellby family maintains a tenuous association with its ancient French connection. Ten miles as the crow flies from the town of Hastings—close to the spot where England's saga was so radically disrupted over nine centuries ago—the old-world Sussex village of Westham sits on the edge of the broad flat lands of the Pevensey Levels. In its precincts stands St Mary's Church, a solid and plainly handsome Norman edifice\*. Within this time-worn

---

\* Constructed in 1080, St Mary's was the first substantial church to be built in England by the recently arrived Normans.

*Captain Montague Sinclair Wellby, 18th Hussars.*

building a tranquil peace is accentuated by the soft light filtering through an elegant array of arched windows. One of these, the stained-glass East window, is of particular note. A close inspection of this fine example of the ecclesiastical window-maker's art will reveal a brass plaque affixed to the wall, on which these words are etched:

This window erected to the memory of Capt. M.S. Wellby, as a loving momento by
his father and mother, was unveiled by Col. E. Paley, 18th Hussars, Aug. 3 1901.

This brilliant window with its simple inscription stands as a poignant memorial to a favourite son from his mourning parents.

In 1820 Montague Wellby's grandfather started a modest jeweller and silversmith business in London, situated in Garrick Street. Little did he know that this venture was to grow into a prestigious enterprise as the years passed. Almost a century later, as D. and J. Wellby Limited, it became diamond purveyor and silversmith to King George V and his Queen, the Prince of Wales, George VI and Queen Elizabeth, and their daughter, Princess Elizabeth. But all this happened long after Montague Wellby was born on 10 October 1866, at 1 Sussex Place, Regent's Park, situated in the elegant terrace laid out by John Nash, who, it is said, had the services of another Wellby in his work. Before her marriage to John Wellby, young Montague's mother had been a

Sinclair, a niece of the Earl of Caithness, since when the name Sinclair has been retained in the Wellby line. Wellby's mother proved to be a prolific producer of children, but of the thirteen she bore only four survived into adulthood, and of these only two lived to reach old age. His father, when business permitted, indulged himself to the full in travelling, a pastime that came to be enjoyed equally well by two of his sons. His lengthy journeyings took him around the world at least three times, while closer to home one of his regular local rambles took the form of an annual Easter walk from Regent's Park to the family home in Westham. When they were old enough his four sons always joined him on those 60 mile (96 kilometre) hikes. In Montague's case it was certainly a prophetic training for what lay ahead.

Montague did not acquit himself well in his studies. While he attended Rugby School there was no indication of any scholarly prowess; in fact, apart from mathematics, he was 'placed very low' in all subjects, and there is even the suggestion that he suffered the indignity of being superannuated when he became too old for his senior class. But aside from his dismal classroom record, he was chosen to play rugby for his house, became a fair cross-country runner, and served as a private in the School Corps—a volunteer battalion of the Royal Warwickshire Regiment. In 1884 he left school, and the following year was enrolled in the Royal Military Academy at Sandhurst. During July 1886 Wellby took his examinations, this time with success, and so became entitled to a certificate of proficiency in Military Administration and Riding. With this somewhat unimpressive record he set out to face the world, one in which soldiering, horses and adventure were all to play important parts.

In 1887 Wellby was commissioned into the 18th Hussars (Princess of Wales's Own) as a lieutenant. For seven years he held this rank, doing most of his soldiering in India, where there was ample opportunity for him to participate in the gentlemanly pursuits of hunting and polo. Short, wiry and very tough, he thrived on the life he led, and in 1895, the same year he achieved his captaincy, he made the first of his sporting journeys—to Somaliland, the up-and-coming playground of the 1890s for the Nimrod type aspiring to shoot lions and other such game. That excursion simply served to whet his appetite for yet more ambitious expeditions, and at the first available opportunity—the very next year as it turned out—he took off on an epic journey in the company of a friend, an officer from the Argyll and Sutherland Highlanders. The aim of their trip was to traverse northern Tibet from west to east, a route which up to that time had not been attempted by any other European traveller. Nine months of grinding slog it took them to complete their project, in the course of which they suffered terrible hardships but doggedly saw it through, and with the aid of Shazad Mir—their stoic Indian surveyor—they returned to their base loaded down with exciting new geographical facts and a storehouse of botanical specimens. The expedition was deemed an immense success and received considerable acclaim, providing the Royal Geographical Society with a wealth of information and establishing Wellby's reputation as an intrepid and thorough explorer.

Wellby was promoted adjutant of his regiment in 1897, a position of responsibility he held for two years. While holding that office he was engaged on several testing military expeditions on India's rugged North West Frontier. At the conclusion of these actions his thoughts turned once more to exploration, and soon enough he was decided on a return to Africa. The account which follows of his history-making journey is yet more evidence of the cavalry officer's tenacity, and the tributes he received on his return to England were further proof of the public's admiration of him as a purposeful explorer. As the *Daily News Weekly* put it: 'There was scarcely standing room in the Geographical Section of the British Association at Dover when Captain Wellby read his paper "A journey in King Menelik's Dominions". Extraordinary interest was excited by a recently-published interview with the gallant officer, and we were all eager to see him in the flesh'.

Wellby was not given much time to enjoy the honours of his success, for the Boer War had just broken out and his regiment was already in the thick of battle. He hastened to rejoin his fellow hussars in Natal, and almost immediately was incarcerated with them in the beleaguered town of Ladysmith, where for several months he and countless others suffered through the seige. Despite this frustration, when relief did finally arrive he was in command of a squadron of cavalrymen and ready for action. Of that there was plenty, and his regiment soon earned a small place in military history by leading the British army's advance from Natal into the enemy's home ground in the Transvaal.

The fateful day of 29 July 1900 found Wellby leading a scouting patrol over the open rolling countryside near Amersfoort in the south-eastern corner of the Transvaal. The peace of the afternoon was suddenly shattered by heavy volleys of Boer rifle fire, which forced him and his men to dive for cover in a convenient gulley. Finding the enemy crowding dangerously close, Wellby ordered his men away to safety while he himself gave covering fire. It was a selfless act, and quite to be expected of the courageous man, but misfortune was soon to follow. Fighting on alone, he was eventually called on to surrender. Heroically, but foolishly, he refused, and shortly afterward received a crippling bullet wound in his stomach. It must have been a long painful night for Wellby as he lay sorely injured and alone in the dark, and how he must have welcomed dawn and the arrival of the regimental doctor. He was then carried off to hospital, but it was too late and on 5 August he died. It was a futile end for a young man of such great promise, but the story does not stop there. Wellby made a final request to his batman as he lay dying, begging him to describe his last days to his father when he returned to England. The man did not immediately keep his promise. In fact it took him seventy years to do so, and by then Wellby's father had long since died. In 1970 the aged ex-soldier arrived at the Wellby shop in Garrick Street and finding his former officer's nephew there, confessed his tardiness and told his tale, thereby at the last salving his conscience. Wellby rests, not as one might wish, in the company of his relatives in the little churchyard at Westham, but in a war cemetery hard by the high-veldt farming town of Paardekop in the distant Transvaal, on the continent he loved so deeply.

\*      \*      \*

By the middle of the 1890s, a short while before Wellby made his appearance on the scene, the era of the adventurer-explorer in east Africa was drawing to a close. The time was over when about all that was required to mount an expedition into the interior of that country was a definite objective, enough cash to finance the journey, and the nerves and desire for excitement, danger and the ever-attendant tribulations. For those restless spirits seeking adventure in far-flung empty spaces, free from the claustrophobia of urban civilisation, conditions had changed, largely caused by the encroaching influences of the great European powers—Britain, France, Germany and Italy—in their predatorial race for chunks of the eastern corner of Africa. At the core of this contest lay two important tracts of country: Abyssinia, and the vast unexplored spaces on the upper Nile. Both, for different reasons, had been partially isolated from the outside world. It was a situation that did not last long, for the arrival of acquisitive white men suddenly focused world attention on the geo-political attractions of these immense tracts. The division of the spoils in the scramble for Africa had added to the complexity of international desires in east Africa. The British imperialistically viewed the north/south spine of Africa as essentially theirs to control—Cecil Rhodes was even then seriously considering the construction of the Cape to Cairo railway—and Britain already tenuously ruled large pieces of east Africa: Uganda, the British East Africa Protectorate, and a desolate section of Somaliland fringing the shores of the Gulf of Aden. Italy claimed interests in the southern parts of Somaliland, and despite their ignominious defeat at the Battle of Adowa, they continued to cast covetous glances on a still largely unknown Abyssinia. France was about to embark on a brave but abortive effort to drive a wedge through the British ambition by establishing an unbroken belt of territory stretching from their west African holdings to Jibouti on the Red Sea. All this political jostling appeared, on the surface, mystifying to the eyes of the watching world. Indeed, it was a situation fraught with international tensions, at least one of them of a major calibre.

Both Cavendish and Donaldson Smith in turn had looked longingly westward from their vantage points at the north end of Lake Rudolf; both planned to return as soon as possible to continue their explorations to the Nile, and both were obstructed by the restrictive powers of a politically sensitive British administration which denied them access to the Nile region. It is important to remember that the late Mahdi's armies still controlled the Sudan at the time, and the authorities in London were uncertain how far south their fanatical domination of that turbulent country extended. Explorers arriving from the east could have had no guarantee of safety, assuming they even reached the Nile, and the Foreign Office was unwilling to accept any responsibility for their safe conduct. Because of this it was unbending in its determination to see that no private expeditions were granted permission to explore towards the Nile. It is easy to see why Cavendish's youthful impatience gave up the unequal struggle against the brickwall created by the British government. Donaldson Smith was older and more determined. He eventually succeeded in muscling his way defiantly through the official barriers and on to the Nile. By then, of course, the political climate had changed for the better, and travel, while still restricted, was not totally impossible.

Into this boiling pot of territorial wranglings came Jean-Baptiste Marchand, a patriotic and enthusiastic French army captain, eager to carry his country's flag from west Africa to the Nile, and then on to Abyssinia via the Sobat river. That he would have to trudge across 3,000 miles (4,800 kilometres) of desert and jungle in mainly unexplored country during the course of his march through the centre of Africa, did not seem to distract him from his purpose. It was a courageous, but ultimately fruitless tramp; his small band of French officers and one hundred Senegalese soldiers covered the ground to Fashoda on the Nile in two years of horrendously hard travelling. The story of Marchand and his isolated post at Fashoda (near present-day Kodok) is well known to readers of African history: how his determined stance was almost the cause of war between England and France in 1898, promoted largely by the jingoistic posturings of the two countries; how Kitchener forcefully, but for once very diplomatically, manoeuvred his ejection; and how in the end Marchand quietly, but with bitter disappointment, vacated his station and departed for Abyssinia, leaving the upper Nile in the hands of the triumphant British forces. The Nile was now assured for Britain; it was one more step forward in the grand imperial scheme.

One other abortive expedition to the area during this period must be mentioned—Macdonald's. A Royal Engineer officer, Macdonald had with considerable success led the team that completed the original survey for the prospective Uganda Railway. Later, in 1892, he was the man detailed by the British government to report on Lugard's supposedly nefarious activities in Uganda. Macdonald could rightfully claim to know Uganda after all that, and with the imminent arrival of Marchand on the Nile generating distinct feelings of nervousness in London, it did not need much persuasion to convince Whitehall that the redoubtable railway surveyor was a suitable man to lead a military force from Mombasa to the Nile. It was ostensibly on a journey of exploration, but its real objective was to nip the Frenchman's plans in the bud. Macdonald's orders from England were to proceed with troops by train to the railhead, then only 70 miles (112 kilometres) inland from Mombasa, and march as fast as he could northwards into Uganda and on to the Sudan; there it was hoped he would eventually link up with Kitchener's army, which was advancing steadily southwards from Egypt to its dramatic conclusion with the Mahdist Dervishes at Omdurman. It didn't work out as planned as the expedition was to be bogged down for almost a year while it quelled the mutiny of Sudanese soldiers in Uganda. Curiously, there appeared to be a tiny element of perfidiousness attached to Macdonald's inconclusive undertaking. The political aspect of the enterprise was skillfully hidden under the guise of an expedition to explore the 'sources of the Juba'. A pithy article in the *Guardian* in December 1898 expressed the paper's point of view: 'Now the Juba that everybody knows is the river of that name flowing into the sea in British East Africa; and the inference left to be drawn was that Major Macdonald's expedition was merely geographical in its objects ... What, then, shall we say of the Government's original explanation of the objects of his expedition? The truth is that there are two Juba rivers. There is the Juba river that flows into the Indian Ocean, and there is a Juba which flows into the Sobat and so into the Nile ... Major Macdonald's was thus as clearly an expedition to Fashoda as Major Marchand's was; and the Government called it an expedition to the Juba in order to mislead public opinion in England and to stifle discussion in the House of Commons on its African policy. All this is as clear as noonday now; but the equivocation was successful at the time'. Maybe this was simply a twist of politics by the press, but in any event Macdonald never did manage to reach the Juba. Worn-out by the rigours of a year's campaigning, and without adequate supplies, his starving column had to return to Uganda. With Marchand already removed from Fashoda, and France's claim to the upper Nile relinquished, it didn't matter much anyway.

Into this tangled web of politics, tensions and military operations Montague Wellby quietly made his entrance and played his little part. As it turned out, his modestly executed expedition was a vivid contrast to the cumbersome afore-mentioned failures. It was a success story that garnered him yet more acclaim as an explorer and diplomat of the highest calibre, and for the eagerly awaiting geographical pundits one that produced more answers for a vital empty space on their maps. It had not been easy to gain access to the prohibited country, as *The Times* observed at the close of 1898: 'But between Lake Rudolf and the Nile there lies one of the most considerable areas of unexplored territory still to be found in Africa. It was across this unknown land that Mr. Cavendish proposed to travel on the expedition which, about a year ago, was countermanded by the Government. Dr. Donaldson Smith and other explorers are known to cherish the legitimate ambition of being the first to open up this most interesting stretch of country, but permission to make the attempt has been refused by the Government'. In spite of all this discouragement Wellby's determination had triumphed, aided undoubtedly by Kitchener's magnificent victory over the Mahdists at the Battle of Omdurman, coupled with the timely intervention of a Captain Harrington, then Her Britannic Majesty's Agent at King Menelik's capital in Addis Ababa. Dame Fortune had also played her part in coming to Wellby's aid, for he too had battled for permission to traverse the country between Lake Rudolf and the Nile, and he too had been balked. Fortunately for him his ability as a explorer-cum-surveyor was known to the staff of the War Office Intelligence Division. They were also aware of his desire to investigate the unexplored tract. Moreover, they felt that Wellby, with his previous experience of African travel, would be the right man to do some work for them. Accordingly, he was given every encouragement to collaborate with Harrington. For Wellby, it was the opportunity of a lifetime. With little time to spare he hurriedly made his preparations and departed from his regimental base in India for the port of Zeila on the bleak coast of Somaliland.

Wellby, in a manner befitting the adjutant of a top-class cavalry regiment, had for some time dreamed about a taste of minor heroics. How glorious, he had pondered, it would be to arrive 'with a handful of men at the south of Khartoum' just as Kitchener's advancing army marched in from the north. It was a dream never to be fulfilled, but satisfyingly for him he could now make the trip so many others envied. On 30 August 1898 he sailed from Bombay, taking with him three carefully selected companions: Lieutenant Vincent—an artillery friend—and two Indian surveyors, Shahzad Mir and Ramji Lal, both from highly esteemed Indian cavalry regiments. Shahzad Mir had already proved himself with Wellby on his gruelling tramp across Tibet, and he was later to accompany the 1903 Boundary Commission Expedition as a plane table man.

Six days after leaving Bombay the quartet arrived with their baggage on 'Zeila's uninviting shores'. It was a hostile and immensely dreary spot, but Harrington had almost completed their caravan arrangements, so no time was lost in shaking off the sands of 'this inhospitable barren maritime station'. The first steps into Africa had been made, but they were not ones that could happily be described as confident. Gloomily Harrington 'could give us very little hope of our being able to travel beyond King Menelik's capital, whilst the other two officers ridiculed the proposition'. A disheartening and hardly encouraging start, further exacerbated by meeting an Abyssinian official who simply repeated Harrington's dampening predictions.

In the face of all this pessimism Wellby and his companions decided on a new strategy. Leaving Harrington they retreated to Zeila and caught a boat to Berbera. With his considerable experience of Somaliland, Wellby considered the best course would be to follow the route Cavendish and Donaldson Smith had taken to Lake Rudolf. But burgeoning officialdom blocked Wellby's new idea, forcing him to reflect disappointedly about the change in Berbera: 'the whole atmosphere has changed—the place appeared to me to have lost its former charm and freedom. To-day every stone of it is strictly under the official thumb, entailing endless rules, regulations, taxes, and certificates from every shooting party'. To add to his despondency he noted that rocketing prices and some of the dubious qualities attached to the norms of civilisation had arrived to spoil the attractions of the place that he had formerly known. To add further to his anxieties, one of the surveyors, Ramji Lal, suffered an eye injury and had to return to India, and Vincent faint-heartedly gave up the struggle to reach Abyssinia. Instead he went off shooting on his own. Wellby then showed his true mettle. Undaunted, he hired eight camels, took four camel-men, a cook and an old Somali acquaintance named Mohamed Hassan. The last was an experienced caravan headman who could claim the advantage of having previously escorted other foreign sportsmen and had even visited England. He was a gem among caravan leaders and proved invaluable to Wellby. In the next few years he towered above all others in his field.

Leading his tiny caravan on foot—horses, he discovered, were not available for purchase—Wellby embarked on his third attempt to reach the Nile, making haste for the border post of Harar, where he hoped to catch up with Harrington's cumbersome party. In the latter's company Wellby resolved to travel to Addis Ababa, where he would make a concerted effort to see King Menelik. He could hardly have chosen a more opportune moment for such a meeting. With Kitchener's devastating victory at Omdurman, British prestige was at a high point in the Abyssinian court. It was a last desperate try for Wellby, and in his characteristic fashion he became even more determined in his effort to succeed where others had failed.

Marching purposefully out of Berbera on 13 September, Wellby was once more on his way. Considering that in the busy two weeks since he had left Bombay he had suffered disappointing setbacks, his extraordinary resilience and willingness to try another plan were ample proof of his ability to think fast, travel light and move swiftly. Climbing steadily into the hinterland of Somaliland, his caravan soon passed the town of Hargeisa, where he paid a cursory visit to Lord Delamere's unoccupied house, scathingly remarking: 'It was a damp and dingy abode, reminding me of an underground dungeon, a most undesirable place of residence; and this appears to be the opinion of the builder, Lord Delamere'. Pounding hard for many miles 'through beautiful park-like land' and 'grassy plain', they next reached Jig Jigga, an insignificant Abyssinian boundary post which 'consisted merely of some feeble stockade'. There he was forced to halt until clearance for his onward journey was received from Harar. Champing at the enforced delay, Wellby was none the less grateful for the kindly entertainment extended to him by the Arab fort commander. Within a few days, which were a 'trial of patience', though not to be his last, a message arrived granting his caravan permission to proceed. On arrival at Harar he was plagued by another irritating delay, but at least he had caught up with Harrington's caravan.

Wellby's second meeting with Harrington marked the beginning of a close friendship between the two men, and had Wellby survived the Boer War, Harrington would have welcomed him on the staff at Addis Ababa. It would have been an eminently suitable arrangement, as Wellby found Abyssinia so fascinating that he made public his desire to spend the rest of his life there. The time he spent in Harar passed pleasantly enough in viewing the local sights, but finally, to Wellby's great relief, Harrington's caravan made a start, marching in procession with a portion of the Emperor's army which was on its way to Addis Ababa. Three weeks of unremitting travel—Wellby still on foot—over rolling and picturesque landscape brought the

RIGHT: *Shahzad Mir, Wellby's trusty Indian companion on two arduous treks in Tibet and Africa.*

FAR RIGHT: *Mohamed Hassan, the invaluable Somali caravan headman, who proved his worth on many testing east African expeditions.*

party to the country's capital. For Wellby a critical milestone had been reached, and he noted that: 'On reaching our tents, I felt with satisfaction that the first stage of my travels had been successfully accomplished'.

The very next day he met the man who was a vital factor in his plans—'His Imperial Majesty, King Menelik II, G.C.M.G., Emperor of Ethiopia, Negus Negasti, King of Kings'. Riding a mule through the streets of the city at 7 o'clock in the morning *en route* to the royal palace, Wellby 'felt very foolish in his evening clothes and felt hat'. Accompanied by Captain Harrington, Wellby's first formal meeting with Menelik was brief. A handshake of introduction and a handshake of farewell—that was all.

He then found himself caught up in a singularly unusual diversion, which kept Harrington and himself distracted for several days. They were requested to accompany Menelik and his army on a punitive expedition against the recalcitrant provincial governor of Tigre province. While this took the explorer in diametrically the opposite direction to the one he wanted to follow, there was no other course since Menelik had still not agreed to his request for permission to travel through Abyssinia to Lake Rudolf. He did not have long to wait though, and the great moment came when 'Harrington, on returning from an interview with the King, told me to my astonishment and delight that His Majesty had not only granted me permission to travel wherever I liked in his country, but had also promised to forward letters to the chief officials of all the districts through which I intended to travel, informing them of the fact. Such kindness surpassed my expectation'. For Wellby this was an agreement of the greatest import. A correspondent for the *Pall Mall Gazette*, on hearing the news in April 1899, wrote encouragingly: 'The captain is the first European who has attempted to reach Lake Rudolf from the north and there seems every possibility that he will succeed in his undertaking'. Following the granting of Menelik's weighty authority, Wellby promptly retraced his steps to Addis Ababa.

Preparations were immediately put in hand for the onward journey. Principally these involved the purchase of transport animals suitable for crossing the mountainous terrain on the route, and the acquisition of sufficient rifles and ammunition with which to arm his men. Fortunately the former were attainable in Addis Ababa, but the latter had to come from Aden. Once more a hurdle had to be crossed, as 'red tape on this occasion caused us to waste six weeks' waiting for the goods to arrive. The time, as at Harar, was enjoyably spent in exploring the neighbourhood, shooting and organising his caravan's requirements. Eager applicants for employment were numerous, and Wellby finally selected a mixed bunch, amongst which were counted Abyssinians, Somalis, Gallas and five Sudanese survivors of Bottego's ill-fated group. In all he recruited a corps of forty-four men, including Shahzad Mir and Mohamed Hassan. On 19 December 1898, four months' supply of food and a light canvas boat were loaded up. With gladness Wellby said his farewells and led his caravan southwards. At long last, after three and a half trying months of delays, uncertainties and changes of plans, Wellby could look forward with satisfaction to his big adventure. It was to be a lonely one, as he would not see a another white man for six months.

With Wellby's skill as a transport officer well proven during the recently concluded campaign on the North West Frontier it was natural for him to organise his caravan on military lines. With the exception of himself, Shahzad Mir the surveyor, his headman Mohamed Hassan and his cook, who each had their own tent, the rest were divided into six sections; each had its own tent, animals and ancillary equipment, and at night their six tents were erected in a tight defensive circle around Wellby's headquarters group. Every section was entirely independent of the others in its duties, and by instilling a strict discipline Wellby managed to maintain a high degree of proficiency in camp conduct and orderliness. Having established this tight routine, he then instructed his men in drilling, musketry and simple military manoeuvres—wise preparations against the unknown dangers that might be lurking ahead. For a month the caravan went through its practice paces, in the meanwhile gradually wending its way southwards to Lake Zwai. There was no immediate hurry, as Wellby's armaments from Aden had still not caught up with them, and in any case there were plenty of agreeable pursuits to pass the time—hunting, local exploring and generally tuning up his men and animals for the long journey ahead. Only one niggling doubt occupied Wellby's mind: how reliable would the Abyssinians on his staff prove to be. It was an understandable apprehension for he was the first white man ever to employ Abyssinians as caravan men far outside their home grounds, and in spite of their willing assurances there was no indication how they would react when it came to leaving the borders of their narrow world. As it turned out his Abyssinians were to allay his doubts with loyal and industrious service, although on occasions in an uninhibitedly avaricious manner that forced Wellby to take severe disciplinary measures.

On 16 January 1899, Wellby's caravan was complete and poised for the trek—'30 Abyssinians and Gallas, 5 Soudanese and 9 Somalis, 31 mules, 19 donkeys and 11

*Emperor Menelik's palace in Addis Ababa, 1898.*

ponies, Shahzad Mir, and my fox terrier, with a litter of three pups'. The thirty-five Martini-Henry rifles plus ammunition had finally arrived and been issued to his men, and from Addis Ababa came the last mail he was to receive for many months. Lake Zwai can be regarded as the true starting point for his journey of exploration into the unknown. For the next month the caravan tramped steadily southwards through a sparsely populated country of rolling open downs and beautiful forest-clad mountains, passing on its route a series of brackish lakes, one of which, Lake Lamina (now named Shala), Wellby later claimed to be the first white man to view. It was a leisurely and peaceful journey; everywhere he was received welcomingly by Abyssinian officialdom—a heartening sign that Menelik's promise of a trouble-free passage through his domain was being honoured. Accordingly, Wellby's little caravan made good progress over hill and dale accumulating a wealth of gifts as it plodded on its way.

Only on dropping down from the cool, damp highlands into the low-lying valley of the Sagan river did Wellby have further moments of uneasiness, 'knowing quite well the hatred Abyssinians have of leaving their hills'. But all was well, and although 'at first we found the plains unpleasantly hot after the cool hills', the caravan by-passed the north end of Lake Stefanie and crossed the Hamar Koke Mountains. On that harsh range the party encountered the most southerly Abyssinian posts, and it was from one of those that Wellby by good fortune released a 'Shankalla'* man from Abyssinian bondage, a man who knew the district well, and who, in his gratitude, offered to guide the caravan to Lake Rudolf—Lake Gallop as Wellby called it—and beyond, through Turkanaland.

While clambering across this rugged mountain range the expedition's first serious problem arose: anthrax began to destroy the transport animals, and to his concern Wellby's best pony was the first to die. Torn between the desire to hunt in the elephant haven they were crossing, or strike for the shores of Lake Rudolf, Wellby elected to abandon his sport and march rapidly to the lake. Even as he travelled on that stretch ponies and mules were dying, and it was with great relief that the party reached the water's edge and set up camp on 'the very spot that Bottego had chosen'. As Bottego

---

*The 'Shankallas' were Reshiat, or Murle people.

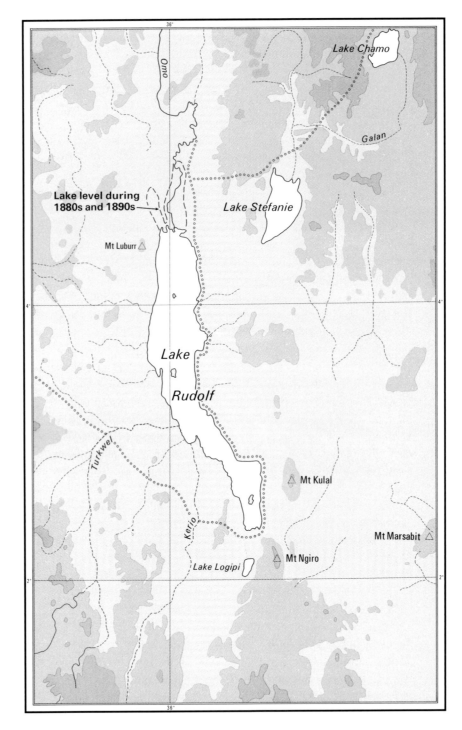

*The route of the Wellby Expedition 1898–9.*

had used the same elevation on which Donaldson Smith had established his base in 1895, it was becoming well-worn ground. But 'this was indeed a lovely camp', with shady trees and cool lake breezes inviting the weary and ailing caravan to rest, so Wellby 'considered the present site suitable and healthy enough for a lengthened stay'.

Like many of the other travellers who had preceded him, he could not resist the temptation to investigate the Omo river mystery, for in his mind 'there appeared to be still doubt hanging over the subject'. His exploration of the Omo river was not an extended one, and most of the four days he allocated for the purpose were taken up hunting elephants, which lived in great numbers along the river fringes. It was while out on one of his hunting sprees Wellby came across a 'snow-white hartebeest', a zoological curiosity, which was, in fact, an albino topi. To his annoyance the unique beast managed to survive his efforts to shoot it, and was still living in the same area when a more successful hunter arrived two years later.

Wellby found none of Teleki's numerous Reshiats at the mouth of the Omo; the Abyssinians in their probing raids had seen to that, and it was only on crossing the river to the west bank that he found a few nervous 'Shankallas' skulking in fear of further attacks. Terror, tragically, had by then taken the place of peaceful existence on the remote northern shores of Lake Rudolf, and the caravan found it hard to obtain sufficient grain supplies for their long onward march.

The brief respite on the lake's shores rested Wellby's men, but the anthrax plague continued remorselessly to destroy his valuable animals. The situation was anything but happy as the caravan resumed its march, down the eastern edge of the lake. The ponies were all dead, so Wellby was walking once again; the mules had been reduced in number to the point that many of his valuable elephant tusks had to be given away, and in desperation his men were forced to break in some of the cattle as load carriers. As if that was not enough misfortune, Wellby, who up to that stage had enjoyed robust health, 'met with an unfortunate accident'. While opening a can the blade of the knife he was using slipped and severed half of the first finger of his left hand. Fortunately he suffered no serious ill effects, but he could use his 'hand but little for the remainder of the journey'. The mishap adversely affected his shooting ability, and as a direct consequence his vital meat supplies. Dolefully Wellby commented: 'I found that my wounded hand was far too painful for shooting, and that without it my firing was far from accurate. My shooting for the rest of the journey was practically at an end and I never dared touch a rifle unless the men were hard up for meat'. The supply of game meat from then on was largely dependent on the unpredictable results of less than adequate marksmen. For Wellby, the endless trudging in slow, short stages in the heat of March days was no pleasure, particularly as it had become a grim race against time to reach the south end of the lake before all his animals died. There he hoped to find fresh donkeys and camels from the 'Lokub'* people. Forced by the caravan's frustratingly slow pace, Wellby decided to take a short cut past the barren Longondoti range south of Alia Bay. Up to that time all other travellers had aimed inland of these forbidding hills, thus avoiding the jagged lava slopes which plunged steeply, and almost impassably, into the lake waters. Wellby, with only a waterless alternative, elected to try the lakeside path. It was a horror, and precious hours were spent in the intense heat frantically forcing a track through the blistering rocks. Later, he wrote:

*The 'Lokub' were the Lokob people (Samburu).

'Even now, in spite of our laborious improvements, I should never recommend this route to any future traveller'.

In a last effort to speed up the drearily slow pace of the march, Wellby ordered Shahzad Mir and the headman Hassan to hasten to the end of the lake and find new transport animals. He was then camped near El Molo Bay, and with the aggravation of his wound compounding the worry brought on by the increasingly weakened state of his transport animals, he decided to await his men's return. In a matter of a few days they re-appeared, and to Wellby's pleasure they were driving before them 'a herd of superb donkeys' and a flock of sheep, all appropriated from their owners. An 'exceptionally lovely spot'—today's Loiengalani—was chosen for a camp, where time was spent in breaking in the new donkeys and repairing worn equipment. But the caravan could not tarry for long in its haven, so the tramp through the unpeopled land continued.

The party reached the south end of the lake without incident, passing on the way one of Cavendish's old camping grounds before clambering round the stark black rubble of Teleki's volcano. Soon after they were 'camped at the south west corner of the lake, our very last halt by the edge of this beautiful water ... In spite of its many attractions ... all of us had had a sufficiently big dose of Gallop'. Following Teleki's route of ten years before, Wellby then struck westwards and away from the lake, a place he would never see again.

Cautiously progressing over the hills, Wellby used small advance guards to probe ahead of the caravan. It was all done in the best military fashion, the faithful Mohamed Hassan leading the scouting party as they searched the arid terrain for water supplies and the Turkana. While on one of these reconnaissances Hassan nearly met with disaster. On trying to capture a Turkana he was speared in the back. But he was tough, and Wellby was a competent bush doctor: 'Although he could scarcely walk for a week or two to come, he eventually quite recovered, and was none the worse for his adventure ... His wound proved his impetuosity, for, totally regardless of results, he had run after six giants armed with spears'. This episode was a serious set-back to Wellby's well-meant policy of peaceful negotiation as an alternative to armed conflict, and it was not the last incident of its kind he experienced. Soon afterwards the caravan encountered more Turkana, peaceably on this occasion, which was fortunate as they were able to trade for a few camels. That they were impressively large people is obvious from Wellby's remarks: 'The Turkana warriors, who strolled among the bushes in groups of four and five, were men of prodigious size, many of them perfect giants in their build, with a mass of thick carefully woven hair hanging over their broad shoulders right down to their waist. They carried extraordinarily long spears, and were magnificent specimens of savage strength'. Shortly before reaching the Turkwel river a further encounter with the Turkana left one of his Abyssinians dead. On that occasion, it was the fault of Wellby's trigger-happy men and they learnt their lesson the hard way. From then on the caravan found the Turkana people friendly and helpful, in striking contrast to the type of reception Cavendish had received at the hands of their lakeside cousins two years earlier.

Wellby's plan now took his party in an unwavering north-westerly direction, aiming for the distant Sobat river where he knew he would find terminal outposts manned by Anglo-Egyptian garrisons. Between the Turkwel and Sobat rivers lay a vast empty space, as yet unmarked on maps. This was the tempting target Cavendish and

Donaldson Smith had so keenly set their sights on. Wellby, to his great satisfaction, was on the eve of being the first white man to make the historic crossing. His own words clearly depict the vacuum he was entering: 'As we continued to travel north or north-west, we were in total ignorance of what we were about to encounter each day, for the only information that the maps afforded us was a blank. The three great questions that were our chief consideration were whether we should find water and grass, whether we should meet people and what would be their attitude towards us, and whether we should come across game we could shoot for food. It was the absolute uncertainty that increased the work of every member of the caravan'. Were they to be blocked by uncrossable mountain ranges, stopped by impenetrable forests, or more likely as they approached the Sobat, held up by impassablle swamps? These were the questions Wellby hoped to answer, much to the envy of other kindred spirits.

The account of Wellby's trek, which ranged over almost 500 miles (800 kilometres) of totally unknown Africa, takes one first into the region of the Lotiggipi Swamp, prehistory's ancient link connecting Lake Rudolf and the River Nile. In this basin Wellby found the headwaters of the 'Ruzi' river, which he eventually followed all the way to its junction with the Sobat. The 'Ruzi' today is known as the Pibor. It soon became known to Wellby that 'Ruzi' was simply the word for river in the language of the people living in the area, as he shortly after found yet another 'Ruzi'. Following the two 'Ruzis'—they flowed parallel with one another for some distance—became one interminable tramp over grassy plains, where streams and rivers meandering at will were the only break in the monotonous flatness. On all sides herds of wild beasts roamed freely over the great expanse, while numberless timid peoples skulked fearfully in the distance. In that region the caravan was forced to make frequent crossings over the tributaries flowing into the two 'Ruzis'. It was hard work pulling camels, mules, donkeys and sheep through these rivers; some were shallow, some deep, but most of them mercifully sluggish and slow-flowing. Inevitably several of their long-suffering beasts met their end in the tiresome business, but by that late stage they were nearing their goal, and many of the animals were no longer needed as load carriers. The further the caravan travelled down the 'Ruzi', the swampier the ground became, and marching degenerated into a horribleness which Wellby's story graphically described. 'On, on we floundered, higher and higher rose the water, until, by the time the sun was setting, frogs were croaking, mosquitoes were swarming, and there was a dampness and chilliness in the air that went to our very bones. To have spent the night in such a quagmire would have meant a stepping-stone to the graveyard ... We could scarcely get any wood for our fires, and the mosquitoes were altogether beyond description. Several of the men were overcome with fever and pains in the back and head. All of them I doctored'.

In mid-June, almost one month after the commencement of their journey from the headwaters of the 'Ruzi', the dishevelled expedition marched in an exhausted state into Nasser, the lonely, furthest afield Anglo-Egyptian outpost on the Sobat river. There Wellby met a fellow countryman, 'the commander of the fort himself striding towards me with a smiling countenance, and in a moment afterwards I was receiving a hearty shake of the hand ... from a Britisher—Lieutenant MacEwen'. And there Wellby could at long last, and certainly with considerable satisfaction, lay claim to have completed his arduous mission. But not his walk. The very next day he was on his way to Sobat, 180 miles (290 kilometres) away on the banks of the Nile. From there

*Wellby's transport animals making one of innumerable crossings of the Ruzi rivers.*

downstream to Omdurman he and his men travelled in style—by paddle-steamer. On reaching the desert town he sold the remainder of his animals, said farewell to his five Sudanese, and boarded the train to Cairo. His arrival there marked the end of yet one more exciting story of exploration, and at the same time the solution to another of Africa's long-hidden geographical questions.

On the morning of the 31 July 1899, readers of the *Guardian* would have come across a short item of news that may have attracted their attention. These were some of the correspondent's complimentary words: 'I learn that letters have reached England from Captain Wellby, whose arrival at Omdurman was announced a few days ago from Cairo, and the greatest satisfaction is felt in geographical and other quarters at the successful termination of one of the most interesting expeditions recently undertaken in Africa. Captain Wellby is to be congratulated on having succeeded where others have either failed or have been denied the opportunity of making the attempt to cover the ground over which he has travelled. The region between the northern end of Lake Rudolf and the Sabat was one of the few large areas in Africa that remained to be explored'. What gratification those lines, and many more of like tenor, must have given the bold captain in the months that followed. It was the second major expedition he had completed in a matter of three years, and both had been of considerable geographical importance.

One can only imagine the heights to which Wellby might have risen in the years ahead, but they were not to be, for within one year of his return to England he lay in a lonely grave in southern Africa. He had served his country to the end with distinction, both as a soldier and an explorer—respected occupations in the age through which he lived. He performed the latter in a style most aptly expressed in one last tribute to his name: 'The deceased traveller had a singularly modest and unassuming manner of describing his exploits, the value of which might thus escape the notice of the chance reader, though fully recognised by the initiated. Another pleasing characteristic was his fairness and tact in dealing with the native races, which enabled him to pass unscathed, where many would have met with obstruction and violence'.

# DONALDSON SMITH
# EXPEDITION II 1899–1900

HAVING twice tasted the excitements and challenges of travel in untamed parts of Africa, Donaldson Smith was still not sated, and furthermore, there was another definite mission fixed in his mind, so 'I continually watched for an opportunity to satisfy my desire'. Ever since his expedition to Lake Rudolf he had set his heart on seeing the wonders he felt lay between the lake and the River Nile. The ambition was not confined to his mind alone, for other explorers had expressed hopes of crossing that African backwater during the last few years of the century, amongst whom Wellby had been the first to succeed.

While killing time between his two major African explorations, Donaldson Smith made a journey to Mongolia in 1897. On that trip he was exposed to the abilities of Indian workers, an experience which undoubtedly persuaded him to try them in Africa. So, when the time came for his second expedition to Lake Rudolf, he recruited nineteen Sikhs and nine Gurkhas as his escort. Unfortunately, as later events were to prove, it was an unwise step.

For his starting point he again chose Berbera. In the five years since he had last been there constricting changes had taken place. For one thing it was no longer a straightforward matter to enlist the Somali camel-men he needed. It must have been a frustrating and difficult time for him as he strove to extract permission to cross the borders of Somaliland from 'incomprehensible officials', and argued interminably with obstructive Somali headmen over staff matters. But despite these trying obstacles he met with partial success in the end, and on 1 August 1899 the caravan slipped unobtrusively out of Berbera. Half the size of his first expedition, it consisted of himself, a companion named Fraser, his small contingent of Indians and seventeen Somalis. On the very first day out eleven Sikhs deserted. It was hardly an auspicious start, but with single-minded determination Donaldson Smith kept the reduced caravan on its way, and as they penetrated deeper into Somali country he succeeded in taking on more recruits, gradually building up his corps into a compact and manageable forty-eight men.

Hurrying along the route he had taken in 1894, and cutting a few corners to save time, he passed through already familiar territory. It was not until he reached distant Egder, near to the place where he had hunted the mysterious 'Thompson's [sic] gazelles' on his first trip, that he entered country new to the white man. Aiming directly for the southern tip of Lake Stefanie, the expedition passed through the district in the neighbourhood of Mega, a delightful land where the friendly Borana tended their extensive herds of stock in 'green upland basins'. Plunging down from the 'delicious cool atmosphere' of these highlands, Donaldson Smith next arrived on the hot, low-lying Golbo Plain. Two weeks later his caravan reached Lake Stefanie. In the course of this uneventful trek he climbed the grassy slopes of Mt Janissa (Jabisa), standing in its lonely isolation at the entrance to the Sele Gublo Pass, a broad open valley dominated by the lofty Tertale Mountains on its north side and the Jabisa range to the south. Clambering to the summit of the dominating peak Donaldson Smith was well rewarded with a magnificent and all-embracing view. From his lofty vantage point he could spot far distant ranges of hills in addition to Lakes Rudolf and Stefanie. On the mountain top he was able to check some of the triangulation survey he had done on his earlier expedition in 1895, confirming the accuracy of his former work, 'which I was most pleased to find correct'. The isolated mountain produced another bonus for him: on it he collected two specimens of the elusive little Chanler's reedbuck, an animal he had not previously encountered in the hills around Lake Stefanie.

Continuing its march in a westerly line, the caravan soon arrived on the shores of Lake Rudolf, where another change was found. The Reshiat seemed to have disappeared from the area, and even the Murle tribe on the River Omo were timid and impoverished. The reason for these changes was soon ascertained—Abyssinian raids. There, too, it appeared, the far-reaching depredations of Menelik's men had ruthlessly exploited the unfortunate inhabitants, causing them to flee the region. Luckily, Donaldson Smith managed to find a few remnants of the tribe, who agreed to ferry his party across the Omo and so towards the land of his dreams. From that point on to the Nile, which his party reached on 14 March 1900, three months later, they traversed a largely unknown region, one in which endless-seeming flat plains were punctuated by isolated and alluring mountain ranges. They encountered strange new peoples of Nilotic character who tended their herds and tilled the soil, and a fauna quite at variance with that of the eastern areas. It was an immense contrast to the desiccated wastes of the Somali peoples, with which they were so well acquainted, but very rewarding for Donaldson Smith's interests as a naturalist and surveyor. His specimen boxes were duly filled with new and rare species, his assiduous surveys cross-checked and corrected the work of earlier travellers, and 'I was enabled to lay down in detail over 500 miles (800 kilometres) of previously unmapped country between occasional known lines'. Furthermore, to his credit, his peaceful crossing of the territory left behind a succession of friendly native peoples.

At the conclusion of his long journey Donaldson Smith could claim once again to have achieved what he had set out to do, and in characteristic manner he had done it with meticulous care. His contributions to the advancement of geographical and scientific knowledge proved to be invaluable, and it was generally accepted that he would return to continue his explorations in those unknown regions. But a new century had started, and with it Donaldson Smith's interest in Africa waned; he had other ambitions to distract him and he never returned on a visit of exploration.

# HARRISON EXPEDITION
## 1899–1900

EXACTLY fifteen weeks after Donaldson Smith had stealthily left Berbera at the start of his second expedition, another party of explorers left the neighbouring maritime station of Zeila with the same goal in view—to cross from the northern end of Lake Rudolf to Fashoda on the Nile. Wellby had triumphed on becoming the first European to establish a geographical link between the lake and the Nile, but there were still many corners into which he had not penetrated, and the next two parties were more than anxious to be the first to visit these unexplored places. While it is not certain whether Donaldson Smith knew of Wellby's success before his departure from Berbera, the second party, led by a Yorkshireman called Harrison, was fully aware of the hussar officer's achievement. It did not deter them from their plan, needless to say, and the seven white men—Harrison, Powell-Cotton, Butter and Whitehouse, together with a taxidermist, Perks, a qualified surveyor, and Butter's manservant, Daniel—sailed to Aden filled with the zeal of those anticipating new challenges, both geographical and sporting. The sporting aspect was foremost in their minds; the geographical interest was supported by the inclusion of a surveyor on the expedition staff. The latter move may have been a form of window dressing, whereby the hunters could justify their pleasures and, if they were deserving, maybe even earn them a touch of fame. As events proved, sport did in fact outweigh geography, but not overwhelmingly. The Royal Engineer cartographer's painstaking work in the field produced a series of exquisite topographical drawings, of such accuracy that the Royal Geographical Society's mapmaker was able to produce useful maps of the country they traversed. In the sportsmen's defence it must be added that they did manage to survey a few corners of previously unknown terrain.

*   *   *

The four leading members of Harrison's group were, despite their differing origins, bound by a mutual interest in big-game hunting. James Jonathan Harrison, the eldest by several years, and with fourteen years of experience in the game fields of Africa and India behind him, was their leader. He was the son of the squire of Brandesburton Hall, a handsome red-brick Yorkshire house hidden away in the tranquil countryside some dozen miles north of the busy port of Hull. Harrison's early life was filled with outdoor activities in keeping with his place as the son of the county's Deputy Lieutenant—shooting, riding and hunting. His education at the famous public school in Harrow was followed by a spell at Oxford's Christ Church, which he entered in 1876. During this period, Harrison struggled with chronic ill health and finally had to leave the college after attending only two and a half terms out of the six he was enrolled, having earned no academic or sporting awards. In 1884 he joined the Prince of Wales's Own Yorkshire Hussars, a local territorial unit in which he served intermittently for twenty-one years, eventually rising to the senior rank of lieutenant-colonel. The first of his many sporting trips overseas was made in 1885, and thereafter he became a fervent hunter. The products of his journeys filled Brandesburton with an immense store of game trophies, which was then considered one of the largest private collections in England. Not only did the larger size specimens stare down glassy-eyed from the walls of his home, but numerous samples of birds and small mammals were present too, all silent reminders of his wanderings in distant parts of the globe.

Although a slight man in build, Harrison was full of physical energy and kept himself busily occupied in a broad range of interests. His regular hunting trips overseas were interspersed with the responsibilities of an officer in the territorial army, and, like his father before him, he dutifully did a turn as a Justice of the Peace. Cricket, the traditional summer game of England, was another of his favourite pleasures. In contrast, between all these activities he even found time to practise the gentler art of the author, writing books on his sporting excursions in India and Africa. The life he led was too full to entertain thoughts of early marriage, and when finally he took that step he was already fifty-two years old. Harrison's life was not overly long in span, but it certainly hadn't been a dull one. He successfully managed to pack in a formidable amount of globe-trotting before his energy and health finally failed him in 1923.

\*       \*       \*

Harrison succeeded in persuading a kindred spirit to join his expedition to Africa. Percy Horace Gordon Powell-Cotton, or plain Percy as he chose to be called by his friends, came from the English county of Kent, and was eight years younger than Harrison. The Cotton family had at one time been wealthy London merchants and had also been closely associated with India, two generations having served as sea captains with the East India Company and one with the Indian Army. On the other hand the relationship with the Powells was established by an early inheritance of estates through a maternal affiliation dating from his grandmother's time. With the Powell connection came substantially more wealth. John Powell had been one of George III's secretaries, and possessed estates in the south of England. In the late eighteenth century he purchased the Kent estate in Thanet which remains to this day in the hands of the Powell-Cotton family. In the latter part of the nineteenth century Percy, in a joint decision with his brother and sister, decided to hyphenate the two family names, and thereafter they used the surname Powell-Cotton.

In a peaceful corner of the Thanet estate, close by England's eastern extremity, a substantial home—Quex House—was constructed by the Cottons in the early years of the nineteenth century. Later, in 1883, it was extensively enlarged and improved. Sitting in the quiet of the gentle Kentish countryside this solid house is a superb example of those comfortable bulwarks from which the English landed gentry of bygone years surveyed the world at large with a self-satisfied and patronising contentment. Quex House was Percy Powell-Cotton's home, and on his father's death in 1894 the young man of twenty-eight fell heir to the house and surrounding estate.

Born to parents who did not excel in business acumen, but were, nevertheless, happily blessed with contented dispositions, it was soon apparent that Powell-Cotton had inherited his mother's restless spirit. The youngster early showed an interest in making collections of natural history specimens, stamps and coins, indicating an ordered mind quite at variance with those of his parents. At twenty-one he made his

*Harrison's party taken in Nairobi at the end of their expedition, 1900. (standing l. to r.) Perks, Clarke, (seated l. to r.) Harrison, Butter, Whitehouse.*

*Percy Horace Gordon Powell-Cotton as a young man.*

first extensive trip out of England—around the world. Significantly, this journey marked the first step in what turned out to be a lifetime of travel through many parts of Asia and Africa, the start of a life dedicated to the collection of ethnic and zoological curiosities. Between 1887 and 1939 Powell-Cotton made the astounding total of twenty-eight collecting expeditions on the two continents. To house his growing hoard of specimens he founded the famous Powell-Cotton Museum based on his home at Quex House. These words from the Museum handbook give a befitting description of this remarkable man's efforts in the field of nature study: 'He made an unrivalled personal collection of the larger mammals of Africa and Asia and, realizing that many species were threatened with extinction, he was concerned to preserve rare and representative specimens for study and popular interest. He was a pioneer in the exhibition of the larger mammals against a representation of their natural habitat'. Powell-Cotton was not only a traveller, explorer and hunter; he also served for some time as a militiaman, eventually becoming an officer in the Northumberland Fusiliers. Furthermore, with his interest in hunting, he trained in, and in turn trained, courses in musketry, a qualification which served him well in big-game country. His activities in public affairs were sporadic, but he did officiate intermittently as a Justice of the Peace over a period of thirty-six years, and at one point even involved himself on the fringe of Conservative politics. His frequent absences overseas, however, interrupted the continuity of these occupations.

He was described by his son as 'a quiet, courteous and kindly man. He ... was observant and thoughtful ... Conscientious in business and in public affairs, somewhat reserved, he did not make friends easily but ... was well-liked and respected'. Powell-Cotton was in essence somewhat of a loner, preferring to travel and hunt by himself, so it remains a mystery how he was talked into joining Harrison's party. Maybe it was simply the attraction of visiting and hunting in a new territory which drew him, reluctantly, into the venture, one that for him personally did not prove a success. But the initial disappointment ended in a favourable outcome, and on his return to England many months later, after a journey which had carried him through a country hardly visited by white man, he took home yet more valuable specimens of rare animals to festoon the walls of Quex House.

*     *     *

The third Britisher in the party, Archibald Butter, came from his estate in the hills of Perthshire. Only twenty-five years old when he was offered a place on the Harrison expedition, a hunting trip to Africa was a proposition he could not resist. Unlike Harrison and Powell-Cotton, Butter had never been to that continent, although, as a keen deer-stalker and bird shooter on the moors and hills of his native Scotland, he felt well-qualified to try his skills amongst the great beasts of Africa. It was, therefore, only natural for Butter to join Harrison's expedition with the enthusiasm of youth on the threshold of high adventure and discoveries. For him it turned out to be an invaluable experience, one that prepared him for a decidedly more important role in east Africa in the years ahead.

*     *     *

The young American in the party, William Fitz Hugh Whitehouse, was born in Elmhurst, Illinois, in 1877. The name Fitz Hugh proclaims his family's English lineage, a connection that was maintained by his father, whose practice as an international lawyer enabled him to spend his winters working in London. Young William was given a stern, disciplined English education: he first attended Cheam School in Surrey at the age of nine, and later studied for four years at Winchester College, the renowned public school which had celebrated its five-hundredth anniversary just a few years before his arrival. William's education was rounded off in his homeland, at Yale, where he graduated with honours in history and economics. As soon as he left he was on his way to England again, this time to join Harrison's party in its preparation for an expedition to Africa.

Whitehouse was by then a sturdy, well-built young man, over six foot in height, and a splendid athlete—he was heavyweight boxing champion of his class at Yale. Moreover, he was a keen and skilled marksman with both rifle and shotgun. Outgoing and gregarious, he was a decidedly popular young man who delighted in the company of his fellow-men. To top it all he had been born with the qualities of a leader, which are clearly evident from his personal account of the journey he took with Harrison. Reading through the slim volume—only eighty pages—one senses that he was a somewhat egotistical individual. He barely mentioned the part his companions played, and gave the distinct impression that the onus of leadership during the whole trip rested on his shoulders alone. But maybe one should be charitable and simply put his style down to the youthful zest of his ilk.

The attractions of life in Africa lured him into another visit to the same region two years later, this time in the company of an English friend, Lord Hindlip. At its end Whitehouse returned to America and settled down to the profession of investment finance in New York. At that stage in his life he counted Theodore Roosevelt among his friends. They shared a mutual love of the great outdoors, and Roosevelt often consulted him on matters relating to hunting in the gamefields of east Africa. Besides business commitments Whitehouse's active nature took him along other and varied paths: he was one of the first to hold a free balloon pilot's licence; he served with the 77th Infantry Division in the trenches of the First World War, where, although mildly gassed, he survived to end the war with the rank of major; and he was twice a successful Republican contender for the seat of Newport State Senator. In addition to his business interests he played an enthusiastic part in community affairs, and busied himself with the activities of a wide variety of institutions, including among them his church, the Boy Scout movement and the Freemasons. When he died in 1953 at the age of seventy-six, Whitehouse was held in high esteem by the members of the Newport society in which he had lived and served so energetically during his busy life.

*   *   *

The direction in which Harrison's expedition intended to travel is clearly defined in Powell-Cotton's words: 'It was at this time that Mr J.J. Harrison proposed that I should join the party he was organising to go from the Somali coast across the north of Lake Rudolf, and through unexplored country between the point where the Omo runs into that lake and Fashoda'. Wellby in fact had already covered most of this ground, and Donaldson Smith—striding immediately ahead of them—would complete even more investigations in the area. As it turned out Harrison never did continue on from the lake to the Nile.

It should be recalled that the four key characters on this trip were all keen sportsmen, two of whom had previous experience in the gamefields of Africa. In the early days of African travel this would have been considered a distinct advantage. In the case of Harrison's expedition it was quite clear that at least one member, Powell-Cotton, considered the shooting aspect of more importance than exploration and survey, his later writings unequivocally showing his personal feelings on the matter: 'At first I feared there would be more exploration than sport, owing to the transport difficulties involved in this tour, but being reassured on this point, I decided to join the expedition'. In the early stages Powell-Cotton was the only member of the party of seven white men who had 'any experience of Somaliland shooting', so, during the planning period anyway, he proved an invaluable aide for Harrison. Indeed, one wonders whether Harrison invited him to join the expedition for this very reason. It is a question that will probably remain unanswered.

A few months before the expedition was due to depart from England, Harrison, in his capacity of chief organiser, tried a little fund-raising. Writing to Dr Keltie, then Secretary of the Royal Geographical Society, in July 1899, he put his case briefly:

Dear Sir,
In case our trip from Berbera to Lake Rudolf and then attempt to explore the country down to the Sobat river, comes off this autumn, could we not interest the Geographical Society to aid us with a grant towards taking out a fully qualified man to map and take observations. I have all but £1000 required for such a trip and it seems a great pity for a small sum in comparison to what we are spending over it, not to take a proper man. Hoping your Society may be induced to give us some financial assistance in the matter.
  Yours very truly,
  James J. Harrison

It was an ineffectual effort on Harrison's part. Keltie responded bluntly, and with good reasons. Firstly, the Royal Geographical Society was not endowed with adequate funds, and certainly not enough to subsidise a surveyor on an expedition to territory much of which was already known. Secondly, Wellby was almost home, having just traversed practically the same route Harrison planned on taking. Keltie's words on the matter of funds were quite explicit: 'You say you have all but £1,000 of the sum required. If this is not a mistake for £100, it seems rather a large deficit. Even if the Council were satisfied that you were likely to do really substantial geographical work, I feel sure they would not be disposed to grant anything like that sum'.

Despite Harrison's fruitless plea to the Society, the shortfall of £1,000 was found from the party's own pockets, and a suitable surveyor signed on. Donald Clarke, a sergeant in the Royal Engineers, was the chosen man. A surveyor with at least twenty years of experience in Africa, he was well-qualified to do his job without complaint. He was a good choice. At the end of the expedition words of high praise came from Harrison's pen: 'I cannot close this paper without once more calling attention to the splendid work done by our Surveyor, Donald Clarke; no day was long enough for him, and no mountain too high to be climbed, after ever such a long weary march and in the heat of the day. One feature we particularly admired was, he never would insert a yard of country unless seen by himself or vouched for by one of us. When in camp his kind cheery manner endeared him to all'. Stored in the depths of the Royal Geographical Society's map room are a set of his topographical drawings. Gems of the surveyor's art, the pencil-shaded features, almost three-dimensional in perspective, rise from the paper and show clearly the nature of the country through which the expedition marched. The Society was not, however, wholly unco-operative with Harrison. While they were unable to assist with the funds, they were happy to provide a set of instruments for Clarke to use in his survey work, and afterwards their mapmaker drew up the final maps.

On 5 November 1899 the four men arrived at Aden on the first step of their long journey. No time was wasted there. The very next day the group landed on the forbidding shore of Somaliland. A further 'five days' hard work' in the dreariness of Zeila completed their preparations. Fortuitously, Wellby's friend Captain Harrington also happened to be in Zeila, and he, too, was making ready to depart with a large caravan for the capital of Abyssinia. In his usual helpful manner he dispensed encouragement and advice to the optimistic group, giving them the good news that Menelik had granted them permission to travel on a road which would take them north of the customary track through Jig Jigga and Harar. This was welcome information indeed, as it gave the expedition the opportunity to visit the little-known valley of the Awash river.

Sunday, 12 November 1899 was a red-letter day for Harrison as he marched out from Zeila at the head of his band of sixty-one Somalis, many of them veterans of caravan life who had been travel-hardened from service with Cavendish, Delamere, Donaldson Smith and Wellby. Leading the men and sixty camels—a compact party compared with Delamere's lumbering entourage—was the redoubtable Mohamed Hassan, only recently returned from his latest visit to England after his success with Wellby. Hopes were high, despite the unfavourable climatic conditions that prevailed: there had been a two year drought of disastrous proportions in east Africa and the land lay parched and desolate before them. This did not deter the sportsmen from pursuing their game as they trudged along, and soon the list of animals felled by their rifles grew; gazelles of various species, antelopes, pigs, hares and sundry birds of all sizes were amongst the specimens quickly skinned out and salted away. Every day, as the caravan advanced deeper into the continent, the barking of guns continued, giving Perks the taxidermist and his assistants work in plenty.

For the first month of the party's march all went well; the sport was excellent, and many specimens were collected. Due to its deviation away from the well-established trading route between Berbera and Addis Ababa, Harrison's caravan experienced some obstruction from the wild and less closely administered tribes living in the region. But they surmounted these difficulties with tact, and on 19 December the group safely reached the banks of the Awash river. Ominously, the approach march to this substantial river—'some 40 yards [37 metres] across and 6 feet [2 metres] deep'—was marked by the first sign of discord in the expedition's story. Foreseeably it arose between Harrison and Powell-Cotton, the two great trophy and specimen collectors, and it clearly indicated the difference in these two men's attitudes towards their hobby. Harrison, it appears from all accounts, was more bloodthirsty about his hunting; Powell-Cotton, on the other hand, was probably more dedicated to the collecting of specimens for science.

Friction first arose after an elephant shoot. Harrison started the action before lunch when he killed two elephants with poor ivory. Anxious to shoot some more, ostensibly with the intention of collecting ivory as a presentation gift to Menelik, Harrison talked the others into an afternoon hunt. It turned out to be a hectic affair: elephants careering through the bush in all directions, desperate charges being thwarted by volleys from large-bore rifles, and hairbreadth escapes by the hunters. Most nerve-racking of all, it took place in thick riverine forest. Powell-Cotton's regretful comments in his later account read: 'The net result of our hunt was, that H. killed five elephants, and W. and B. one each, while I had also seen two drop. As none of the natives here eat the flesh it seemed a pity to have killed so many for the sake of such small ivory, and I was sorry I had taken part in the hunt'. Powell-Cotton's thought was well warranted. On weighing the 'small ivory' it only came out at a paltry 17 pounds (7½ kilograms) per tusk, an embarrassing fact for which Captain Harrington later made apologies to Menelik, adding that he had reprimanded the hunters for their thoughtless action. That night, in the quiet of his tent, Powell-Cotton wrote tersely in his diary: 'J.J. and I had words apropros of shooting elephants whether with tusks or not'. He was on his own in his feelings, for the other three were euphoric, Whitehouse and Butter having triumphantly bagged 'their first tusker'.

While the expedition rested for one week on the banks of the Awash river, Christmas Day 1899 was celebrated and a sumptuous dinner was enjoyed in traditional manner, followed by toasts in champagne to the success of the trip. The very next day Harrison ordered a quick detour march to Addis Ababa so the party could pay their respects to the Emperor. As the capital was just 100 miles (160 kilometres) away, only a small escort of six men was needed to accompany the white men there, the rest of the caravan remaining in camp under the charge of Clarke, who was 'glad to have time to go over all his work, and complete his mapping work up to date'.

In the previous two weeks Clarke had been successful in making an accurate survey of a little known tract of country, a wild stretch hardly visited even by the Abyssinians themselves. It was there that a trait peculiar to this expedition first showed itself—giving the names of expedition members and parts of their home country to topographical features. The practise was, of course, not unusual, for countless other explorers had done the same thing around the world, and even Donaldson Smith on his first expedition had given his name to two features. However, on this occasion, the difference appeared in the sheer number of prominent landmarks that received alien names. As the caravan proceeded on its way down the spine of Abyssinia to Lake Stefanie, names were liberally handed out, appearing on the final map as Clinton Range, Edith Lake, Brandesburton Range, Whitehouse Range, York Range, James Peak, Mt Clarke, Mt Faskally—the name of Butter's Scottish estate—and Harrison Range, to mention but a few. It was self-gratification in an almost puerile form, and quite uncalled for, especially if one bears in mind that Bottego, Donaldson Smith and Wellby had covered much of the same ground and found no cause to indulge in such an orgy of name-giving. The matter did not pass unnoticed. Eyebrows were later raised in the Royal Geographical Society—Dr Keltie's among others. Forthwith he wrote to Harrison on the matter, outlining the officially recognised procedure for the naming of newly discovered places. Clearly, it was a formality Harrison should have checked on before leaving for Africa. In due course Harrison replied, apologising for the *faux pas*, but writing defensively: 'I regret the enclosed notes on "naming places" has never been given me before, but you can rely on Clarke having retained every name known or used by natives. He always tried both Abyssinian and Galla for every place—and kept a careful list of anything without any local name'. This was a very diaphanous cover for someone's peccadillo. Had Clarke been slack in his questioning of the natives, or had Harrison indulged in a series of ostentatious declarations? More probably the latter, as after all he was master of the exercise.

On New Year's Day 1900 the Harrison party walked into Addis Ababa, where they were welcomed by Captain Harrington. While in the capital Harrison was forced to reach two important decisions. The first one came as a result of a warning from reliable sources that the drought in the south of the country and around Lake Rudolf would create problems for his journey; it was an unavoidable circumstance that prevented them making the crossing to the River Nile, and forced the caravan to proceed at a pace faster than the eager hunters intended. Consequently, Harrison decided to forego his hunting ambitions until he reached more hospitable country. This led to a second problem—Powell-Cotton. Hunting was his main interest, and the thought of being deprived of this was the last straw for him. Ever since the Awash river he and Harrison had not seen eye to eye, and with the prospect of limited hunting opportunities ahead, Powell-Cotton, a lone wolf at the best of times, decided to leave the expedition. His diary entry for 1 January was terse: 'off at 7.30 after a row with J.J. about his way of running things'. On 3 January another entry finalised the issue: 'I drop out of trip as J.J. and I can't hit it off'. One last meeting on 17 January between the four principal members of the party discussed the winding up of their financial arrangements, and the very next day they parted company—Powell-Cotton to pursue his lonely course and hunt ibex in the remote and almost unknown Simien Mountains in the north, and Harrison, Butter and Whitehouse to continue on their march to Lake Rudolf in the south.

From Addis Ababa to the end of their journey Harrison's expedition could claim no discoveries of great significance. Its route to the south end of Lake Rudolf was

*A typical camp scene with Clarke posed by his theodolite.*

almost a carbon copy of Wellby's march of exactly a year before, following the well-worn native tracks that wound their way across the mountains. Climbing the prominent Mt Zukwala south of Addis Ababa, two members of the party, Butter and Clarke, visited the crater lake in its centre, which Wellby had described as a 'lake of wonderful beauty'. Despite Wellby's earlier visit the explorers were eager to give it another name, so it was duly 'called by us Butter Lake'. Harrison's route to Lake Rudolf was not overly ambitious, and his written account added little that was new. He travelled under Menelik's aegis, as Wellby had done the year before, so there were no obstructions of human making on the road. Nevertheless, the physical ones remained, and it was hard work for the camels as they clambered over the steep and often slippery mountain ranges. With a great sense of relief the caravan eventually descended to the hot lowlands in the vicinity of Lake Stefanie.

One great disappointment for the hunters on approaching the once elephant-rich country to the north of the lake was to discover that the Abyssinians had made severe inroads into the population of these beasts in their pursuit of ivory. Mournfully, Harrison noted: 'alas! they are a thing of the past, cleared out by the constant shooting of Abyssinian soldiers'. The southernmost Abyssinian posts on the Hamar Koke range had been deeply involved in the massive slaughter, and tragically it had all happened in a matter of three or four years. Fifteen hundred soldiers were employed in killing elephants for the Emperor, and in the two months prior to Harrison's arrival they had despatched one thousand, five hundred tusks to Addis Ababa. In the year Harrison made his journey, ivory represented over 20 per cent of Abyssinian exports from Addis Ababa and Harar. It was a significant statistic, and with the Abyssinian budget leaning so heavily on them the elephants had poor hopes of survival.

The excessive drought had created a desolate wasteland around Lake Stefanie at the close of the nineteenth century, and Harrison's caravan was discouraged to find the lake and its environs desiccated. Even its feeder, the Sagan river, was bone dry, and had it not been for several violent thunderstorms the party's position would have been critical. Pushing on over the Hamar Koke range, now abandoned by the Abyssinians on account of the severity of the drought, the natives disheartened Harrison with the depressing and unnerving information that his next target, Lake Rudolf, contained water 'unfit for drinking', and anyone 'drinking from it died'. The expedition was fortunate enough to have experienced exceptional rainstorms during the height of the dry season, for without this supply of water there would have been no possible way across the desolate lowlands between the sister lakes. It took the party four days of hard trekking to reach Lake Rudolf's shore, where it found, providentially, the water was far from poisonous.

Harrison had now reached an important milestone in his travels, and it turned out to be full of surprises for him. One of these was the famed Omo river. For all previous explorers the river had proved to be an obstacle, but for Harrison it turned out to be a decision maker in a quite different way. He had earlier decided that if it was found flowing strongly the expedition would make an attempt to march on the Nile. He did, however, have a suspicion of what he might find: 'On March 31 we left camp early and rode up to visit the Omo and Murle, having decided, if this big river was dry, to work out south by the lake to the Uganda railway. All the thick scrub and timber which should have been alive with elephant, was almost dead, with never a sign of living beast or bird. Passing villages, we came on to the banks of the Omo, and with sad hearts ate our lunch in the middle of the dry stream, while our mules fed on the green luxuriant grass, which had covered the whole dried-up bed'. His mind had been made up for him, and he opted to return homewards by the well-worn route down the east side of the lake.

*Harrison's armed Somali escort, which accompanied him on the six month journey.*

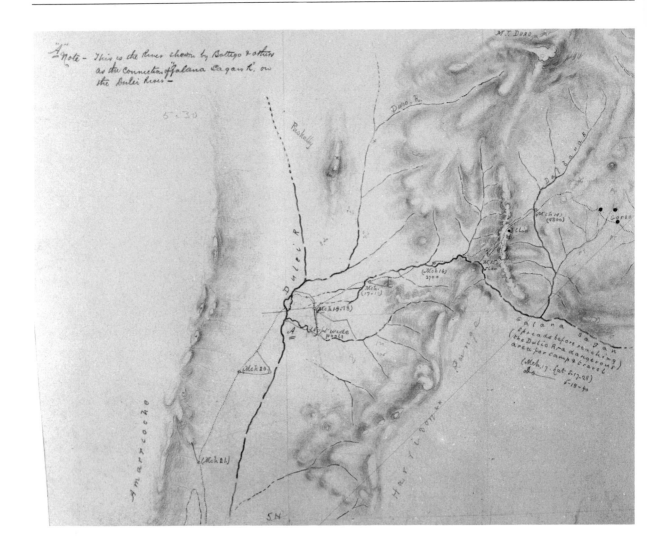

*A sample of Segt Donald Clarke's immaculate topographical drawing.*

While on his short visit to the Omo, Harrison undertook a little chore for his Queen. Sending his men up a tall acacia tree, 'we hoisted the English flag; doing so at the request of Colonel Harrington and with the acquiescence of the Emperor, to denote the Abyssinian and English boundary line'. While the flag was being raised 'God save the Queen' was sung by the little band of white men, followed by a toast with champagne. It was all the heady stuff of empire building. The flag raising was a token gesture, but historically it was the very first official element of boundary making by the British in the vicinity of Lake Rudolf. The event was to prove especially significant for Butter, who unbeknown to him at the time, was two years later to lead an extensive boundary commission survey through the region.

Another surprise for the expedition was the complete dearth of human inhabitants—a striking contrast to the scene which had welcomed Teleki, Neumann and others in earlier and more hospitable years.

The third surprise was the wealth of game, and with this Harrison and his party were certainly pleased. One trophy in particular they looked for—Captain Wellby's famed white topi. Mohamed Hassan had often talked about the deviant animal, and to

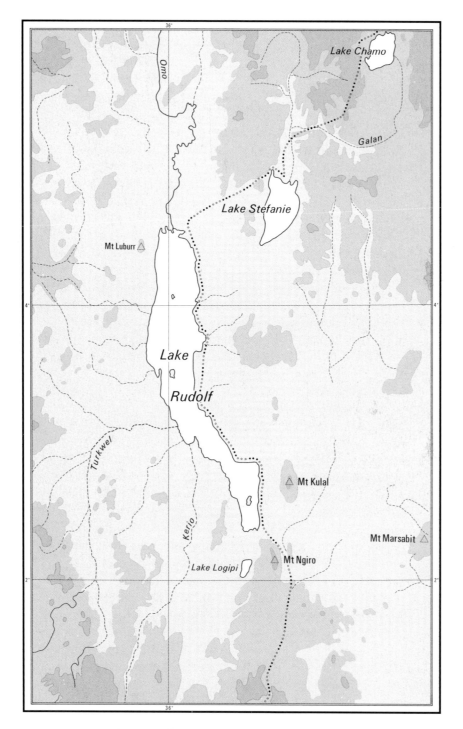

*The route of the Harrison Expedition 1899–1900.*

their amazement, there it was waiting for them on the shores of Lake Rudolf. Harrison had first stalk and, like Wellby before him, failed. Butter made the next attempt, and succeeded. 'Splendid luck!' Harrison exclaimed. Today the extraordinary beast may be found standing in an annexe of the Royal Museum of Scotland at Newbattle on the outskirts of Edinburgh, a reminder, along with Butter's other trophies, of his sporting activities in Africa.

It was obvious the expedition could not stop for long on the Omo. With no Reshiat food supplies to replenish its stocks, the caravan was forced to make haste southwards and homewards. Eighteen days of steady marching brought it to the southern extremity of the lake, and on 19 April Harrison's party finally left the lake shore and struggled up the lava-strewn hill Teleki had first descended twelve years before. Winding past Mt Ngiro, over the grass-covered Elbarta Plains, on up the long wooded slopes onto the Lorogi plateau, down the steep escarpment to Lake Baringo, the caravan finally reached the railhead in the vicinity of Naivasha. There, Harrison disposed of his transport animals: the mules went to the railway, the camels and donkeys to some itinerant Indian traders. The expedition members then boarded a train to journey down the last lap to Mombasa. Their travels had lasted exactly six months, in the course of which they had covered a distance of almost fifteen hundred miles. Their health record had been good, for only one man, a Galla, had died on the way, and with the exception of Clarke's single attack of fever, the white men had enjoyed robust good health throughout. In that respect, at least, the expedition had been a resounding success.

On reviewing Harrison's exploits through the words of surviving documents one feature stands out: the speed with which the journey was done. Nowhere does one read of camps made in one spot for several weeks, giving men and animals a chance to rest and recover their strength. Harrison must have been a hard driver, and speed appears to have been the rigid rule, a fact his computations seem to confirm: 'Pushing on we reached Railhead on May 15, having done 103 miles [165 kilometres] from Baringo in four and a half days—a fine performance, after our camels had done 1,453 miles [2,325 kilometres] at an average of 11½ [18½] a day'. It had been a cracking pace indeed, and the industrious Clarke would have been hard put to it on occasion keeping up with his surveying work. One can only admire the diligence he must have applied in the course of this frantic tramp across the wilds of Africa.

While Harrison's expedition may not have returned to England with a surfeit of new geographical and scientific facts, excepting the animal specimens for Brandesburton Hall and Quex House, one vital function was served: the grounding Butter received for what was probably the most important mission of his life. What Archibald Butter learned on this expedition proved of immense value in 1902, when he led the crucial survey of the boundary territory between Abyssinia and the British East Africa Protectorate. Looked at in hindsight, this reason, if no other, could be said to justify Harrison's expedition in the eyes of the geographical world.

There is one last comment to make on Harrison's journey. It may rightfully be regarded as a watershed in the annals of exploration in eastern Africa, forming a link between the pioneering days of the nineteenth century explorer and the age of the twentieth century traveller, when blackpowder guns were finally deferring to cordite rifles, and territorial rights were moving out of the hands of the original landowners into the grasp of the imperialist powers.

# AUSTIN EXPEDITION 1901

IN the closing decades of the nineteenth century, the British showed increasing interest in the specialised science of geography. It was almost an acquisitive interest, engendered by Britain's scheme for continued expansion in its imperial possessions. One distinguished member in the circle of Englishmen who made a close study of the subject was Sir Cuthbert Peek. Before he died at the early age of forty-six, he gave generously in his patronage of scientific research. A large share of his enthusiasm was channelled into the activities of the Royal Geographical Society, which he had joined in 1875: he lent much of his time serving on the council, and in his latter years was appointed as one of the Society's trustees. During the same period, he had, coincidentally, made a few minor exploration journeys of his own. As a result of this deep involvement with geography, Peek saw fit to offer the Society a sum of money 'to aid in the advancement of Geographical research'. He instructed the Society to invest the funds and use the annual interest to reward 'explorers who do not receive a money grant from the general funds of the Society'. The recipient of his prize—the Cuthbert Peek Grant—would receive a certificate signed by officials of the Society 'testifying (1) that he has sufficient practical knowledge of astronomy to enable him to fix positions with regard to their latitude and longitude; and (2) that he is able to survey, and make a sketch map of a tract of country'. The winner of the Grant also had to possess an adequate knowledge of geology and economic botany. In 1906, following the council's ponderous annual deliberations, the Cuthbert Peek Grant was awarded to a deserving officer from the Royal Engineers, in recognition of the 'high geographical value of your various expeditions between 1891 and 1901'. During those years the industrious engineer had worked on several arduous expeditions in Africa and India. Into the bargain, most of them had involved him in extremely hazardous situations, with considerable danger to his life. The major, when asked whether he had any preference for his prize, responded that a gold watch and chain was the very thing he wanted. His request was granted, and he duly received a handsome gold half-hunter.

*The gold half-hunter inscribed and presented to Austin on his receipt of the Cuthbert Peek Grant in 1906.*

Many years after Austin received his gold watch, Sir Frederick Jackson wrote a brief personal reminiscence of the young engineer officer he first met at Tsavo in East Africa: 'During our enforced stay at that dreary spot (Tsavo river, 1892) our spirits were never allowed to flag, as we were fortunate in having the most irrepressible and cheerful companion I ever travelled with, H. H. Austin R.E. supported by his delightful little fox terrier and a banjo'. At the time the two men met, Austin was on his second major railway survey, and just at the beginning of a long and successful military career.

\*     \*     \*

The second son of a colonel in the Indian army, Herbert Henry Austin was six years old when he left Burma, the country in which he was born on 1 June 1868. The first stage of his life, as he moved with his parents from one military cantonment to another, was a

*Major Herbert Henry Austin, R. E.*

happy, carefree existence. His mother, from his own description, must have been a wonderful woman: bright, cheerful, totally unselfish and highly revered by her burgeoning family, she ended up producing a brood of six boys and one girl. It appears from all accounts that young Bertie, as he was known to the family and friends, was fortunate in having his mother's pleasing nature, a godsend that must have stood him in good stead during the many trying periods of his busy life. In 1874 he travelled to England in the company of his mother and an elder brother, and there he was put to school. Although no scholar, by dint of sheer hard work, young Austin made the grade in the succession of schools he attended, ending with Clifton College in Bristol. The two and a half years he spent there were undistinguished, but he did achieve positions in his house teams for his ability at cricket, football and fives, and even represented the school at gymnastics.

Austin had by then decided that his future lay in an army career, and to that end he studied for the entrance examinations with a driven intensity far in advance of his years. Without question he was both diligent and industrious; they were facets of his character that enabled him to overcome his scholastic difficulties, and rewarded him with an acceptance to a course at the Royal Military Academy in Woolwich.

At the famous academy Austin excelled, but not without considerable effort, as his own words express: 'I must confess I never ceased slaving deep into the night, and nearly nightly'. In the field of sport, too, he achieved a modicum of brief fame, receiving colours for his place in the cricket team—wicket-keeper was his position—and being capped for representing the academy at rugby. Those days were contented ones for Austin, but financially somewhat cramped. They could not have been otherwise, as his father, despite the rank of colonel, had to bring up a family of seven solely on his army pay; there was neither family wealth and influence nor substantial private income to ease the way. That state of affairs may have been one reason why Austin aimed to join the Royal Engineers. Undeterred, his industry finally earned him a place on the list of successful candidates for the School of Military Engineering at Chatham in Kent. The two years he spent at that celebrated army institution were satisfyingly busy—'the cheeriest of my youth'—filled with all the work and social pastimes a young second lieutenant could want.

Austin's working life began shortly after the completion of his course at Chatham in February 1889, the same month that Teleki and von Höhnel were visiting Abyssinia on the way home from their east African expedition. His first posting was to India, and it was there he met the man with whom he was to share a great friendship and many adventures in the years to follow—Lieutenant J.R.L. Macdonald. Under his command Austin was engaged in strenuous survey duties in the rugged mountains of India's North West Frontier, while at the same time tolerating the occasional ministrations of local tribesmen who took pleasure in sniping at the British working parties. A brief break with India in 1891-2 took him, again under Macdonald, into the depths of east Africa, on the preliminary survey of yet another famous railway line—the Uganda Railway. In 1897, after a few more years of work in India at his forte—railway survey—Austin received another call from his old compatriot Macdonald, now a colonel. He was asked to join the British expedition to Fashoda, a request he accepted with delight: 'Thus it came about that I was once more to resume my acquaintance with the African continent, for which I often sighed in vain when bored by the ordinary dull routine of cantonment life in India'. Despite the expedition's failure to achieve its main objective, Austin was successful in his leadership of a digression to Lake Rudolf in 1898. Marching up the western side of the lake, he and his caravan arrived at the mouth of the Omo river, which they then followed for three days before shortage of food supplies, and more threatening, the presence of smallpox in the Murle people, drove them back. It was a three-month tramp, mostly through Turkana country, where the inhabitants forcibly tried to obstruct him, and, in turn, were forcibly dealt with. For Austin, the journey, although a short one, was important in that it introduced him to the region lying to the west of the lake, a tract of country which he was destined to visit again a few years later.

Following his last major African expedition in 1901, Austin was awarded the C.M.G. (Companion of the Order of St Michael and St George). It was an honour earned the hard way, and complemented the military award of the Distinguished Service Order he had earlier received for actions in the Uganda Mutiny. By then he was a brevet-major. All those distinctions had been achieved by hard, trying work: of the thirteen years he lived in the tropics, at least eight and a half had been spent under canvas, and he couldn't accept a Boundary Commission job in 1901 because 'I was still convalescing from the effects of scurvy, and had partially lost the sight of my right eye,

due to haemorrhage in the retina when the attack was at its worst. This has never cleared'. Austin journeyed to England in 1903 to attend Staff College, and on the completion of his course he returned to duty in India. For the rest of his army career he served in a variety of places and posts, steadily rising in rank and experience. In 1919, one year before he retired, he received the C.B. (Companion of the Bath) from King George V, and the following year he left the army a brigadier-general. Austin's career had been a fine one, embroidered by the publication of a series of six 'vivid and humorous' books, all from his own pen, describing various stages in his active life. He did not live to a great age, dying in 1937 at the age of sixty-eight, but he kept publicly active to the end.

\*     \*     \*

In the three-year period between August 1898 and August 1901, Austin was busily involved in a series of important survey tasks in the vast empty region which stretched between the western shores of Lake Rudolf and the Sobat river in the Sudan. They were not easy years for him, and during their course he led three important expeditions: the short journey already mentioned to the Omo river in 1898; a survey in the eastern Sudan down the Pibor river to the Akobo river in 1899; and the last and most extensive, which took six and a half months and almost cost him his life. The final trip was Austin's swansong in Africa, and its story is unparalleled among the annals of exploration in the precincts of Lake Rudolf. The grim hardships and unprecedented mortality experienced by Austin's party exceeded by far those which had afflicted Teleki's caravan in 1888.

*Austin's companions on his disastrous expedition.*
LEFT: *Major R. G. T. Bright and* RIGHT: *Dr J. Garner.*

Just a year after Wellby had completed his famous crossing of the unknown territory between Lake Rudolf and the Nile, followed by Donaldson Smith's successful negotiation of another section of the tract, Austin was offered the command of an official survey expedition, with instructions to traverse the same general area. From his previous travels in the region, the northern and southern extremities of his brief were familiar to him, but the politically important portion that lay in between needed a connecting survey. The British government could have found no better man for the task. In October 1900 he willingly accepted, with no reason to anticipate the appalling losses the expedition would suffer before its end.

Selecting an assistant for the new adventure was easy. Major Richard George Tyndall Bright of the Rifle Brigade, a companion of two former excursions, one of which had been the Uganda Mutiny, was Austin's choice. It was a good one, for they were old friends, and moreover Bright could boast of similar service on previous survey expeditions in the region. In later years he was to earn even more distinction on such assignments, accompanying several Boundary Commission surveys in east Africa, principally along the Anglo-German and Anglo-Congolese boundaries. Coincidentally, in 1906, the same year Austin received the Cuthbert Peek Grant from the Royal Geographical Society, Bright was awarded the Back Grant from the Society for his outstanding contributions to geographical survey. One other white man joined the party at Cairo—Dr J. Garner, a medical doctor attached to the army in Egypt.

For the three officers the journey started at Cairo, with orders to complete their mission at Mombasa, a distance of almost 4,000 miles (6,400 kilometres) in an anticipated year of travelling. The first leg, of 1,350 miles (2,172 kilometres), was relatively easy, transportation as far as Khartoum being by rail and river steamer. There the party gathered its forces: 21 Sudanese soldiers as an escort, 32 Jehidia (former Dervishes), 2 interpreters and 4 servants. For transport Austin took 15 camels, 12 mules and 125 donkeys. With that compact and well-organised group went three months' food supply, enough, the planners felt, to keep the party fed—with a little to spare—as far as the grain-growing area at the mouth of the Omo river. Unlike Lord Delamere's caravan, with its reserve of foodstuffs plentiful enough for a prolonged stay in the wilds, Austin was reckoning on restoring his food stocks *en route*. Having failed to find food in Murle country on his previous expedition, it was a chance he should not have taken. He was also relying on replenishing his stores from a rendezvous with a British food supply expedition at the north end of Lake Rudolf, another risk compounded by the small, and very inadequate, reserve he carried. Travel in the remoter parts of Africa in those days was full of imponderables and gambles, so Austin may be forgiven his optimism, but it was to have dire consequences for his party.

On 29 December 1900, the expedition was ready to start its journey, and on that day they embarked at Omdurman on the stern-wheel gunboat *Fateh*, towing behind it two barges and two sailing boats, all of them loaded down with the expedition personnel, animals, supplies and equipment. Almost two weeks later they reached Nasser Fort on the Sobat. They had been fortunate in being able to travel so far upstream by boat; with the commencement of the dry season the river was dropping in level and was almost unnavigable in parts. Nine miles further upstream from Nasser the caravan eventually disembarked, and on 14 January the boats retired, leaving Austin and his men on the riverbank, and to their fate—they were to be out of touch with the outside world for almost seven months.

Though the first part of the expedition's route was familiar to Austin and Bright, the going was by no means any easier, with the long rank grass not yet burned off by the Nuers and swampy ground on the river fringes frustrating their progress. It took almost a month of horrendous struggle to escape the flat, dreary, mosquito-ridden swamp-lands. In the last miles of the hard tramp the caravan covered ground Bottego had walked over nearly four years before, and Austin had a chance to check the earlier explorer's map-work. Apart from the placement of a prominent mountain on the wrong side of the Akobo river, Austin found Bottego's maps 'very reliable'. This was a compliment to the excellent work done by Bottego's expedition cartographer, Vannutelli. Parting company with the Akobo river, which they had followed closely for three weeks, and parting too with the route they had shared with Bottego, Austin's party struck south into unexplored and hilly terrain. What a huge relief it must have been after the noisome pestilence of the swamps: 'As may be imagined, mosquitoes tormented us almost beyond human endurance at night-time, and even our transport animals were driven nearly frantic by the persecution of these myriads. After the molestation of dreadful night one welcomed dawn and the rising sun more than I can describe'.

The adjacent hills, and the lofty Abyssinian mountains in the distant east, made a welcome and beckoning change to the scenery, but the going, instead of changing for the better, became harder: the rainy season had started early and daily downpours flooded the rivers, turning the ground into a slippery morass over which Austin's transport animals floundered and struggled. The atmosphere, however, was beneficially cooler, a contrast to the hot dank airs of the lowlands. Rather than clamber through the mountainous terrain, Austin decided to turn onto the 'dead level vast plain, extending as far as the eye could see ... away to the west'.

Assuming by the presence of the huge herds of wild animals that there must be substantial supplies of water in the area, he was encouraged to plod on across the flats in a southerly direction. Near-disaster then struck them, as no water was found on this 'burnt-up plain'. In desperation, and with men and animals showing severe signs of distress, he ordered his Sudanese officer, Mabruk Effendi, out on a search party. They disappeared westwards, into the shimmering haze. As the daylight hours passed and night fell without their return, Austin had awful forebodings: 'a horrible idea seized me that we must be in the middle of the desert—where Mr. Donaldson Smith's expedition for three days had experienced such dreadful torture for want of water—in which case the Ruzi II was here non-existent. I firmly believed then I had sent off the unfortunate search-party to their utter destruction'. Morning dawned with still no sign of the water party, but providence was on their side, for shortly after sunrise the Effendi and his tiny party returned—with an ample supply of water. That occasion marked the expedition's first confrontation with near-tragedy. Another waterless march southwards, under the guidance of two local inhabitants brought them to a substantial water pool on the Karuno river. On the ephemeral stream's banks, Austin found signs of an old camp—it could have been either Wellby's or Donaldson Smith's last hill-fringed camp, before they started out across the flat arid desolation on their separate ways to the Nile the year before. Austin was in well-trodden country once again, but it was certainly new for him, and just to add to his burdens he could detect a distinct feeling of apathy growing among his men, fostered by their continuous anxiety over the shortage and nerve-racking unpredictability of water supplies.

Turning south-eastwards, he followed the foothills of the looming Boma Plateau, an elevated tableland on the slopes of which he had found a wealth of wildlife, a cooler climate and most important, generous water supplies.

When Austin at last spotted the mountain he had named Mt Naita in 1898, it was a red-letter day for him: 'Its culminating point is a magnificent pinnacle of solid rock, sheer as a steeple, which attains an altitude of over 7300 feet [2245 metres] and towers majestically above all surrounding eminences. For the next five weeks we seldom lost sight of this striking feature'. Comforted by the familiar landmark, Austin led his caravan confidently towards Lake Rudolf and, he expected, fresh supplies of food. Soon enough they reached the Sacchi river, in full spate after recent heavy falls of rain. Ironically, after the previous weeks of thirst, they then had to struggle through thick forest and swamps before a crossing could be effected. One last twenty-mile march separated them from the site of Austin's most northerly camp on the Omo in September 1898. The expedition reached that critical point on 6 April. As a reward for his labours, Austin was delighted to find that on concluding his survey line from Nasser he found: 'The closing error was less than half a mile, which was highly satisfactory, as the original starting points of the surveys—Mombasa and Omdurman—were some 2,500 miles [4,000 kilometres] apart by the routes followed'. What satisfaction he must have derived from the amazingly accurate conclusion. His duty done there still remained the homeward journey, and, as had been the experience of so many of the earlier explorers who found themselves on the remote and intensely hostile shores of Lake Rudolf with a long march ahead of them, prospects looked grim indeed.

The first complication to affect his plans was the absence of the relief expedition with a store of badly needed food supplies, which Austin was relying on, and hoped would be waiting for him on the Omo river. It was not there, and it never appeared.

The next move was to make contact with the Murle. On the caravan's arrival in the district the natives had all fled, doubtless perturbed by the presence of an armed force which they feared might be another band of predatory Abyssinians. Austin never managed to communicate with them, and just to add to his dilemma the Omo was flooding heavily, proving a most effective barrier between the two parties. Not that it mattered much anyway, for in the course of their foraging excursions Austin's men found all the crops in a state of unripeness and quite unready for consumption.

The expedition's position had now become very grave, and Austin's words clearly showed how he felt: 'Our efforts proved futile, and the extreme gravity of the situation could no longer be concealed. Unless we could obtain food further north in the Mursu district, or were shortly met by supplies, our position would be wellnigh desperate'. One last frantic wriggle in the search for food took the party north to Mursu country, where Donaldson Smith had found meagre supplies the previous year, but it was in vain, for the 'Goshen [the Old Testament land of plenty] we hoped to find was absolutely deserted'. Into the bargain their misery was compounded by the torrential rainstorms which had reduced the terrain to a mass of bogs and swamps. Tersely, Austin wrote: 'To continue was useless and hopeless'. With that numbing realisation in his mind, he ordered a return to the point where the relief expedition was supposed to have rendezvoused with his party. But there was still no sign of the vitally needed succour. Sixteen precious days had been spent fruitlessly scouring the countryside for food, days he could ill afford to spare with their sparse stocks. The position was intensely bleak, a fact he later noted: 'On full scale rations the food was barely sufficient for ten or twelve days, and it was more than three months before we were fated to reach safety!' As if to augment the feeling of imminent doom the caravan suffered its first mortality with the mysterious disappearance of a Jehidia transport driver. He was never found, and Austin could only assume that the man had been speared and thrown into the Omo river, where the ever-ready crocodiles would have made short shrift of his body.

On the afternoon of 25 April the expedition started its dolorous journey homewards. Austin had at the beginning estimated losing 'about one-quarter of our men and half the animals' before he reached the end of his journey; it was probably just as well he could not at that stage know of the final toll. It might have distracted his determined spirit. From then on to Baringo the caravan was to have a stern fight for survival, and it was only the beginning of the long trek. To make matters worse, it took three days instead of one to return to the Sacchi river, which in the meantime had flooded its banks, 'for the next week we were struggling midst swamp and bog, subjected to heavy rains, and try as we would, we could not penetrate that belt which separated us from the lake shores we were so anxious to reach'. Finally, on 5 May, ten days after their departure from the Omo, the exhausted caravan found itself free of the interminable swamp-lands and on firmer ground. Relief was short-lived, for that very afternoon three more of Austin's men were found dead; speared by 'the Marle natives, who [although they] had been extremely friendly in 1898, were bitterly hostile'. That night the superstitious amongst Austin's Sudanese had much to mutter about: they found an evil omen in a bright comet which flashed swiftly through the constellation of Orion. Soon after, their worst fears were borne out with a full-moon attack by a 'band of forty to fifty warriors . . . yelling like demons as they charged'. Fortunately the sentries were alert and the attack was thwarted, but all through the following day the bellicose natives lurked in the vicinity, and that night it was necessary to build a strong zariba for shelter from further attack.

Three days after this episode Austin's party reached the foot of Mt Luburr, well inside Turkana territory, and there he himself was struck down with a violent attack of gastritis, forcing a two-day halt. By then the expedition members were subsisting mainly on the flesh of their emaciated camels, and the effect on the men was beginning to tell. Not only was Austin, in his weakened state, compelled to ride, but at least ten of his Jehidia were put on donkeys, as they no longer had the strength to march. They were the lucky ones: three more men had died of malnutrition by then, and one other was speared to death by the stalking Turkana. It was a debilitated party of men in a 'wretched condition' that reached the Turkwel river on 22 May, and turned inland away from the brackish lake. Austin may have been in familiar territory, but his experiences with the Turkana were no better than in 1898, and their treachery was as evident as before. Staggering up the open bed of the river to avoid its foes lurking in the riverside bush, the expedition 'crawled painfully along day after day, hampered by ten or a dozen sick riding in the rear, who collapsed sometimes in batches of three or four. It was truly an appalling business'. With Austin's plight becoming mortally dangerous, surplus equipment was discarded to 'lighten the work of the men'. Two more disquieting, but by now routine notes by Austin, record the daily occurrences: on 24 May 'a further large consignment of tents, trophies, spare saddles and many other things no longer indispensable, were committed to the flames', and on 27 May, 'we had a dreadful march, and four men died after we got them into camp'. To make matters worse, 'the ever-present Turkana following us incessantly greatly added to our difficulties'. On 2 June Austin wrote with sadness in his diary that the: 'original force of fifty nine blacks . . . had been reduced to thirty eight', and they still had two months of travelling ahead of them. Their rations, or rather their lack of them, were of serious concern. There was no flour left, there were no camels—they had all been eaten—and the expedition members were 'all living on donkey now, and these poor, humble carriers provided for all of us for a space of two months until we reached Baringo. We slaughtered those that we anticipated would not last out the coming march, and who already had about three of their four legs in the grave. It was poor fare—they were horribly tough, and in spite of running our share of the haunch through a mincing machine, and then currying the result, we never really got to be fond of the gentle moke's flesh'.

A welcome change in the countryside coincided with their departure from the inhospitable banks of the Turkwel river. Signs of agriculture raised the party's hopes, which were almost immediately dashed by the unripeness of the crops. At last they were almost out of Turkana territory, but the latter had their final throw, and with it they speared one of Austin's few remaining Jehidia. That was on the 13 June when two more men were buried, leaving only twenty-nine. The next day, on the road up the Wei Wei river, in the vicinity of the Marich Pass, seven more men died. Time was running out for Austin's men: within the next few days, as the remnants of his expedition dragged their exhausted bodies southwards, yet another four died, and to crown it all, Austin himself fell victim to the ravages of scurvy: 'I became so virulently attacked by the disease that I nearly succumbed to it, and at one time my life was despaired of by our medical officer'. It was touch and go for him during those dreadful days, but he struggled on, leading his ragged column onwards, sometimes doing a mere five miles a day before his men collapsed from fatigue. On 28 June they were eventually in no fit state to travel further, and a halt had to be called. Their plight was critical and all seemed lost, when by good fortune they found a paltry source of grain from the local 'Suk' (today's Pokot). Following an enforced twelve days' rest, the caravan, or what was left of it—seventeen men—started once more on its way. Creeping along at a rate the failing strength of the men and Austin's weakened condition could cope with, it took ten days to cover a mere forty miles. In spite of the gentle pace, three more men succumbed and Austin hovered for a week between life and death: 'my vision was rendered almost useless, and I became nearly stone deaf'. He still possessed, however, the same brave spirit which had helped him over so many formidable hurdles in earlier years, and it was not to fail him then. As the leader of the expedition he had heavy responsibilities, which his stern self-discipline would never consider dropping: 'In the bitterness of my spirit I would almost have welcomed death to free me of so much suffering, had it not been that the lives of the few remaining survivors were dependent on my knowledge of the country to guide them through to safety'. From its camp at Kisite waterholes on the north-eastern footslopes of the Tugen Hills, the greatly reduced caravan was led towards Baringo by a 'Suk' guide who told them of a British post at the south end of the lake. By his hand a note was despatched forthwith urgently appealing for help. On 2 August, at the end of six and a half months of body-shattering travel, relief finally located the pathetic, scarecrow remnants of Austin's expedition—only seventeen men had survived. Under the efficient care of

Hyde-Baker, the Collector for the Baringo district, the party gradually recovered enough strength to continue with its last march—75 miles (120 kilometres) southwards to Nakuru. There the train for Mombasa was boarded, and as they rattled down the line, Austin could at long last be sure that his few surviving men's hardships were over. His final African expedition had turned out to be a hideous experience, and left its mark forever on his health.

Austin's ill-fated journey was in a way a paradox, since it was acknowledged as a complete success, with an exceptionally accurate survey line through hitherto unknown lands completed by a competent and professionally trained surveyor-engineer. Many others would follow to fill in the blanks, but Austin had formally joined the Sudan survey with recognised points in British East Africa, and by doing so had added important data to the world's geographical banks. Yet the venture might almost be considered a failure: too many men had died for it to be termed otherwise, especially when compared with the performances of other expeditions through the lonely region. Moreover, the relief expedition had failed to put in an appearance on the Omo, and Austin, too, had made a miscalculation in hoping to find grain in the Murle country at the end of the dry season. The expedition organisers had clearly cut their planning too fine in arranging food reserves grossly inadequate for a lengthy journey in such isolated territory. Might it have been caused by bureaucratic parsimony? It matters little now, but one thing is clear in the final analysis: it was Austin's determined and experienced leadership which saved the party from total annihilation, a fact that was recognised by the President of the Royal Geographical Society when he concluded his appraisal of the story with these words: 'that during the severe hardships and the anxieties from attacks of natives, and the terrible sufferings during the latter part of the journey, these officers, and especially Major Austin, should have continued to take observations regularly and with accuracy, so that he has been able to construct a valuable map of the region a portion of which is quite new. For this . . . he deserves our admiration'.

*Count Eduard Wickenburg*

# WICKENBURG EXPEDITION
## 1901

'WENN Dante diese Gegend Gesehen hätte, er würde gewiss in seinem Inpferno irgend einem Prinzipe folgend unausgesetzt wesen über diese heissen Felsmassen spazieren lassen.' (If Dante had seen this region he would certainly have made some of his characters walk over these rocky masses in his *Inferno*). When Eduard Wickenburg wrote these words expressing his heartfelt feelings on the appalling stretch of country he had stumbled over during the first days of August 1901—four days of ghastly marching, when he and his caravan picked their way across the barren lava-rubble wastes on the footslopes of the Hurri Hills by the northern border of British East Africa—another kind of terrible inferno was looming ahead. It was one that would end the era of gracious living in which he had grown up, and in turn revolutionise the world's ambitions and ideals. The war to end all wars, the 'Great War' of 1914–18, caught him up in its agonies, along with many millions of his fellow men. In it the rocky sun-blasted terrain of his African journeyings was replaced by the dreary mud and sickening misery of the front-line trenches, and the sighing desert winds were substituted by endless whipping streams of slaying enemy bullets. Wickenburg was doubly fortunate to survive both. One of the world's most tireless wanderers, his seemingly endless travels on foot and horseback were hard to best, even by the greatest names in African exploration, and the journeys he completed over vast unfrequented tracts in out-of-the-way quarters of the globe were impressive. Little is generally known of his exploits today, for he was a modest and unassuming man, far preferring the exhilarating examination of the earth's more remote corners to the search for worldly riches and fleeting fame. A restless wayfarer, he never travelled with companions of his own kind. Wickenburg was a man of many parts: an intensely resolute explorer, an unpretentious and brave soldier, a true sportsman, an impeccable aristocrat, and above all fiercely loyal to his homeland of Austria. The lengthy journey he made from Jibouti to Lamu in 1901 was just one more triumph in his growing record of successes. It was also a worthy addition to the register of white man's early wanderings in Kenya's northern desert lands.

\*     \*     \*

The chronicle of Count Eduard Wickenburg's forebears begins centuries ago in the ancient cities of Rimini and Venice. His paternal ancestors, the famous and highly positioned Capello family, were already well-established in senior government seats and naval posts as far back as the sixteenth century, when Venice was the most powerful of the Italian states. In the late 1600s one bold member of the influential family, a youth by the name of Francesco Maria Capellini, left home to do service as a page in the distant court of Hanover. His career was marked by success from the start. Steadily he climbed the ladder of fortune, finally being appointed Prime Minister to the Duke of Hanover—the future King George I of England. It was not the only high-ranking position Capellini held; the posts of Minister of Finance and Postmaster-General had also been put in his capable hands. Moreover, it was at that stage in his career he was honoured with the title of baron, and at the same time awarded the ownership of an extensive estate called Wickenburg, which the new baron adopted as his name. In the years that followed more estates in Austria were purchased to add to the family's growing landholdings. Another step forward came in 1708, when Count Wickenburg was appointed General in the Royal Bavarian Army, followed later by his attendance at the court of Catherine the Great of Russia in the capacity of ambassador.

Although the Wickenburgs came originally from Venice, and were firmly entrenched as a family of prestige and power in Austria, Eduard Wickenburg's maternal great grandfather was a man of wealth and importance in Burgundy, owning a vineyard and large tracts of land. During the French Revolution he lost much of his wealth. As an aristocrat he determined to fight for his King. He left for Austria where he formed his own Regiment of Chevaux-legers to continue the losing battle against the French revolutionaries. But it was all in vain, and at the last he returned to Burgundy and his home.

Years later one of the Frenchman's granddaughters, Countess Bussy de Mignon, married a Wickenburg; an illustrious soldier who was at the time a major general in command of an elite Austrian cavalry unit, the 11th Ulanenregiment. On 3 July 1866 Eduard Wickenburg was born to these aristocratic parents.

With such a redoubtable martial background it was fitting for young Wickenburg to attend first a cadet school followed by a military academy. He was a skilled horseman, and it was while at the academy he achieved a certain degree of renown by winning the arduous long-distance horse ride between Vienna and Berlin, a hard test calling for the qualities of a top-class horseman and great physical stamina. On the completion of his academic career he was posted to the 3rd (Count Hadik) Hussars as a lieutenant, a move which coincided with a turning point in his remarkable life. A strong desire to travel had now manifested itself, and the remainder of his life was to be divided between spells of military service, extensive journeys to distant parts of the world and restless periods at his home in Austria.

The scope and extent of Wickenburg's global wanderings was quite extraordinary. His quests took him to India and the Himalayas, Ceylon, Indo-China, Siam, Malaya, Sumatra, Java, China, Japan, Australia, New Zealand and the Americas, all before he had even attempted the hinterland of Africa. His father died while he was absorbed in these endless expeditions, and the running of the family estate then fell on his mother's shoulders, a task she undertook with characteristic competence. It was as well she managed, for it enabled her son to indulge himself at will in his restless preoccupation. In the end, however, she was forced to sell some of the family lands, partly to alleviate her burden, partly to finance her son's fund-consuming pastime.

Wickenburg made his first visit to Africa in 1897, and he did it with a calculated thoroughness. In April of that year he left Zeila for a visit to Abyssinia, but was peremptorily halted at Harar by the authorities. Backtracking, he headed east and instead went lion hunting in the Jig Jigga district. On his return to Harar in June the road to the interior was still blocked, so, disappointed but far from defeated, he returned to Zeila and organised a new caravan with which to explore the unknown parts of the Ogaden country in Somaliland. Five months later, having traversed and mapped stretches of country mostly unknown to white men, Wickenburg reached Berbera.

By then Wickenburg's appetite for African travel had been thoroughly whetted, so, with ample supplies in hand, he immediately sailed for British East Africa. He disembarked at Mombasa and set off across the Taru Desert to Taveta on the footslopes of Mt Kilimanjaro. For the next six months he diligently collected specimens of all kinds, did meticulous survey work, and walked extensively in the environs of the mighty mountain. On his way home he travelled by way of Tsavo, spending some time assisting in the search for the dreaded man-eating lions of railway construction fame. He returned to Austria in May 1898, loaded down with valuable ethnographic and scientific specimens. Shortly afterwards he had the satisfaction of handing over his detailed survey material to a Professor Paulitschke for analysis. It was just the first geographical contribution Wickenburg made to institutions in Vienna. During the next two years, while he restively lingered at home, he found time amongst other things to publish a full account of his wanderings in east Africa—*Wanderungen in Ost Afrika*. It was the only publication he ever made relating his African travels.

In 1901 Wickenburg was back in Africa on what was to be his longest, and last African expedition. For some unknown reason he never published a book on his most important African exploration. Lamentably, all his diaries disappeared in unfortunate circumstances at the close of the Second World War, so the full story of his experiences will never be known, but a satisfactory account of his lonely walk can be pieced together from the material that has survived. His journey matched all others as an example of stoicism and self-discipline in the face of extreme hardship.

Several years after, in 1911, Wickenburg made an extended investigation of South America. He was then forty-five years old and looking for somewhere to settle down. His preference was for Argentina, but to make sure of his choice he visited the Falkland Islands, Chile, Peru, Colombia and Brazil as well. This amazing hike took him three years to complete, all on horseback over 5,000 miles (8,000 kilometres).

All Wickenburg's plans were rudely interrupted by the onset of the First World War in 1914. Hurriedly catching a boat to Europe he immediately rejoined his hussar regiment with the rank of captain. But it was not long before he was dissatisfied with his situation. It was characteristic of his make-up that on recognising the obsolescence of cavalry in modern warfare he should resign from that arm and join the infantry instead. It did not matter to him that he had abandoned the prestigious world of the Austrian cavalry officer for the mundane life of a foot-soldier, for he was primarily a man of action, patriotic, and devotedly admired by the men alongside whom he fought in the war. By the end of the holocaust he commanded an infantry regiment, he had survived the horrors of the Isonzo battles against the Italians and been highly decorated for his bravery in the front line. Count Eduard Wickenburg could well claim to have maintained the standards of his forefathers.

After the war Wickenburg finally settled down. Marriage came in 1919, and later two children—a son and a daughter—arrived to complete his family. By that stage in his life he was content to spend his time writing articles on his many travels, and climbing in the nearby mountains. But even late in life his wandering instinct continued to draw him from family and home on excursions which lasted anything from a few days to weeks. Suddenly unable to tolerate the claustrophobia of home and the presence of people, he would disappear into the neighbouring woods and mountains on his solitary walks. His roving career was destined to end on one of those lonesome treks. In his seventieth year, alone and high on the mountains he loved, Wickenburg died as he had lived—on the move.

\*     \*     \*

When Wickenburg first tackled Africa, in 1897, he had definite aims in mind. His main scheme was to travel through Abyssinia and visit the Galla people, possibly check the Omo river and clear up some of the mystery still attached to its mountain course, travel down the west side of Lake Rudolf, then through to Uganda and back to the Indian Ocean. He calculated on spending two years in the bush and accordingly arranged for sufficient provisions to last that length of time, 'as well as a large number of guns and many thousands of rounds of cartridges'. These ample stores were packed in more than a hundred crates and shipped off to Aden. He followed soon after, in March of that year, 'with a deep desire to explore in then unknown areas'. After all that meticulous preparation it must have come as a bitter disappointment when he was foiled by Menelik's outright rejection of his application for permission to cross Abyssinia on his proposed route through to the south. Obviously Wickenburg had been unaware of the fact that Abyssinia and Austria were not then on the best of terms. Regrettable as the set-back was, it didn't deter him from trying again in 1900. By then he could claim to be a well-salted African traveller and admirably equipped for the nine-month-long slog he had before him. When word came that Menelik had agreed in principle to his journey through the lands of the Galla people, the Austrian count wasted no time in departing with his stores and equipment for Jibouti.

By coincidence Wickenburg arrived at the Red Sea port in January 1901, the same month that the French explorer de Bozas and his party also landed there, with remarkably similar aims in mind. The two parties must have missed each other by a hair's breadth. De Bozas arrived on 30 January, only a day or so after Wickenburg had left for the hinterland. There is no mention in the de Bozas chronicle of the close meeting, but this is understandable, for the Red Sea ports of Zeila, Jibouti and Berbera were busy centres for European travellers and hunters in those days, and Wickenburg's small party would hardly have caused much of a stir.

Towards the end of January Wickenburg's caravan was prepared for its journey. The country ahead, certainly as far as Harar, was familiar to him from his previous travels, so to save time he took the train to Douadle, then the railhead on the new line being built by the French from the port of Jibouti to Addis Ababa. This convenience spared him 63 miles (100 kilometres) of marching across a desperate stretch of waterless terrain. At Douadle he hired a bunch of pack camels from the Somalis. From there his expedition started in all seriousness. Departing on 2 February, Wickenburg hastened through the bleak country of the predatory Issa-Somali and on to Gildessa, a centre he knew well. There an old friend, the governor Ata Masha, was waiting for him with the excellent news that he could proceed forthwith to Addis Ababa. Progress was briefly delayed, however, as a new train of camels for the next stage had to be recruited. But within a few days his caravan was on its way again, and Wickenburg then elected to follow a rarely used road to the country's capital. When he decided on this he was of the belief that the Italian traveller Cecchi had been the last European to travel that route—in 1877. He was not aware that he would be following the same line to the Awash river as Harrison's expedition had done only fifteen months before, into the lands of the Danakil tribe, where their notorious chief, Tombacco, held sway. This rascal had earlier tried to obstruct Harrison, but Menelik had warned him not to repeat the performance with Wickenburg, whose own words best describe the creature: 'Soon the chief, Tombacco, came to my camp. He was feared by all caravans. A small cross-eyed wild looking man with a foxy face and greasy hair. Unexpectedly, he behaved quite politely and promised, after a good baksheesh, to bring camels the next day'.

Continuing his tramps with his new lot of camels, Wickenburg took five days to reach the hot springs of Bilen, close by the Awash river, and there, as Harrison's party had done before him, he spent some time elephant hunting.

In the stretch of territory between Gildessa and the Awash river he covered the same ground as Harrison, and it is interesting, but at the same time confusing, when comparing their respective maps of the region to find a marked lack of conformity in the names given to places. It is mystifying, even allowing for the distinction between pronunciation in the Austrian and English languages, how such disparities could have arisen. Considering the two explorer's achievements, their temperaments and their ambitions, one inclines to the conclusion that Wickenburg was undoubtedly the more meticulous, and certainly not blinded by the fatuous desire to donate alien names to key points, as was Harrison's wont. Wickenburg's designations also bear a closer relationship to current names, although many of his have been lost in subsequent changes.

On 5 March Wickenburg's expedition reached the well-used caravan camp of Tedech Malka on the high road between Harar and Addis Ababa, and shortly after it started the sharp climb into the cool hospitable Abyssinian highlands. In this beneficent climate the party would wander for the next three months, before plunging once again into the desert lowlands. In the mountain-top station of Balchi, Wickenburg had to change his transport animals yet again, exchanging his Danakil camels for the surer-footed donkeys and mules of the region. From Balchi he made a deviation to Addis Ababa, 56 miles (90 kilometres) distant, for the purpose of discussing with Menelik the reasons and intentions of his visit.

By then Menelik was quite familiar with the wandering habits of the white man. With his astute mind conscious of possible gains, he was usually only too glad to fall in with their requests. Wickenburg was no exception, and he was met with civility and interest. Menelik had heard of the Austrian's skills at lion hunting on his earlier trips, and with their mutual interest in the chase a happy accord was soon reached. To Wickenburg's relief 'the Negus accepted my application with great politeness and promised to give his backing to my plans'. Wickenburg's good rapport with Menelik encouraged him to spend a month and a half in the district, in the course of which he made a detailed study of the Amharic people, writing copious notes on their history, customs, politics and religion. Menelik, too, was included, and Wickenburg included such facts as the blackness of his pock-marked negroid face, that his mother had been a slave, that his lively eyes indicated a sharp intelligence, and how his gracious and friendly manner, combined with cheerful nature, made him easily approachable and sympathetic in discussion. Underlying these features, he noted, lay a character of great strength, filled with exceptional energy, qualities that stood him in good stead as the leader of a huge country.

While in Addis Ababa Wickenburg also busied himself with final preparations for the long journey ahead. With a wealth of experience in such arrangements he had equipped himself well. In addition to the customary accoutrements of African travel—a serviceable selection of firearms—he had brought along a formidable set of surveying instruments with which to pinpoint the geographical features of his route. Survey work was in fact his main concern, and in his unflagging production of sketch maps in the field—mostly drawn to the scale of 1:75000—he turned out one hundred and eleven sheets covering the ground between Gildessa and his terminating point on the Tana river, a distance of 1490 miles (2400 kilometres) by his pedometers' reckoning. All this work was done with the instruments he listed:

'A sextant by Negretti and Zambra
An artificial horizon by L. Casella
A nautical compass on a tripod, fitted with a diopter and spirit level, which enabled surveys to be made to within a degree (at an estimate to within ⅓ of a degree)
Neuhofer's metal barometer nr.6820 for calculating altitudes
A compensated ditto
Two pedometers

Besides the above I took with me a surveyor's table complete with diometer, several watches, a thermometer, psychrometer and photographic apparatus.'

With this comprehensive set of gadgets he proceeded, through thick and thin, to record over 3,000 azimuth (true bearing) angles, 330 barometer readings for elevations, and take countless photographs with a magnificent Kodak folding camera*. On only one section of his journey did Wickenburg fail to set about his careful plotting, as his diffident words explain: 'unfortunately, along the Gidabo [near Lake Abaya] to Lake Stefanie route I was unable to plot any azimuth angles as the result of a not inconsiderable injury to my hand from an exploding cartridge'. It was the type of accident one had to be prepared for in African travel.

The result of all Wickenburg's industry is represented by a set of five immaculate maps drawn up by Herr R. Dokaupil of the Military-geography Institute of Vienna. In an appropriate summing up of the problems besetting the many amateur or professional surveyors in those far-off days, Wickenburg's words indicate the difficulties under which they laboured: 'Should one or two inaccuracies nevertheless come to light, the excuse may be put forward that the conditions under which such surveys can be made in Africa differ fundamentally from those prevailing in Europe. Quite different factors are involved out there which can only be appreciated by someone who himself has carried out surveys in unexplored and uncivilized territories. The dangers arising from hunger, thirst and attack by hostile inhabitants sometimes allow the traveller no time to stay long enough in one place; exhaustion or illness hamper his activity, and very often the nature of the area concerned is such that vegetation, mountains and the like deny him an exact study of it'. How hard it is today to appreciate the obstacles early surveyors struggled to surmount, displaying a stern determination of purpose, and a hardy endurance in the face of seemingly overwhelming odds, without all today's modern aids and conveniences.

Towards the end of April 1900, Wickenburg had mustered the caravan that would struggle through with him to the end of his course. Assembled back at Balchi, its manpower consisted of 45 Somalis and Abyssinians, with an animal train of 40 camels, mules, donkeys and a few horses. From 20 April, when the expedition finally started

---

*This venerable camera was brought to Kenya by Wickenburg's daughter eighty-four years later, in 1985, and used along part of the Austrian's route.

out on its southwards trek, until the middle of June when they arrived at the southern end of Lake Chamo, Wickenburg followed in the footsteps and general directions of Harrison and Wellby, trudging along the broad rift valley which holds the fascinating chain of Abyssinian lakes. While the caravan wandered down the mountain-skirted valley, the rainy season started with a vengeance. Rivers rose in bank-overflowing spate and in places the going became appalling for the unfortunate transport animals, particularly the camels, which found the cold, wet and often hilly terrain so testing. Many of them were to die in the mountains. Canoes were hired from the local natives, rafts were constructed from drums, and tracks were cleared through bush and swamp. Finally, in early June, the caravan leader was forced to call a halt on the shores of Lake Abaya, the same locality that Bottego's party had visited exactly five years before. Wickenburg's men and animals were by then totally exhausted from their strenuous exertions, and a rest of several days was badly needed. The short respite revived man and beast, but the relentless march had to be resumed, despite the continuing rain. Their troubles continued. A new obstacle in the form of the Sagan river appeared. It was now a deep torrent and quite impassable except by boat. With the aid of a native craft, bodily carried overland from the lake shore, stores, men and animals were eventually ferried across. It turned out to be a hazardous crossing, and not without incident. One of Wickenburg's horses was lost when attacked by a crocodile.

By the middle of June the thoroughly exhausted group had reached the southernmost shores of Lake Chamo, and there Wickenburg was at last relieved to find herds of wild game and fields of cultivated millet. He described the lake as 'the most beautiful of all Abyssinian lakes'. Its beauty was not enhanced by the 'legions of crocodiles' and the 'many hippos', but it did remind him of the Alpine lakes of his homeland with its crystal-clear waters and surrounding fog-covered mountains. However, all this did not encourage him to tarry. Soon he was on his way again and into the rugged mountains of the Konso people, where, to add to his trials, more camels died. After dropping down into the Sagan river valley, in desperation Wickenburg decided that his best strategy would be to follow the river to its meeting place with nearby Lake Stefanie. But the same barrier which had defied Donaldson Smith years before lay in wait: dense riverine bush and the narrow steep-sided gorge stopped all further advance along the riverbanks. Three days later the caravan struggled wearily out of the valley on an alternative highland route to the lake. It took another six days to reach the lake shore, by way of a high pass on the Tertale range.

Wickenburg's feelings on his arrival at one of his main targets were a blend of disappointment and satisfaction. It did not please him to find that the water in the lake had been concentrated into a salty and quite unpalatable liquid, totally unfit for human and animal consumption: 'we found to our sorrow that the water was very salty and polluted by swamp birds'. It was a bitterly ironic situation. Fortunately, the men he sent back into the hills found an ample supply of fresh water in a cave. The compensation for this set-back is best described by the expedition leader's own words: 'During the last month we had travelled in a moist and beautiful mountain region, but now we were suddenly in a bare dried-out semidesert land, surrounded by mountains devoid of any vegetation. In front of us lay a lake of undrinkable water. None the less we looked with deep satisfaction onto the water surface because I had reached the first goal of my lonesome journey. With excitement I thought of my two brave fellow-countrymen, Teleki and von Höhnel, who were the first Europeans to reach this lake after considerable hardships and named it Lake Stefanie'. Walking on to the southern end of the lake took two more days, and there the caravan stumbled on a blessing in that arid land—a potable spring. For many the desolate scene would have been depressing: 'The scenery at the lake showed a distressed picture; the plains were covered with yellow dried out grass and leafless sunburnt trees and bushes. The sun's rays sent down a baking heat'. For Wickenburg's irrepressible spirit there was, however, a satisfying reward: 'In spite of the unfriendly character of this area there was a lot of game; thousands of oryx, zebra and ostrich inhabited the lake shores. Even rhinos and elephants lived there, and at night we could hear lions roaring. On the shore-line there were wide stretches covered with pelicans, geese and all sorts of ducks'. The explorer's hunting instinct soon decided him in favour of a protracted halt in the sultry heat-laden valley, where he had water and a wealth of sporting prospects with its consequent food supply for his weary men: 'As the remaining transport animals were completely exhausted, and half of them already dead, I decided to have a long rest on Lake Stefanie'. He was the only explorer who spent any length of time in the vicinity of the lake; he stopped there for three weeks, devoting most of his time to hunting, but also taking a quick side trip to Lake Rudolf, which he summarily dismissed in these terse words: 'As this trip was not in my original expedition plan I don't make any comment on it'. And that was that. Apart from Delamere, Wickenburg was the only other explorer to the region who did not regard Lake Rudolf as a Mecca to which all efforts should be applied. He had the distinction of being the second Austrian to visit the great lake, but he felt there were other, less known, fields to be explored, so he wasted little time on its shores.

Wickenburg had now stepped into territory under the embryonic British East Africa Protectorate's jurisdiction, although at that time no one in government headquarters in Mombasa knew much, or for that matter, probably cared too much, about the distant northern frontier land.

Wickenburg's next objective was to find the Rendille people, a tribe whose reputation intrigued him in much the same way as it had attracted Chanler's attention several years before. It was a search which would shortly involve him in considerable effort and suffering, but in the end success.

On 26 July Wickenburg loaded up his surviving camels and left Lake Stefanie. The effects of the humid dusty camp were beginning to tell, and with many of his men suffering from malarial fevers it was clearly time to leave. Heading in a south-easterly direction and following for a short distance in Donaldson Smith's tracks of twenty months before, the caravan marched through the lonely Sele Gublo Pass, under the towering grass-covered massif of Mt Jabisa, and on across thickly bush-covered plains to the shallow river-bed wells of Saru. The land over which he marched was empty of people except 'one starving and emaciated Boran family'. To them he donated a rhinoceros he had just shot. The Saru bushlands were a haven for these archaic creatures, and in the space of less than an hour he killed three of the beasts as they crossed his path. Four days after leaving his camp on the lake he arrived at the unprepossessing wells of Dukana, situated in a shallow windswept valley on the edge of the flat, almost treeless Dida Gola Plains*. The exquisiteness of this great stretch of

---

*In the Gabbra language the word 'gola' means 'at the edge of the wilderness', or alternatively, 'the boundary'; an old name suggesting the limits of their former territory.

country is best seen after good rains, when the wheaten-coloured grass ripples in the wind for as far as the eye can see, disappearing to distant horizons quivering in the hazy heat of midday. Under this benign-seeming cloak lurks a foot-traveller's Nemesis, as Wickenburg found to his cost. 'Soon we came to one of the most terrible areas I have ever seen. In a true stone desert in front of us lay an endless grass region which was covered with lava rocks'. Four days of stumbling across this misleading stretch found the expedition at the famous wells of Balessa, ancient holes in the dry river-bed of that name, bored down by a long-forgotten race of people to Stygian depths close on 40 feet (12 metres) below the surface of the earth.

Wickenburg was poised on the edge of a horrific experience. One must recall that he was crossing an unpeopled land, where no guides were available to advise him on the best route. This should be considered in vindication of his next, and near lethal, decision. Instead of following the acacia-shaded river-bed where he was camped, down to the desert and the perennial springs of Kalacha Goda, Wickenburg chose to make a bee-line for the southern foothills of the distant Hurri range. Whatever decided him on his course, once started he felt committed to completing it, through a savage terrain which he graphically described on his return home: 'Very often there were walls of lava blocks piled three metres high for wide stretches, which almost looked man made. Or there were long sections of irregular lying rocks which may have come from a stream of solidified lava. The sun's rays beat mercilessly down on this sea of stones. In the afternoon the whole area was covered in a haze and in the evening the sun went down blood red . . . Over this burning hot, sharp-edged stone mass we had to walk, and the camels too had to clamber over the stone walls. After the first marches my horses and mules started to die of thirst. Often the camels fell between the rocks and lost their baggage. We only rescued them with much trouble and effort. Quite a few fell down and were unable to rise again, and we had to shoot them. Many of my men could no longer follow the caravan through lack of strength and thirst. Some of them just lay down and said they would rather die'.

August 7 should forever after have been deeply imprinted on Wickenburg's memory as a day of salvation. On that date the caravan found water. It had taken them four long days to stagger across the waterless wasteland, and with everyone on the point of dehydration and in the final stages of collapse they reached a waterhole, hard by the red volcanic hill Afgaba. It was a stroke of sheer good fortune, for there is no other waterhole for miles around, excepting the springs at Kalacha, 10 miles (16 kilometres) down the hills, and of which Wickenburg had no knowledge anyway. Afgaba waterhole can easily be missed. It is a deep hole carved out of the volcanic rock by aeons of scouring seasonal torrents, and it lies completely hidden from view until almost the last step, when it is suddenly revealed nestling in its cliff-fringed chasm. That it has succoured countless herds over the millenia is clear from the animal pictures etched on the surrounding rocks by artists of bygone ages. It must have been with a sense of deep gratitude that the hard-pressed explorer peered down into this pristine haven; it had been an extremely close call, as his words laconically explain: 'Accidentally we found a waterhole on the edge of a chain of hills. I don't think the caravan would have been able to survive one day longer. I gathered the scattered remnants of my caravan and gave them two days' rest to recover. More of the camels were useless, so I had to shoot them. Now I had a shortage of pack animals, and I was forced to abandon some of my baggage. Bails of cloth, boxes of glass beads, and some

*Situated exactly on the border of Ethiopia and Kenya, Mt Foroli (Wickenburg Berg) dominates the vastness of the Golbo Plain.*

of the nonessential stocks which were reserved for my use were discarded. Quite a few boxes of ammunition we blew up'.

With his depleted transport in desperate need of replenishment Wickenburg set out to find some Borana, from whom he hoped to be able to buy replacements. Marching along the spine of the refreshingly cool, but almost waterless, Hurri Hills, the caravan took only four days to reach the foot of Mt Foroli*. A day's march north of the lofty mountain the caravan found the first Gabbra encampment. Apart from the starving Borana family at Saru, the Gabbra were the first humans the expedition had come upon for eight weeks, and it must have been a heartening sight to view 'thousands of camels' browsing round the Gabbra villages. The people were friendly, too, a fact Wickenburg put down to their hopes that he had come to protect them from Abyssinian oppression. He very badly needed camels and sheep, but the presence of Abyssinian soldiers prevented the Gabbra from selling anything, and it was only after he had issued peremptory warnings to the soldiery, showing them his letters from Menelik, that they acceded to his demands and allowed him to purchase ten camels and eighty sheep. Wisely he also signed on two Gabbra guides to travel with him on his way eastward along the row of granite hills—El Dimtu, Kwial, El Ebor and Turbi—that rise out of the great empty plain. At each of these he was grateful to find pools of rainwater.

Leaving Turbi, Wickenburg then struck directly south, towards the faint blue range beckoning on the hazy skyline 70 miles (112 kilometres) away. Four days of intense marching across the flat boulder-strewn grasslands of the Dida Galgalo—the vast desiccated plain that isolates Marsabit from the Abyssinian hills—brought him to the foothills of the lone mountain. All the while the dominating thought running through his mind was to find the elusive Rendille, an ambition that received fresh impetus when the caravan accidentally came upon an immense volcanic crater (Gof Barachuma) near which was found a waterhole where mobs of camels and their herders had recently drunk. This was an exciting find, so forthwith 'I sent some of my men in all directions to search for the Rendille, and for the same reason made a desert march'. His march took him back down the hill and off on a westerly tangent, directly away from Marsabit. But his diversion was rewarded two days later when he finally came up with the very people he had been so ardently searching. They lived in a harsh inhospitable terrain, hardly the place to expect humans in, but 'after we marched for seven and a half hours we finally saw huge herds of camels, and soon after half naked savages came running, with bows and arrows in their hands ready for shooting. I immediately stopped my caravan and let them know through an interpreter we were not coming as enemies. I am convinced that had a gun gone off accidentally we would have had a fight with these savages. Slowly everyone calmed down and we made friends . . . I stayed several days with the Rendille to trade for camels and sheep'. While staying with them Wickenburg paid a short visit to the springs at Koroli on the floor of the Chalbi desert, and observed that 'there were several clear, but salty springs, similar to the dried out areas of Lake Stefanie. One could envisage in this dried out lake a picture of the future of Lake Stefanie'. Prophetic words if one compares the sameness of the two features today. After his three-day sojourn with the Rendille, profitably spent in studying their habits and customs, and purchasing additional stocks of

---

*Wickenburg, or more likely, his cartographer Dokaupil, named this mighty bastion Wickenburg Berg.

camels, goats and sheep, it was time to move on again. Having satisfied his curiosity and replenished his herd of pack animals, Wickenburg set off back towards Marsabit, where for ten days he wandered amidst forest, craters and grassland, enjoying the peace of the hunters' El Dorado where elephants, rhinoceros, antelopes and buffalo abounded. As it had been for previous travel-weary explorers, so the tranquil spot was a haven of rest for Wickenburg's party, giving it a chance to recuperate and prepare for the remaining stages of the journey to the Tana river.

Leaving the sanctuary of Marsabit on 19 September, the expedition tramped south, crossed the sun-parched wastes of the Kaisut Desert and reached the springs at Laisamis three days later. There, Wickenburg found Rendille, and from them he hired a guide who agreed to accompany him to the Uaso Ngiro river. Following almost the same line Donaldson Smith had taken exactly six years before, the caravan reached the flowing stream after five hard marches. Wickenburg noted in his record that 'it was also three months since we had seen flowing water'. On the banks of the river he found yet more Rendille, living peacefully alongside 'Laigop' villages. He made an interesting observation when he wrote that the Rendille living there were not in fact true representatives of their tribe, but were the cross breed between the 'Laigops' and the Rendille—the Ariaals. The 'Laigops', or Samburu, he found living all the way down to the Lorian Swamp, and he further noted that they were said 'to be great robbers'. It was a reputation probably earned from the efforts of the thieving 'Dthombons' of Chanler's writings.

At the beginning of October 1901 the Lorian Swamp was dry, apart from a few stagnant pools of water, but nevertheless it was the home of great herds of wild animals, and in this rich gamefield Wickenburg, in the same way as Donaldson Smith before, enjoyed one last hunting spree, shooting among other things 'two of the biggest elephants I ever shot'.

On the eve of the last leg of his journey one wonders whether Wickenburg had ever read Donaldson Smith's graphic description of the desperate stretch of country he had crossed in his march to the Tana river in 1895. If he had read the account, then he was prepared for the worst; if he hadn't then he was not prepared for one last unpleasantness on Africa's part. In seven days' travelling through the 'completely sunburnt endless bushland' the caravan found water only once, and with four days separating it from the great river the party suffered horribly yet again: 'Because our water supply was completely finished after three days, the whole caravan badly suffered from thirst, and once more we saw the spectre of death by thirst. Many of my people fell exhausted on the way, and could only be persuaded by force to continue the march. On the evening of the fourth day we once again reached a dried out river bed, but nowhere was there a trace of water. Slowly I began to doubt whether it would be possible to reach the Tana river with this totally exhausted caravan, but all of a sudden we heard the roar of elephants, and as we followed them we found the place in the river where these intelligent animals had dug deep water holes. Once again we were rescued by sheer luck from death by thirst'.

The very next morning fortune smiled on them again as they came in sight of the snaking green band of trees bordering the Tana river, and 'with delight' Wickenburg realised his trials were at long last over.

With all the anguish and worry of the past nine months behind him, it only remained for Wickenburg to purchase a number of dug-out canoes from the Pokomo

*The busy watering place by Afgaba Hill still succours thirsty men and beasts, in the same way it did Wickenburg's desperate caravan in 1901.*

and paddle down the river to the sea. The final lap was completed in the remarkable time of eight days, six days less than Donaldson Smith's performance on the same stretch. It was an amazing feat, achieved by frantic paddling day and night, with only brief stops of an hour or so twice a day to cook a meal. Now he was in well-known territory it appeared the explorer was anxious to finish the journey in the most expeditious way. The remainder of his men and his baggage camels followed at a more sedate pace overland, meeting up with him at Lamu.

Wickenburg arrived in Lamu to find a telegram from Austria awaiting him. It bore a grievous message, informing him that his mother had died in his long absence. One can only speculate on the lone explorer's thoughts as he sat in the sultry heat of Lamu. It was then the end of October, the south monsoon was nearly dead, and the still, hot days in the decadent old port may have hung heavy on him as he contemplated the uncertainties of the future. His mother, the mainstay of the family and its estates, was gone. Would he be shackled to his homeland from now on, unable to travel as he willed; would he be bound to the sedentary life and tasks of a landowner, always restlessly champing to be on the move again? Whatever his thoughts, his travelling days were far from over, although they may have been less frequent than before.

# DE BOZAS
# EXPEDITION 1901–3

THE opening years of the new century saw Abyssinia and Somaliland becoming increasingly powerful magnets for adventurers from Europe and officers on furlough from India. Enticingly for them there were still many uncharted corners to explore in those territories and the gamefields were naturally popular with the keen sportsman. Abyssinia in particular had much to offer the enterprising traveller who had been attracted by the writings of pioneers like Powell-Cotton, Wellby and Wickenburg, to name but a few. A young French nobleman and his syndicate of scientists were among these latter-day explorers. By good fortune they had chosen an opportune moment to journey through Abyssinia. It was opportune for the simple reason that the French government was in the course of constructing a railway line from Jibouti to Addis Ababa. With this diplomatic lever Vicomte de Bozas had no difficulty in extracting the required district passes from Menelik. Times had changed since Bottego met his tragic end in Abyssinia five years before. Instead of obstruction, bona fide expeditions were being given every encouragement by the Emperor to explore his huge country. The de Bozas scheme clearly fell into this category. It was an important project, sponsored by himself, supported by the moral backing of his government, and staffed by a group of skilled scientists with a well-defined programme. On the completion of its first year in the field an entry was made in the expedition journal, proudly proclaiming: 'Le Vicomte du Bourg est un explorateur dans la plus belle acception de mot' (The Vicomte du Bourg is an explorer in the finest sense of the word). By the time their journey in Africa was over, the Frenchmen had spent more than two years on the continent, crossed it from the Red Sea to the Atlantic Ocean, collected a mass of valuable geographical and ethnic information, and, regrettably, lost their young leader to fever. It was tragic that de Bozas should lose his life almost in the final steps of his great adventure, so missing the ennobling rewards of success, and his country's highest acclaim. But, while worldly awards eluded him the expedition rendered him one important service: the opportunity to prove his worth.

\*     \*     \*

Pierre Marie Robert was the second son of the Marquis du Bourg de Bozas, a status which accorded him the title of Vicomte in that well-known family of French aristocrats. Their line can be traced back to 1276, when a tenuous thread attached one of their ancestors to an heir of the famous Comtesse de Poitiers: a former Queen of England, whose husband, Henry Plantagenet, had succeeded to the English throne in 1154. With the passage of the years the Vicomte's forebears steadily rose in prominence, and by the late fourteenth century the du Bourg name had become well-established. Three hundred years later, in Louis XIV's reign, the title of Marquis de Bozas was bestowed on the family's head, upgrading the du Bourgs further in the

*Vicomte Robert du Bourg de Bozas.*

ranks of French aristocracy. Since then the family have been distinguished by the full name du Bourg de Bozas.

Robert de Bozas was born in 1870, into a life of comfort and ease. The family home was close by the town of Neuvy-sur-Barangeon, in the department of L'Indre, not far distant from their Anjou ancestors' lands. In his early adulthood he acquired ownership of an estate, Chateau de Prye, situated close to the small town of La Fermeté lying snuggled in the valley of the River Loire. Life for him was not overburdened with difficulties, and it was simply a matter of course for the young Vicomte to take on his bounden duties. Amongst others, he served for a spell as Mayor of La Fermeté, and as a lieutenant in the Reserve of the 31st Dragoons. One can be sure the social round took him regularly to Paris during the season, there to consort with his contemporary 'mondaines'. While at home, sporting activities doubtless helped him to pass the time agreeably. But on the whole he found it an irksome existence, filled with empty social talk, pointless entertainments and seemingly inconsequential matters: it was a drearily monotonous life for a young man anxious to channel his energies in other directions. Written a few years after his death these words summed up an outsider's view on how the ungratified de Bozas must have felt before the great African adventure came to change his life: 'La monotonie d'une brillante et vaine existence pesait sur son esprit lassé du déjà vu et des banalités somptueuses' (The monotony of a luxurious and futile existence weighed on his spirit bored with familiar and lavish trivialities).

Robert de Bozas was endowed with many of the physical and mental characteristics that made him a suitable candidate for the leadership of a lengthy African journey. Of above average height, he was slim and tough in constitution. From his finely featured face gazed a pair of bright, perceptive eyes. In speech and manner, too, he displayed a marked maturity: the former was quiet, intelligent and filled with authority, the latter courteous and undemonstrative. A man of dignified bearing, he was regarded as a future 'chef' of ability, and one of the 'aristocratie authentique'.

But, like his English contemporary Lord Delamere before him, he wished desperately to escape the dull routine and shallowness of his life in rural France: to find some activity which would stimulate him and remove him from the tedious bondage of his narrow world.

Poring over explorers' maps helped sow in his mind the seed that, on blossoming, would release him and afford the opportunity to travel abroad—in his case expressly, to 'l'Afrique Orientale'. Two aspects of African exploration particularly appealed to him; the value and importance of such an enterprise for the science of geography and natural history, and the thrills of hunting the seemingly endless variety of big game. Shooting was in his blood and was probably the principal attraction which drew him to Africa, but science was far from forgotten. When he turned his mind in 1900 to making a plan for his ambitious programme, a team of talented scientists was without question included; moreover, he promised that all specimens collected—zoological, botanical and ethnological—would be presented to 'le museum d'histoire naturelle'. Generously, he asked for nothing in exchange except the support of the government in granting his expedition the status of an official mission. Needless to say, his request was supported with enthusiasm. For de Bozas the expedition turned out to be the most important event of his short life. Liberated from his constraining existence, he was finally in a position to prove his mettle, not only to the world, but more importantly, to himself. It was an opportunity, too, to validate his family maxim—'Lilium inter spinas' (A lily amongst thorns).

\*    \*    \*

By 1900, the year in which de Bozas considered the possibilities of a serious expedition in east Africa, the countries of Somaliland, Abyssinia and British East Africa were becoming well known to the outside world. While a number of Frenchmen had explored in Abyssinia, the lands to the west of the Nile basin seemed more attractive to the French than those on the eastern side of the continent. There, British, German and Italian interests asserted a near monopoly, thereby inhibiting French involvement. De Bozas's geographic researches instilled the hope that his fellow-countrymen would make more effort to explore the eastern parts of Africa, and it was this desire that finally drove him to plan an expedition of his own in 'l'Afrique Orientale'.

De Bozas did his homework thoroughly, scrutinising maps, reading reports and accounts by all the leading explorers and naturalists of the day and consulting senior officials of La Société de Géographie in Paris. With the encouragement and assistance of that esteemed and old-established institution, an ambitious programme was jointly prepared. He intended travelling through territory previously unvisited by French travellers, and decided that the expedition would commence from Zanzibar, the age-old departure point for countless other journeys. It was a curious decision. Might his reason to use the somewhat outdated and inefficient starting place possibly have been born of a romantic impulse? The decidedly more practical alternative, Mombasa, was by contrast a thriving metropolis in 1900, with substantial port facilities and railway access to the hinterland. It would have been an infinitely better place to prepare for an extended inland journey than sea-locked Zanzibar. Whatever his reason for this first step, de Bozas proposed that on reaching the mainland his party would march to Mt Kilimanjaro, which he intended ascending, traverse Maasailand towards Lake Natron where he would survey the lake shores, and cross over to Lake Victoria to determine the courses of all the streams and rivers flowing into the lake from the adjacent highlands on the east and north. He would then proceed to Lake Rudolf, travel round it and on into Abyssinia which he aimed to cut through on his way to Jibouti.

On the off-chance that he might feel unsated at the conclusion of these peregrinations, de Bozas tacked on an addendum to his ambitious plan. He optimistically considered that a diversion to Madagascar for a bit more exploration would neatly round off his excursion. It was certainly a strenuous proposition, and although much of the country he proposed visiting had already been looked over by earlier travellers, none the less, from the very thoroughness of his geographical, scientific and ethnological coverage of the region he hoped to return home with a mass of new material for the scientific world.

De Bozas was not without personal apprehension over his ability to command such a formidable operation. He was, after all, without any experience of African travel, apart from the knowledge which he had assimilated from books. Up to then he had lived only the life of an urbane aristocrat, accustomed to the niceties and comforts of a gentle existence. To counterbalance this disadvantage he possessed enthusiasm and energy, and was a keen sportsman. He would need all of these qualities in the months ahead. On the eve of his departure from France his latent abilities of leadership were suddenly put to the test. He was warned that the lands under British administration in east Africa—from Somaliland to Lake Victoria—were in a state of unrest, and that he might come up against considerable diplomatic obstacles if he persisted with his original plan. This meant a complete change of programme. Undaunted he promptly telegraphed Zanzibar, where all his stores, arms and expedition equipment had been shipped, and ordered their immediate movement to Jibouti. For the young man this was a set-back, both administrative and financial, but the first could easily be overcome, and the second he light-heartedly dismissed with the remark: 'mais plaie d'argent n'est pas mortelle' (but the wound [loss] of money is not the end).

Before he could leave the shores of France de Bozas was required to produce a revised itinerary that would meet with the Minister of Education's satisfaction. His new route would commence at Jibouti, from where the party would travel to Harar and thereafter spend time in the blank spaces between the Shebeli river and Addis Ababa, principally in the almost unknown Galla and Arussi lands. After that the expedition would advance southwards and follow the Omo river to its confluence with Lake Rudolf. From there he would then march the group to the Nile. Having arrived on the

*Members of de Bozas's team in 1902.* ABOVE: *Lt Burthe d'Annelet.* ABOVE RIGHT: *Dr Brumpt.*

river he was uncertain in which direction he would lead the party; it all depended on such circumstances as time, health, supplies and enthusiasm. But at the back of his mind was a notion to continue across the continent by way of the Congo river to the Atlantic seaboard.

On 10 January 1901 de Bozas and his carefully selected companions sailed from Marseilles. It must have been a moment of great satisfaction, particularly for the young and uninitiated 'chef de Mission', but more than likely his equally youthful staff— none of them were over thirty years old—shared his sentiments. They were an experienced trio: Dr Brumpt, a versatile scientist who included in his skills that of geologist, botanist and tropical disease specialist; Lieutenant Burthe d'Annelet, a baron in his own right, and a soldier whose experiences with the French Spahis in the Sahara had familiarised him thoroughly with all aspects of life in the desert, making him eminently suitable for the positions of second-in-command of the expedition and official cartographer; and Zeltner, a reliable and proven zoologist, and an expert in the world of ethnography. While waiting in Jibouti another capable man was recruited: a Swiss, Golliez by name, whose previous travels in Abyssinia had given him an extensive knowledge of the country and its peoples—an asset which was to prove of inestimable value to the team.

During the two month wait for the stores to reach Jibouti from Zanzibar, de Bozas tended to the recruitment and training of his mixed troop of seventy-three men, made up of Somalis, Sudanese, Abyssinians, and Swahilis. His choice of transport animals

*Members of de Bozas's team in 1902.* ABOVE: *Golliez.* ABOVE RIGHT: *Zeltner.* FAR RIGHT: *Didier.*

was also diverse: camels for his desert travels in the Ogaden, and donkeys and mules for the mountainous regions ahead. On 1 April all was finally ready, and the next day de Bozas marched his men out of Jibouti at the start of a journey that lasted two years, and from which he himself would not return. Unlike Wickenburg, de Bozas did not use the railway to assist him in his first steps into the interior. He elected, rather, to trudge across the rough desert roads. D'Annelet had left earlier with vital letters of introduction to Menelik. In them were listed the plans and itinerary of the expedition, and a request for passes through Abyssinia.

Three weeks later the main expedition arrived at its first major stop, Harar. There the party was held up for three weeks while they waited for d'Annelet to meet them with the clearance to proceed. This unwanted delay was, nevertheless, put to good use. Zeltner was able to improve his knowledge of Somali customs and collect botanical specimens; de Bozas, with Golliez coaching him, continued his study of the Arabic and Abyssinian languages; and Brumpt made a quick survey of the district's geology. Their patience was rewarded, and with the required authority from King Menelik in their hands, the expedition headed off in a southerly direction. Seven months later, on 28 December, having wound its way across unknown stretches of the Ogaden and Galla countries, made a sizeable collection of zoological and ethnographical curiosities, and mapped many uncharted tracts, de Bozas triumphantly led his men into the capital city of Addis Ababa. All this had been accomplished without a single shot being fired in defence or anger. Moreover, they had successfully managed to examine much of the country in the blank space Donaldson Smith had vainly attempted to penetrate in 1894, exactly seven years before. In all, the first leg of the journey had been an enormous

success, and reflected highly on de Bozas's by then well-proven competence as a leader. Of equal satisfaction to him was the three-week side trip he took to appease his hunting instinct by shooting many elephants.

On 4 March 1902, following two months of pleasurable pastimes and scientific work in the vicinity of Addis Ababa, the reconstituted caravan set forth on its southerly march. Changes in the staff had been forced on de Bozas, caused by the loss of Zeltner and d'Annelet. Zeltner, the invaluable ethnographer, had developed a chronic ailment which necessitated his return home, and d'Annelet had been called back to military duties in France. It was fortunate de Bozas had obtained the services of Golliez, but a further stroke of luck in Addis Ababa made good his staff losses. A young man named Didier, an employee of the telegraph company, asked to join the expedition. He was promptly signed on to serve as secretary. At that point de Bozas's party consisted of forty Abyssinians, in addition to his other men. With the experience gained from the Wellby, Harrison and Wickenburg journeys, the Abyssinians were fast becoming seasoned caravan men. With his expedition aiming to travel through their territory in the next several months, de Bozas felt it politically expedient to employ them anyway. Camels were discarded, and instead a transport unit comprising 20 mules and 110 donkeys took the field. Again, it was a wise decision on his part. He had obviously learnt from the lessons of earlier travellers, and foreseeing difficulties with the camels in the endless mountain chains he intended crossing, he prudently elected to use the surer-footed equines instead.

The route de Bozas took to Lake Rudolf roamed over country already familiar to the outside world from the reports of former explorers. It meandered down the central

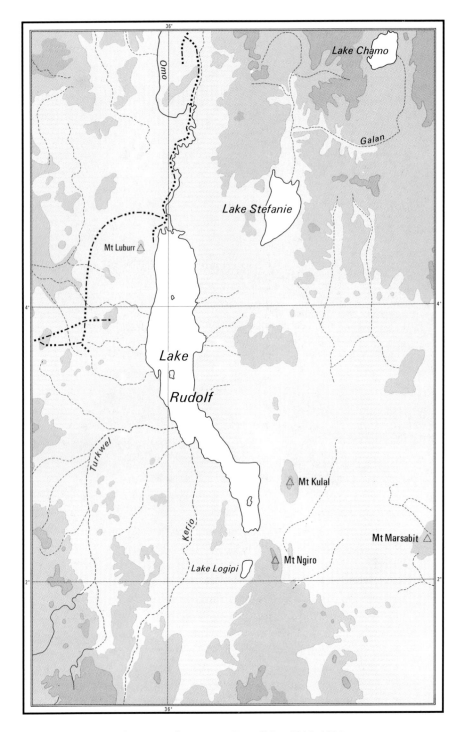

*The route of De Bozas Expedition 1901–1903.*

*Murle canoes ferrying the caravan across the Omo river.*

line of lakes to Lake Abaya (well known from Bottego's extensive survey), westwards across the mountains, touched the Omo river briefly, and then ran southwards through more mountainous terrain to the river which Donaldson Smith had in early 1895 erroneously described as the Omo. Several days' march down that stream brought the caravan to its junction with the true Omo. There the first Murle people were found, now a pathetic tribe living in constant fear of Abyssinian raids and most reluctant to extend any welcome to strangers. Despite this unfriendly attitude, the Frenchmen were jubilant, for they had at last reached the famed Omo river which Bottego had so successfully surveyed six years before, and they were also on the point of reaching the northernmost shores of the fabled Lake Rudolf. Lashing a few canoes together to make a raft took little time, and soon the whole expedition had been shuttled across the river to the west bank, and the last lap of their march to the lake was started.

The expedition had left Abyssinian territory behind, and was on the threshold of Turkanaland, a waterless and arid environment inhabited by a bellicose people only too ready to spear strangers straying from the safety of their camp. Sure enough, it was not long before de Bozas suffered his first fatalities at the hands of the Turkana warriors, losing two men and several animals to their spear thrusts. Even the few villagers who consented to communicate with him refused to barter for food supplies. For de Bozas the region held little attraction, and his visit to the lake's environs was therefore brief. Like Wickenburg, de Bozas did not view the lonely lake as more than a passing curiosity, and with the prospect of his next target, the River Nile, drawing him on, he continued his course, taking a south-westerly direction to avoid following the same route Donaldson Smith had pioneered three years before.

For the next five weeks de Bozas and his caravan trudged across the hills of northern Turkana country, crossed Wellby's old tracks at right-angles, and onwards into Karamojo territory in northern Uganda. There the white men enjoyed more fruitful elephant hunting, in the same region that was shortly to become one of the favourite shooting grounds of the renowned elephant hunter W.D.M. ('Karamojo') Bell. On 8 August the party marched into Nimule, a British military post on the Nile, where they were given a handsome welcome by the two officers in charge. De Bozas could with deep satisfaction consider that 'La seconde partie de la traversée de l'Afrique, la plus périlleuse, la plus neuve, était terminée' (The second part of the crossing of Africa, the most perilous, the most recent, was ended). Since leaving the dusty sun-scorched shores of the lake, it had been a productive journey for hunter and ethnographer alike, and the expedition could claim with a feeling of well-being to be half-way across the continent.

At Nimule de Bozas prepared himself for the third and final leg of his long journey. First he paid off his band of Abyssinians, Somalis and Swahilis, and set them on their road to Mombasa under the care of his faithful Abyssinian interpreter, Daniel Tassama. This task completed, he made the necessary arrangements for the next stage of his journey across the Belgian Congo. Before moving he despatched a formal application to the distantly stationed provincial governor for permission to pass through the vast territory. A heel-kicking month in the company of the hospitable English officers at Nimule, plus several more days with the Belgian officials at Dufile Fort, a few miles further up the Nile, were spent while he impatiently waited for a reply. At long last, on 16 October, the expedition started out once more on its marathon trek.

Ten days later the first signs of fever struck de Bozas, a malevolent ague that never left his system. For the next two months he suffered from a succession of attacks, and finally his tough constitution failed him. At 11.50am on 24 December the Vicomte succumbed to the ravages of his ailment. On Christmas afternoon he was laid to rest in the little mission cemetery at Amadis, with all the honours the lonely Belgian outpost on the Ouelle river could muster. For the other members of his expedition it was a heart-rending loss, and Didier sadly recorded their mutual sentiments in his diary: 'Nous sommes atterrés ... Je voudrai avoir le talent d'un écrivain pour dire son intelligence, sa fermété, sa large tolérance, son héroïsme et sa simplicité. It était notre chef et il était notre ami' (We were dismayed ... I wish I had a writer's ability to tell of his intelligence, his steadfastness, his great fortitude, his bravery, and forthrightness. He was our leader and he was our friend).

His untimely passing was to rouse some bitter feelings when it was revealed how long he had been held up on the Nile while waiting for the necessary pass for the Congo. The question why the provincial governor, Monsieur Hanelot, had not acted more promptly was repeatedly asked in official circles. In their reply to a letter from the Secretary to the King of the Belgians, the Société de Géographie suggested in blunt words, touched with personal experience, that tropical dilatoriness in an apathetic colonial civil servant might have been the reason for this uncalled-for delay. And there the matter was laid to rest. The French had made their point.

It was a tragic and inopportune end for the young man who had set forth so full of energy and good intentions, just when he was on the threshold of fame.

# STIGAND EXPEDITION
## 1909

'WELL, Stiggins, I expect you will be pleased when you are out of it and don't always have to leave for Egypt or some other b..... country at 8 in the morning'. These outspoken words of a friend to a major in the Royal West Kent Regiment were made on the eve of his return to duty in the southern Sudan in 1919. The major was going back, very reluctantly, and certainly not in the best of health, to his tropical post. There was a tragic twist attached to those laconic words, for just four months later to the day the officer was dead, speared in an ambush laid by a rebellious mob of Dinka warriors in the far distant region of the upper Nile. His death marked the premature end of a truly remarkable life, in which almost every moment of adulthood had been put to profitable use. Major Chauncey Hugh Stigand was not a Wickenburg, the loner whose horizons stretched without limits to far-off corners of the globe; nor was he a de Bozas, the leader of a group of highly trained savants in the sciences. Yet in many respects he resembled both those men in character, profession and in purpose. Like the Austrian count, Stigand was a brave and diligent soldier, a keen sportsman and filled with wanderlust; like the French Vicomte he was possessed of an immense desire to improve the world's store of knowledge in the widest possible range of subjects. In contrast to his two aristocratic contemporaries, whose contacts with Africa were only transitory, Stigand spent most of his adult days in that land, where, like de Bozas before him, he finally lost his life to another of its innumerable perils. Over the many years he lived in Africa, Stigand participated fully in the unique and fascinating ways of that continent, giving his most useful years to its service. One feels sure he would have approved of these words written to his widow by a brother officer: 'I cannot help thinking that, as it was willed that he be taken, he would have liked to die, as he did, in the wilds of Africa where he had spent and enjoyed so much of his life'. He would not have been alone in this desire; countless others have had the same inclination.

\* \* \*

Stigand has already been compared with Wickenburg and de Bozas, but there was another parallel to their stories in their comparably ancient backgrounds. While not of aristocratic ancestry himself, Stigand could trace his forebears back to the eleventh century, when they inhabited the Medway region of Kent. One prominent early family member even held the exalted positions of Bishop of Winchester and Archbishop of Canterbury in pre-Norman days.

Chauncey Stigand was born on 25 October 1877 in Boulogne, where his father was acting as British Consul. Shortly afterwards his parents' relationship began to fall apart, and young Chauncey's early life became a turbulent affair, further aggravated by his parents' eventual separation when he was only four years of age. The ensuing bickerings raised by parental claims for rights to the children led to a series of exciting and somewhat slapstick kidnappings and counter kidnappings, with Chauncey and

*Major Chauncey Hugh Stigand.*

his elder brother Almar in the centre of it all. For his first few years, during an endless legal tug-of-war, Chauncey remained in the care of his father and aunt. His father's life was a round of diplomatic transfers, first to a post on the Dalmation coast, which Stigand years later was to describe as 'one of the most beautiful spots I have seen . . . it is probable that the environment of Gravosa has influenced me in later life more than any place I have been to, and given me that passion for mountains and wild rugged spots which I have possessed ever since'. While there he first became fascinated by animal life: 'on the walls and terraces of the garden bright green lizards used to play, and I would watch them by the hour and try to make friends with them'. When he was seven years old his father was moved to Venice and then Trieste, where he met the renowned Arabist, Sir Richard Burton. The famous man 'was a friend of my father, but was connected to us on my mother's side'. That meeting made a deep impression on the young lad. In 1884, after travelling by way of Paris, the Stigands reached London, and there Chauncey changed parents.

From that moment young Stigand came under the care of his mother and grandmother. He did not see his father again for twenty-two years. By good fortune the Reverend George Squibb, an elderly cousin and retired missionary from South Africa, came to the rescue and acted as surrogate father to the boy. Squibb was an unusual man, kindly, humorous and a veritable encyclopedia of information and worldly anecdotes. For the child, mollycoddled by a household of women, Squibb's influence could hardly have been a better antidote; in fact he might even be regarded as the youth's saviour. About then Stigand's years of schooling started in earnest, and a series of long-suffering institutions took up the difficult task of educating him. The boy's relief from the exasperations of the classroom were the holidays the family took in the pleasant countrysides of Wales, Scotland, Devon and Cornwall, endless delights of nature study and specimen collecting. These were the formative years for his future interest in the wonders of the outdoors, an all-absorbing involvement that continued to the end of his days. All through his schooling Stigand looked upon himself as 'a particularly lazy boy' who made little effort with his studies, a shortcoming which undoubtedly contributed towards his failure to gain a place in the military academy at Sandhurst. There were, however, some things he did not neglect: the study of tales of adventure and travel in far-off lands, and equally important, learned works on science and nature.

A career in the army had long been Stigand's goal, so it was fortuitous when a friend managed to offset the Sandhurst disappointment by finding him a place with the Warwickshire Militia. Through academic indolence he had failed to achieve entry to the army by the customary means, and although he 'was thoroughly ashamed of . . . not getting into Sandhurst' he was content with 'this back door into the Army'. In military service Stigand at last found his true vocation, and henceforth he threw himself into the activities of his new life with zest and enjoyment. As an extra-curriculum, and with a view of building up his rather sparse frame, he took up Sandow exercises: 'After two years of hard physical training I developed enormous muscles'. The formerly 'lank overgrown youth' duly received a medal from Dr Sandow for his perseverance at body building, but more important, he had learnt many strong man tricks with which he would entertain and impress future audiences. His groundings in army affairs came to a satisfactory close when he was commissioned as a second lieutenant in the Queen's Own Royal West Kent Regiment on 4 January 1899. He was now prepared and eager to face the outside world—first in Burma.

While Stigand remained an officer in his regiment for the last twenty years of his life, only eleven of these were actually spent on military duties, out of which several were on secondment to other units. After his death a brother officer and lifelong friend, Colonel Thorp, wrote of him: 'Stigand was a man of wonderful physique, well proportioned and finely developed; a true model for a sculptor ... He was of commanding presence, with firm countenance and clear, piercing eye ... Every spare moment was devoted to his favourite pursuit as a field naturalist and hunter ... As one would expect, he was a keen practical astronomer and field surveyor ... Duty was his watchword. His every undertaking was characterised by thoroughness and a marked power of organisation and endurance'. Even these compliments did not include his remarkable ability in the field of languages, or his deep interest in ethnic matters. Hardly had he reached Burma than, 'with his characteristic zeal and thoroughness he at once began to study the language'. Later, after five years of service with the King's African Rifles in central and east Africa, he could claim to having passed the set of examinations in all the recognised regimental languages—Arabic, Chinyanga, Hindustani, Somali and Swahili—and was already regarded as an authority on six Swahili dialects. As if that impressive array did not satisfy his linguistic ambitions he later went on to acquire a good working knowledge of Amharic as well. Despite his dedicated studiousness Stigand was a perfectly human person who possessed a delightful sense of humour, a deft gift of narration and a flair for descriptive writing. Furthermore, not only was he an immensely brave individual and fearless in action, he was also a man with the highest sense of justice.

Stigand worked in Burma, Aden and Somaliland before being seconded to the King's African Rifles in December 1902, and for the following three years he soldiered, hunted at every possible opportunity, studied all forms of life, both human and wild, and wrote copiously. In 1905 his battalion left Nyasaland (today's Malawi) and moved to British East Africa. There too he was hyperactive in all his interests, soon acquiring a widespread knowledge of the region through his employment with the Protectorate survey. The three years he spent in East Africa were filled with industriousness: two more books were published, and another was ready for the printer; the Swahili language had been mastered; and he had survived more hunting forays, including a severe mauling by a lion. In August 1908 his term with the King's African Rifles came to an end, and with some leave in hand he set forth on a long trek past Lake Rudolf, across Abyssinia, and on to the shores of the Red Sea. On the successful conclusion of his expedition Stigand briefly rejoined his parent regiment in England, and while with them his knowledge of East Africa was put to good use by the War Office in the compilation of an important military handbook of that country. Life had not been dull for him during the first ten years of his army service, nor had he wasted a minute of his time, as his publications were clear proof.

In the spring of 1910 Stigand was on the move again, this time to an appointment with the Egyptian Army, which ultimately took him into the most southerly limits of the Sudan. It was at this stage in his career that his occupation metamorphosed from that of soldier to one of administrator, and for the rest of his life he served in the Mongalla Province in the latter capacity. His energies were boundless, and sickness from fever, near death from the pounding of an irate elephant, and the endless labours of his profession did not prevent his continued outpouring of books and articles in an extraordinary variety of topics. In 1913 the rigid rules of the Sudan were generously waived for him, and he was allowed to marry a spirited American girl from Washington with whom he enjoyed a whirlwind two-week romance whilst on leave in England. It was a happy, but sadly a short marriage, for when he embarked for Africa in July 1919 it was to be a final farewell. His last months as Governor of Mongalla

Province were disturbingly active ones. With the recalcitrant Aliab Dinkas storming round the region in rebellion he had much to do, and on the morning of 8 December he was with the advance guard of his military escort when a seething mob of warriors attacked through the tall rank grass. They were driven back, but Stigand lay dead, speared through the chest. That he had fought to the end was clear from the empty cartridge cases scattered by his body, and he had died as one might have expected, in the forefront of battle. It was one of those tragedies of empire building, in which England lost a magnificent man who was best described in the words of his memoirist, Sir Reginald Wingate, Governor General of the Sudan at the time: 'A man of splendid character and of almost unique experience of Africa and its people and languages, he had made his mark in the line of life he had chosen, and for which he was fitted as few men are'.

*　*　*

In 1938 von Höhnel wrote an article for the *Journal of the African Society* in which he summarised the results of the earliest expeditions to the Lake Rudolf basin. It was appropriate that he, as one of the first white men to have visited the lake, wrote this paper, which still serves as a useful inventory of travel in the region. The last on his list was Stigand's 1909 journey. Stigand was very much a latter-day explorer, though the idea had been in his mind for several years, and but for the demands of his surveying duties he would have undoubtedly made the journey long before.

Stigand may not have arrived in time to find much new territory, but on making a careful study of earlier explorations he managed to plan a route that, in parts at least, took him off the beaten track. Just as Teleki had done over twenty years before, Stigand proposed approaching the Lake Rudolf region from the south, from the British East Africa Protectorate. But, unlike the other explorers he planned to travel inland and east of the lake, reaching its shore at the mouth of the Omo river. To consider following a line away from the lake, and through such a wild tract with no known water supplies was an ambitious idea. Following the Omo for a short distance only, he then aimed to advance along the high mountain ranges to Addis Ababa, but west of the commonly used road down the chain of Abyssinian lakes. Thereafter his goal was to reach the port of Jibouti by the quickest means possible.

Towards the close of 1908 Stigand was ready for his journey. It was to be a lonely one, as his companion had to drop out through ill health contracted while they were elephant hunting in the Congo, a side trip forced on them by the need to augment funds for their expedition.

Stigand was fortunate in enjoying two distinct advantages over former explorers to Lake Rudolf. Having served for several years in East Africa he was fully *au fait* with the habits of the the local natives, and moreover, he was a competent linguist, fluent in several of their languages. Next, and vital for his limited funds, he was already on the spot, and so was able to equip his caravan with the minimum of fuss and expense. In Nairobi he soon had his stores and rifles organised, plus twenty-two loads of trade goods, weighing 60 pounds (27 kilograms) each, and a crew consisting of his old gunbearer Tengeneza, a Somali named Abdi who had formerly served in the King's African Rifles and gave sterling service as donkey headman, and a motley bunch of Wanyamwezi porters, several of whom had served in the army. Stigand started with twenty donkeys and a bag containing one hundred Maria-Theresa dollars for use in Abyssinia.

Travelling on the train from Nairobi to Gilgil with Stigand were his mule 'Nairobi' his dog 'Narok' and his personal servants. At Gilgil station they found the caravan waiting for them. It was an exciting moment, as the eve of departure on any African expedition, however modest, usually is, and Stigand, a veteran of many such occasions, still savoured the sweetness of the moment: 'As I stepped into my tent, a place already associated with many happy memories, I felt as if all the fetters of civilisation and its abominations slipped from me'. The very next day the group left Gilgil. Including Stigand himself, the party numbered thirty-four, of whom twenty-one bore loads. It took five days' marching to reach Rumuruti, then the northernmost administrative post in the area, situated on the edge of a land that was still largely unknown. There, another twenty porters were enlisted—Kikuyu men this time—to hump the extra food loads as far as Barsaloi. One of these men, Macharia, was to remain staunchly to the end of the long road to Jibouti, proving in Stigand's estimation 'to be the only reliable Kikuyu' he had ever met.

On leaving Rumuruti Stigand could at last feel 'his journey had begun in earnest'. Steadily tramping across the windswept Laikipia plateau, a landscape made up of vast grass-covered plains stretching to the furthest limit of vision, the caravan encountered few people. A sparse population of Maasai and a handful of Wandorobo were all the column met as they tramped from waterhole to waterhole. Camping near places long familiar to the northbound traveller—the springs at Suguta Naibor and Suguta Marmar, and the stream Ngare Narok—Stigand's party penetrated steadily northwards and up to the head of the valley where the small town of Maralal now stands. At that point he followed his guide's advice and clambered over the Lorogi mountain range in a direction which he had been assured would take him to the 'Samburr' (Samburu) people living in the valley far below. After a waterless two-day slog across these heavily forested hills, the road dropped steeply into the Operoi valley, a place unvisited by white man. Even Neumann in his wanderings through the district over ten years before had not seen this peaceful re-entrant valley. In this hidden corner Stigand found the 'Samburr', a people who accepted him in peace and called him 'Sirrgon', after the hills he had crossed to find them.

With Barsaloi only one day's march away, the Kikuyu porters were paid off and Abdi opened negotiations with the Samburu elders for the purchase of donkeys. It turned out a time-consuming process and only the first of such parleys, but eventually, after hours of deliberations the Samburu agreed to lend Stigand six donkeys and two men to guide the party as far as Rendille country, where they hoped to find plenty of camels.

Travelling by way of the waterholes in the sandy beds of the Barsaloi and Suiyan rivers, it took Stigand and his men four days of long hard marches to reach the foothills of the Ndoto Mountains, finally arriving at Lesirikan as night fell. There a meagre supply of water was found in a set of narrow rock-sided clefts hidden in a shallow hillside valley. In those days it was a lonely spot, perched on the edge of the rolling Elbarta Plains. Today, an embryo township has sprouted up close by, boasting a few corrugated-iron-roofed shops, a school and such nuclei of civilisation's intrusions. The scant water supply for the recent settlement comes from exactly the same sources that Stigand used so many years before.

After a day's rest at Lesirikan Stigand decided to deviate from his course slightly and visit another notable spot named Baragoi. There a series of waterholes in the dry river-bed were used by both the Samburu and the Turkana, who lived near one another in a delicately balanced state of armed truce. Enough time was spent in this place of fragile politics for Stigand to purchase a few donkeys from the Turkana, and shoot a fresh meat supply for his caravan from the herds of wild beasts that roamed over the plains. Leaving Baragoi, the expedition headed once more in a northerly direction, towards the looming massif of Mt Ngiro, the stronghold of the Samburu people. Following the same road Teleki and Neumann had travelled years before, it took Stigand two days to reach his next halt at Naisichu waterhole, close by the foot of the great mountain mass.

Camped on these well-known wells, Stigand was perched above the rim of rambling hills bordering the low-lying Rendille country to the east. He had now reached an important milestone on his trek, and was expectantly looking forward to venturing across a land where few, and in parts, no other white men had left their footprints. The Rendille there told him he had a choice of three different routes to the north. Characteristically he settled for the hardest one, knowing that it would, most likely, take him into little-known territory. But first he had to find the camels he needed for his desert journey. Dropping down through arid broken hills, Stigand soon found himself in rugged terrain: 'If the low thorn country under the Lorogai had seemed an inhospitable desert to us, it was only because we had not seen the Rendille country . . . A bare desolate waste, covered with rocks and dust, and dotted with little stony hills, was the country we struck at the foot of the descent'. In sharp contrast to this unfriendly prospect was the warm welcome given to him by the Rendille, which immediately raised his hopes of success.

Stigand was without any doubt a talented communicator, and a man who could tolerate the seemingly endless harangues, arguments, discussions and interrogations which early travellers in Africa were more often than not drawn into when dealing with the country's native population. His transactions with the Rendille over the sale of their treasured stock was no exception, and he had to use every ounce of patience he could muster during the negotiations. But even then he was not overly successful when 'At last, after prodigious trouble and incessant talking, and visiting different kraals, we managed to collect eleven camels in all . . . I had hoped to obtain about fifty . . . I now had to do the best I could with these eleven'.

Stigand's hard-earned purchases were made in the neighbourhood of Arsim and Ilaut waterholes, at the northern end of the majestic Ndoto Mountains. After ten tedious days spent in haggling for a modest mob of camels, he was only too glad to march away from the mountains, across the barren bush-clad Elgess Plain, an intensely hot and waterless stretch 'over which travelling is very laborious'. The first water they would reach, his youthful Rendille guide reassured him, was Laipera well. It took them well over two days marching, mostly during the cool of the night and by the light of the full moon, to reach the single well. The solitary twenty-foot-deep hole was situated in a desolate little depression, surrounded by a terrible barren waste of rocks, sand and dust. But it was 'the only place at which water may be obtained for miles around', and as it was fifteen days since the expedition had been camped by the waterhole at Naisichu, the party was 'delighted to be once more near water'. The name Laipera means 'round' in the Samburu language, and to this day the solitary well of that description supplies the local community, now centred round the village of Kargi. It is a cheerless spot, surrounded by bleak lava-shingle hills, sand dunes and dust, and

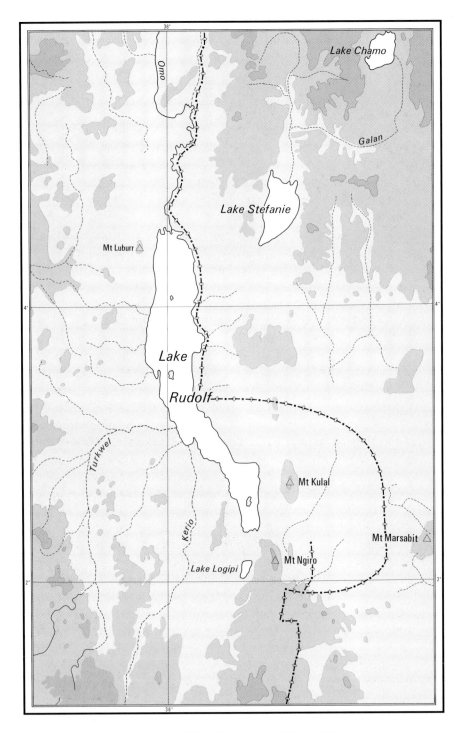

*The route of the Stigand Expedition 1909.*

desiccated by the searing winds that regularly pour across the land, baking everything in their path as they drive on northwards over the heat-radiating Chalbi Desert to the parched shores of Lake Rudolf. Today, the Rendille still congregate round the well, just as they did when Stigand found them watering there in 1909.

The Rendille at Laipera adamantly refused to sell Stigand any camels, but they assured him there were 'Gabbra Boran' in the neighbourhood of Koroli, and from these people, they were certain, he would be able to buy all the camels he needed. By then Stigand was experienced enough to be sceptical about success, but with no reason to tarry any longer at Laipera, he set out to find the Borana. It was only a short journey to Koroli, and he was duly rewarded on reaching the brackish springs to find numberless 'Borana camels being watered'. But his relief was short-lived for no amount of persuasion would encourage the Borana to sell their camels. Aside from their stubbornness, Stigand was not overly impressed with these people, and noted that 'they did not seem to be, on the whole, very hospitable'. This was further borne out by their reluctance to supply him with a guide. The day was saved, however, when two youths came into the camp and volunteered to show him the way to the wells at Maikona, some 30 miles (48 kilometres) northwards.

In the year Stigand first set eyes on the bubbling springs at Koroli, the only other white men known to have visited them were Delamere, Atkinson and Wickenburg, and he himself was on the point of starting a series of history-making marches across the desert. Koroli is situated at the southernmost end of the Chalbi Desert, the extraordinary feature that lies in the shimmering heat between Marsabit and Kulal mountains and the rambling Hurri Hills. Flat as a billiard table over most of its surface, sun-blasted and in places crusted with a brilliant snow-white layer of salt, its unrelieved deadness is only enlivened by occasional glimpses of thirsty wild animals wending their way to water or the spiralling columns of red dust which twist skywards as they travel sedately across the barren desert floor. Thousands of years ago it was a lake, a fact proven by scanty signs of an ancient aquatic fauna scattered sparsely on the ground: black-stained bones and teeth of fish, crocodiles and turtles tell their tale of bountiful times long past. One redeeming aspect of this unfriendly place is the succession of refreshing springs that well up from under the forbidding lava wall that fringes the desert edge. Nurtured by rainwater percolating slowly underground from the cloud-catching heights of the Hurri Hills and Marsabit mountain, the water sources appear as green oases in this desolate land of rocks and sand. Through that starkness Stigand's caravan walked, led by his Gabbra guides. He had willingly accepted their offer to lead, for no other white man had travelled the length of the Chalbi Desert.

Taking advantage of the full moon's brilliant light, Stigand's caravan trudged along, stopping to rest and water at the springs of Maidahad, the wells at Maikona, the water pool at Gamura with its bountiful supply of the sweetest water on the desert, the dense palm forest at Karauwi where close to camp he shot a savage old bull buffalo, and on to the hot springs at Burgi. Finally he reached Kalacha Goda, where abundant pools of water lay among shady groves of rustling palms and stands of spreading acacia trees.

While at Kalacha Stigand rested his caravan and interrogated the local Gabbra elders on the most suitable route for him to follow on his northward tack. Once again he was faced with alternatives. He could either strike due north and follow the string of wells that would take him into Abyssinia, or he could head in a westerly direction towards a waterhole named Horr, vaguely remembered by his advisers from their visits many years before. Wisely, he chose the latter, and with the assistance of two new guides he struck out over the soft dusty desert flats on a direct line to a distant landmark quivering in the mirages of the molten day. Dabandabli Hill was the lonely beacon, a tortured excrescence of twisted black lava standing near the springs of Horr—pools of 'quite the best' water tasted by the party for many weeks, lying on the edge of a small colony of glaring white sand dunes. Stigand had reached another important milestone in his journey, but his satisfaction must have been tempered, no doubt, by the uncertainty of the problems ahead. At least he could claim to be the first white man to have walked the full length of the Chalbi Desert, and had carefully plotted all previously unmarked water points on his map.

Now that Stigand had reached Horr and the last source of water he knew of for miles, he was presented with a tricky problem. The men from Kalacha would go no further, and decided to leave for home. This was the first time on his journey he was without a guide. A decision had to made, and quickly, as food stocks were running low. Stigand decided on a dash for Lake Rudolf, where at least water would no longer be unpredictable. Having made his computations, he reckoned on arriving at the lake's

*'after crossing another tract of loose, soft dust, steering for an isolated little hill called Daban Dabli, we arrived at . . . Horr'. (Stigand)*

*'I also noticed a rocky peak in the distance, which might serve to guide us'. (Stigand)*

shore in the neighbourhood of Moite hill, the bastion landmark that stands close to the southern end of the Longondoti range. He was fully aware that the main problem he would face in the unexplored country between Horr and the lake was the constant one in that baked land—lack of water.

Following the departure of the two Gabbra guides a sudden fear of the unknown made itself felt amongst Stigand's men. How could they go on, they asked, in this waterless lion-infested desert, without a leader who knew the way? It took all of Stigand's determined coaxing to persuade them to hoist their loads and follow him. The benevolent moon, now waning, still gave enough light for the caravan to hasten on by night. Using the distant lava-capped peak of Kinu Sogo as a beacon, Stigand led his men off on their westward course. A day and a half of rigorous marching brought them to an insignificant, but adequate waterhole in the neighbourhood of Wano, where, thirsty and exhausted they made a halt in the spot Stigand named 'Tumepona Camp'. It was an appropriate name, for the word 'tumepona' in the Swahili language means, 'we have recovered', and indeed the welcome water had been reached just in time to save the party from a desperate fate. The Rendille water containers had almost disintegrated by that stage, and consequently the caravan's range was severely restricted, a position that was worsened by the men's habitual incontinence in the use of water.

From 'Tumepona Camp' three days' stiff marching brought Stigand and his men to Lake Rudolf. Unlike his predecessors, he arrived at the water's edge in the darkness, finding that the lake level had receded considerably since Teleki's time, noticeably in the place where the shore was flat. As a consequence Stigand's caravan found their 'way led over dry, sun-cracked mud for a couple of miles, and at last we reached a fringe of grass and reeds and the lake'. They may have reached a source of unlimited water, but by that particular spot 'it was very vile', so the next day they decamped to a rocky point where at last they found clearer water. Now that he had reached the lake, Stigand was on ground well known to the white travellers. It was twenty-one years since Teleki had first struggled along the shore-line, and many others had followed in his steps before Stigand's arrival, but the region still remained very much a backwater, and the problems of travel had not changed a jot. Despite his comparatively small group of men, he agonised over his dwindling food supplies in the same way as Teleki before him, and of this vexatious problem he later wrote: 'To me, however, the daily increasing dread of seeing my last ration given out before we had reached an inhabited country was an ever-present source of anxiety'. So, he hurried on up the lake to find the Reshiat and their sustaining grainfields. The elephant, rhinoceros and buffalo meat supplies of Teleki's and Neumann's day were long gone, so once more Stigand had to contend with a race against time, hoping to reach the rich food region of the Omo river before starvation took its toll. Unlike Austin and de Bozas before him, Stigand was fortunate in finding both hospitality and ample sustenance amongst the Reshiat. Contentedly, he was able to stock up for the last stage of his journey through Abyssinia.

By the time Stigand made his trek through Menelik's territory there was little of that country unexplored, so he hastened to Addis Ababa by way of the mountain ranges to the west of the central line of lakes, down through Danakil country to Dire Dawa, where he finally parted with his long-suffering mule 'Nairobi' and boarded a train for Jibouti to complete his journey in comfort.

Chauncey Stigand could not claim to have exposed much that was new to the world, but the up-to-date information he took back to England was of considerable intelligence value to the British government, especially as it came right on the eve of the administration's arrival in the British East Africa Protectorate's neglected northern district. More important for him personally, he had satisfied his desire to traverse 'nearly the only large tract of unknown country in British territory on the eastern side of Africa'.

* * *

When Stigand turned and had one last look at Lake Rudolf before disappearing into the hills of Abyssinia, he was in effect closing an important chapter in the story of British East Africa's remote northern corner. It had been twenty-one years since Teleki and von Höhnel first saw the lonely lake, and in doing so unwittingly opened a new chapter of exploration. Late as he was in the roster of explorers to the region, Stigand earned credit for determining one last untravelled route to the lake's shore-line. After that there was little else left to learn about the broader aspects of the district's lakeland geography.

The story of Lake Rudolf's exploration would not be complete without a few words about the two expeditions arranged by Emperor Menelik from his base in Addis Ababa. They were unusual in that, although Abyssinian in concept, they were led by Russian officers. Towards the end of the 1890s Russia was covertly viewing colonial prospects in Abyssinia, and with this in mind quietly advanced its political influence and commercial interests in that land. Menelik, on the other hand, watched British progress towards his territory, principally from the west and south, with anxiety. Macdonald's approach from Uganda particularly worried him. For the Russian government, which found British power distasteful anyway, an alliance with Menelik seemed most convenient.

Abyssinia and Russia allied themselves in a small way when a young Russian nobleman, Lieutenant Alexander Xavierovic Bulatovich of the Imperial Guard, was asked to join a military force under the leadership of the governor of Menelik's southernmost province, on its march to Lake Rudolf. He was away from Addis Ababa for four and a half months. In all that time the highland-loving Abyssinians spent only one day on the desolate shores of the lake. But it was, however, enough time for an important event to take place: Bulatovich symbolically raised the Abyssinian flag on the spot. Menelik had quite emphatically staked his claim, and with the help of a Russian. Bulatovich later wrote an exhaustive account of the journey in his native language, but it remained untranslated for many years, and hence of little value to the outside world.

The next Russian to exert influence on Menelik was yet another nobleman, Captain Nicholas Stephanovic Leontieff. Rising rapidly in the Emperor's esteem, he was eventually honoured with a senior rank in the Abyssinian hierarchy. On 1 June 1899 he marched southwards from Addis Ababa at the head of a powerfully armed body of men. His brief was to establish a strong military presence at the north end of Lake Rudolf. This he did in a brutal and unmerciful style, tramping over all resistance as he travelled, and finally reaching the lake on 21 August. His first action was to tear down the British flag that Austin had raised in place of Bulatovich's Abyssinian one and raise Menelik's standard again. Shortly after, he returned to Addis Ababa, but not before ordering a contingent to advance to the Turkwel river and there construct a fort in Menelik's name. In the King's view this last act was rather too provocative, and shortly after Leontieff's popularity began to wane.

As the years went by, others of many nationalities came and went on Lake Rudolf's shores, and soon it became better known to the outside world. Later on, administrators, soldiers, scientists and even casual visitors arrived to inspect the mysterious place. But despite them all the lake and its savage, inhospitable surrounds did not change, and if von Höhnel were to visit it today he could well repeat the horrified words he wrote in March 1888, when he bemoaned the full significance of the 'utterly barren, dreary nature of the lake district'.

*Archibald Edward Butter: painted on the occasion of his 21st birthday by C. M. Hardie, R.S.A.*

# THE THEODOLITE BRIGADE

'They're marching through the jungle, mate,
With theodolite, compass and chain,
They're driving us further back, mate,
Alas, it'll ne'er be the same again.'

Unknown East African poet

A N ancient Abyssinian legend had this curious tale to tell. Many centuries ago the first king of Abyssinia, Menelik I, self-styled the King of Kings and remembered as the son of King Solomon and Mikeda, the Queen of Sheba, went forth on a conquering expedition. His Tigrean army was all-powerful then and Menelik, despite his advanced years, was determined to overpower the lands to the south of his mountain fastness. In this he succeeded mightily, his campaign ruthlessly crushed all opposing forces as he steadily advanced; first Shoa fell into his clutches, then present-day Somalia, followed by all of Kenya, and finally the northern parts of today's Tanzania. Triumphant, satisfied and far from home in the mountains of Tigre, Menelik called a halt. His conquests were enough, he declared, and he was old and tired and ready to die. Addressing his men, he said: 'King I am and as a King I wish to die'. Escorted by his senior lords, and with a small band of slaves to carry his jewels and treasure, Menelik proceeded to ascend the steep slopes of Mt Kilimanjaro, climbing ever upwards until he disappeared from sight in the clouded summit snows. In the evening his lords returned without him, to tell his followers their king had gone for ever, to sleep amidst the ice and crags on the loftiest of all African mountains. In time to come, the legend continued, an ancestor would return there to seek the treasure, and in so doing find the seal ring of Solomon. With this token he would be endowed for the duration of his life with the infinite wisdom of the ancient king.

There the legend ended, and the real story began. White men eventually came to exert their rule over the land in which the great mountain sits, but still the Abyssinians believed it was theirs, and moreover, they were convinced Menelik II was the rightful man to re-occupy the lands of their ancient conquests. Menelik never lived up to the predictions of the old legend, or the hopes of his people, but he made a modest move in those directions. It was a move forceful enough to subjugate the once powerful Galla people, and cause consternation as it encroached on the claims of another and far greater imperial power.

During 1888, the historic year when Teleki exposed the hidden 'lake Samburu' to the outside world, two far separated events were taking place in east Africa. In Abyssinia King John's tenure of the throne was becoming precarious; by the next year Menelik II was established as the new King of Kings. Far to the south the Sultan of Zanzibar had finally prevailed on the Scottish businessman William Mackinnon to take over the management of his mainland estate, under the auspices of the Imperial British East Africa Company. Significantly, these seemingly unconnected incidents were the beginnings of two paths which would eventually join as time went by. Menelik's imperial expansion southwards would soon conflict with British imperial expansion in its sluggish northerly movement. This confluence started in the fulcrum year of 1888.

During the closing decade of the nineteenth century, events moved rapidly towards a confrontation between Abyssinia and British East Africa. Menelik had by then found his feet as a ruler and was relentlessly overpowering his internal adversaries. The astute King led his mobile army in campaigns to destroy all resistance from the once powerful, but now woefully underarmed Galla, the belligerent Tigre and the nomadic Somalis in the Ogaden. These rampaging Abyssinians were the very forces Donaldson Smith, Bottego and Cavendish either met or avoided. Ruthless, predatory and destructive, the Abyssinians terrorised the former owners of those great tracts, remaining there to enslave the land for their emperor and country.

Conveniently for Menelik his advancing armies found certain useful assets in the recently conquered territories. Gallaland was, despite the ravages of the rinderpest plague of the 1890s, still a region wealthy in cattle, and the tributes exacted from the Borana people were used to feed his armies and enrich its leaders. It was also a country in which enormous numbers of elephants lived. For Menelik, who needed cash to arm his soldiers with foreign rifles, this was of great benefit, and soon the Amharic hordes were slaughtering the innocent creatures in their efforts to swell the country's coffers. The accumulation of further possessions had another distinct advantage. The king was able to satisfy some of his more restless and ambitious officers with appointments to posts of senior administrators in the new provinces.

Whilst all this rapacious activity was taking its toll in Abyssinia, Mackinnon's embryonic company was pushing ahead with its programme in the Sultan's provinces. Primarily, the intention was to establish trading and political ties with Uganda, while at the same time attempting to put an end to the slave trade from that same region. For six difficult years the Company worked towards these objectives, but rewards were elusive and in the end, with its capital exhausted, all efforts to cope with the financial losses, the political frustrations and the general immensity of its task, fizzled out. The long arm of its influence did, however, manage to reach into the heart of Uganda. It also built a functional road for a considerable distance inland along the line of the old caravan route—the famous Mackinnon Road—and made a modest start in the construction of a light railway. Of particular value was the assistance the Company gave the British government in a railway survey to Lake Victoria. But it was all in vain, and with Mackinnon's death in 1893 the mainspring was gone; it was then just a matter of time before the demise of the Company.

On 1 July 1895 the Company handed over to the British government the burden of running all of the territory stretching from the coastline to Uganda*, including the financial millstone. It was a heavy responsibility, which the government had undertaken with considerable reluctance, and from which they would not escape for almost seventy years. Apart from the country in the vicinity of the Uganda road it was a wild untamed land, of unknown economic quality and certainly of unpredictable prospects. On that mid-year date Arthur Hardinge, Her Majesty's Agent and Consul-General at Zanzibar, formally opened the administration of the new British East Africa Protectorate. With it came a powerful influence on the east African scene.

On the day that signal change was taking place, Dr Donaldson Smith was far away in the no-man's land between Lake Stefanie and Lake Rudolf. What he observed disturbed him in no uncertain way. He had personally experienced frustrations in his dealings with Menelik's officialdom, had seen signs of the Abyssinians' aggressive advances, and later, on his return to civilisation, learned of the Protectorate's official formation. All three facts prompted him to write these warning words: 'It behooves England to act at once. If she does not immediately check Abyssinian advance, it will only be a necessity deferred, and then when finally she is obliged to possess herself of the country to the east of Lake Rudolf, she will have lost all of ... that ... country of great commercial value, extending a hundred miles [160 kilometres] north of Lake Rudolf'. This was only an outsider's opinion, but it came very close to the mark. Donaldson Smith's hint was not heeded, and by the time any action was taken

---

*Up to 1902 the boundary between the East Africa Protectorate and Uganda stood at Naivasha.

Menelik's men were deeply dug in and ready for the ponderous British approach.

Forewarned of the great European powers' territorial aspirations in eastern Africa, Menelik had stolen a march on at least one of his frontiers, and the bone of contention which arose from his land grabbing was one which would be gnawed on for many decades thereafter.

The remaining five years of the nineteenth century were to witness an increasing flurry of interest in the borderlands dividing the two principal claimants, Abyssinia and the embryonic British East Africa Protectorate. Abyssinia's claim was based on its ancestral traditions of an ancient ownership. Britain, as a newcomer carried along on the wave of Europe's imperial expansion in Africa, was not on such firm ground. In attempting to follow the story of the border dispute a review of the historical background is vital.

The first European explorers to visit the mountain fortress of Abyssinia were Portuguese. They spent several decades wandering through that region in the years at the end of the fifteenth and the beginning of the sixteenth centuries. After their initial probings they departed, and a long lull followed. Not until the Scotsman James Bruce arrived in 1772 was the veil lifted from that extraordinary country of forbidding mountain barriers and curious customs. Whilst it is true that Bruce's reports met with ridicule and disbelief, nevertheless a sure foundation had been laid, and it was not long before foreign travellers and missionaries in ever increasing numbers dared to penetrate Abyssinia's lofty seclusion. At that early stage English visitors predominated, and not until later, in 1835, did French explorers start to arrive. It is historically significant that the first foreign country to make a treaty with Abyssinia was Great Britain, in 1841. In 1843 the French followed suit. The British treaty was simply one of friendship, and was endorsed some eight years later. From the time of those early treaties England never exhibited any territorial desire for the ancient kingdom of Abyssinia. This was a policy quite the opposite of the French and Italian schemes that came to the fore in the latter part of the century. The Italians, who had already established control of Eritrea and the seaport of Massawa, were covertly planning the formation of a protectorate in Abyssinia, while the French had designs on a belt of contiguous possessions right across Africa from the Congo to their tiny portion of Somaliland. It was all very stealthy, and quite in keeping with the imperialistic machinations of that age.

With Menelik's coronation the picture was to change drastically. Revered as the descendant of Abyssinia's ancient rulers, the forty-five-year-old King felt committed to his sacred trust, and that trust was to regain all the territories which traditions had ascribed to the long-lost Abyssinian empire. On 10 April 1891, in open declaration of this fervent desire, Menelik wrote a circular letter to three major European powers, in which he directly contested two important international agreements.

The first, the Anglo-German Treaty of 1 July 1890, defined the northern boundary of British influence as: 'commencing on the coast at the north bank of the mouth of the river Juba; thence it ascends that bank of the river and is conterminous with the territory reserved to the influence of Italy in Gallaland and Abyssinia, as far as the confines of Egypt'.

The second, the Anglo-Italian protocol of 24 March 1891, was even more specific: 'The line of demarcation in Eastern Africa between the spheres of influence respectively reserved to Great Britain and Italy shall follow from the sea the mid

*Emperor Menelik surrounded by a group of senior officials on the occasion of Butter's visit.*

channel (thalweg) of the river Juba up to latitude 6° north . . . The line shall then follow the 6th parallel of north latitude up to the meridian 35° east of Greenwich, which it will follow up to the Blue Nile' (see map on p. 302).

This went on to add that should geographical conditions necessitate a change in the line it would be amended by 'common agreement'.

Menelik's challenging letter to Europe made his territorial claims quite clear*, defining the southern boundary in his considered opinion as: 'Towards the east are included within the frontier the country of the Borana Gallas and the Arussi country up to the limit of the Somalis, including also the province of Ogaden'. Having staked his claims formally, Menelik concluded with this pragmatic declaration: 'If Powers at a distance come forward to partition Africa between them, I do not intend to be an indifferent spectator'. He then went on to add, presuming somewhat on Divine co-operation, that: 'As the Almighty has protected Ethiopia up to this day, I have confidence He will continue to protect her, and increase her borders in the future'.

It could almost be said that the battle for Gallaland commenced on that date. Menelik took it all very seriously, and swiftly initiated the first moves in a southerly direction. Britain and Italy on the other hand complacently popped their copies of his letter into the depths of their Foreign Office files and took no further action. Why should they, the diplomats reasoned, for Abyssinia would soon be under Italy's wing

---

*See Appendix 2 for full contents of Menelik's circular letter.

anyway; the British government, confident of this conclusion and friendly with Italy, could see no reason to pursue a matter which had already been resolved by treaty. In five years' time, practically to the month, a military confrontation was to take place which would make both these nations sit up with a start, but before then Menelik had much to do to implement his letter's resolute stance.

For the next decade the term 'effective occupation' was to prove a significant one in the unruled land between Abyssinia and the British claims, and it was in proof of his determination that Menelik instigated his oppressive 'effective occupation' in Gallaland and the Ogaden. The British on the other hand did nothing to stake a claim to the property formally acceded to them in 1891. In any case the I.B.E.A. Company was far too harassed to cope with anything beyond its two immediate problems—Uganda and remaining solvent. Meanwhile, Menelik enjoyed a few years of free reign.

In their humiliating defeat at the Battle of Adowa on Sunday, 1 March 1896, many Italians were slaughtered. Concurrently, some European pretensions were humiliated, albeit only to rise again at a later date. This battle, a disaster as it was for the Italians, was quite the opposite for the Abyssinians*. All at once Abyssinia was recognised in Europe as a force, and a realm, to be viewed with cautious respect. From that moment representatives from the main European powers came scurrying to set up their legations in the nascent town of Addis Ababa, a sure indication that the sovereign state of Abyssinia was at last truly on the map.

In 1897 Sir Rennel Rodd led a British diplomatic mission to Abyssinia, with instructions from the Foreign Office to discuss various affairs of state with Menelik. Low on the agenda was the touchy question of the southern boundary, a problem the pundits in Whitehall now deemed to be a matter between Italy and Abyssinia. With the bitter lesson of Adowa barely a year old, and the Anglo-Italian protocol clearly a dead letter, this was a remarkable act of self-inflicted blindness on the British part. While Rodd talked, two of his intelligence officers learnt the sombre truth: that the Abyssinians were by then far into the British sphere of influence as defined by the Anglo-Italian protocol of 1891, encroaching even then into the upper Nile regions and Uganda, as well as Gallaland in the south. Menelik, triumphant after his amazing success at Adowa, was on the move, and flaccidly Britain stood by, trusting even then on the outmanoeuvred protocols to stand firm. Even Captain John Harrington's appointment in 1898 as England's first diplomatic representative to Menelik's court could do nothing to stem the flood†.

By 1899 Menelik's tide of 'effective occupation' had spread to the extent that even the itinerant Wellby was forced to comment: 'in order to put a check on their raiding, there is, in my opinion, one speedy and effective method, and that consists in fixing a frontier line around the Abyssinian domain'. He also stressed the necessity for effective occupancy and patrolling thereafter to ensure an observation of the rules. In

---

*On this occasion ill luck befell the Italians. They were not to know that in another few days the enormous Abyssinian army would have been forced to retreat from Adowa for lack of food. As it turned out the appalling leadership of the Italian General Baratieri lost the day with 4,034 Italians—including two generals—and 2,600 native troops dead.

†Sir John Lane Harrington, the son of a surgeon, first served in Somaliland with the army. Later he transferred to the consular department and was stationed at Zeila from 1895 to 1898. The most important part of his career was at Menelik's court, where he represented Britain for ten years. For his outstanding efforts he was made a K.C.M.G. in 1909.

that same year, Menelik, by then highly satisfied with his advances and supremely confident he could continue to sidestep the British, who up to this stage had appeared to him remarkably weak and dilatory in their claim to territory, approached Harrington with a proposition. It was an opportune moment, as his western boundary line with Sudan had finally been settled with the British, and it was now time, he felt, to finalise matters in the south. Accordingly he drew his proposed boundary on the map for Harrington to see; an ambitious line far to the south of the 6° latitude previously agreed on by Britain and Italy. His line in fact ran from the southernmost shore of Lake Rudolf across to Somaliland, acquisitively including the whole lake in the territory he claimed for Abyssinia (see map on p. 302).

Harrington then showed his true mettle, bluntly telling the king that it would be quite impossible for his government to accept the line suggested. This parry was just the start of a protracted sparring match between those redoubtable men in their long drawn-out contest over the southern boundary, and with it Harrington won a point. Menelik's proposition had merely been a feint to test British reaction, and this time he had met his match. Almost immediately he came up with a more serious proposal, one that was within the limits of reality. Harrington's response was to accept the idea in principle, but, he declared, his acquiescence was not to be considered binding on the British government. At last a glimmer of light could be seen, but there were still many sharp bends to be negotiated in the long tunnel ahead.

Harrington was in a tricky position, for he knew full well that not to accept such a proposition might only provoke Menelik into another burst of expansion southwards, into a country as yet not occupied by the British Protectorate's forces. There was also the threat that Count Leontieff, the colourful Russian opportunist acting as an Abyssinian governor, might push Menelik's influence and claims through the land of Kaffa and further down Lake Rudolf's shores. By agreeing to Menelik's line Harrington displayed cool-headed diplomacy; he had achieved a tacit settlement which he felt even Menelik's greed might respect for a little while. If nothing else it turned out to be a satisfactory staying action. Harrington was not fighting his battle entirely alone. Many senior British officials in London were aware of the problem and knew its only solution was 'effective occupation' of the border lands, but the British Treasury was tight-fistedly unwilling to disburse any funds towards the policing of an unconvincing cause in the remote depths of east Africa. It would maintain this stubborn stance for many years to come.

The whole boundary affair was reaching a head in 1899, and Menelik's proposal should have been leapt at with alacrity. Instead, the British government procrastinated. They were reluctant to accept Menelik's new line because it meant a considerable loss of the territory included by the Italian protocol. On the other hand they were reluctant to spend funds on border patrols to prevent further Abyssinian invasion. It was an awkward dilemma, and certainly not one that encouraged instant action. As was to be expected, Harrington was issued orders to continue with his delaying tactic. Britain, in doing this, unwittingly played once more into Menelik's hands, and so he continued with his territorial accumulations. In fact, Britain's parsimony gave Menelik time to tidy up loose ends and appropriate the desirable little remaining corners on which he had set his sights. Powerless to interfere, Harrington nevertheless continued to ply Whitehall with exhortations for action, but in vain, for an atmosphere of torpor seemed to invest the Foreign Office over this particular affair, so nothing happened.

In June 1900, a year after he had made his first serious boundary proposal, Menelik presented yet another plan. In desperation Harrington advised his seniors in London that the new boundary line represented the maximum the king would yield. It was, quite simply, a case of now or never. But still the Foreign Office made no move. Indeed, the situation was now proving a nightmare to poor Harrington, who wrote anxiously in 1901: 'Until some sign of our authority, however small, exists in the northern portion of our B.E. African Protectorate, it is hopeless trying to prevent the Abyssinian raids and . . . when a raid takes place it is a waste of time complaining'. It was a cry repeated by an administrative official in the Protectorate to his Commissioner, when he announced the Abyssinians' arrival that same year at a point on the Juba river *south* of Lugh, and reported that they were full masters of the situation there. This encroachment was an ominous one, deep into Protectorate property, and called for urgent action.

At long last a breath of fresh air whispered through the musty rooms of Whitehall, and the British government finally paid heed to the calls from east Africa. It was now 1902, and, belatedly, the Foreign Office wanted to do something about negotiating an official boundary between the Protectorate and Abyssinia. It was agreed that diplomatic backing should be given to a formal survey of the districts in the region of Menelik's suggested border line. But stingily only diplomatic assistance was proffered; the rest of the burden was to fall on the shoulders of Archibald Edward Butter, the eager young Scottish sportsman who had travelled so light-heartedly with the Harrison expedition in 1899. It is hard to believe that the government of the greatest imperial power of the day could stoop to such niggardliness as to accept private financing for an official expedition whose sole purpose was to define one of its possession's borders. One wonders just how much longer the government would have delayed before undertaking this critical task if Butter had not been forthcoming with the necessary funds and enthusiasm.

At the time Butter volunteered to lead the Boundary Commission survey, he was laird of Faskally, the magnificent 33,000 acre Scottish estate whose bounds ranged over the rugged hills and glens of Perthshire. Born in 1874, he inherited the lairdship from his father at the tender age of six, and with it a deep love for the wild countryside which the Butter family had owned for over a hundred years. Schooled at Eton, where he proved a mediocre scholar and athlete, young Archie's main interests included the challenges of the outdoor sportsman—shooting, fishing and the breeding of gun dogs*.

Butter made several trips to Africa in a very short period, the first with Harrison, and the last on his boundary expedition, which ended in 1903. The final journey seemed to sate him, and he never returned to that continent. For Butter, 1910 was a notable year in which two events of importance took place: Faskally was reluctantly sold, and he married. Moving to the Borders of Scotland he continued with his dog breeding, but with the change his interest shifted to sheepdogs, as farming had become his main occupation. The First World War saw a spell as a captain in the Scottish Horse, but a breakdown in his health prevented further front-line service, and

---

*Butter was one of the top Labrador retriever breeders of the times, and was responsible for much of the pioneer work on improving the quality of the breed. One dog, 'Peter of Faskally', became famous as a champion in its class during the early years of the century.

he ended the war as an ambulance driver. For the rest of his short life, which ended early in 1928, Butter suffered poor health, a misfortune which may have had its origins in his African travels, particularly on his last expedition in 1903, which turned out to be an unduly stressful experience for him.

When Butter volunteered to sponsor and lead the boundary expedition he was only twenty-eight years of age. There is little doubt that the immense pleasure he had derived from his previous experience of life in the African bush induced him to offer to lead this expedition. There is also no doubt he was quite unaware of the trials in which he would shortly be ensnared. It was a challenge he had 'been incessantly longing to do for nearly two years', encouraged by his involvement in 1901 on one of the two abortive War Office attempts to do the job. On that occasion he had accompanied a man named Darrah and two plane table men on their fruitless effort. It was an ill-prepared trip, which foundered soon after leaving the port of Zeila. Instead the party abandoned all thoughts of further work, and applied their energies to shooting game in Somaliland, such was the light-hearted mood of that luckless enterprise. Shortly after his own successful survey journey, and in recollection of the Darrah failure, Butter wrote these frank words of appraisal: 'I can truthfully say I don't believe a W.O. [War Office] Expedition on hard and fast rules would have had the ghost of a chance of getting through'. He was probably a bit over-zealous in his statement, but if one remembers Austin's disastrous expedition, and views it as a yardstick of officialdom's apparent shortcomings at organisation, then Butter had good reason to write as he did.

It appeared the young Scotsman had at that stage in his life discovered a social conscience, and a need to prove his worth as a useful citizen. He earnestly wanted to establish a new image, distinct from that of the landed gent, whose presence on the shooting moors, attendances at official county council meetings and sporting disappearances to the Dark Continent, seemed to be his sole concerns. Several times he brought up the subject in his diary during the stressful months while his expedition laboured through the unsurveyed terrain of the border region. One entry in particular bears out his moral obligation to the task: 'I would give anything to be out of Africa . . . but I am far from kicking from it. On the contrary, it was the best day in my life that I ever took the job on. It is one of those things that it is ripping to have done but pretty damnable in doing, but I guess anything worth doing or having is in the same category . . . I only hope I can get through this expedition as it is the only thing I have ever undertaken that really matters'.

On reading through Butter's diaries and letters one becomes increasingly aware of the motivations which led him to subscribe his time and financial backing to the survey expedition. From these records it is quite apparent that he had no real inkling of the immensity of the task which lay ahead of him, a fact he later divulged in a letter to a friend when he wrote: 'If I had known what was in front of me I wouldn't have touched the job for anything on earth and let the govt do their own dirty work'. While it is true that the desire to tackle something of real value was paramount in his mind, there most certainly lurked an ulterior motive—big game shooting. Already besotted with the thrills of the African chase, Butter could not resist the temptation of a return trip to his favourite hunting grounds. It was a happy coincidence for him that they lay for a great part in the border region to be surveyed, and there is no doubt this influenced his decision. Time and time again his lengthy diary entries confirmed his relish for the hunt. A brief note on the topic written early in the journey was quite explicit: 'Though sport is not the object of the expedition and though everything is to be sacrificed making a satisfactory frontier, still as we go through unknown Africa there must be plenty sport'. The anticipation was reinforced by his personal armoury of five sporting rifles.

In mid-1902 a memorandum from the British Embassy in Rome reiterated England's earlier promise 'to act in agreement with the Italian government' in any disputes over the boundary's delimitation. It went on to state that the Anglo-Italian protocol would continue to be observed in all future discussions, and furthermore, agreed that support should be given to the Italian representative in Addis Ababa on any border matters linked to his nation's interests. It was a harmonious accord, in which Italy also agreed to support England 'such as to strengthen their common interest at the Court of Menelik for the purpose of safe-guarding their reciprocal rights and interests'. Yet Britain and Italy continued to pay little heed to Menelik's self-asserting circular of 1891.

Into this stew-pot Butter blithely stepped. By early 1902 diplomatic wheels had been set in motion, and plans were afoot for his expedition. Butter was issued with a clear-cut set of instructions by Harrington, including a request that sufficient information be placed in his hands which would enable him to negotiate the final demarcation of the border with Menelik. Where possible the survey was to follow a line defined by obvious natural features, which as far as possible was not to interfere with tribal limits*. One final requisite before work could commence was Menelik's permission for the party to travel in his southern territory. Harrington, in his formal application, carefully explained the British government's need of more detailed information about the country at stake. Menelik readily agreed, being fully confident that his policy of 'effective occupation' had by then swamped all the territory previously claimed by Britain under the Anglo-Italian protocol.

With the groundwork completed, Butter set about recruiting a suitable team for his challenging assignment. Above all, it was vitally important for him to have the services of a professional surveyor with previous experience of such field-work. Butter needed 'a real hard man, as perfectly correct work was required'. His special request for Captain Philip Maud of the Royal Engineers was readily granted by the Foreign Office, and in him Butter could hardly have found a more fastidious and industrious worker.

It might confidently be said that Maud's family background had imparted in him the spirit of an earnest and tightly self-disciplined martinet. At the time of his birth, in August 1870, his father was the Rector of Sanderstead, his mother the daughter of a colonel in the Rifle Brigade. On the completion of his schooling at Leamington College, where he had proved outstanding in the classroom and on the playing fields, Maud's great ambition was to join the Army.

Unfortunately his father could afford him only a meagre allowance of £50 a year, so, like his contemporary Austin, he opted to join the Royal Engineers. During his spell with the Royal Military Academy at Woolwich he turned out to be an exceptional cadet, excelling at both bookwork and sport. By the age of nineteen he was in the

---

*As it turned out this didn't entirely happen, and to this day the Borana overlap the boundary between Ethiopia and Kenya.

*Captain Philip*
*Maud, R.E.*

Engineers, and again proving his skills as a first-class rugby player and cricketer. Standing just over six feet, his stern blue eyes and rugged physique projected a formidable force on the rugby field, and by the time he was twenty-three he had twice been capped to play for England's forward line in international matches.

Following a military stint in England Maud was posted to India, where he excelled himself doing survey work on the testing North West Frontier. There he gained the experience which was to prove its worth over and over again on Butter's 1903 expedition in Africa.

While Maud was enjoying a period of leave in England Butter made contact and offered him the post of expedition surveyor at £60 per month. On his acceptance, a partnership was formed which at times proved upsettingly turbulent, fraught with clashes of their widely divergent natures. It said a lot for the self-discipline of the two men that their efforts were ultimately rewarded with success.

In 1910, after a period as a Staff Officer, Maud retired from the Army and joined the London County Council as Chief Officer of their Department of Parks and Open Spaces. Apart from five years of service during the 'Great War', when he attained the rank of Brigadier General, the remainder of his life was devoted to the improvement of the London Parks, and activities centred round the interests of sport and youth.

When Butter, the relaxed and easy-going country squire, employed Maud, he had been told of the engineer's skills at surveying, but was quite ignorant of his character. Many years later the stern unbending man earned this filial description: 'My father was an outstanding man ... He had a first class brain and was something of a mathematician. As a sportsman he was not only a Rugby international, first class cricketer and good racquets, squash and golf player, but also a good big and small game shot and horseman. He was very meticulous and thorough, and set the highest standards over all things for himself and others. He was inclined to be rather strict but was very fair minded with a great sense of duty and justice'. Under the stresses and strains of travel other facets of Maud's character would come out, but in a final appraisal of his meticulous work, Butter generously wrote: 'Maud's work is accurate enough, I believe, for a Govt. survey map of England'. He was certainly well qualified to bear one of the Royal Engineers' two mottos during his working life—'Quo Fas et Gloria Ducunt' (Where Right and Glory lead).

To assist him in his labours Butter was loaned the able young man who was Harrington's assistant at Addis Ababa—John Lawrence Baird. Exactly the same age as Butter, and an old school friend from Eton days, Baird was an invaluable support to the expedition leader, displaying a forceful ability in his capacity of political officer; it was an attribute which stood him in good stead in later life, as he climbed up the ranks through a variety of parliamentary posts in London, eventually becoming Baron Stonehaven and Governor-General of Australia. Baird's position on the boundary survey was at times an intensely trying one, but he had benefited from a stiff training under Harrington, and his results more than justified this brief appraisal from Butter: 'John has done more than any of us for the success of this show'. That remark was, just possibly, tinted with a shred of old school tie loyalty, for Maud too could legitimately claim to have played a vital role on the expedition.

One other man of note played his part: the Somali Butter had met on the Harrison expedition, who had previously served Wellby and others so magnificently and the paragon of caravan leaders, Mohamed Hassan. His labours during the months of travel

*Count Guiseppe Colli de Felizzano.*

on the survey's routes were prodigious. To Butter he was worth his weight in gold: 'My headman . . . I think the best headman in Somaliland . . . He is a first rate man . . . and in my opinion there is not his equal in Africa'.

To complete the party Butter was lent Dr Wakeman, the British Residency doctor in Addis Ababa, and two Indian plane table men, Khan Sahib Sher Jung of the Survey of India, and Shahzad Mir of the famed Bengal Lancers. The latter could well claim to be a veteran of travel hardships after his two testing journeys with Wellby. One other person joined Butter's caravan—the handsome secretary to the Italian legation in Addis Ababa, Count Guiseppe Colli di Felizzano. He had no function except that of observer, and before the end caused Butter no end of irritation, but at the time it was deemed politic to take him along: 'I took him to save complications with the Italians, to make the survey more pukka and that is the only object of the expedition'. The spirit of the Anglo-Italian protocol clearly still prevailed.

On 6 November 1902, after two months of preparations, everything was finally ready. That day the advance guard left Addis Ababa for its first base camp at the foot of Mt Zukwala. Three days later Butter and Baird joined it there. For the first time the whole force was together in one place, and Butter could take stock of his small army: five Europeans, 2 Indians, 70 Somalis and 12 Abyssinians. To carry the equipment and stores for his entourage, 160 camels, mules and donkeys were used. Twelve ponies, of which eight were Butter's own, accompanied the tightly knit force. To round off the list Butter took with him three half-bred dogs from Scotland—Flint, Hector and Soldier.

Butter's expedition was not travelling on its own. An Abyssinian delegation travelled with it to see that fair play was observed, and to ensure that the prying eyes of the British did not reach into corners they were supposedly not meant to see. Three officials of importance represented Menelik's government. Two bore the senior military rank of Kanyazmach, and had been sent as observers. The third was a man named Ato Mama, who had spent six years in France and was considered educated enough to act as the official Abyssinian recorder on the trip. They in turn were escorted by a motley band of camp followers, which brought the combined total of Abyssinians and Butter's party to a ponderous two hundred souls.

Zukwala marked the first important survey point of Maud's assignment. As he was anxious to continue the line he had started at Addis Ababa—a point already established by earlier surveyors—through the summit of this 10,000 foot (3,000 metres) high peak, he ascended it in the company of Baird, only to spend several bitterly cold hours perched on its exposed summit, buffeted by a gale of wind. While Maud carefully took his star bearings through chinks in the clouds, 'Baird took time completely covered by a rug', but by one o'clock in the morning they had had enough, so hastily retreated to their camp in the shelter of the crater. They deserved success, but to Maud's chagrin all this hardship on their first working day was worthless; he found Baird had used the wrong chronometer, so 'the lat was no use'. After continuing their observations the next day in cold misty conditions, a further irritation arose on their return from the mountain when they found the mule detailed to carry the cumbersome surveying paraphernalia had left with the departing camp. It was hardly an auspicious start, and must have tested Maud's temper greatly, but it was early days and tolerance of mishap was still at a high level. Those few days in fact gave Maud ample opportunity to assess the expertise of his two Indian surveyors, and his diary entry described their abilities: 'Jemadar Shahzad Mir ... He is imaginative but I know he is not accurate. He however will always produce a map of something. Sher Jung is a good surveyor, works systematically and clearly and has an excellent eye for country'. Right up to the end of the survey Maud never found any cause to alter his first opinion of those two willing men, and as time went on Maud developed an increasing admiration for Sher Jung: 'The more I see of this man the more am I pleased. His energy, the accuracy and neatness of his work, his pleasant manner, the extraordinary knowledge of country all go to make him the most valuable asset to the expedition'.

On 12 November the caravan left Zukwala camp and headed south, marching for the first time as one body; but not before Butter could record that he had managed to shoot '19 hartebeests, 11 Grant's gazelle, one cock ostrich and 3 reedbuck'. He justified this week's slaughter by the need to feed 'about 200 men' daily, and in common with the practice of the times, when there was plenty of game around he took advantage of it to conserve his other rations. From the hunting angle it was certainly an exceptional start to a non-sporting expedition, but a sour note had already struck as Butter noted in his diary with some bitterness: 'Colli ... said he was coming too to hunt as he is only with us for political reasons, as a guest and only a passenger, to say the least of it most caddish. It is the devil to have to race with him for game, and at the same time work the survey and look after the caravan ... It is annoying however, as without him Johnny and I might get a little good shooting and there would be none of this nasty and bad feeling'. Already Butter's hunting appetite had created a disturbing effect on himself and some of the expedition members.

Butter's party had a specific point to look for as its starting base for the boundary survey. This important spot lay at the intersection of the 6° latitude and the Ganale river, and it was, by chance, coincident with a distinct bend in the river's course. That was the point where the tentative Anglo-Italian protocol boundary left the river and followed the 6° parallel westward. The crucial bend was the expedition's first main objective, and could clearly be seen on Bottego's map of the river. The fact that the Ganale had a surfeit of dramatic bends as it tumbled down on its escape route from the mountains of Sidamo, coupled with the discovery that Bottego's survey had only been done with a prismatic compass, so was not entirely accurate, made the expedition's task far from easy. To complicate the matter further Ato Mama had been told by Menelik that 'we were to start the survey at the junction of the Ganale and the Daua just above Lugh'. Whichever was the correct starting point, one thing was clear: a broad strip of country in the general region of the proposed border would have to be surveyed in order to satisfy everyone.

As the caravan progressed on its way southwards, passing Lakes Zwai, Langano, Shala and Awasa, the mountains of Sidamo rose forbiddingly ahead. The route to the Ganale lay across those endless ranges, which at that time of year were shrouded in chill mists and sodden by torrential rainstorms. It was miserable going for everyone, but particularly the desert-loving camels, who started to collapse and die. That first crisis struck the party only one month after its departure from Addis Ababa, and remedial action was urgently called for if the expedition was to survive.

Butter made the correct decision; he had to split his party. He himself hurried on ahead with the camels, leading them to a warmer district, while Maud plodded along behind at his own pace, religiously carrying out his difficult survey line through the monotonous miles of rain-drenched and densely forested mountain. He only caught up with the main party some two weeks later, having 'plane tabled as much of the country as was possible on the march down'. A letter from Butter awaited Maud on his arrival in camp. The contents did not please the diligent surveyor. Butter and Baird had left camp that day on a jaunt, and his letter explained: 'The camels will require a few days rest here and I have allowed 8 days for this, and Baird and I are going off this morning on an 8 days hunt to Ganale and also to prospect the country'. Grumpily, Maud commented in his diary: 'Butter and Baird have gone off shooting leaving camp "in the air" in the middle of a practically pointless country . . . a place which hinges on nothing—I can do nothing here'. Despite Butter's truancy and Maud's disgruntled feelings, there was good reason for a respite: the camels badly needed a rest, and it gave Mohamed Hassan time to bargain for more beasts from the local Borana. As it turned out, Butter and Baird were back in four days, having found no elephants to shoot.

Christmas Day found everyone united at Darar. It was the last time they would be together for several weeks, for they had now reached the proximity of the Ganale river and the serious work of the expedition was about to begin. Butter had been successful at Darar with his purchase of replacement camels from the Borana. As fortunate had been his second lucky escape from the attack of a wounded elephant. On both occasions he had missed death by a fraction, and one can well appreciate Maud's

*A group of Gallas (Borana) as they were found by the Butter survey expedition in 1903.*

feelings as he contemplated the thoughtlessness of the expedition leader's continued gambles with mortal danger: 'Butter following some others [elephants] to a bad place, narrowly escaped being killed—That's twice'.

An insidious state of affairs developed at that pivotal stage. The Abyssinian Kanyazmaches now displayed their true colours, but not in an obvious manner. Despite the letters of authority Butter carried from Menelik, allowing him to travel freely wherever he wished, granting him permission to hunt at will, and ordering everyone in his path to give him all the assistance they could, the first signs of obstruction became apparent. The survey had by then reached the Borana part of Gallaland, and was camped on the edge of Menelik's claims. Judging by the signs passed on the road, some of the so-called occupation was very recent—an indication of a token last minute extension of Abyssinian-held ground to best the survey party. The country was at the time virtually unexplored by white men and not well known by the Abyssinians either. For those very reasons Butter planned on using the resident Borana people as informants on the local geography*. An unpleasant disclosure then revealed the first of the Abyssinian officials' calculating moves. It was Colli who divulged that: 'the Gallas had orders not to speak to us or come near our camp, and if by chance they couldn't avoid speaking to us, to give us all the misleading information they could. If we asked about game they were to tell us the exact opposite to the fact. Colli says that this is done by Dugafu's [one of the Kamyazmaches] orders. He says

---

*The Borana lived in three different regions: Liban—the northern section lying between the Ganale and Daua rivers; Dirre—the southern section between the Daua river and the Megado (Goro) escarpment; Tertale—the western section, up to the Tertale Mountains.

that if Dugafu can keep to the letter of the King's orders and still bitch our show he will do so'. All that was amply confirmed by the faithful Mohamed Hassan and the Amharic-speaking Dr Wakeman. For the next few months Butter experienced endless efforts on the part of the Abyssinians to hide facts, obstruct and mislead where they could, and generally display a deviousness which nearly drove him to despair, forcing him to record some testy thoughts in his diary about the unwanted passengers he had been required to take along: 'The case is really the Abyssinians insist on taking us for fools . . . It isn't their game to incense us, and if they see they can't play tricks with us, they will give in absolutely. So they live for intrigue and can't see straight if their lives depended on it, but their intrigues and lies are so palpably childish'. Once, on being forced to give the Abyssinians a particularly severe dressing down, Butter ended by telling them: 'In the King's [Menelik's] own words—anyone who interferes with us, let him beware'. That helped clear the air for a while, but another factor had by then crept in to add to Butter's exasperation: Colli was bent on his own little Mediterranean-style intrigue. Once more Butter committed terse observations to his diary: 'Colli is very busy getting me all the information that he can from the Gallas . . . Colli gives me the impression of being as keen as the Abyssinians to prevent the Gallas of speaking to Wakeman, Mohamed or me'. All that and more provoked Butter into writing dejectedly: 'Ye Gods! what a life of intrigue and lying I have been thrust into'. Most fortunately the beleaguered young Scot had an able and potent assistant in John Baird, his political officer, for he alone was able to cope with the twisted machinations of Abyssinian subterfuge. His tough diplomacy stood the expedition in good stead on many an occasion, and the C.M.G.* he later received was a hard-earned reward for all his efforts.

With the end of the brief Christmas respite at Darar the critical part of the expedition's programme started in earnest. Perched as he was on the fringe of Boranaland, Butter's first concern was to decide on the best means of surveying the vast Liban and Dirre region. Under the Anglo-Italian protocol this land had been allocated to Britain, but Menelik also claimed it as his land by his right of 'effective occupation'. The situation was a tricky one, compounded by the overall lack of knowledge of the region—apart from the recognised through trade routes and Bottego's rough guide-lines along the Daua and Ganale rivers—and the unco-operative tactics of the Abyssinian escort. Time was too valuable, as the work had to be completed as far as possible before the onset of the rainy season in April. Accordingly, Butter decided to split the party once again, and for the next four months the detached groups ranged back and forth over an area of 3,000 square miles, meeting up every few weeks for an exchange of news before departing once again on their spider-web pattern of trails. The connecting links between those industrious parties were Somali runners who travelled prodigious distances bearing messages and letters between Butter and Maud. Baird alternated between the two men, and on one occasion he spent two lonely weeks on his own preoccupying the Abyssinians, and by doing so enabled the others to go unhindered about their tasks.

In his capacity as leader Butter was often sorely tested by the administration of his widespread operation: 'It is not the actual work but I cannot get my mind off thinking about this show . . . wondering whether Maud is going on alright, or when I get back to

---

*A civil award—Companion of (the Order of) St Michael and St George.

camp whether he will be indignant with me . . . how the camels are . . . how the food is going to work out . . . and the same interminable round till I almost believe I am frantic, going mad, and begin to believe I will go on thinking of nothing else all my life'. It was quite understandable how Butter, only just twenty-nine years old, suffered such mental nightmares as he carried that weighty responsibility on his youthful shoulders. By his own admission: 'I have been a drone all my life and still not used to thinking of one thing i.e. the b..... frontier and all the incidents connected therewith, and have occasional lapses'. For a man whose great love was hunting, and who claimed 'the very sound of a lion roaring banished all thoughts of survey or frontier matters from my mind altogether', he had to exert on himself an immense amount of self-discipline and determination to keep his 'show' on the road: 'This is partly owing to this trip being so full of nothing but worries, produces nerve strain, especially to a fellow like me not used to this sort of life'. All in all, it was to his great credit that the work continued so successfully.

Two important tasks had to be completed in Boranaland, and both of them were time consuming. The survey work was the party's main assignment, but it also had to 'get to the bottom of the tribal situation' in the district. The first was Maud's paramount concern, and he, laboriously dedicated to exactitudes in his triangulation and survey duties, set his own pace in his pursuit of precision. A meticulous worker, more often travelling apart from the main body of the expedition, he often appeared to his compatriots to be progressing at a snail's pace. He was not, however, to be rushed, and although at times his fastidious nature was strained to the limit by the ineptitude of his assistants on the one hand, and personality differences with members of the survey group on the other, through thick and thin he assiduously applied himself to his task; he would check and recheck his base points to such a fine degree that in the end he achieved exquisitely accurate results. Despite that, the continued reflections in Butter's diary displayed a vacillating opinion of Maud: 'Maud is such a keen and enthusiastic worker and never spares himself or cares how often he spends nights sitting on the summit of some infernal mountain . . . whenever I have constrained to tell him to mind his own business he had of course always given in, or else I would have sent him home . . . He is as hard on himself as he is on others, and no man could work harder or better . . . He is older than I am and thinks himself perfect in all things . . . I have a great respect for Maud in many ways, but he is annoyingly small minded in some things'. For Butter—he admitted he was 'too good natured'—coping with a man of Maud's keen mentality and often self-righteous stances must have been an immense headache. There can surely be no doubt that Maud, the older of the two, must have on occasions appeared a terrifying individual to the amiable easy-going Butter.

The second thing Butter had to deal with in Boranaland was a thorough investigation of the Borana people, including their distribution. It involved extensive interrogations, all done as the expedition groups went about their daily survey chores. Butter, Baird and Maud were equally occupied in that painstaking duty, often hindered by the underhand tactics of their Abyssinian escort. Despite that hurdle they gradually accumulated enough information from which to draw a picture of the Borana society's position in the region, and in doing so they laid a foundation for future ethnographers.

By the end of February the expedition had completed an overall survey of Liban and Dirre. The country had been methodically criss-crossed, most of the main features triangulated, the Ganale and Daua rivers traced for many miles, Bottego's map corrected, and the Borana questioned at length. Out of all that effort one clear fact emerged: there was no possibility of making a frontier based on the original proposals, and anyway, as Maud frankly noted on finishing his survey of Liban: 'The country gained by us, ie, the bit N of Daua, simply isn't worth a damn. It is habitable only in the rains, and then the whole country must be damnable'. In any case, the Abyssinian penetration had proceeded far too deeply into the district, and it was obviously determined to stay. One other influencing factor appeared: there was a marked lack of prominent features with which to demarcate a boundary line. This would result in an expensive and difficult border to police. It was also clear that such a line would split the Borana, which Britain wished to avoid.

Butter would have been in a predicament had Mohamed Hassan not returned from an extensive side trip to the south with some intriguing information. He had learnt from the Borana 'of the existence of a remarkable escarp running for a considerable distance east and west, which marked the limits of the plateau inhabited by the Galla Borans'. Surprisingly, none of the party seemed to have heard of that striking feature before; surprising, because Delamere had seen it in 1897 and Donaldson Smith in 1899, and, moreover, both men had actually descended it in the course of their travels. Anyhow, at the time the news was greeted by Butter with enthusiasm, and soon he and Maud were marching there by separate paths, full of hope and expectation. Maud approached it from the east, first arriving at the cluster of wells by Gaddaduma, nestled in the foot slopes towards the scarp's lowest end. This was a strategic spot, which in years to come would be striven over by Abyssinia and Britain. Turning west at that juncture he followed along the top of the escarp until he met up with Butter and Baird camped on its crest. For the next 70 miles (112 kilometres) the united caravan trudged along the edge of the hills, taking their bearings, and with satisfaction noting the eminently suitable line of the mighty landmark.

The expedition was now entering its third and final stage, and although there was still much territory to be surveyed before it reached Lake Rudolf, with the clarification of the Boranaland question and the discovery of a very workable frontier along the scarp, Butter could at long last see some light. The latter event particularly pleased him: 'I have now to recount the ... best ... news on the whole expedition so far. The ... escarpment Johnny heard about not only exists but does so in a manner to exceed our most sanguine expectation ... It is a sheer escarpment about 1,000 feet [300 metres] and the most perfect natural frontier possible ... It is absolutely the luck of the world to find this escarpment'.

At that point some careful decisions had to be made. It was now late in March and the rains were beginning to threaten. Butter arranged that Baird, Wakeman and Colli, together with the major part of the expedition, should break away and proceed to the north end of Lake Stefanie, where it was hoped they would meet up with Captain Arthur Duff and the resupply caravan he was bringing down from Addis Ababa. Duff, in fact, had kept impeccable time, and rendezvoused with Baird as planned. Butter and Maud in the meantime struggled along with one another's temperaments, and successfully managed to map the rest of the all-important scarp.

At Lake Stefanie Count Colli considered his usefulness over, and with alacrity he packed up and left with his group for Addis Ababa. His relationship with the expedition had not been an altogether happy one; his conflict with Butter in the field of hunting ethics was a continual bone of contention, producing marked ill feelings. That state of affairs, however, had come abruptly to an end on an elephant hunt in early February, when Colli had his left hand shattered by a misdirected bullet. The unfortunate Count had all along been regarded as a rather unwanted hanger-on, imposed on Butter by the suspicions of the Italian representative in Addis Ababa, Major Ciccodicola. Regrettably, Colli had been fully aware of the unpopular arrangement. For him it had been an uncomfortable few months, knowing that he was an undesired guest, and it must have been with a sense of great relief he finally left the Britons and headed for home and creature comforts.

Just to add to Butter's distress he was struck down in early April by sunstroke. While recuperating he had ample time to analyse his innermost thoughts on many aspects of the expedition. Of himself he wrote: 'I was always told I would pay for it [travel in tropical Africa] sometime ... and it would be terrible if I personally on account of my wretched body, interfered with its ultimate success. However, we are within a month of Rudolf and once there, nothing matters'. The magical lake was by then not far off, and Butter, teamed up with the irascible Maud, was about to start the approach march to Lake Stefanie. Although Maud had tended Butter in his sickness 'as if I had been his brother', working with him was still the same old trial: 'I think Maud, though he is a first rate fellow and works like a fiend, gets on my nerves worse than all the rest put together, as I am in a constant state of apprehension about him'. Poor kindly Butter endured that exhausting state of affairs right up to the end of the expedition. It was clearly a case of tender heart versus iron spirit.

Butter's indisposition caused him to be laid up for sixteen days in the Ronso camp. Baird and Dr Wakeman had promptly retraced their steps from Tertale 'by double marches' on receiving 'the melancholy intelligence ... that Mr. Butter was seriously ill'. As soon as the doctor was in attendance, Maud was able to continue his mapping of the escarpment. Another 35 miles (56 kilometres) further on he 'skirted round the end of the great natural balustrade ... and descended by a long easy slope to Golbo'. On 29 April he rejoined forces with Baird and the newly recovered Butter, and three days later the party had crossed the Golbo and were camped by the wells of Saru, near where Wickenburg had camped in 1901.

At that stage in the expedition's long trek Butter was confronted with a major decision. In Addis Ababa Harrington had described an unsurveyed section of Abyssinia's western border, stretching between the Sacchi (Kibish) and Akobo rivers. Austin, on his distressing journey through the district two years before, had not managed to include that line in his survey, and it had now become a matter requiring urgent attention. Butter agreed to try his best to do the additional chore, knowing it would 'save the Government an expedition costing some thousands—it will cost me some hundreds extra'. But it was all dependent on the surveyors' rate of progress on their principal assignment. Moreover, the state of the rains had to be taken into consideration. If Bottego had found himself heavily bogged down in the Akobo Swamps at the peak of the dry season, obviously it was out of the question for Butter to try during the height of the wet season. As it had turned out, more time was spent on the Boranaland survey than Butter budgeted for. Because 'Maud travels of a necessity with his careful work fearfully slowly', and Shahzad Mir had suffered a breakdown in health and was no longer able to assist. Before Butter left Addis Ababa it had been agreed that 15 April was 'the latest date which we should leave Lake Rudolf if this extra work was to be done'. And it was then the beginning of May, the rains had started in earnest, and Maud had not even reached Lake Stefanie. After lengthy discussions with Baird and Maud, Butter wisely decided to forego that added task. As if to reassure himself, Butter noted in his diary: 'When I was ill at Ronso John wrote to me in the strongest possible terms advising me not to attempt to do this work'. Butter discussed the problem with Maud who said: 'it would be pure madness to attempt it, but if I liked he would go. I naturally said I would never ask a man to do a thing that before starting he had stigmatised as pure madness'. With the scrapping of the Akobo journey, Butter's mind was made up; he would complete his survey journey at Lake Rudolf, and return home by way of the eastern lake shores, through Baringo and Nairobi, and embark at Mombasa.

On 1 May 1903, Maud and Butter once more took separate paths: Maud to climb Mt Jabisa and Butter to travel to Lake Stefanie in search of Duff's caravan. Maud made his ascent of Jabisa, and Butter luckily found Duff at the south end of the lake. Exultantly, Butter wrote: 'It is a rum thing to be at Lake Stefanie again after four years . . . The whole place is swarming with game . . . For the first time on this trip I really feel I am in Africa and that all the terrible country we have been through must be some other country . . . by God, it is a relief to feel that our work is practically over, and well over too . . . A few days ago I was still thinking everything was rotten—we had no shooting and a stinking six months. Now the frontier is done . . . Now we [Butter, Baird, and Duff] never mention the word frontier and we have dinner parties when we talk of shooting here and at home'. His jubilant words were soon put into effect as the three young men set about their hunting with a will, the pages of Butter's diary being crammed with tales of gripping lion hunts in the neighbouring bushlands.

Meanwhile Maud plodded on with his chores, fixing his points, ascending the Tertale Mountains to the summit of their highest peak, and squaring away the remaining details of the frontier survey. But it was not just work that occupied Maud, for he too was a keen shot, and on his trek he was fortunate in bagging a magnificent leopard with his little .256 Mannlicher rifle. On 8 May he rejoined the others in their main camp. Stopping only briefly to discuss further plans, Maud was on his way the next day, leaving the three enthusiastic sportsmen to continue with their hunting spree—Butter was anxious to 'get twenty lions between us'.

Clambering into the hills rising to the west of Lake Stefanie, Maud made his last few frontier triangulations. Hills marked on his 1903 map as South Hill and Rocky Hill are still shown by these names, and it was from the summit of the latter that the industrious surveyor made his terminal triangulation station. From that isolated prominence he could see the waters of Lake Rudolf's northern tip shining some 20 miles (32 kilometres) to the west*.

When Maud finally caught up with the main caravan on 24 May his mammoth task was completed, except for a few verifications he wanted to make on the homeward stretch. As Butter noted: 'Maud is very pleased with his work—all his triangles perfect and checks working out to fractions'.

After nearly five months together the party was now breaking up. Colli had already left for home, and now that the Abyssinian entourage had reached their

---

*Since Maud's day the lake has receded greatly, and the north end is now some 35 miles (56 kilometres) to the south.

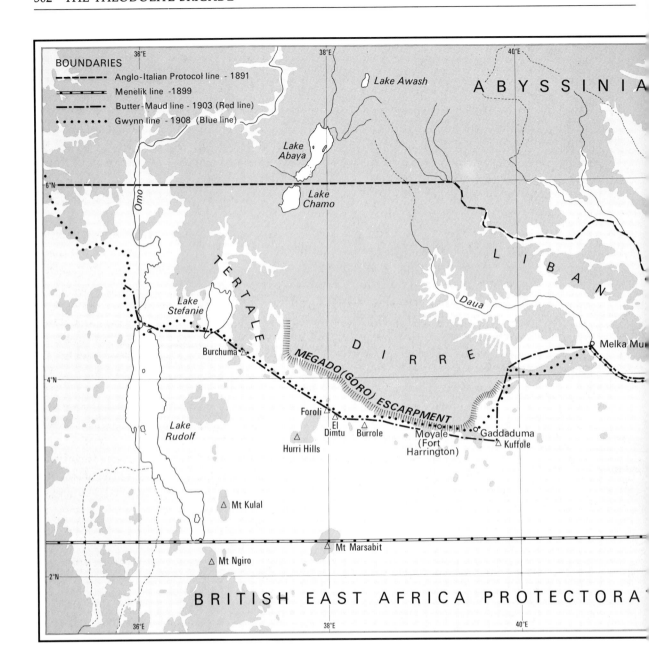

*Boundaries proposed between Abyssinia and British East Africa.*

country's southern limit, they also departed, laden with gifts and goodwill. Butter's group, delayed for a few days to allow Baird to recover from a minor lion mauling, then made a start on its homeward march down the lake shore. Butter was now on the eve of finishing his journey: 'Marching is not amusing in Africa or anywhere else ... even marching in Africa is good enough, and heaven compared to the damnable civilised life in Europe. I simply dread the idea of going back to it. Every step homewards towards boiled shirts and respectability ... gives me cold shivers'. There was a touch of irony in those words, if one recalls Butter's lamentation during the preceding months. The indefatigable Maud, however, was not tired of marching. The dedicated surveyor twice broke away from the main party to investigate landmarks far to the east

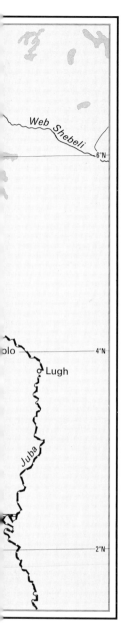

of the lake-shore route. He was the first white man to walk round the prominent red hills of Shin, Derati and Kubi Algi, sited far inland from Alia Bay, and further on became the first to reach the summit of Mt Kulal.

On 18 June the whole expedition, which at that stage included ninety camels and a hotch-potch of three hundred donkeys, mules and sundry livestock, clambered up the steep slopes and out of the lake basin. A few days were spent in the picturesque valley entrenched between Ol Doinyo Mara and Mt Ngiro, where the animals rested and the white men hunted to their heart's content. Only one month after leaving the lake the party were sitting in Mombasa. They had travelled uneventfully by way of Baringo to Nakuru, where Butter had sold all his animals to some Somali traders for over ten thousand rupees*, and then caught the train to the coast.

Butter could justly contemplate his expedition's triumphs with pride, especially in the light of others' failures. Despite the stresses and strains, which on occasion came close to overwhelming him, success had been his reward. It had certainly been a severe test for the young man, one which probably would not have proved as formidable to an older and more experienced person, but he had won through, assisted by the tireless efforts of his industrious colleagues, Maud and Baird. In a stiffly formal letter from the Foreign Office, the Marquess of Lansdowne wrote to Harrington: 'I request that you will convey to Mr Butter the thanks of His Majesty's Government, with an expression of their high sense of his public spirit in undertaking this expedition, and of the perseverance, courage, and judgement with which he has carried it to a successful conclusion'. It was the very least he could have said, for Butter had most generously provided almost two years of his time and at least £10,000 from his private funds for a purpose the procrastinating British government had seemed reluctant to tackle.

When Butter sailed from Mombasa on the Deutsche Ost-Afrika Line's steamship, the *Kronprinz*, he travelled together with his full compliment of Somalis. Thanks to the ministrations of the conscientious Wakeman, not a single man had been lost and, incredibly, he was able to report that none had suffered from either malaria or dysentery, the two malevolent spectres that haunted most expeditions travelling in east Africa in those years. When they disembarked at Aden, Butter could proudly claim that: 'I brought every single one of them back to their homes fit and contented and none left behind'. It was a most creditable achievement for all concerned, and a highly satisfactory note on which to end such a testing expedition. Equally satisfying to Butter, the sportsman, was the party's bag of game trophies. He himself had slain a gigantic elephant with tusks weighing 134 pounds (61 kilograms) each, and had personally accounted for nineteen of the thirty-nine lions shot. All in all the shooting had been a great success with, amongst other animals, twenty rhinos and forty-two species of assorted antelopes falling to their guns. So in the end Butter could not complain, for he had realised his sporting desires.

On reaching England, Butter and Maud each went their ways: Butter back to his Scottish estate, where the grouse shooting season had just begun, Maud to his desk in London. The engineer's job was not yet over, as the serious business of compiling a report and preparing the long-awaited maps still had to be done. By late September everything was finished and the completed report presented to the authorities. In a

---

*Up to 1921 the rupee was standard currency in East Africa. In 1905 a cental coinage was adopted with 100 cents to a rupee. At the time the rupee was worth 1s 4d.

letter introducing it to the Foreign Secretary, Harrington ventured 'to suggest to your Lordship that the services of Messrs. Butter and Baird richly merit recognition by His Majesty's Government'. As one delves deeper into the facts behind the communication, it becomes apparent that of the forty-six pages in the official report, Maud wrote twenty-eight, Baird twelve and a half, and Wakeman only three and a half*. Furthermore, Maud compiled the all-important maps attached to the written report. Butter, the expedition sponsor and leader, wrote a short covering letter. It is strange that while Harrington acknowledged the minor authors, Baird and Wakeman, in his communication, he made absolutely no mention of Maud, the chief subscriber. Unfortunately, it is impossible to account for that regrettable and very obvious omission. Was there a possibility that a tiny whiff of tendentiousness surfaced to tarnish an otherwise wholly commendable performance, or was it that Harrington simply regarded Maud as a fellow soldier who was duty bound to do his job without expectation of bureaucratic praise? Whatever the reason, in the end all was well, with both Butter and Maud receiving the C.M.G.

With Butter's report in their hands, the British government at last had a sound guide-line to assist them in their arguments and substantiate their claims at the negotiating table. The surveyors had done their bit, and now the long drawn-out struggle between the diplomats commenced. Menelik had already declared he would never relinquish any part of Liban, and into the bargain he had dropped an ominous hint to Major Ciccodicola that all would not go Britain's way in future boundary line discussions. The situation was not made any easier by the separate proposals put forward by the two principals, Butter and Maud. Butter suggested a boundary which followed physical features and separated the Gallas from the non-Galla peoples. Maud saw it in a slightly different way; he felt that Menelik's 'effective occupation' should be given consideration. A communication between the Military Intelligence Division in London and the Foreign Office encapsulated his viewpoint: 'Captain Maud's frontier involves the surrender to the Abyssinians of all the country of which they may be said to be in occupation at the present time. Should it be successful as a barrier to prevent them from pressing further south, the sacrifice of territory to which the British Government has claims would be worth the advantage gained'. Maud could foresee clearly that any attempt to make Menelik return to the line of the Anglo-Italian protocol would prove fruitless. Moreover, he warned that the enforcement of his line might require at least three posts of one hundred armed men, supported by constant patrolling.

A telegraphic report to London from the British Legation in Addis Ababa confirmed that Menelik intended squeezing every drop out of the still fluid position. First of all it was confirmed that the King would 'repeat the orders already given by him, that until the frontier has been determined no movements south are to be made by his troops'. A confidential note attached to the report insinuated this might be a smoke screen: 'The southern Chiefs are aware that the Emperor is better pleased by their disobeying his orders not to advance ... His Majesty ... feels that the more territory he can show to be in actual Abyssinian occupation the stronger will his position be when the frontier comes to be discussed here'. That was the latest opinion

---

*Butter's report was presented to both Houses of Parliament in November 1904—Africa No. 13 (1904). Butter had his personal copy bound in pillar-box red leatherette with gold lettering.

in early December 1903; the deft manoeuvres that would continue for many decades had only just begun.

One other problematic ingredient in the approaching boundary discussions was the Italian interest. Nervous lest Britain should make an agreement with Menelik behind their back, the Italian government requested that the British 'should, before actually negotiating the frontier with Menelik, refer to them the proposed modification and obtain pro forma their consent to any changes in the line of the Protocol'. It was an outdated aspiration which Harrington, the man in the forefront, could recognise: 'I cannot see what right the Italians can claim to interfere with any frontier we choose to make with Abyssinia ... The sooner the farce of regarding Abyssinia as an Italian sphere of influence is knocked on the head, the better'. Lansdowne, sitting in his Whitehall ivory tower, did not see it that way, and thereby added to the delay. Higher politics prevailed over the views of the man in the field and by order, before any conclusions were reached, the Italians had to be consulted.

On his way back to Abyssinia at the end of 1903, Sir John Harrington—he had been knighted while in England—stopped in Rome to discuss the Abyssinian case with the Italian government. After somewhat unsatisfactory talks they agreed to the British boundary proposals, but only on the condition that Britain would assist Italy in its claim for Lugh. At that point Harrington was poised at the start of a long exhausting barter session with the Abyssinians and the Italians. At the same time Menelik was busy altering his claims to include tribes and territory hitherto assumed to be outside his province.

The whole of 1904 was taken up with endless inconclusive discussions, and by the middle of 1905 Harrington was deeply concerned. Continued reports of frontier disturbances finally forced him to beg for the employment of a boundary official. The Colonial Office agreed to the request, creating the post of Abyssinian Southern Frontier Inspector with an annual budget of £1,200, which rightly, the British East Africa Protectorate had to meet. It was a frugal amount to pay for the defence of its long and still undefined northern frontier. None the less, it was a step forward, and Harrington already had the right man in mind for the delicate position. Curiously, the candidate was a Greek citizen, Fotios Zaphiro*. He was to prove a wise choice, filling the vacuum perfectly in the four years prior to the advent of the British administration in the Protectorate's northern district.

Zaphiro was an unusual man of many parts, resourceful, politic, and filled with the guiles of the Levant—ideal qualities for coping with his ponderous responsibility. Born in Constantinople (Instanbul) to Greek parents, Zaphiro, after his parents' death, grew up in Cairo in the care of an aunt and uncle. For a while two interests kept him occupied: tending his uncle's shop, and working in the Cairo hospital. By the age of twenty his adventurous nature could no longer take the life in Cairo, so he headed south for Abyssinia. His first step was Harar, where he set up practice as a charlatan doctor. There, with his flair for languages, he soon picked up Amharic to add to the Arabic he could already speak. His scant medical knowledge quickly won him grateful patients among the Abyssinian highborn, an advantage which eased his paths in the years ahead. Harrington first came to know him when trying to obtain special passes

---

*Fotios was the correct Greek spelling, but Zaphiro also signed his name Photius. Later he was known as Philip.

for the McMillan expedition. Zaphiro, with good friends in high places, was just the person to help and swiftly expedited the matter. So impressed was Harrington by this that he asked the young Greek to join the expedition. That event started an association with the British which would continue to the end of his life. For two years he worked as interpreter, negotiator, taxidermist and animal trapper to McMillan, the bulky American millionaire, and at the end he escorted a shipload of wild animals destined for the London Zoo.

Zaphiro had by then developed the talents which were later to stand him in good stead. Sturdily built, he possessed a quiet, jovial, kindly disposition. As the years went by he built up an influential reputation among the Abyssinians, fostered by an excellent knowledge of the local languages and his uncommon ability to handle the peoples of the region. It was fortunate for Harrington that the young Greek was on the spot, and more so that he was willing to accept the role of Boundary Inspector with an annual wage of £200.

In November 1905 Zaphiro started work for the British government. His lonely demanding job lasted until the arrival of the Protectorate's administration in late 1909, when he was called back to Addis Ababa. For his extraordinary service on the frontier he was awarded the C.M.G., a well-deserved reward earned in the hardest possible way. In 1913 he became a naturalised British subject, and for the last fifteen years of his life, which ended in 1933, he was Oriental Secretary to the British Legation in Addis Ababa. Highly respected amongst Europeans and Abyssinians alike, Zaphiro left a heritage of sayings which he had made up in the Amharic language. One he coined in 1909 was still being used many years after his death. It had a practical Levantine flavour: 'Ganzap alle samai mangat alle' (If you have money you can find a way even in the sky).

As soon as Harrington had established Zaphiro as frontier patrolman, he felt on firmer ground. It could hardly be termed solid ground, for Zaphiro had only about £900 a year to run his show, which included a tiny rag-tag army of about two dozen untrained Abyssinians armed with ancient Martini rifles. But he was not daunted by these inadequacies and soon put into practice one of the strategies he was noted for—bluff. First he found a suitable site for his headquarters. It was on a high healthy piece of ground, and he had the local Boranas' agreement on its position. Only later did the authorities find it was almost five miles inside Abyssinian territory, a matter which led to considerable argument. Respectfully, he named his modest stockade Fort Harrington. It was not a place he could spend much time in, as his frontier stretched from Lake Rudolf to the junction of the Ganale and Daua rivers, a distance of almost 500 miles (800 kilometres). The station he built on Churre Moyale hill was almost at the centre of the 'Red Line', the boundary proposed by Maud's survey.

Zaphiro's efforts to patrol the border included fighting bands of Tigre hunter-raiders, halting larger mobs of trespassing Abyssinians, protecting fleeing Borana refugees, controlling the trade routes, and generally trying to keep the peace between the Abyssinians and the British, both of whom had his sympathies. It was certainly not a task for the average man. In a memorandum addressed to the Foreign Office in 1909, Major Gwynn wrote: 'Mr Zaphiro had in many ways done extraordinary good work ... It would be impossible to replace [him] by any one man, his experience and knowledge of languages is unique. But he cannot go on for ever; the loneliness of his position, his health ... may at any time cause him to throw up his appointment'.

Zaphiro never did resign. Instead, through thick and thin he used his amazing skills and tact to hold the line, and while he may not have prevented every incursion and infraction of the law along the boundary, the gradual lessening of activity by the Abyssinians indicated their growing awareness that some form of boundary existed. Zaphiro did in fact construct a few rudimentary beacons along the 'Red Line'. Although the battle was not yet over, between them Harrington and Zaphiro had managed to stabilise the border zone. It was an amazing accomplishment for the two men, and at long last, after years of patient striving, Harrington could see an end to his problems. The great moment arrived on the morning of 7 December 1906 when Menelik and Harrington finally agreed on a formal acceptance of the 'Red Line'.

Hardly was that done than Harrington was on his way to London. The agreement was not deep rooted; the southern chiefs were still agitating for further expansion south to Wajir and El Wak, and there were signs that Menelik's health was beginning to fail, so no time could be wasted in bringing the matter to a close. It took all Harrington's powers of persuasion to pressure the reluctant Colonial Office into accepting the terms, his forceful words clearly indicating a desperation to progress matters: 'It has taken nearly eight years hard fighting to get this frontier, and no time should be lost in sending Mr Clerk telegraphic instructions to sign, as any delay will probably mean we may not get the frontier settled for a year or two more ... In my opinion, we have been a great deal luckier that I ever thought we should be over this border'. With the Colonial Office's approval, a hurried message was sent to his deputy in Addis Ababa ordering him to sign the agreement with Menelik. Needless to say, Menelik balked, and it then took another eleven months of dreary argument, with claims and counter-claims by both parties before he realised that this time the British were adamant in their refusal to be moved from Maud's 'Red Line'. In the end, and with reluctance, Menelik lifted his pen on 6 December 1907 and signed the agreement, exactly one year after his first approval of the terms. At long last Harrington could heave a sigh of relief, for that most protracted of border disputes seemed to be near resolution. Menelik, having finally committed himself, was then anxious to implement the clause in the agreement ' which declared: 'Both Governments shall send Commissioners, who shall, in concert, delimit the exact line of the frontier which is above described, and which is marked ... with a red line'.

Six months later, in May 1908, the British government appointed Major C.W. Gwynn as their Commissioner. The selection of that competent man was reinforced by Menelik's personal desire to have him included in the team—Menelik and Gwynn were old friends. Gwynn was also generally recognised as a highly skilled surveyor; he had earlier worked on three British survey expeditions demarcating the Sudan–Abyssinian frontier, and on the final one Menelik had even gone so far as to entrust him with representing Abyssinian interests too. With his wealth of local experience, he was undoubtedly the best choice to lead the critical assignment on the Southern Frontier Boundary Commission.

Gwynn was a person with a decidedly intellectual background, a man destined to rise to great heights in his lifetime. Only four months older than Maud—he was born on 4 February 1870—his father, like Maud's, was a man of the cloth, and a very esteemed one, having been at one time Professor of Divinity at Trinity College, Dublin. The reverend's son, Charles William, was born in Ireland, and was the third of five brilliant brothers who later all became exceptional men of letters. Gwynn was the odd man out as regards his profession, electing to join the army and become an engineer rather than follow a scholarly bent, but like Maud and his own brothers, he too had been blessed with an incisive intellect. Gwynn and Maud were contemporaries and studied together at the Royal Military Academy in Woolwich. They were later commissioned into the Royal Engineers at the same time. Unlike Austin, who had preceded them by two years, both men excelled in their studies, and like Maud, Gwynn shone on the field of sport—he was one of the gifted few who represented the Corps in the cricket, football, rugby and golf teams.

On completing his course at the School of Military Engineering in Chatham, Gwynn served briefly on the staff there before being posted to Sierra Leone in 1892. After two very active years of field service, which saw him wounded three times, mentioned in despatches and awarded the Distinguished Service Order, he was invalided home. On his recovery another short assignment in Sierra Leone followed, but already his outstanding ability had been noticed, and in 1897 he was appointed to the geographical section of the Intelligence Branch at the War Office. His commanding officer, also an engineer, and late commandant of the school at Chatham, had been greatly impressed with Gwynn's talent as a student, and had made a mental note to watch the young man. He was not to be disappointed.

In 1899 Gwynn was posted to the Sudan. Kitchener had defeated the Dervishes the year before, and the British were busy tying up the loose ends. One of those ends was the survey of the boundary between the Sudan and Abyssinia, and on this exacting duty Gwynn was occupied for four years. For his efforts he received the C.M.G.

On his return to England Gwynn entered the Army Staff College at Camberwell. That step marked the beginning of an illustrious career in the military administration, and excepting the years he was employed as Commissioner on the Abyssinian–East African boundary survey, his professional life was principally taken up with staff appointments. A spell in Australia as acting commandant in the new Military College introduced him to the Australian as a soldier, a relationship which continued into the First World War when he commanded an Australian brigade and fought with them over the infamous battlefields of Gallipoli. He ended the war with the rank of Brigadier General, and in 1918 was created a Companion of the Bath (C.B.). For the latter thirteen years of his active military life Gwynn held a variety of distinguished positions: in 1923 he was A.D.C. to the King, in 1925 he became a Major General, and in 1926 came his last important office—Commandant of the Staff College. In 1931 he retired, earning at the same time a well-deserved knighthood with his promotion to the Knight Commander of the Bath.

During his remaining years Gwynn devoted considerable time to writing and editing articles and books on military subjects, an industry which kept his agile brain fully occupied to the end. He died at the great age of ninety-three, leaving behind him an exemplary record of achievements and honours.

When Gwynn arrived in Addis Ababa at the end of August 1908 he was head of an impressive contingent. The British government, which was determined to conclude the protracted affair, had provided him with a most able team. It consisted of a fellow officer, Captain R. Waller, as his deputy; a transport officer, Captain G. Condon; a medical doctor, Dr R.E. Drake Brockman; and two non-commissioned engineers, Corporal Carter and Sapper Favier, as assistant surveyors. Drawing on the experience that he had gathered on his earlier boundary expeditions, Gwynn procured a herd of

*Major General*
*Charles William*
*Gwynn, R.E.*

Charles Gwynn.

'about one hundred camels, with a dozen riding mules and ponies'. To manage the caravan he elected to recruit a staff consisting of ninety Somalis, led by the steadfast Mohamed Hassan. Of that extraordinary man Gwynn later wrote how much of the expedition's success was: 'due to his immense power of work, loyalty and intelligence'.

Gwynn's first serious problem arose immediately on his arrival in Addis Ababa. He found his friend Menelik was ill. It was the beginning of the final run-down in the old King's health, and unfortunately its effects were to cause the expedition considerable inconvenience. To start with Gwynn found that without Menelik's authority no one could act in his place. As he had not appointed a deputy Gwynn realised nothing had been done to nominate any Abyssinian representatives on the Commission, and as long as the King's indisposition continued it seemed that no progress was likely to be made. For two months Gwynn kicked his heels impatiently in the capital before British patience finally ran out and Gwynn was ordered to continue his journey without an Abyssinian contingent.

Menelik had been advised that Gwynn could not wait for forever. There was a good reason: if his start was delayed later than the end of October the April rains would eventually impede the completion of the survey. With still no response from the Abyssinian government, Gwynn assumed, erroneously, that Menelik's lack of assent was tantamount to consent. Looked at from the Abyssinian viewpoint the British had exhibited arrogant presumptiousness in their approach to the matter, but on the other hand it could be argued that Menelik had entrusted Gwynn with full responsibility on the execution of the Sudan border survey, so why not this one as well. Moreover, a border treaty laying down clear guide-lines had already been signed by both nations, so it should have been simply a matter of finalising the chosen marks on the map. It was quite understandable why Gwynn could only view his predicament as intolerable; after all, he had under his command an expensive commission, and valuable time was running out. The thinly veiled words he wrote at the time clearly displayed his frustration: 'No Abyssinian Minister . . . could take any action when the Emperor was ill. For several days none of the Ministers was transacting business, as they were employed in personally superintending the Emperor's hay-making'.

Hurrying from Addis Ababa on 24 October, Gwynn caught up with his waiting caravan at Ginir, some 200 miles (320 kilometres) south east of the capital. He found his men and animals in a 'deplorable condition'. During their long wait a third of his Somalis had gone down with fever, and despite Condon's ministrations many of the transport animals were suffering as well. Ginir was no longer the rich trading centre it had been when Donaldson Smith first visited it in 1897, and Gwynn found few replenishments for his supplies and transport. It is understandable why he was glad to leave the run-down place and move on towards the starting point for his boundary delimitation—the junction of the Ganale and Daua rivers. Five weeks after leaving Addis Ababa he arrived at that critical point, and there he found the first feeble signs of a British presence. Two lonely white men, representatives of the Boma Trading Company, and in effect the forerunners of the British administration in the district, tended their remote post at Dolo on the river banks. It was there that Gwynn first met the irrepressible Zaphiro, and heard that he was to have his company for part of the boundary route. For both men it was a beneficial alliance. Gwynn then had the assistance of a most able person, well versed in all aspects of border matters; Zaphiro gained companions, and a small army to add to his arm.

Gwynn's job, like Butter's had been before, was twofold. He had to relate the line surveyed by Butter to the rights of the tribes along its course. In the five years since Butter and Maud had done their investigations, regional movements among the tribes had taken place, and it was of vital importance for Gwynn to extend the Commission's knowledge of their boundaries. While Waller moved westwards and verified Maud's stations along the 'Red Line', Gwynn and Zaphiro made a southerly detour to the wells of El Wak. There, they had heard, Abyssinian encroachments had affected the distribution of the Garre and Somalis living in the area. Gwynn found worrying signs, notably the westward pushings of the Somalis, pressured by Abyssinian influxes and the depredations of the Mad Mullah's campaign.

On finishing that task Gwynn rejoined the main expedition at Banissa. He arrived there to find a major set-back; the doctor's health was in jeopardy from the scourge of black-water fever. His case was so bad that he had to be sent back to Addis Ababa, and henceforth home. With the expedition on the eve of entering the most critical stage of its survey, his departure was disturbing.

From Banissa the surveyors moved to Malka Murri on the Daua river, the point at which Maud had begun his line in 1903. Gwynn began his survey along Maud's tracks at the beginning of 1909. Before leaving he reported again to the British Legation that there was still no sign of the promised Abyssinian representatives. Bluntly he wrote: 'In any case they cannot possibly arrive in time to do any work'. Undeterred by their absence, which in a way was a blessing, Gwynn's party commenced their task. Moving with swift efficiency, and with Maud's accurate maps to guide them, Gwynn and his crew travelled steadily westwards. With a view to the future requirements of the border patrols, a special effort was made to determine the positions of vital water supplies on the 'Red Line', and several adjustments in Maud's line had to be made to take this fundamental need into account. At Moyale Zaphiro left the expedition to attend to other pressing matters, and here Gwynn diverted from Maud's route. Instead of marching along the top of the Goro escarpment as Butter had done, he chose to follow the foot of that great feature. It was now late January and the hot unhealthy Golbo lay parched and empty around them. But with no Abyssinian officiousness to hinder them, and by dint of forced marches, the surveyors continued to make excellent time.

For the sake of diplomacy, Gwynn had made persistent efforts to contact the Abyssinians, but eventually, when Fitaurari Waldi of Gardula failed to arrive for a meeting with him in early February, he sent word to Lord Hervey, the British Minister in Addis Ababa, with a brusque comment that: 'He [Waldi] however, evidently is desirous to avoid meeting me and sent an excuse for not coming. I shall not make any further effort to get into direct communication with these Frontier Officers as this is the third failure I have had and each involved expenditure of time'. Waldi's indifference was simply a reflection of the worsening state of affairs in Abyssinia as Menelik's grip on his administration loosened; and the situation was gradually to become even worse.

Gwynn was then at the western end of the Goro escarpment, and at that point he was again in country previously surveyed by Maud. From here there was no need to divert or delay on the final leg to Lake Rudolf, as he was not 'breaking new ground, and making few additions to Captain Maud's map'. Unlike Butter, Gwynn's inclinations were not towards sport, and one feels that the militarily minded Maud would probably have preferred working with that tightly disciplined group. It was due to Maud's pioneering work that Gwynn covered ground so expeditiously, arriving at Lake Rudolf on 22 February. He had taken barely two months to reach the lake from Malka Murri on the Daua river. Gwynn's main task was now done, and there remained only a few points to check in the region north of the lake before he made his way back to Addis Ababa. His journey ended on 20 April 1909. The round trip had taken only six months, despite most of the latter part being undertaken in trying drought conditions, and Gwynn could look back on his team's field work with considerable satisfaction.

In the final analysis Gwynn's expedition was not entirely successful. Granted, the management had been faultless, the survey had confirmed Maud's work and added some further details to the map, and more useful information was collected about the distribution of the tribes in the boundary's vicinity; but regardless of all that, the Abyssinians disputed the findings. Gwynn, it is true, had seen fit to make a few alterations to Maud's 'Red Line', but on an equitable basis, exchanging territory he had excised from Abyssinia with corners he had removed from British claims. Encouraged and advised to do this by Zaphiro, he had thus given the British a series of water points, vital for future boundary patrols. Unfortunately for Britain, on signing the treaty in 1907 agreeing in principle to the 'Red Line', Menelik had already set his mind on Maud's line. Even Gwynn himself conceded this: 'I am afraid these deflections will not prove acceptable to the Emperor and I have been very unwilling to make them as they may appear to be a departure from the Treaty . . . On the other hand I found that at all a literal acceptance of the treaty line would have given us a frontier absolutely impossible to patrol or watch'. On the subject of patrols Gwynn had already expressed the urgency of policing the boundary. Whilst on his march he had intercepted and arrested several gangs of elephant hunters; significantly, most of them were under the orders of their Abyssinian officers. Menelik's discipline was distinctly on the wane, and the need of an obvious British presence on the frontier had become even more imperative. Sir John Harrington, then based in London, had these warning words to say: 'It is absolutely necessary, in my opinion, for us to practically demonstrate with as little delay as possible to both Abyssinians and natives that we really consider the portion of the Protectorate now subject to Abyssinian raids our territory'. Gwynn was also worried that not only would the border patrols be severely hampered by the lack of water points, but the inhabitants of the Golbo on the British side would lose their vital wells to the Abyssinians. Maud had not taken either of those matters into consideration when he drew his line.

The two salient diversions Gwynn made in the boundary were at the all-important well of Gaddaduma and Zaphiro's base at Moyale. Both were in so-called Abyssinian territory, and both were essential for the British administration. Gwynn hoped for an Abyssinian relinquishment of them, and for this he was relying partly on Zaphiro's unique relationship and influence at Menelik's court. He was, however, fully aware that his proposals stood on unsure ground: 'I hope therefore the Emperor may be induced to accept my settlement. At the same time I realise that I may have acted beyond my powers and should the Emperor object it would seem better to throw over my work and leave matters as they were before rather than to deliberately accept an unworkable line'.

Meanwhile, the Abyssinians had obtained the services of a German to act as their boundary Commissioner. Lieutenant Schubert of the 12th Regiment of Artillery (Reserve) was their chosen man, and he was ordered to undertake the independent survey of the 'Red Line' under the supervision of an Abyssinian contingent. Schubert was in an awkward position from the beginning. Employed on the one hand by the Abyssinians, on the other he was under strict instructions from the German legation in Addis Ababa to send them regular reports. To add to his predicament, the Abyssinians, who mistrusted all Europeans, denied him an interpreter, so he was unable to communicate with any of the tribes on his route, and had to listen to the Abyssinian point of view alone, a decidedly one-sided state of affairs. Hindered from starting his work by the non-arrival of his surveying instruments, coupled with difficulties in obtaining transport and equipment, Schubert was still sitting in the capital when Gwynn returned. By then it was the end of May, and with the onset of the rains it was several months before his work could be finally completed.

Gwynn left Addis Ababa after carefully explaining his demarcation to the Abyssinian authorities. His proposals were rejected by them, needless to add, on the grounds that the Commission had not been properly represented by both parties. Britain retorted to this accusation by blaming the Abyssinians for their dilatoriness in providing Commissioners, despite Menelik's express wish to conclude the matter. The bickering was to go on for years, but in 1909 the British at last put their feet down firmly, and declared the limits of the Gwynn line to be an acceptable frontier. Abyssinia never approved this boundary—the 'Blue Line'—and carried on determinedly with their infringements on the Protectorate territory, but now it was against increasing resistance. It was a contest which would continue for another sixty years.

Gwynn's Commission report, meticulous but disrupting, earned praise from the Colonial Office, and as one senior civil servant minuted: 'It is impossible for one sitting in an office at home to criticise a piece of boundary work like this. But Major Gwynn's report makes an excellent impression, and satisfies one that he has weighed very carefully the considerations involved, and that his recommendations deserve acceptance'. He ended by saying: 'We should also tell the W.O. [War Office] that the S. of S. [Secretary of State] appreciates very highly the excellence of Major Gwynn's work, and the value of the advice which he has given'.

After years of side-stepping and manoeuvring, some semblance of order was at last in sight on that most fluid of east African boundaries. Harrington, Butter, Maud, Zaphiro and Gwynn had been the principal participants on the British side; Menelik and his ministers represented the Abyssinian side. Both parties had proposed, procrastinated, counterproposed and protested, to the point that no true conclusion was reached. In the end the British Lion stood its ground against the Lion of Judah and an uneasy status quo came into existence, but at a cost. Britain, as a result of its tardiness, had lost nearly 50,000 square miles of the territory it had stood to gain from the Anglo-Italian protocol of 1891.

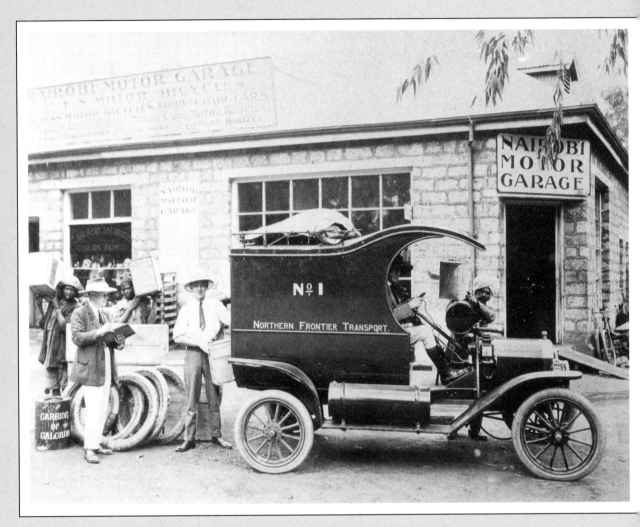

*Loading up one of the first Fords used in the Northern Frontier District – June 1914.*
*(l. to r.) unknown, Jack Boulton, Clement Hirtzel, garage proprietor, behind wheel.*

# PAX BRITANNICA

*'How much European heroism has to spend itself in obscure battle, to sink in mortal agony, before the jungles, the putrescences, and waste savageries can become arable.'*

Thomas Carlyle, *Selected Essays*

'IT is a spacious kingdom. It is a country within a country . . . of vast plains of lava, of sand, of thorn scrub. There are the traditional deserts of Horr and Koronli and the Kaisut; there are the great areas of sterile and blasted earth, where no blade of grass can live; there are the vast steppes as void and unsubstantial as a shadow. It is a country bereft and stark. Its suns and winds set their mark on the lean faces and spare bodies of the people; and its grievous dearth of water makes of them plotters and quarrellers, every one'. Bitterly graphic words these, as true today as when they were first written nearly fifty years ago by Major Eric Dutton, an old-time traveller in that desolate district. Teleki, with sharp memories of his own ordeals, would surely have endorsed them, and indeed countless others who strove thereafter to introduce the elements of law and order in the Protectorate's desolate north lands. Not a place for faint hearts and spirits, it was a country intolerant of those who lacked resolve and cynical of those who tried to change its ways. Its obstacles were regarded by many as a testing challenge, by others, a thrilling adventure, and for a few, a task to be treated with an earnest dedication. The administration of the Northern Frontier District was certainly never a light undertaking.

Britain assumed a vague proprietorship of the immense tract of land lying between the Juba river and Lake Rudolf during the period when Teleki was undertaking his great journey of exploration in east Africa, at the same time as Mackinnon's infant company was committing its energies to trade in the region. Teleki was a transient in the desert north, foremost in the procession of equally transient hunters and travellers who visited that country in the 1890s. Mackinnon, who stayed longer, eventually failed in his purpose, and his men never even came close to the inhospitable lands far to the north of the Uganda road. When Hardinge was given the reins of command over the newly declared British East Africa Protectorate in 1895, he promptly made the first serious efforts to establish orderly rule. But Britain, the new European landlord, still made no move to encourage any control over the northern portion of its accession, a far-off corner encompassing nearly 100,000 square miles of raw Africa. Hardinge, for his part, was not in a position to change that state of affairs. Battling with the parsimony of a home government reluctant to increase its overseas possessions, he was hard put to consolidate his position, even in the more profitable districts closer to his base in the southern part of the country.

In 1897 Hardinge appended a simple map of the Protectorate to his annual report. It illustrated the provincial and district boundaries as they were set out in those embryonic years. Significantly, his map showed an unmarked region north of a line which snaked along the northern Uaso Ngiro river's course to the Lorian Swamp, and from there directly east to the Juba river. Printed on the map's empty space was the information: 'Territory of East Africa Protectorate', and in parenthesis was added 'Not yet organised in Provinces or Districts'. Hardinge had thereby clearly registered a recognition of the Protectorate's responsibility over that desert tract*. It was a responsibility the British government was unwilling to meet, particularly in view of its 'mark time' policy for the new Protectorate. For some years nothing more was done to change the situation, and the blank space on the map continued to lie untended and hardly known.

---

* A War Office map printed in the same year titled the little-known region—'Future Boran District, Jubaland Province'.

Late in 1900 Hardinge left the Protectorate to take up a diplomatic post in Persia. He could look back with satisfaction on his five year spell in East Africa, for which he had received a knighthood. Apart from the establishment of a stable administration on the coast, the main achievement had been the progress in the construction of the Uganda Railway, which by then had traversed the whole Protectorate. With that useful tool available it was up to his successor, the scholarly Sir Charles Eliot, to continue with the country's development, which Hardinge had so energetically set in motion.

Eliot took over in hard times. The Boer War was then a major preoccupation of the British government, its expenses siphoning off vital Treasury funds which only helped to sustain the niggardly policy for East Africa. Despite that, the steady advance made in extending British control over the districts in the vicinity of Mt Kenya brought the administrative influence ever closer to the northern parts of the Protectorate. Eliot's name will be linked for ever with a significant factor in the growth of the country—his enthusiastic promotion and encouragement of the country's settlement by white men. By doing so he hoped to make the country justify itself economically, and so vindicate the costly construction of a railway that critics had unflatteringly dubbed 'the lunatic line'.

The railway, and Eliot's policy, succeeded in bringing a steady flow of prospective white immigrants to the country. They were a multifarious collection, all eager to try their hand at whatever opportunity arose, and it was only to be expected that amongst them there were a few who envisaged their fortunes being made from the lucrative ivory trade. It was a business which attracted the straight and the unscrupulous. The reports brought back from east Africa by Thomson, Teleki, Neumann, Donaldson Smith, Delamere and Atkinson were glowing—Lake Rudolf's environs were an elephant paradise, and ivory could be purchased from the local people for a few strings of beads. Elephant tusks were there for the asking, and one enthusiast was optimistic that a railway to the interior could even make a profit from the haulage of the stuff. The dream of this wealth in the northern districts of the Protectorate tempted many white men to try their luck. Indeed, such high hopes had been engendered by Thomson's report that the East Africa Ivory and Rubber Company was incorporated in England in 1891 to exploit the new El Dorado of elephant teeth. The monopolistic Imperial British East Africa Company promptly blocked that threat. Later, in 1894, following the demise of the latter enterprise, a trading concern in Zanzibar, Hansing and Company, sent an agent into that remote country to trade for ivory. It could almost be stated with certainty that the lure of the valuable commodity directly contributed to the early infiltration of the Protectorate's north by white men. Of the many who dabbled in the industry, two were prominent—Atkinson and Neumann. Prior to 1900 both of them had travelled extensively through that territory in search of elephants. Neumann, the recluse, on his return to East Africa from the Boer War in 1901, resumed his hunting activities. Following the practices of the gentleman-sportsman, he self-centredly regarded the north as his own special domain. Atkinson, after his successes on the ivory trail with Delamere, viewed the business in a different light. To him it was all hard business. His methods were not always the most scrupulous, and eventually they brought him into a Nairobi courtroom for the cold-blooded murder of a group of Rendille tribesmen who had frustrated him in his attempts to purchase their cache of ivory.

Atkinson's crime was not smiled on by the authorities, and especially not by Eliot, who found the idea of bloodsports highly distasteful anyway. He wasted no time in despatching an expedition to visit the scene of the crime and make an investigation. The journey was significant for at least one good reason. It marked the very first visit to the northern frontier country by an official of the Protectorate administration, into the vacuum inhabited by nomads, wild animals and rumours. Leading the pioneer caravan was a District Officer by the name of Harold Tate, aptly nicknamed by his men 'Bwana Kongoni'* on account of his sandy kongoni-coloured hair, doleful long face and nose, and hartebeeste-like gait. Tate led his men out of Nakuru on 14 August and marched across the empty plains of the Laikipia plateau to Meru, before turning north to Laisamis and Marsabit. He spent six days camped on Donaldson Smith's Crater Lake, where he proceeded with his investigations amongst the Rendille. On 29 September, having collected evidence and witnesses, he started his long trek homewards. Returning by way of Meru and the east flank of Mt Kenya he was able to reconnoitre country that was then little known. One month later he was back in his office at Fort Hall (Murang'a today). There, Tate could proudly make a unique claim—he had been the first government officer to reach Marsabit Mountain.

Early in 1904 Eliot tendered his resignation to the British government. His latter days had been difficult ones, and his conflict with the Foreign Office over the intricate problems relating to white settlement led him to no other conclusion. The following year his appraisal of the country in which he had served as Commissioner was published†. Its pages roamed the length and breadth of the Protectorate and even included a brief assessment of the still little-appreciated northern wastes. Eliot himself had never visited them, but his informants‡ had given him reason to write some cautioning words of advice: 'The northern boundary of the Protectorate also presents political problems, as it is not fixed for a great part of its length ... We have no pretence of administration or authority in this district, and the Abyssinians have advanced far to the south of our supposed limits ... This southward movement of the Abyssinians is a serious matter'. After expanding on the Abyssinian threat Eliot went on to make a statement which, while apt in his time, also applied for many decades thereafter, and even to this present day is relevant: 'It is true that all this region is very distant. People hardly think more of it at Mombasa than they do in London, and an expensive extension of our power and responsibilities ... is to be deprecated'. Damning words, which he quickly went on to redress: 'Hitherto our experience in East Africa has not been one of disillusion. As a rule we have not found that supposed valuable lands were deserts, but rather that supposed deserts were valuable lands'. There was little else Eliot could add about the northern district, for there were still few white men who could advise him of its potential.

Sir Donald Stewart, who stepped into Eliot's shoes, served as Commissioner for a brief period of only fifteen months. He was a very different type of person from his predecessor. A soldier and a disciplinarian, he was also a keen sportsman, convivial,

---

*Kongoni—the Swahili name for the hartebeeste family in general. The droll, long-faced creatures were formerly found in great numbers on the plains of East Africa. A great-nephew of Tate's claims he was also a dreary conversationalist, adding further to the comparison with the melancholy-looking antelope.

†Eliot's book, *The East Africa Protectorate*, was published in 1905.

‡One of Eliot's most direct sources of information was Butter, who discussed with him the observations made by the 1903 Boundary Survey expedition. Butter visited Eliot in Nairobi while on his way home.

hard drinking and indolent. Nevertheless, with his military frame of mind he appeared to be the right man to place in a country filled with rebellious spirits, whether they were indigenous peoples or recalcitrant white settlers.

During Stewart's short tenure of office—before he died of pneumonia in October 1905*—an important event came about which had a direct bearing on the administration of the Protectorate. On 1 April 1905 the Foreign Office handed over its responsibilities for East Africa to the Colonial Office. This changeover did not in fact disrupt the flow of management, as the two offices had previously enjoyed a close working relationship on Protectorate matters, nor did it seem to make any difference to the disinterest shown over the management of the northern region. Continuing bureaucratic ignorance of the district was made obvious in the classic little volume, *Jubaland and the Northern Frontier District*, published in Nairobi in 1916. This small handbook, bound in a drab institutional olive-green cloth cover, became the Bible of the north. It was, and still is, fascinating reading—a compendium of history, advice and anecdotes about the remote desert districts. Its contents, in minute print, were required reading for countless young officers posted to the administration in those lonely parts. Looking back on earlier days, one snippet of information from its pages was a clear admission: 'Prior to the latter part of 1905, practically nothing was known of what is now called the Northern Frontier District. The officers in charge of Jubaland Province from time to time mentioned in their reports 'a country . . . vaguely believed to be immensely rich'.

The hardy characters who had an inkling of the possibilities in the 'immensely rich' land north of the Uaso Ngiro river included Atkinson, Neumann, John Boyes and a few others of similar bent. Otherwise, it was still strictly a no-man's land.

Two months after Stewart's death, in December, the ruling Conservative Party in Britain fell. In the latter month Stewart's successor, Colonel James Hayes Sadler, arrived to take up his post in the sprawling tin-shanty town of Nairobi. At the same time, taking his seat as Under-Secretary for the new Liberal government in the rooms of the Colonial Office was a young man of extraordinary ability—Winston Churchill. The two men, Hayes Sadler' and Churchill, could not be compared. The former, described as a 'charming old gentleman' by one of his staff, and by another as 'industrious, kind and hospitable, but weak and vacillating', was not of the same fibre as the younger man, who 'made his mark with originality and zest, not least in the affairs of the East Africa Protectorate'. Those two men, of such opposite temperaments, were destined to meet in the Protectorate in 1907, when Churchill made his whirlwind two-week journey round the country. Originally planned as a sporting trip, it developed into a quasi-official visit, and from this about-face he gained the notable distinction of being the only political head to make an extended tour of the country in its formative years.

The inexorable advance of government control was all this time creeping steadily closer to the Protectorate's lonely northern district. Towards the end of 1906, a station was established at Embu on the southern slopes of Mt Kenya, under the care of a young District Officer called Horne, aptly nicknamed 'Shorthorn' because of his short stature, compared with that of his tall brother, who was popularly known as 'Longhorn'. The chameleon-like progress of government next saw Horne move round

---

*His grave may be found in the old Nairobi cemetery below the hill.

the eastern flank of the mountain in late 1907, when he reached the Meru peoples' country. There Horne paused and consolidated his position. Perched on the north-eastern slopes of the mountain, he could see far to the north, into the haze of the unknown. His new post was later to prove of strategic importance, as a recent historian has described: 'its geographical situation made it a natural gateway to the north, and to the vast unadministered areas that stretched up from Mount Kenya to Ethiopia, a shadowy land in the far distance'*. Even Sadler well appreciated Meru's tactical value, when he saw it as an excellent base for future expeditions heading into the 'shadowy land'. Horne, sitting on the fringe, thus became the first agent of the government to watch over happenings in that remote desert region, and as such he played a valuable part in its conquest.

Some eight years before Horne entered Meru country and made his mark by unwittingly opening a door to the north, destiny was drawing three young men to the bottom of the African continent to fight in a war against a common enemy. Destiny had also ordained that Horne and the trio would meet before another decade was over. George ('Jack') Hutton-Riddell, Hamilton Frederick ('Freddie') Ward, and the Marquis Ralph Gandolfi Hornyold were the three who found themselves involved in the Boer War at the turn of the century, and whose paths were later to meet on the same continent, but far to the north in the fledgling East Africa Protectorate.

Jack Riddell came from a family steeped in old English history. His forebears could be traced back to Norman days, when a baron in King Henry I's court was granted huge tracts of land in the dale of Rye, from which he derived the name Ryedale, shortly to become Riddell. Much later, the Riddells were further honoured—this time by King Charles I—with a baronetcy and more estates, in the Borders of Scotland. Still proud of their Norman origin, the family retained its ancient motto—'Habshar' (I hope to share) and somehow it also managed to maintain the classic Riddell characteristics: 'men of high stature and of strength almost herculean ... The race has always been rich in distinguished men ... usually dark or sandy, and of the Norman Type'. True to form, Jack Riddell, with his aqualine features, hardy nature, six foot (1.85 metres) height and courageous spirit, displayed many of the qualities of his ancestors.

Riddell was born in 1878 at Bragborough Hall near Rugby. His father, at one time a captain in the 16th Lancers, ranked himself as a 'gentleman'; his mother was the daughter of the 2nd Earl of Craven, of another outsize family. Young Riddell was surrounded by sportsmen and horses. In those days the hunter of renown in Africa was the unrivalled Frederick Selous, a man who the boy reckoned was 'responsible [indirectly] for my African career'. Riddell's parents hunted 'the fox as often as possible. But all sports came equally under their approval'. Young Riddell thrived in that atmosphere, and its effect on him was the influence which eventually took him to faraway places in his search of sport, adventure and trade. But before his travels came his education, which started at Eton, followed by a spell at Sandhurst military academy. By the end of the 1890s he was a junior officer in his father's old regiment, then stationed in India. He first became conscious of east Africa when a brother officer returned to India laden down with game trophies from a three-month hunting trip to the rolling Athi Plains, on the edge of which Nairobi was soon to rise. It was then Riddell made a vow to himself: 'Someday, somehow, I'd be there'.

---

*This reflection was made by Dr Gordon Mungeam in his scholarly treatise *British Rule in Kenya 1895–1912*.

About this time Riddell earned a most unusual award when he received the M.V.O. (Member of the Royal Victorian Order) from Queen Victoria. This special decoration, which may only be granted by a member of the Royal Family, he received for courageous action when a bomb was thrown at the Royal Carriage carrying the Queen's daughter on the occasion of her marriage in Madrid to the King of Spain. Fate had ordained that young Riddell would be one of the select few chosen to ride as a close escort alongside the coach.

Riddell attained his dream of reaching Africa by the same route as so many young men of his generation. His regiment was mobilised in 1899 to fight in the Boer War, and 'for two and a half weary years' he pursued the elusive Boers across the endless plains and hills of South Africa. Surviving 'that grim period of misery' he returned to peace-time drills in India. But he yearned for an opportunity to return to Africa, and through a stroke of perverse good fortune his 'dream came true four years later as a result of a badly broken leg'. Declared medically unfit for further military service, Riddell then determined that regardless of his physical incapacity he would spend his leave in East Africa following his desires.

In 1906 Riddell at last reached the Protectorate, and so achieved his goal. For six eventful months he wandered over the remote tracts of the northern region, Abyssinia and Somaliland. By the end of that time he had learnt much. Amongst other things he had gained a sure grounding in the management of men and camels, acquired a working knowledge of the native peoples and their languages, and most important, he had made an assessment of the country's trading potential. Armed with his new expertise, Riddell decided to start his own business with a view to trading in whatever he could find to sell—cattle, horses, ivory or any other products of the land. His new enterprise, aptly named the Boma Trading Company, was to become a well-known name in the tiny world of commerce in East Africa during the trail-blazing days before the First World War, and its many ramifications provided Riddell and his associates with toil, hardships, losses and gains, for a few hard years.

Freddie Ward came to East Africa in mid-January 1904, a good two years before the arrival of his future partner, Jack Riddell. He was then twenty-three years old, had attended Eton at the same time as Riddell, and like him had fought in the Boer War. In the early months of 1901 Ward held the rank of lieutenant in the Oxfordshire Light Infantry, shortly after transferring to the recently formed Irish Guards. In the war he served under John Ponsonby, who was in command of a special unit, the 2nd Guards mounted infantry. It was Ponsonby, and the stirring tales he recounted of his experiences while serving with the Uganda Rifles, who fired Ward's imagination with the prospects of big-game hunting in East Africa. At the first possible opportunity after the war was over, Ward organised a shooting party of fellow officers to go there on a hunt. So attractive did he find the country that a second trip was made early in 1905. Eighteen months later, having restlessly longed to return, he managed a secondment to the King's African Rifles, but in 1908 he had had enough of army life, so resigned. By then he had made Riddell's acquaintance, and as a first step towards earning a civilian livelihood, he invested in the Boma Trading Company, which was then actively engaged in outfitting shooting safaris and general trading. For Ward it was a faltering start to an industrious life in the new Protectorate, a life that was to be notable for its variety of interests and achievements.

The third of the trio, the Marquis Ralph Gandolfi Hornyold, came from a family with a very mixed ancestry. Although not able to compete with the Riddells in age, the Hornyolds could similarly claim a French connection. In 1547, the year after King Henry VIII died, they acquired Blackmore Estate in Worcestershire, a county in which the family had owned property since the thirteenth century. At the time of that new acquisition the head of the family was the Receiver of Normandy; later, he became the Governor of Calais. But bad times for the staunchly Catholic Hornyold family came in the seventeenth century Civil Wars during which, and for some time after, they had to lie low.

Ralph Hornyold was born in 1881 to parents of quite different backgrounds. His father was English, his mother the daughter of Conde de Morella, a Carlist general who had abandoned Spain for England and married a wealthy Englishwoman. The Gandolfi name came from a titled Italian family of Genoese origin, which had arrived in England at the beginning of the eighteenth century. By the time a Gandolfi married a Hornyold in the middle of the nineteenth century, they had become completely anglicised. Their title they continued to use, and it was buttressed even more when the Pope made Ralph Hornyold's father a Papal Duke for his sterling service to the Catholic Church.

Despite his varied antecedents, Ralph was thoroughly English, had been brought up in England, and then educated at a well-known Catholic institution, Beaumont School. Of average height, muscular and well-built, he was gregarious, sociable and had many friends. He also possessed an adventurous spirit, which soon manifested itself when he left for Africa, first to the Boer War with the Worcestershire Regiment, then into a short-lived mining venture in North Africa with a friend, followed by his arrival in East Africa at about the same time as Riddell and Ward. There his enjoyment of riding and shooting soon found ample scope for fulfilment. On his arrival in the Protectorate he, too, joined the Boma Trading Company. This was only to be expected, for the Riddell and Hornyold families were old acquaintances, and it was quite on the cards that Jack Riddell gave his young friend every encouragement to join the new venture.

It was Riddell who laid the foundation stone of the Boma Trading Company, and it was he who recruited Ward and Hornyold as assistants in his enterprise. Later, others joined—among them, William ('Billy') Gilman Sewell, the wealthy Bostonian whom Ward met by chance in a Zanzibar club; Alec Roy, whose job was Company secretary; and his brother Frederick, who through thick and thin spent many lonely months keeping open the remote trading posts at Marsabit and Moyale. Conveniently placed next to the Norfolk Hotel was their little office of substantial stone and tile construction, conspicuous in a town of shops and dwellings built mostly of dreary corrugated iron.

Riddell's business experienced some competition in the diminutive shape of the irrepressible John Boyes, the trader-adventurer who, denied a chance to join in Riddell's first big trading expedition to the north, defied him, and in late 1906, on his own initiative and to spite Riddell, brought down a whole caravan of ivory, horses, mules and donkeys from Abyssinia. Riddell, as it turned out, never reached that country; his well-equipped group was not officially permitted to travel beyond Marsabit. Halted there, it then created history when it established the Boma Trading Company's first field base in the north. During the opening months of 1907 young Hornyold set to and constructed a humble trading post on the forested edge of

Donaldson Smith's Crater Lake. Those simple buildings of mud and thatch represented only the second settlement of substance—Moyale was the first—in the vast empty space which was shown on later maps as the Northern Frontier District.

When Riddell and Hornyold marched into the north and established their trading post at Marsabit, they had the blessings of both the Protectorate government and the Colonial Office. Their company was unique as the first European enterprise to be permitted entry into that remote district. It was an ambitious undertaking, typical of those far-off days when opportunities and hardship went hand in hand, tempting many a hardy young man to try his luck. Riddell and Hornyold were undoubtedly members of that adventurous group. While the latter hacked away at the forest and built his depot, Riddell returned to Nairobi, and on 18 June 1907 he wrote a long letter to the Sub-Commissioner reporting on his first official journey to the north.

Riddell's four page letter was of prime importance in that it gave the government in Nairobi an up-to-date and comprehensive appraisal of a vital part of their unadministered northern district. Amongst other details it gave information on the best route to Marsabit, the trading possibilities in cattle (good) and ivory (poor), the state of the native tribes (friendly) and suggestions for further operations. It was well received in Nairobi and immediately despatched to London in its entirety. The Protectorate officials were quick to catch on to the usefulness of the Company as their source of information on the state of affairs in the district, a point Dr Mungeam emphasised: 'The chief importance of the company, so far as the Government was concerned, lay in the fact that it provided, at no expense to the authorities, a useful method of penetration into the comparatively unknown north'. In a nutshell, the Company's activities in the shadowy land to the north were a distinct advantage to the government.

As a result of that encouraging start, Riddell took on his payroll another young

*The Boma Trading Company base adjacent to Crater Lake, Marsabit, 1909.*

man, Frederick Roy, who had recently arrived in the Protectorate. The brother of Riddell's secretary, Alec, he had arrived in the country only the year before. The brothers had a useful business background; the Roy family came from Angus in Scotland, and the young men's father had worked for their grandfather's shipping business, based in London. Of much the same age as Hornyold, Fred Roy had been old enough to join the Imperial Yeomanry and participate in the Boer War. Footloose after that episode he took off for Canada, where he spent a few years drifting between the life of a lumberjack and the existence of the hobo. It was then he lost his left eye through a kick from a horse. Thereafter he sported a glass eye, a disability that didn't seem to disturb his marksmanship against even the most dangerous of wild creatures. On his arrival in East Africa good fortune smiled when Riddell offered him a job in the Company with the meagre wage of 100 rupees per month. Readily he jumped at it, and on 16 May 1907, at the head of a trading caravan, he marched northwards out of Nairobi on the road to Marsabit. Fred Roy proved a diligent, careful employee, and over the next three years he laboured faithfully and with great fortitude for the Company.

Roy's caravan reached Marsabit in the middle of June, and there he met Hornyold for the first time, as a letter to his mother related: 'Hornyold who is . . . a fairly decent fellow, and of course no ceremony was made on our meeting. During his two months up here he has built 1 mud house for self and rush houses for porters'. Simple as the structures may have been, they represented, significantly, the first headquarters for the region's surrogate administrators.

While all this was going on, Riddell had returned to England to register his business as an English company. He, of course, still aimed to hold the reins as managing director. In his arrangements he was successful, and the Boma Trading Company became a respectable institution in the government's eyes, registered at

Somerset House with a capital of £10,000. There were six directors, all in England, and five principal shareholders, including Riddell, Hornyold and Ward. Prospects appeared good and enthusiasm was high; even minutes by Colonial Office staff on communications relating to Company matters showed a benevolent tolerance for the young men's plans and rather monopolistic aims.

Back at Marsabit Roy relieved Hornyold, who not long afterwards returned to Nairobi after investigating trading prospects with the Borana. Roy continued Hornyold's pioneering work and completed the trading post, while busily haggling with the Rendille for camels, cattle, sheep and goats. Later, his slow return trek to Nairobi, trading as he went, took almost two months, but his six-month sojourn was deemed a success; the animal stock and ivory brought back by him appearing to justify all the Company's efforts.

Riddell, however, had higher ambitions than simply trading out of Marsabit. In 1906 he had become aroused to the attractive prospects of trade in Abyssinia, and that had always been his main objective. In late 1907 a timely event helped him to achieve his aim: Winston Churchill arrived on his brisk visit to the Protectorate. Riddell, an old 16th Lancer, knew Churchill, a one-time 4th Hussar, from the days when they served together in India, so it was quite understandable for Churchill to ask Riddell to guide his party on its hunting expedition. While on this trip Riddell quickly seized the opportunity to tell his former comrade about the Company's ambition to carry trade into Abyssinia from East Africa. As he had hoped, the response was encouraging, and following Churchill's consultations with Hayes Sadler, the Colonial Office, undoubtedly pushed by their forceful Under-Secretary, agreed to the Boma Trading Company's operations in the northern part of the Protectorate, but only subject to certain conditions.

Initially, the terms laid down were simple. Firstly, Riddell was asked to provide the government with the maps he made of the region in which he ran his business. Secondly, he had to lodge £1,000 as a surety against the Company's good behaviour. Thirdly, the Company had to be a registered English business, trading strictly through British territory. Fourthly, Riddell had to provide the government with intelligence and trade reports of the country in which his men travelled. Last, and most important, he had to obtain permission from King Menelik himself before entering Abyssinia to trade. All these conditions were swiftly accepted, and Riddell and Ward left promptly for England to complete the final details. For the next few months Ward, from his address at the Guards Club in London, determinedly bombarded the Colonial Office with correspondence on Company matters.

Ward's protracted dealings with the Colonial Office went on for several months. It was not until 28 April 1908 that a formal agreement between the officers of the Company and officials of the Crown Agents for the Colonies was signed and sealed. Prior to this, however, there had been considerable wriggling on the part of Riddell and Ward over the terms of the bond, but in the end the matter was resolved to everyone's satisfaction, and the Company was granted permission to trade between Nairobi and Marsabit, and in the east, on the Juba river. As part of the updated deal the British government increased the surety bond to £2,000, and repeated their insistence that Menelik's permission be received before trade could commence over the border with Abyssinia.

While the dry formalities of law were being enacted, Riddell, Ward and Sewell were already in Abyssinia, wrangling over a permit from Menelik. Fortunately, they were young, audacious and resilient, and with a little judicious greasing of palms the vital document was soon in their hands. On 9 May 1908 Harrington officially notified London that the transaction had been finalised with Menelik. Riddell wasted no time in acting. He immediately arranged for Ward and Sewell to advance southwards, to Dolo on the Juba river. They traded as they went, and at Dolo they confidently set up a trading post. Riddell struck north to Berbera by himself, purchasing on the road one hundred Abyssinian horses for sale in East Africa. Both journeys experienced their ups and downs, but both, through the boldness and initiative of their respective leaders, were successful.

Meanwhile, in East Africa, the Company had not been idle. Roy started back to Marsabit in early February, leading a caravan heavily laden with trade goods and food supplies. He was still not permitted to carry on beyond his base at the Crater Lake on Marsabit, but he had plenty to do there anyway, refurbishing the neglected post, and erecting stables and outbuildings. He was not to remain there long, though, for new orders arrived from Riddell on 11 July. At last the Company had been given permission to break from its mountain barrier, and it could start trading with the Abyssinians from a base at Moyale. Promptly, Roy handed over the station to his new assistant, Watson Taylor, and moved north, along the Hurri Hills and bypassing the dreaded lava-studded desert of the Dida Galgalo. Three weeks after leaving Marsabit, he reached Fort Harrington*, the lonely British outpost on the border, and there he met Zaphiro, who was to be his sole European companion for the next eight months.

While Zaphiro jealously guarded his position as Frontier Inspector, Roy carried on with his trading, based on the wells at Waye in the lowland below Moyale. Zaphiro's attitude to Roy and all he stood for—competition in the form of the Boma Trading Company—was mercurial. At times accommodating, polite and even generous with gifts, on other occasions he was egotistical, obstructive and threatening. It was not an altogether happy situation, but nevertheless Roy steadfastly continued with his business, and whenever conditions permitted sent down mobs of cattle and mules to the staging post at Marsabit. Above all, he did his best to observe Riddell's implicit instructions not to quarrel with Zaphiro. Roy needed every shred of patience he could muster as the months dragged on, with almost no contact with fellow Europeans, and little mail, to dilute the dreariness of his solitary existence. During a two-month wait at Waye he wearily noted in his diary: 'The monotony is getting unbearable. I have nothing to read, no tobacco, my chief occupation is to watch the lizards catch the flies about the house'. On another occasion he admitted: 'I have been sitting in the dark to save candles, but now have six packets'. They had been a gift from the better supplied Zaphiro in one of his amicable moods.

The Protectorate government may have regarded the Boma Trading Company as its agent in the north, but the British government in London viewed its operations with considerable suspicion. In a brief letter from the Colonial Office to the Foreign Office, a request was made to provide Major Gwynn of the Boundary Commission, who was then approaching Dolo, with all correspondence dealing with the Company's affairs. Gwynn in turn was ordered to determine what game the Company was playing. In effect, Gwynn the surveyor was expected to act as Gwynn the spy, a

---

* Fort Harrington was by the village of Moyale.

position which belied the trust Riddell's Company had in the British government's goodwill. To confuse the matter further, Zaphiro approached Roy on 21 November and asked him to caretake both Fort Harrington and British interests in the area while he went to join Gwynn at Dolo. Loyal as always to the Company, Roy noted: 'I agreed to do so as long as it did not interfere with trade'. On 24 November Roy took up his 'official position as resident in the fort'. And there he stayed for many weeks, trading on the Company's account and administering the border in Zaphiro's absence. For that brief spell the Boma Trading Company could claim to be more than just a listening post for the Protectorate authorities; it became the government's direct agent. One could argue with justification that the tenuous link represented the first murmurings of administration in that vast tract of desert country.

By late 1908, when Roy and Hornyold were busy in their posts at Moyale and Dolo, the Protectorate government under Hayes Sadler had already become aware of the need to take control in the northern district. Winston Churchill, in his encouragement of Riddell's company, had without any doubt made a direct contribution towards an awareness of the region by the authorities, and there was a strong feeling that something should be done. That same year saw two changes which were to influence affairs in the Protectorate. In May, Churchill was replaced in a reshuffle of Whitehall staff, and some months later, Hayes Sadler, the unfortunate Governor whose ability for hard work did not compensate for his timid vacillations, came to the end of his term in East Africa. In February 1909 he left the country on a posting to the Windward Islands.

After much deliberation the British government selected Colonel Sir Percy Girouard to succeed Hayes Sadler. By then the country was badly in need of a leader with the combined qualities of strength and diplomacy to handle its problems, and in Girouard it would have been hard to find a better person to drag the Protectorate out of the doldrums. He was a railway specialist, soldier and administrator, he had fought with Kitchener's army against the Mahdi's men, worked for many years as a director of railways in Egypt, South Africa and the Sudan, and latterly had served in West Africa under Lugard, whom he had succeeded as a Governor in Nigeria. Moreover from his marriage to a girl from Transvaal society, Girouard had gained an inkling of the problems facing white pioneer settlers. With all that formidable experience behind him, coupled with a tremendous energy and enthusiasm for his new position, Girouard arrived to resolve the confusion left behind by the amiable Hayes Sadler.

The control of the Protectorate's remaining unadministered region had been clearly in Hayes Sadler's mind before he left the country, but the Colonial Office pundits had not concurred with his design. They were waiting, they said, for Gwynn to complete his survey before making a commitment. So, once again the matter was shelved, but not for long. In July 1909 Gwynn produced his confidential report, a document that was precise and to the point. Two matters he raised had a direct bearing on the administration of the border zone. First, he was emphatic that Zaphiro should be removed and a British officer installed in his place. Next, Gwynn declared that the Boma Trading Company was quite open in its aim to keep a monopolistic hold on the district. He also described the bad relations that existed between Zaphiro, Company staff and itinerant Somali traders: 'The former [Company] undoubtedly resent being under the control and criticism of a man who they consider a Greek adventurer, and whose honesty they profess to distrust. The latter [Somali] also dislike and distrust Zaphiro on account of his nationality and partiality for Abyssinians'. Another terse comment did not help to untangle the three-cornered web of suspicion: 'Mr Zaphiro is excitable and suspicious to a degree, and cannot be said to handle the situation with tact'. Gwynn ended his castigations with an obvious death-knell for the Company: 'The position of the company's officers is undeniably invidious ... It can only be hoped the company will shortly abandon its unsuccessful venture'.

Whilst all these secret exchanges were taking place, Roy struggled on in his lonely station, but against ever-increasing difficulties, trading in ivory, stock and a new possibility—coffee from the highlands of Abyssinia. His trade goods had virtually run out, and by selling 'my personal property to Zaphiro and giving him a cheque [Roy's personal one] I have been able to keep trade going without a scrap of help from Nairobi'. By early April 1909, Roy had accumulated enough ivory, coffee and mules to justify his return to Nairobi. On 22 May, after nearly sixteen months in the wilds without a break, he reached Naivasha, and 'handed over entire safari to Ward and was extremely pleased to do so'. With a light heart Roy then sailed to England for a well-earned respite.

Hornyold, meanwhile, had been centred at Dolo, his remote station on the Juba river. During the time Roy tended Moyale, Hornyold and his assistant Vincent traded with the Somalis in the far north-eastern corner of the Protectorate. His labours did not, however, seem to be any more successful than Roy's, and it was now becoming obvious that the Company would be forced to close down its operations in the north before much longer.

Gwynn's confidential report to the Foreign Office was the catalyst that finally activated Colonial Office support for a more effective administration in the northern district of the Protectorate. In fact, the government there had already moved in that direction, and before Girouard arrived in September 1909 a young officer by the name of Geoffrey Archer had established an advance base on the summit of a low flat-topped hill perched strategically on the northern bank of the Uaso Ngiro river. Called Lgirrgirr, meaning in the Samburu language 'barbed arrow', the isolated hill was to

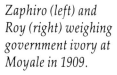

*Zaphiro (left) and Roy (right) weighing government ivory at Moyale in 1909.*

330 · PAX BRITANNICA

play a vital part in the story of the Protectorate's northern district. Situated just a few miles downstream from Neumann's last camp on the river, Archer's tiny base was made up of a collection of huts built from locally obtained materials—doum palm logs and thatched roofs. Later, appropriately, it bore the name Archer's Post*, a name that survives to this very day. One traveller through the area in 1913 described it in these words: 'A few miles from Kampi ya Nyama Yangu [Neumann's old camp] is a little fort, surely one of the most desolate of all the defences of the Empire. Some day . . . this cluster of huts, hemmed in by barbed wire, and with one or two black "askaris" (police) as custodians, may play a minor part in a Colonial Tragedy, but for the present it is more of a store and half-way house between Meru and Marsabit'. The government's move had come in the nick of time, precipitated by the increasing problems of Abyssinian and Somali incursions and raids along the Protectorate's borders.

When Archer strode out of Naivasha in May 1909 at the head of an immense procession made up of two white army officers, a medical assistant and a Goan clerk, together with a company numbering seventy-five King's African Rifles and nearly six hundred porters, he already had eight years of service in East Africa behind him. He was then twenty-seven years of age, and had been a District Commissioner for two years.

Frederick Jackson, a keen sportsman, enthusiastic naturalist and an administrative officer of many years' standing in east Africa, was the person directly responsible for encouraging his nineteen-year-old nephew, Geoffrey Francis Archer, to leave England and visit him in Uganda. Later, it was undoubtedly Jackson's solid reputation that influenced Eliot in his decision to recruit Archer for the Protectorate's administrative office. It was an exceptional engagement, as Archer, at twenty, was six years under the minimum age for acceptance to the service. Clearly, Jackson's position and good name had played a part, although there appeared to be no hint of nepotism in Archer's premature appointment. The young man, without any university education, had by good fortune managed to steal a march on his contemporaries. The luck of that start was compounded by his subsequent two-year spell in the Secretariat, which gave him a solid grounding in the workings of the Protectorate's administration. But he found being office-bound an irksome existence, and not in keeping with his love for the outdoors and sport. By good fortune all that changed in 1904, when he became, of his own wish, an Assistant District Commissioner in the Lake Baringo area. In 1907, at the early age of twenty-five, Archer was promoted to a fully-fledged District Commissioner.

It was at this point in his life, and while on leave in England, that he decided to learn the rudiments of the surveyor's skills. Painstakingly he studied draughtsmanship at the offices of the Royal Geographical Society and, complementarily, attended their plane table classes in the field. For the next few years Archer made good use of his new talent, and applied himself diligently to his survey work, producing immaculate maps

* Abandoned during the mid-1920s in preference for the new station at Isiolo, Archer's Post fell into decay, and today all that remains of this once important spot are faint signs of the log walls, a solitary cement floor where the transport shed once stood, overgrown vehicle tracks, and artifacts ranging from spent cartridges to broken china. It is a bleak, but haunting place, with magnificent views in all directions, an obvious choice for such a post in the pioneering days at the turn of the century.

*Geoffrey Francis Archer on survey duties in the Northern Frontier District.*

of the Protectorate's northern frontier district in the course of his duties.

In 1909, much to Archer's pleasure, he was selected to lead the government's first large-scale expedition into the north. By then he was fully qualified to head the force. Physically, too, he was well-endowed for the task: an impressive six feet, seven inches (2 metres) in height, he had captained his school football team, had already proved a good leader of local tribesmen, and was a keen observer of country and nature. In his policies he was a man who thought ahead of his times, proving sympathetic and considerate to the peoples he administered. He was not, it is said, overly popular with his white staff, being branded as egotistical and pompous. By all accounts he was a vast hulk of a man, stupid, opinionated and conceited, who never listened to advice, an accusation that was not entirely without foundation. His character did not, however, prevent him from attaining the governorship of Somaliland, Uganda and finally, though briefly, the Sudan. From the last post he decided, judiciously, to resign.

While Archer was busy entrenching the Protectorate government's post on Lgirrgirr hill, Riddell was trudging round his Company's trading grounds further north, making an inspection of his spread-out chain of stations. By then they comprised a shop in the government post at Embu, a possible new site near Horne's base at Meru, the little centre on Marsabit Mountain, and the remote encampment close by Moyale. Riddell had decided it was time for a critical appraisal of the position, and what he found was not altogether pleasing. He arrived at Embu to find 'the B.T.C. Duka [shop] with the shutters up and trade finished a sad sight and I trust not an omen for the future'. At Meru his plans for a trading centre were obstructed by bureaucracy in the shape of Horne. In his effort to avoid the cramping shackles of official interference, Riddell had tried hard to place his post some distance from Meru government station, but Horne, with reasons of his own, put his foot down and refused permission. All that was discouraging for Riddell, but none the less he moved on north and spent six weeks at Marsabit, using some of the time in supervising the preparation of a patch of ground on which to grow maize, and the rest in hunting over the game-rich country on the mountain. In mid-July Riddell departed for Moyale on the final leg of his inspection journey. Ten days later he reached Fort Harrington and reported to Zaphiro, who 'was dressed in white drill uniform with very large gold buttons—overalls strapped at the foot and over all a black "Italian brigand" hat'. A week later, having checked the trading post's accounts and stocks he departed for home, but not before he had left 5,000 dollars (Abyssinian) of the Company's funds in Zaphiro's safekeeping. In the months to come Riddell would sorely regret that last arrangement. He never visited Moyale again on Company business, a prospect he was probably not fully aware of then, but on reading through his diary one feels sure he must have had a sneaking suspicion that time was running out for the northern branch of his business.

On 6 September, whilst camped at a lonely waterhole south of Laisamis, Riddell chanced on an old employee, 'Ibrahim Aden lately my headman and sacked for gross dishonesty and blacklisted among all Nairobi agents turned up in charge of a Government Safari from Archer ... Aden now occupies the proud position of Political Officer'. For Riddell the meeting carried an ominous warning, which was reinforced two days later when he staggered into Archer's Post and met for the first time the man who would in the end prove to be his *bête noire*—the lofty Geoffrey Archer.

To start with Archer 'was very friendly', and Riddell on his part sportingly joined in games of football on the two evenings he was camped there. But after a full day of discussions, when the two men, of such opposing aims, tried to thrash out their interrelated problems, Riddell noted tersely in his diary: 'Not very successful. Archer I believe wants to be friendly but his views are the same as all his confrères and if persisted in will inconvenience trade considerably. He also threatens to take our site at Marsabit'. Archer's plans must have made Riddell think hard. Were all the Company's efforts to come to no avail after all, and was it to be forced out of the northern frontier, despite the agreement signed with the British government? No longer would Riddell and his men range freely on their business in the unchecked spaces of the north; dedicated officials like Horne at Meru, and the newly arrived Archer on the Uaso Ngiro river, had come to interfere with their carefree life.

In the same month Archer and Riddell were weighing up each other's intentions, Sir Percy Girouard arrived to commence his duties. Flinging himself into his new job with a feverish enthusiasm, he shortly afterwards stunned his seniors in Whitehall with a voluminous report on the state of the Protectorate. One thing was clear; Girouard viewed the administration of the northern frontier in the same light as

Gwynn. Both were soldiers and both were aware of the dangerous situation building up with the Abyssinians along the border zone. Immediate action was called for, and Girouard could see only one of two alternatives; either he must operate with a minimal force of troops to back up his administrative officers and practise a policy of observation, or he had to follow his instinct and advance a strong military contingent to combat, physically if needed, the Abyssinian raiders. There were on his staff protagonists of both these strategies, but before he could make a move Girouard deemed it necessary to begin a formal assessment of the situation.

Even before Girouard's all-embracing report reached London, the Protectorate authorities had listened to Zaphiro's pleas for assistance on the border. Increasing Abyssinian raids, elephant poaching and abductions of Borana people from British territory, had become a serious threat to life in the region. To try to control this gloomy state of affairs a contingent of sixty men of the King's African Rifles (the K.A.R.) under the command of Captain Leycester Aylmer was ordered to march forthwith from the seaport of Kismayu in Jubaland to Fort Harrington. With them travelled Captain W.E.H. Barrett, lately an officer in the regiment, and now an Assistant District Commissioner. His instructions were clear—he was to replace Zaphiro as Political Officer at Moyale.

At the time of this move Aylmer was twenty-seven years old. He had already been in the country, attached to the K.A.R., for a few years. The son of a former colonel in Riddell's old regiment, the 16th Lancers, Aylmer joined the King's Royal Rifle Corps just in time to see a little action in the closing days of the Boer War. And, as had so many others who participated in that pointless war, he fell in love with Africa. After that episode he, like his contemporary Freddie Ward, asked for and was granted a posting to the K.A.R. in the East Africa Protectorate. There Aylmer happily spent his years of service soldiering, exploring and writing articles about his trips for the Journal of the

Royal Geographical Society. Except for a brief spell back in England with his parent regiment, Aylmer spent the rest of his short life in the borderlands of Abyssinia and East Africa. Six feet, six inches (2 metres) tall, good humoured and ideally suited to life in the wilds, the young man from Risby Manor in Suffolk resigned from army life on his return from England, to join the civil service as a Political Officer back on the familiar ground of the Abyssinian frontier.

The day Aylmer's force marched into Fort Harrington marked an all-important turning point in the story of the Protectorate's northern frontier. That day, 23 October 1909, saw at long last the arrival of an effective British presence on the border. It was none too soon. A worrying letter to the Foreign Office from the British Legation in Addis Ababa had already reported one month earlier: 'He [Zaphiro] reports over two thousand hunters in the Golbo and the vicinity of Fort Harrington, who daily loot the defenceless Boran Natives in British territory; if these show any signs of resistance in protecting their homes and their stock, they are shot down without mercy ... News had also arrived that Walda Gabriel's [the Abyssinian leader in the area] soldiers had crossed the line with instruction to arrest and chain up all the native chiefs at Debel, and bring them north'.

Four days after Aylmer's arrival in Moyale, Zaphiro departed for Addis Ababa. When Zaphiro left the frontier at the end of October 1909, he had, unknowingly, reached the end of his term as Frontier Inspector. He had served British interests well, as a letter to the Foreign Office from Sir Herbert Hervey, Harrington's successor in Addis Ababa, detailed: 'I venture to bring to your favourable notice the activity and zeal displayed by Mr Zaphiro in the protection of British interests on the frontier. His mastery of native languages ... his unique knowledge of Abyssinian laws and customs have together once more carried him through a most delicate and even dangerous situation, and great credit is due to him for attaining his object without getting into awkward conflict'. There were many who had doubted the wisdom of having a Greek in charge of Britain's interests. Lord Delamere had querulously voiced his opinion on the matter at a dinner party in Nairobi held in honour of Winston Churchill; members of the Boma Trading Company had frequently muttered among themselves about the man's behaviour towards them, adding biting notes in their diaries; and doubtless there were a few office-bound pundits in London who had considered it a most unusual arrangement. But all in all Zaphiro had filled a difficult position with tenacity, forbearance and an abundance of aplomb. When he retired from his lonely post he had already become a legend, a unique one, which survives to the present day*.

Archer's advance from the south, Aylmer's arrival at Moyale, Zaphiro's departure to Addis Ababa, and Riddell's realisation that the future for his Company was poor, all marked the close of an era. No longer would the endless seeming deserts and wastes of the north be free from human management. A new authority had arrived there, signalled by the disciplined tramp of martial boots, barked orders and resonating bugle calls. Clearly, they heralded the end of the old *laissez-faire* order.

'The history of the Administration of the Northern Frontier District may be said to commence with the appointment of Sir Percy Girouard as Governor of the East Africa

---

*Today, the only visible sign of Zaphiro's presence in Moyale is a plaque affixed to a low wall which states: 'This plinth marks the site of the doorway of the house occupied in 1905 by the late PHILIP ZAPHIRO, C.M.G., the first frontier agent at Moyale'.

*Civil administration warrant officer and N.C.O.s based at Marsabit, 1910.*

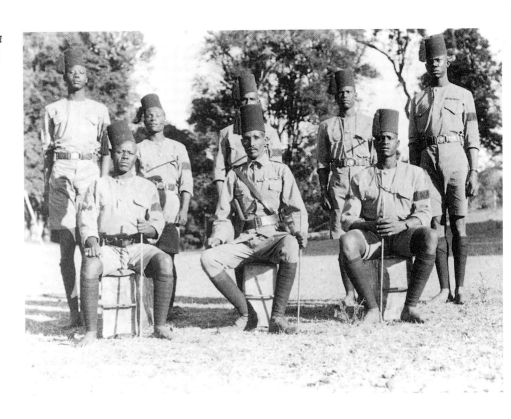

Protectorate in October 1909'. That to-the-point sentence appeared at the opening of chapter five in the authoritative little manual, *Jubaland and the Northern Frontier District*. The tentative probings by the early explorers and hunters, the commercial efforts of John Boyes and the Boma Trading Company, the sporadic visits by officials*, and Zaphiro's solitary activities, had each in their different way played a vital part in opening up the district, but it needed a man of Girouard's energy to promote a full-scale take-over by the government.

In late October 1909 Fred Roy arrived once again at Marsabit, on what was to be his last trading safari in the north. When he found Archer had pitched his camp next to the Company's depot by the Crater Lake, he wrote dejectedly to his mother: 'The Govt have made a station at Marsabit and now in occupation. This will make quite a bit of difference for we will not be able to shoot . . . as we used to do. In fact we are getting altogether too civilized'.

Further north, at Moyale, Aylmer had received orders from the War Office to remain where he was and do garrison duties for at least three months. To occupy his time he built his own strong point facing the hills of Abyssinia, described as: 'a good fort close to the Boma [Moyale] which could easily be held by a few men. In one corner of it he had made a tank which would hold a large supply of water'. Zaphiro's old fort—Fort Harrington—consisted at the time of 'two thorn bomas one inside the

---

* These included Tate's visit to Marsabit in 1902, and the journey undertaken by Captain J. Bois of the K.A.R., who spent three months in 1907 making an official survey of possible routes in the country between Baringo, Rumuruti, Meru and the Lorian Swamp, Merille and Baragoi.

*Aylmer's little fortification at Moyale.*

other. The outer one is 400 yards [370 metres] square, and the inner one about 100 yards [92 metres] square. In the space between are built the men's houses—round huts of wattle and daub and thatch roof. In the inner boma there are six round huts of wattle and daub and one oblong one. These are the officer's and their servants quarters, and store rooms. The wells are about a quarter of a mile away'. Those two frail constructions were the sum total of the fragile British defences, built to face the Abyssinian hordes perched in the hilly country to the north.

Although Boyes, Neumann, Riddell, Roy and others managed to pursue their interests without the security of a military escort, the newly arrived administration, which had a far sterner task ahead of it on a much broader front, felt it advisable to provide their political officers with sound support. That stiff backing was given by the 3rd (East Africa) Battalion of the King's African Rifles. It was, as the name suggests, an infantry unit, whose history stretched back to 1877, when the first armed contingent of Zanzibari troops was formed by a young Royal Navy lieutenant, Lloyd Mathews, to assist in the suppression of the slave trade*. In the following years, when first the Imperial British East Africa Company controlled the interior, and later the East Africa Protectorate authorities ruled the land, the embryonic regiment gradually matured. Under proper soldierly leadership it grew into a disciplined body of fighting men, and in 1895 became the East African Rifles. As the years went by the War Office realised that an amalgamation of all the east and central African army units into a single

---

*This was the same man who had assisted Teleki in Zanzibar in 1887, chivvied Chanler in 1894, and later became the Sultan's First Minister.

regiment would be administratively wise, and on New Year's Day 1902 the King's African Rifles was formed. The Regiment would gain fame in many a skirmish in its homelands, and in later years even more laurels on battlefields in alien lands. Men from the East African Protectorate made up the 3rd Battalion, comprised of eight companies, one of which was a camel company specially recruited for service in Jubaland. Raised from a wide cross-section of tribesmen, the Battalion's loyalty in the early days was at times unpredictable, and the occasional mutiny was not unusual; sometimes they took the form of a harmless demonstration, at others they proved fatal

*King's African Rifles badge at the time of the First World War.*

for their British officers. But serving with and leading them in those pioneering days was a profession eagerly sought by many a young British officer, all anxious to find the adventure, action and challenges for which East Africa was then renowned. And their men, armed with .303 Lee Enfield magazine rifles and a few not altogether reliable machine-guns, faced up to their potential foe in the north, the fiercesome Tigre bandits from Abyssinia, most of them armed with the outdated but lethal French 1874 Gras rifle, firing a slow-moving, flat-headed heavy lead slug.

Towards the end of 1909 Girouard was prepared to act. His deliberations were over, and he had arrived at some definite conclusions. One crucial matter was the pressing problem of the north. Having decided that it was time for something positive to be done, he called a meeting of senior officials and recommended the formation of a new district, with a central station at Meru, and field stations at Marsabit and Moyale. The district would be called the Northern Frontier District, and he had already drawn up its boundaries and a few simple rules for its conduct. From that moment the northern wastelands were no longer regarded as the Protectorate's Cinderella.

Girouard opened the year 1910 in his characteristic fashion. In early January he put his proposals in front of the British Secretary of State. Bluntly he warned him that the frontier line as defined by Gwynn would have to be held; Moyale and its water supplies should be retained in Protectorate territory; Zaphiro retired from boundary duties; and a strong British presence maintained to combat Abyssinian aspirations and encroachments. For the last purpose regular patrolling along the border was imperative. With Menelik's increasingly poor health causing chaos in Abyssinian politics, discipline in that country was waning, and border raiding and encroachments had become even more frequent than before. The situation clearly needed a strong, positive-thinking man at the controls, and in Girouard the British Government had chosen wisely. The actions taken by him in 1910 marked the year as one of exceptional importance in the history of East Africa's north lands.

In the meantime, Roy, continuing with the Company's chores, could see the writing on the wall, and from his camp, now shared with the forces of authority, he wrote on 30 January to his mother in England: 'I have not kept a diary this trip, being totally disgusted with the whole show ... I have had the usual trouble in feeding the men and now the puzzle is to feed myself. The Company have refused to supply any more stores'. Appalled by the changes, Roy went on to add: 'How different this place is now to what it was last year when we had the whole country to ourselves. The Govt have a company of soldiers here and it is one continual bugle call from morn to night. The Govt have also given us notice to quit our present site, a pure case of the "dog in the manger"'. No longer could Roy look across the lake at herds of peacefully grazing buffalo and elephant, or the occasional shuffling rhinoceros. The noisy busyness of the new encampment had doubtless forced the great beasts into the quieter parts of the neighbouring forest. His closing words to his mother were a certain predication of the Company's final spasm in the district: 'Now that things are rather dicky I will proceed to the Border and sell or leave everything, square up and return to Nairobi'. He did just that when he 'bought a few mules and closed the Moyale Depot'. On 18 April he left the border and marched for Marsabit, where he wound up his business, and on the morning of 15 May, Roy and the Boma Trading Company abandoned their mountain base for ever. Sometime later, as a final pay-off, the Company received a paltry £100 from the authorities for its humble buildings. The Company's working days in the lonely place were over, but its struggles with the region's new masters were not quite done. In December 1909 a mutiny of soldiers at Moyale caused the Company an unwanted loss: the 5,000 dollars Riddell had left in Zaphiro's care was with the loot taken by the absconding miscreants. But hard as the Company's officers strove in their claims for compensation, the authorities' evasions defeated them.

On 16 February 1910, Girouard wrote a confidential letter to his Chief Secretary in Nairobi*. The letter, remarkable for its brevity, contained simple, emphatic instructions for the establishment of the proposed Northern Frontier District, and guide-lines for the officer appointed to run the new district. The man chosen for the challenging task, John Owen Webley Hope, was already familiar with the problems of administering desert lands; he had been transferred from a senior post in Jubaland to do the job. Girouard chose wisely when he selected Hope, for he was a proven administrator of widespread experience, and had eleven years of service in East Africa behind him. A gregarious, highly popular man, of great charm and ability, the words

*For the full contents of this communication see Appendix 3.

*Senior Protectorate administration officers outside the District Commissioner's office, Nairobi, circa 1915. (seated extreme left) J.O.W. Hope, (seated extreme right) H. R. ('Kongoni') Tate.*

on the memorial plaque to him, pinned to the wall of Nairobi Cathedral, give a clear indication of the respect in which he was held: 'in the course of 28 years of public life conspicuous no less for his unfailing courtesy, hospitality, generosity and charity than for those distinguished services which he rendered to the state in the provinces of Seyidie, Ukamba, Kikuyu, Jubaland and the Northern Frontier . . . won for himself the profound esteem and lasting affection of whatever race with whom he came in contact'. Those words were written in 1927, the year of his death, but in 1910 he had just been given a task of the highest responsibility, and he had much to do in the months ahead.

Most of Hope's time in 1910 was spent in making a thorough investigation of his far-reaching domain. Girouard badly needed a full picture of the situation there before he could proceed with his policy for the district. His aims were, in fact, quite simple: most important, to establish law and order along the boundary line with Abyssinia; to encourage friendly relations with the indigenous tribes living in the region; and to assess trade possibilities. Putting those fundamental aims into practice did not prove to be easy, especially with a financially hard-pressed government showing reluctance to add further strain to its skimpy budget. All this meant months of wearisome travel, plodding countless miles by camel caravan across the dusty, rock-strewn, thorn-covered wastes, and calling at the lonely posts in Moyale, Marsabit, Dolo and Wajir along his way. Fortunately for Hope, he had ample experience of that way of life, but for a man of sociable inclination with a yearning for the company of kindred spirits, it was a trying existence. In those early days life could be intensely lonesome on the remote frontier stations; where months might be spent on one's own, and only brief spells of contact with fellow white men punctuated the monotony of endless empty days. There were a few individuals who tolerated the position with equanimity, but for most, companionship was essential. Hope was one of the latter group, and it was said he would prefer to delay a journey and wait for a brother officer to join him, rather than travel on his own.

As Hope commuted round his far-flung district, a steady stream of intelligence reports indicated his progress to Girouard, but it was not until August that he finally completed his circuit and returned to Nairobi. What he told Girouard was not altogether pleasing.

Everywhere there was disturbance. The Turkana were proving troublesome along the east side of Lake Rudolf; the Abyssinians were being as obstreperous as ever on the central section of the border, with elephant poaching by bands of Tigre outlaws continuing unabated; and to the east the Somalis were becoming better armed. The fact that the resident tribes were friendly and welcomed the prospects of better security under the new administration, coupled with reasonable prospects of trade with Abyssinia, did not lessen the worrying feeling that a formidable and expensive job lay ahead for the Protectorate government.

Continued hawk-like warnings from Colonel G.H. Thesiger, the Inspector General of the K.A.R.*, that a policy of observation would not help to clear the region's ills, did not seem to make an immediate impression on Girouard or Hope, who still wished to try a peaceful approach to the problem. Apart form anything else, they argued, their method was considerably cheaper. Thesiger, a practical man, was altogether sceptical about the policy of observation, and said as much to his equals in the Colonial Office. His warnings did not go unheeded, and Girouard, who then had Hope's full report in his hands, compromised, and proposed that a full battalion of the K.A.R. should be deployed along the border in small garrisons posted between the Juba river and Moyale. His request could hardly have come at a more inopportune moment.

The military authorities were busy whittling away at their budget, and at the time of Girouard's request were even contemplating the disbandment of one whole battalion of the regiment. Girouard's decision to have a series of army detachments strung out along a 500 mile (800 kilometre) border, itself situated hundreds of miles from the Protectorate's capital in Nairobi, met with stiff resistance from the army powers. Apart from anything else, the problems of resupplying such remote posts with the poor means of transport available on non-existent roads, was enough to make any office-bound quartermaster shudder. Money was tight, as was obvious when the Inspector General himself applied for a new watertight despatch box to take the place of his worn-out wreck. Earlier repairs to the old box had cost £5.10/-, an expense apologetically explained away by the official comment: 'I am afraid this is an unusually heavy bill but the kit got very heavy work in Somaliland, mainly on riding camels, which are a peculiarly destructive form of transport'. On that scale of skimping, Girouard had a hard time ahead of him finding sympathy in the War Office for his cause.

---

*Thesiger had held the post of Inspector General since September 1909. Although he had no previous experience in East Africa, he was a redoubtable soldier, and familiar with wars in other parts of Africa. As a young officer in the Rifle Brigade, he had served at the Battle of Omdurman and in the Boer War. In both he had been mentioned in despatches, and in the latter he was severely wounded. He was killed at the Battle of Loos in 1915.

The year 1910 had proved an eye-opener for the Protectorate authorities. Hope had shuttled round his bailiwick, making his observations, writing his advices, and above all doing his best to maintain peace along the fermenting border zone. Spending most of his time in Moyale, when not on the move, he successfully managed to restrain the Abyssinian politicians from further land grabbing, but not the Tigre raiders, who continued with their troublesome forays. Despite this last irritation, by the end of the year a state of uneasy calm prevailed in the district, and for some months after Hope could sit back and take stock. The British presence, civil and military, had finally brought a modicum of peace to the region, but it was only a lull before the storm.

By May 1911, when Hope reached Nairobi on his way to England for a spell of leave, he could report favourably to Girouard on the developments in his immense district. Moyale with its fortifications was well garrisoned. At Marsabit, Archer had pulled down the ramshackle Boma Trading Company buildings and erected a well-laid out station made up of mud and thatch residences, stores, offices and staff lines; in addition he had constructed a solid log-walled blockhouse, and work was in progress clearing some acres for crops in the vicinity of the camp. A small military expedition, which had been despatched in late 1910 under the command of a white officer to position a garrison in the neighbourhood of Mt Kulal, had successfully completed its assignment. Even the country's wildlife was benefiting from the presence of government agents, as was evidenced when Hope met up with Blaney Percival, the Protectorate Game Warden, on his round of the recently declared Northern Game Reserve. Trade was also showing encouraging signs of improvement, with horses and mules from Abyssinia being moved southwards in their hundreds for sale in the Protectorate, and for the future there was growing optimism that as communications improved trade goods would flow in ever-increasing quantities

*Blockhouse constructed by Archer next to Crater Lake, Marsabit, 1910.*

through the border post at Moyale. All in all, after a year of testing work, prospects looked good, but satisfying as all that may have seemed, Hope must have heaved a huge sigh of relief when he handed over his duties in the Northern Frontier to Archer, and boarded the mail train to Mombasa on his way to a furlough in England.

If 1910 could be described, in military terms, as the year of reconnaissance, then 1911 could equally claim to have been a year of consolidation in the Northern Frontier District. But the severe cuts in the K.A.R. establishment had adversely affected the 3rd Battalion's recruiting programme; and to make matters worse they had reduced any incentive for old soldiers wishing to sign on for another spell of service. All this came at a most unwanted moment in the Protectorate's history, because necessity required a full-strength battalion of ready troops. Situations demanding a practical demonstration of military might existed at several critical points: along the Protectorate border zone with Abyssinia; in Jubaland, where the Somalis were becoming increasingly acquisitive and aggressive; and on the eastern shores of Lake Rudolf, where there was an upsurge of Turkana and Dasenech raids. Somehow those problems had to be dealt with by a heavily depleted battalion of doubtful loyalties—in May 1911 'A' Company was made up of 60 Abyssinians and 40 Meru, of whom the latter had proved a failure as soldiers; of the other six companies only three comprised seasoned soldiers of dependability, and in the camel company many of the men were Somalis, of dubious fidelity.

When Hope left in May 1911 a state of false peace existed in his district. Girouard, who preferred to continue with his policy of observation, allowing the nomadic tribes to enjoy their way of life as they felt inclined, did have an alternative proposition. It was a disastrous sounding idea: he suggested that if all else failed the government should simply shrug its shoulders and walk out of the district, abandoning it to the forces of disruption once again. Whether it was born of defeatism or desperation was irrelevant; the very thought was abhorrent to baffled Colonial Office officials who, already weary of the dilemma, promptly passed the message on to the determined Thesiger for an answer.

Thesiger was then on board ship, travelling to Kismayu in Jubaland. He was on the eve of commencing a thorough inspection of the K.A.R. detachments in East Africa, and before too long the wires would be crackling with his caustic comments on the gloomy situation in the Protectorate.

Girouard cannot be castigated too harshly. He had taken what action he could to bolster the strength of his administration, which in turn was doing its best to guard the interests of the native peoples in the Northern Frontier District. It was unfortunate he had been caught up in a time of untoward financial constraint for the military. As a consequence he had been forced to position the meagre forces he was allowed in the best way possible. Positive evidence of his dispositions were to be seen in the garrison at Moyale, and the new army post at Loiengalani. The construction of the latter in October 1910—a flimsy fortress though it was, near the shore of Lake Rudolf—was an event heartily welcomed by the Samburu and Rendille, who lived a state of permanent terror of rapacious Dasenech and Abyssinian (Sidam) raiders and elephant hunters.

As a first step towards countering those marauders, Hope had ordered the small garrison of K.A.R. based on Marsabit, under the command of Lieutenant Bockett-Pugh, to move to Lake Rudolf. There, on a bare windswept ridge overlooking the oasis of Loiengalani, Pugh decided to put his base. It was a barren spot, worse even than

*Loiengalani military base in 1910.*

Archer's Post; the only redeeming features were the crystal-clear springs of fresh water bubbling out of the wilderness of rocks and sand, and the shade of spreading acacia trees mixed up with groves of sheltering doum palms. Pugh did his best to make his dreary position more homely; a vegetable patch was prepared, but soon failed on account of the sour salt-impregnated ground, and two cows were kept for milk. Meat was supplied, very reluctantly, by the Samburu and Rendille. It must have been a great relief for him when he handed over the cheerless post seven months later, in April 1911, to another young K.A.R. officer, Lieutenant A.C. Saunders.

Saunders was an energetic man who soon found much to satisfy his interests: wildfowl to shoot, hippopotami to hunt for the Elmolo, antelopes to stalk on the slopes of Mt Kulal, and fishing in the lake waters, apart from regular foot patrols into the broken country under his jurisdiction. Loiengalani, despite the beauty of the springs, was not a healthy spot, and with the tiresome recurrence of fever attacks amongst his men, added to which his camels were struck down with sickness from eating a poisonous shrub growing in the neighbourhood, Saunders decided a move to another site might be prudent.

He had two suitable alternatives in mind: either the post was removed to a well-watered place a few miles inland from the lake's edge—Teleki's delightful springs at Mouwoligiteng—or it had to be put close to Pugh's highland camp on the cool forested slopes of Mt Kulal. Saunders decided to try the former, and in mid-1911 he organised the construction of a modest fort on the crest of Teleki's ravine, dominating the tree-fringed springs. Apart from the restful green smudge of grass bordering the perennial water, the land around was, if it was possible, even more bleak than at Loiengalani. Strewn with lava boulders and studded with burial cairns*, the desperate landscape provided unlimited building material for Saunders' men in their hot work. Today, the lonely little square fort with its low crumbling walls, still stands, a silent monument to a solitary white man's efforts to assert his authority in that terrible countryside. As one contemplates the stony relic, with the blue-green waters of the

---

*The cairns at Mouwoligiteng are by far the largest of their kind seen by the author on the east side of Lake Rudolf. Of the mound type, and no more than 5 feet (1.5 metres) high at the centre, they are often at least 80 feet (25 metres) in diameter.

*Mouwoligiteng fort constructed by Lieutenant Saunders in 1911, and abandoned shortly after.*

lake to the west, the magnificent pyramid-shaped profile of Mt Kulal rising 6,000 feet (1,846 metres) into the sky to the east, and over it all the furnace-like wind blustering by, it is not hard to imagine the feelings of the young officer who built the insignificant stone bastion. It would have been for him, one must remember, a hard three-week slog to reach Nairobi; mails were erratic; and the fellowship of his own kind rare.

Thesiger's journey to the Protectorate's Northern Frontier District started on the day he left Serenli, an isolated British post on the Juba river. The date was 6 November 1911. To accompany him on his two-month fact-finding tour of the border region he took along a top brass team, made up of Archer, the senior administrative officer of the district; Lieutenant Colonel Breading, the commanding officer of the 3rd Battalion, K.A.R.; his adjutant; and, most important, Thesiger included a staff officer, Captain Charles French, to assist him in his work. The first garrison he inspected was at Dolo, 150 miles (240 kilometres) up the Juba, and here, the Somali camel-men deserted, taking their camels with them. The infuriating incident certainly didn't augur well for the success of the trip, and as it turned out later, it was not the last occasion on which the camel transport let the party down. Needless to say, Thesiger was not impressed with that experience, and nor indeed with much more of what he found as he made his careful scrutiny of the border garrisons.

On reaching the British fort at Moyale he made a terse note on its value: 'A large amount of labour had been expended on a small fort about twenty yards away from the boma, but I fail to see what can be the practical good of it'. Despite that, Thesiger complimented Zaphiro on his wisdom in siting the post on such a strategic spot, and recommended that it should be kept as a permanent station. Moyale, however, was not the right place to garrison with Abyssinian troops, whom he regarded as very unsatisfactory material to man an alien fort on the fringe of their homeland. He had previously reported unfavourably on them as soldiers, and at the end of December 1911 he had clearly not changed his mind, as his blunt words intimated: 'I am totally opposed to getting more Abyssinians as I regard them as unreliable and we cannot employ them near Abyssinia'.

Thesiger's tour ended at Marsabit towards the end of December. He had seen much that alarmed him, had learnt a great deal more about the precarious situation on the border and had written copious notes for the Colonial Office. For the recipients sitting in Whitehall they were depressing reading, providing them with warning of the serious state of affairs: 'something will have to be done ... unless we are going to be content to sit on a powder magazine and smoke pipes until something happens'. Those words of Thesiger's summed up his feelings, and he concluded his assessment by saying: 'There are many most serious problems in this country'. He had solid grounds, backed by plenty of evidence, for his forthright remarks: on the road between Moyale and Marsabit his martial procession had been subjected to the indignity of a hold up by an impertinent handful of five Abyssinian bandits, and at Marsabit came the final straw—the camel transport completely broke down, forcing him to write drily that there appeared to be an 'ignorance of everything to do with camels'.

Back at his office in London Thesiger had plenty to write about, so he promptly set to and produced an exhaustive memorandum on both the plight of the country and conditions in the K.A.R. Covering everything from suggested future policies to regimental footwear, his reports and memorandum gave many officials good reason to ponder deeply. One of them wrote: 'The outlook on the northern frontier of the East African Protectorate is far from pleasing'. Winding up his written appraisal, Thesiger gave the Colonial Office three alternatives for future policy. Firstly, it could follow Girouard's face-losing suggestion and withdraw completely from the district. Secondly, the rather feeble practice of observation could be continued; or thirdly, the policy Thesiger himself advocated, a more vigorous course of action should be taken, with military backing.

Two mundane but important recommendations from the Inspector General's pen were implemented without question. The soldiers in the K.A.R. were issued with the comfortable footwear he had suggested: 'as the natives of this Protectorate seem unused to wearing chupplis, and usually wear sandals in the bush and rock country I have authorised the C.O. to keep sandals instead of chupplis'. His thought was both practical and economical: sandals were cheaper and also made locally. The other, and vital change needed in the men's equipment was for the latest weapon issued to infantrymen: the famous .303 S.M.L.E. (Short Model Lee Enfield) rifle. First made available to the British army in 1907, the up-to-date military arm, complete with bayonet, cost £4.5.10d in 1911, and that same year the Colonial Secretary gave his personal assurance it would be made available to the K.A.R. battalions as soon as enough were available. So, even if the politics of the Northern Frontier were in confusion, at least the soldiers of the K.A.R. were promised the right equipment with which to march and fight.

*Belt buckles for the Northern Frontier Transport Corps and Constabulary.*

Early in 1912 Hope returned from leave and again took up the reins of his job as officer in charge of the Northern Frontier. Archer, to his credit, had held the position capably through a difficult period, and before he left for Jubaland he wrote a report for Hope, full of practical suggestions. One in particular received Girouard's encouragement—the creation of an armed constabulary to provide escorts for administration officers working in the field. It was essential in those turbulent and lawless days to have such a force, especially as the K.A.R. was so low in strength. Already a body of fifty armed men—the Northern Frontier District Transport Corps— existed, whose tasks were to operate and guard the transport system in the region. Its success was quite evident, and later inspired Girouard to recommend the formation of a brother unit to assist in the protection of the region—the Northern Frontier District Constabulary. Initially, the plan was to recruit one hundred and twenty Somalis and Sudanese for the force, men who were used to living in the desert lands, and traditionally well-versed in handling camel transport. In July 1912, after personal discussions with the Secretary of State in London, Girouard announced the formation of the Constabulary. Captain Barrett, an ex-army officer turned District Commissioner, was given the job of administering and training the new unit at its base on Marsabit. The raising of the Constabulary was one of Girouard's last significant services to the Northern Frontier District; that same month he resigned as Governor of the Protectorate.

Shortly after Girouard's departure another step forward in frontier affairs was made with the appointment of a transport officer to spruce up the service Thesiger had found so grossly inefficient. Progressively, as the administration of the district tightened, more officers with specialist experience and intellectual ability were recruited, with orders to improve the government services. In one of them, Captain Charles Alexander Neave, the district profited greatly: he was an experienced man with many years of active military service in East and South Africa to his credit. Neave came from a respected old English family: his father was a Lincolnshire vicar, and his great grandfather, Sir Thomas Neave, had been at one time High Sheriff of Essex and a Fellow of the Royal Society. Tall and athletic, Neave had attended the Royal Artillery

*Captain Charles Alexander Neave.*

School at Woolwich, where he captained the college's rugby fifteen. He was thirty years old when he went off to the Boer War in South Africa with the gunners, and there he stayed for the duration of that conflict. After the war was over he trekked north, arriving in the Protectorate in time to take part in the Nandi Expedition in 1905. In 1914, following several years of a full, but chequered life, Neave was offered the position of Northern Frontier Transport Officer. His acceptance gave him the chance to leave his marks, literally, on the rocky thorn-clad surface of the district. They took the shape of narrow winding roads, radiating from Archer's Post and Meru, stretching to lonely stations as far afield as Wajir and Marsabit, and other lesser ones closer by.

With Sir Conway Belfield's arrival in October 1912 as the Protectorate's new Governor, a more positive attitude to the problems in the Northern Frontier District was taken. After careful consideration of Thesiger's reports and memorandum, Belfield expressed his agreement with the parlous state of affairs in the district, and concurred with the Inspector General's opinion that the K.A.R. badly needed its numbers boosted. Promisingly, too, the Colonial Office was of the same mind as the two men, and with its backing the day was saved for the K.A.R. From then on the regiment's ranks were replenished with more recruits, and patrolling of the border trouble spots was stepped up. It happened only just in time; at the end of 1912 an intelligence report bluntly declared: 'The whole of the Abyssinian Border is infested with Abyssinian Tigre elephant hunters. They have been repeatedly warned'. Apart from that thorny

*East Africa Protectorate boundaries in 1912.*

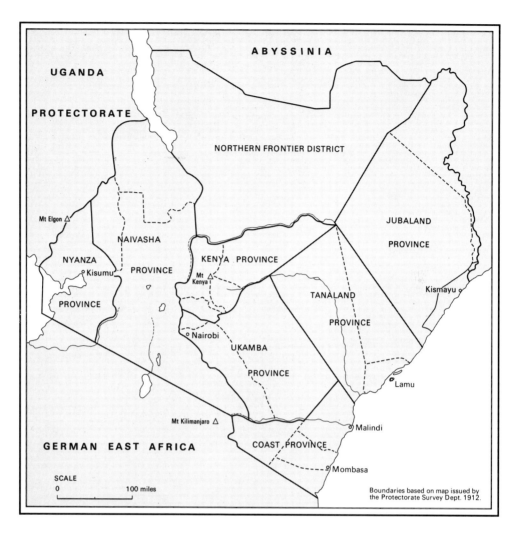

problem, the authorities had an equally delicate one farther east—the need to disarm the increasingly belligerent Somalis on the border of Jubaland.

Belfield, the new broom, had arrived in the nick of time to refresh flagging spirits in the Northern Frontier. The Colonial Office, too, was anxious to put things in order there, and with more reinforcements to Hope's field staff, it seemed as if the untidy situation was going to be straightened out at last. Neave's appointment to transport duties in the district in 1912, Aylmer's service throughout the year as a political officer to the Garre people in the east, and the arrival of Harold Kittermaster, a singularly large man in all senses of the word, as Assistant District Commissioner to Marsabit, were all visible signs of the government's readiness to exert a tighter grip on the running of the region's affairs.

There is no doubt Kittermaster was one of the greatest of all Northern Frontier administrators. On his untimely death in 1939, when he was Governor of Nyasaland (now Malawi), the obituary written for *The Times* of London had these words to say of him: 'Sir H. Kittermaster was a huge and rugged man, direct and forcible. Yet he is chiefly memorable for his great gentleness ... Personal ambition never swayed him. Bitterness and prejudice were wholly foreign to his nature'. A solid man, down to earth and lacking in any suggestion of pomposity, he was in essence the ideal type of man for the hard grind of life in the frontier district. The story of that large man's life is not an unusual one, but it is well worth knowing.

Of all the giants described within the covers of this book, Harold Baxter Kittermaster was without the slightest question physically the largest. Born under the sign of Taurus, he was a veritable titan, attaining in adulthood the mighty stature of six feet, eight and a half inches (2 metres). Towering over his contemporaries, he was in his time reckoned to be one of the tallest men in the British Colonial Service. The words of a fellow officer fittingly described his first meeting with the magnificent man at Archer's Post in 1913: 'As I was nearing the river I saw what at first I took to be a giant walking through the bush, lightly swinging a young sapling. This turned out to be K the Political officer from Marsabit ... He stood several inches over six feet and was built in proportion ... Trotting along beside this son of Anak I felt very small indeed, and began to think that only big men could live in the Northern Frontier District'. Those words came from the pen of an officer in the K.A.R., Lieutenant W. Lloyd Jones, who a few months later had his life saved by the man he wrote about.

Born on 14 May 1879, Harold Kittermaster grew up in the vicarage at Baystonhill near Shrewsbury, one of the Reverend Frederick Kittermaster's family of eight. When he was old enough he attended nearby Shrewsbury School for five years. There, although only a fair scholar, he managed to develop considerable skill as a sportsman, and in his final years played for his house in the cricket and football teams. His forte was, however, the field of rowing, an activity in which he excelled, and before he left he was pulling for the Shrewsbury crew with both enthusiasm and skill. By then he was head and shoulders taller than his schoolmates, having, from the age of fifteen, shot up a preposterous two feet in two years. Together with his homely craggy face, steady blue eyes and head of curly hair, went a quiet, amiable and generous nature. Beneath it all lay a determined disposition, supported by a splendid sense of humour.

Kittermaster's next step in life was to Oxford, where he arrived in time for the Michaelmas term of 1898. For four pleasant years he studied in the mellow gracious halls of Christ Church, working at his studies in Literae Humaniores, and rowing. Kittermaster's loyalties were divided during his time at Oxford between his academic toils and his sporting inclinations. The conflict as to which pursuit should receive the most attention resulted in Third Class honours in his subjects, but considerable distinction in the boats, for which he was awarded a rowing Blue. It was a formidable training.

A Third Class honours degree from 'the premier school in dignity and importance' may not have placed him in the upper echelon of intellectuals, but he read expansively, and the prose he wrote was on occasion charming, even Biblical at times. When it came time for him to seek his fortune he used those skills, firstly as a schoolmaster in the Transvaal, a land sadly devastated by the Boer War. It was into that despondent scene that young Kittermaster arrived, and it was there he found a job with the Transvaal Education Board, teaching in the small corrugated-iron school in the high veldt town of Ermelo, a hundred miles east of Johannesburg. Pictures of Ermelo as it stood in those days show a bleak-looking village, sparsely planted about with eucalyptus trees and surrounded by stark, treeless plains stretching in endless monotony to far horizons. Life, however, must have had its compensations for the young teacher, as he seemed content to work there for four years, teaching the children from a district renowned for

*Harold Baxter*
*Kittermaster.*

producing one of the most formidable Boer commandos in the recent war.

It will never be known what influenced Kittermaster's next move, which changed his whole life, developed the latent forces in his character, and ultimately brought him into the topmost ranks of East Africa's administrators. Maybe he had heard rumours of the marvellous sporting possibilities in the Protectorate, so, with some leave in hand, he decided to travel there and see the newly opened up frontier for himself. In July 1907 he joined a friend from Oxford days, and for six glorious weeks they indulged themselves in an orgy of hunting and bush life on the upper reaches of the Tana river.

The pleasure he derived was obvious from his delightful phrases, written after the event, when his mind had been totally converted to the immense exciting panorama of the Protectorate, with its exhilarating possibilities for sport and work. His lyrical words, annotations in a photograph album, clearly showed his sentiments at that stage: 'At last, the march begun; in front a life of free enjoyment and nature; wild nature, as it was in the beginning, is now, and shall be only a little longer . . . And so from day to day we wander on by shaded stream, or smoothly flowing river, by hill or plain, through thick bush or open veldt, in a country where man is not to be seen nor man's handiwork, where the fowls of the air and the beasts of the field roam at their will, and the peace of the African bush, the embodiment of God's peace, broods over all creation'. For the rest of his life Kittermaster remained a lover of the outdoors and an enthusiastic sportsman.

On his return to England after his first experience in East Africa, he had one compelling desire: to find some reason to take him back to the marvellous new Utopia he had found. He promptly applied to the Colonial Office for service in the Protectorate, and to his delight was accepted. He arrived in East Africa in 1908 with the rank of Assistant District Commissioner, and in 1912 he finally reached the Northern Frontier District. There he lived for seven satisfying years, toiling through the difficult times of the First World War when supplies and staff were at a premium in the Protectorate.

In musty dog-eared files, buried deep in official archives, will be found the evidence of Kittermaster's presence in the Northern Frontier District. They are rarely looked at, except by the serious researcher bent on some specialist task, and were it not for a tiny geographical feature, one of East Africa's finest administrators would remain forgotten. The feature appears on the map as a point some 50 miles (80 kilometres) downstream from Archer's Post, on the Uaso Ngiro river. Its name, Kittermaster's Camp, came from an incident involving Kittermaster himself. One morning, many decades ago, while he was camped on the river, a shirt of his was hung on a bush to dry. In the rush of departure it was overlooked and left behind. On the party's return to the same spot several weeks later, there, much to everyone's surprise, was his shirt, still hanging exactly as it had been left. From that day the camp earned its name, a small reminder of the tallest man ever to administer the vast northern area.

By the end of 1913 Aylmer was dead and Lloyd Jones, the officer in command of the lonely post at Loiengalani, had been crippled for life. For those grievous losses ugly lead bullets from Tigre rifles had been responsible.

Tucked away in a quiet corner of Nairobi Cathedral may be seen an elegant memorial plaque, attached to the building's grey stone wall. Inscribed on the tablet are these words: 'And this man died leaving his death for an example of a noble courage and a memorial of virtue, not only to young men, but unto all his nation'. Also written is the fact that the man died in action, far to the north on the Southern Abyssinian Border. Seventy years after his death he was still remembered by the very elderly in Moyale. Aylmer, for it is his memorial, met his death at the age of thirty-one while on border patrol far to the west of Moyale.

On the morning of 1 May 1913, two Transport Corps scouts brought to Aylmer's camp news of fresh human tracks they had found at the foot of nearby Gudderh Hill. Having little doubt they were Abyssinians' marks, Aylmer promptly set out in advance of his main force, accompanied by ten of his K.A.R. escort, his cook and Tzamma, his

Abyssinian orderly, in the hope of finding where the gang was lying up. By mid-morning they had reached the foot of Gudderh, and there they spotted a lone sentinel, perched high up among the boulders. With alacrity, Aylmer deployed his men in a circling movement, but the sentry's signals had already warned his comrades, who agilely clambered up the slopes and settled themselves behind the rocks on the rough bush-covered slopes. Insolent replies to Aylmer's shouts demanding their identity provoked the K.A.R. to open fire, and soon the bullets were flying thick and fast. During a lull in the firing, Aylmer moved his position to a convenient tree, thereby giving his rifle a better rest. His improved aim brought him an immediate result with the despatch of one of the enemy, but almost instantly he himself received a bullet through the chest. He only had time to utter the words: 'Tzamma, I am killed', before he, too, died. For the next seven days his men faithfully carried his body along the road to Moyale, but heavy rains finally blocked their way. There, in a lonely place called Kuffa, they were forced to bury him. Three days later they tramped into Moyale and made their tragic report to Captain Barrett, the District Commissioner.

Barrett acted swiftly. With a mixed force of K.A.R. soldiers, and a band of Transport Corps riflemen, he went on a hunt for Aylmer's killers. Barrett and Aylmer had been good friends, and had done much pioneer work together in the early years on the frontier, so one can well imagine the determination with which Barrett set out to seek revenge for the death of his companion. On 15 May, two weeks after the skirmish at Gudderh Hill, Barrett caught up with a party of Tigre, engaged them in battle, and succeeded in killing nine of them. The leader, badly wounded as he was, managed to escape, but died a few days later. Sometime after, reports came in that he had been the one who had fired the fatal shot at Aylmer, so Barrett could claim with satisfaction that scores had been evened.

Aylmer's death caused ructions in high places, and soon the wires were humming with talk of compensation, retribution and disciplinary action against the Abyssinians. The British Minister in Addis Ababa made strong remonstrations to the Abyssinian government, and asked the British Foreign Office for permission to demand blood money to the tune of at least 200,000 dollars. But none of that made up for the loss of Aylmer, the young officer who had given his life for the district which he had so enthusiastically volunteered to serve. Seven years later, in 1921, he found his final rest, when his remains were brought to Moyale and buried with full military honours.

At the time of Aylmer's death the border lands were beginning to suffer from the effects of growing political chaos in Abyssinia, a condition which had slowly been deteriorating since Menelik's abdication. Disorder had started in 1910 when the King became too old and sick to continue ruling his country. For the next three years Abyssinia was ineffectively ruled by a Regent. By 1913, the year the King died, discipline in the outlying provinces had dropped to a distressingly low level, a state of affairs that affected the boundary region for many years thereafter. Poorly disciplined and ineffectually led Abyssinian troops, avaricious provincial officials, plundering elephant hunters, stock thieves and refugees fleeing from them all, contributed to an endless nerve-racking existence for the lonely administrators and army officers stationed in the northernmost limits of the Protectorate. Behind the turbulence lay a scene of near anarchy, aptly expressed in *Jubaland and the Northern Frontier District*: 'As regards Abyssinia . . . The general attitude was that of people waiting for a crisis which they knew to be inevitable . . . The chiefs were in a state of uncertainty and while they detested the existing form of Government ... their own personal jealousies and intrigues, united with their rooted mistrust of their colleagues, prevented any combination for the purpose of joint action'. On the face of it there existed a sure recipe for disaster.

One sturdy by-product of the state of unease along the border came about when Lieutenant Rose of the K.A.R., who took command of the Moyale garrison at the beginning of June 1913, built a proper fort, complete with a square tower, crenellated walls and loopholes. Fort Rose, as it was then named, was of substantial build, made of poles, mud and stones, and stood for many years as the visible token of a determined British presence on that lonely extremity of the Protectorate. An engaging little aside in an official report of 1924 warned the fort's keepers that it was essential to keep a good supply of ant heap soil—a material with excellent binding qualities—available for application to the fort's walls, otherwise they would suffer considerable damage from rain erosion. Of such stuff was one of the British Empire's bulwarks built. Several years later, Major Dutton, on a visit to Moyale observed that the fort was: 'the very counterpart of an English country church in red sandstone ... There I read a framed notice, which hung in the old Mess ... It read, "The outer wall is loop-holed to fire standing. The inner wall of the guard-room proper is battlemented to fire kneeling: access to the roof is gained by a ladder and trap-door. There are 78 loop-holes in all" ... the notice was embellished with a rough perspective of the building, whose architect was a young officer named Rose, long since killed in some frontier fight'.

The establishment of a garrison at Loiengalani, the construction of Fort Rose at Moyale, the formation of the armed Constabulary, and the increase in military strength, were all stabilising influences desperately needed on the border in that period of flux. Flimsy defences they may have been for such a vast region, but they did represent an obvious British effort to stem the rising flood of border raids. That the available forces were inadequate was made quite clear in reports written by district officers at the time: only an increase in staff would alleviate the pressing problem. Anticipating its deeper commitment, the government had already made moves in that direction.

With the deteriorating political scene in Abyssinia came an increase in border incidents; already roaming bands of Tigre and undisciplined units of Abyssinian soldiers were penetrating ever deeper into Protectorate territory, but an added worry for the hard-pressed administration was the newest threat in the shape of rifle-armed Gelubba (Dasenech, Reshiat), who were stepping up their raids down the shores of Lake Rudolf, and across to the easternmost waterholes on the Chalbi Desert. As if those problems were not sufficient, a further one presented itself as numbers of Borana and Gabbra people fled to the Protectorate searching for sanctuary from enslavement and exploitation at the hands of Abyssinian soldiers and officials.

In 1913, a series of disastrous attacks on the Gabbra and Rendille living along the Chalbi Desert waterholes took place. The marauders were mostly Gelubba, aided by a sprinkling of Abyssinians. Swooping down from the north they first savaged the weakly defended Gabbra settlements at Kalacha springs, killing thirteen, and then one month later, they attacked them at Maikona wells, killing a further twenty-three. Thousands of head of stock—cattle, sheep and goats—were driven away from those bloody one-sided encounters, and with no resisting government forces nearby, the culprits contentedly escaped scot-free.

*Moyale fort (Fort Rose), constructed in 1913.*

Occasionally, however, all did not go so well for the plunderers, as was described in a letter from Kittermaster to Lloyd Jones, who was then based at Loiengalani. The communication reported on a raid in April 1913 when 'some 30 Reshiat and 8 Abyssinians' audaciously attacked a Rendille encampment only 12 miles (19 kilometres) from the Marsabit station. By a lucky coincidence three of Kittermaster's armed men happened to be staying at the camp, and although heavily outnumbered, they pluckily engaged the enemy, killing twenty of them in a running gun battle. Reinforcements rushed down the hill from Marsabit, and helped to chase the enemy out of the area and westwards to Mt Kulal. All the stolen cattle were recovered, and four rifles captured. The action was a resounding success for the government; the only person to lose out on the excitement being Kitters (Kittermaster's nickname) himself. Ever anxious for such adventures, he could only write: 'And I was on safari, blow it'. Still hoping for a piece of action he added: 'At the earliest possible moment I will raise some camels and come across to you [Lloyd Jones] and we will make a patrol northwards'.

Kittermaster's opportunity to deal a blow to the bands of Gelubba roaming his district came in August 1913, when he joined forces with Lloyd Jones at Loiengalani. The two men then marched northwards along the lake shore, accompanied by a strong column of thirty-three K.A.R. men plus a few Constabulary. As they trudged up the lake-side to Alia Bay, through country new to both of them, Kittermaster made constant reference to the pages in Stigand's book, which described the latter's journey through the same region only four years before. From Alia Bay the party struck eastwards, away from the lake, into a rough, waterless land, and straight for disaster. On 3 September, two days' march from the lake, Jones's scouts unexpectedly came on a

*King's African Rifles on camel patrol in the frontier district.*

*Captain W. Lloyd Jones, D.S.O.*

thorn zariba hidden away in a lonely little valley. Next to it lay a tiny pool of water*. A solitary rifle-armed man and a few donkeys were the only signs of life. The herder, on seeing the strangers approach, bolted. A shouted order in Abyssinian to those who might be inside the zariba to surrender produced neither reply nor movement. Jones, having made his formal challenge, ordered several volleys of fire directed at the grass hut in the centre of the compound. An ominous silence was the only reply. The bugler then sounded the charge, and Jones, with a few men, rushed the stockade. Only then did a wicked rifle fire meet them full in the face, and Jones, as he struggled to tear down the gateway, was struck down by a heavy bone-shattering bullet through his ankle. The bugler, too, fell with a bullet in his chest, and another of the men was killed. Despite the losses the fight was soon over, and the enemy, eight in number, all lay dead. For Lloyd Jones, the next six weeks were unmitigated torment, suffering continually from intense physical pain and bouts of delirium as his men carted him bodily on a stretcher, first to Loiengalani, then over to Marsabit, down to Meru and

---

*This is Wano waterhole, much increased today from what it was at the time of the incident in 1913, but still well off the beaten track. From the clusters of burial cairns and ring graves on the surrounding hillslopes, the waterhole must have been a steady source of water even in ancient times.

finally, by way of Nyeri, to hospital in Nairobi. For two agonising weeks he was nursed by Kittermaster at Loiengalani, before the Indian doctor eventually arrived from Marsabit. Captain Barrett later wrote of those first days: 'Lloyd Jones owes his life to the careful and skilful nursing of Mr. Kittermaster'. For his bold action in the fight, and fortitude in the subsequent gruelling journey back to civilisation, Lloyd Jones received the Distinguished Service Order. The three devoted soldiers who made the final attack on the zariba and wiped out the enemy, each received the Distinguished Conduct Medal. The military decoration was a poor compensation for Lloyd Jones, crippled as he was for life, and no longer able to continue his active military life in East Africa.

The year 1913, eventful as it had been, ended quietly, but the two main problems affecting the practical side of administration stubbornly persisted: the shortage of, and difficulty in finding, adequate and suitable transport for the district's needs; and the provision of enough food to keep the garrisons at Archer's Post, Loiengalani, Marsabit and Moyale going.

An efficient transport service in the Northern Frontier District was of vital importance. Its upkeep, however, provided the authorities with constant frustration. In the earliest years the system of moving supplies was a complex manoeuvre involving several different means of carriage. Between Meru—the district's headquarters—and Archer's Post the carrying was done on the heads of Meru porters. From there on to Marsabit everything went on the backs of camels and donkeys. At Marsabit a team of camels took over and did the final stretch as far as Moyale—only camels could cope with the waterless five-day haul across the Dida Galgalo. As time passed, and roads cautiously reached out across the bushlands, more use was made of waggons pulled by straining spans of oxen. As early as 1913 an Afrikaner by the name of Bothma, using two waggons, contracted to move supplies as far as Merille, 65 miles (106 kilometres) beyond Archer's Post on the road to Marsabit. He, in his humble but essential task, may not have been aware at the time that he was one of the stalwarts who pioneered the way for all future wheeled traffic in the Northern Frontier. But despite the advent of Bothma's ox-drawn carts, and later, motor-powered transport, the complaining camels and donkeys would remain for many years the main load carriers on the district's long winding supply routes.

The Boma Trading Company, which was the first to use the route to Moyale on a fairly regular basis, usually managed to find enough camels for its needs by a system of forcible purchase from the Rendille. The government, although at first expressing their disapproval of such tactics, was soon driven to procuring the beasts by a highly unpopular taxation, which took the form of camels. Eventually, through the Rendille's skill at hiding their best animals when the call went out for more, the system proved a failure. The Gabbra, another potential source of camels—and larger and stronger ones—lived too far afield to be a reliable source. The authorities were finally forced to alter the arrangement: from then on camels were rented from their owners at fifty cents a day. In the event of death, which regularly happened, an agreed compensation of thirty shillings, or its equivalent in cloth, was paid. By that means the transport deficiency, although never entirely eliminated, was lessened. For the last desperate stretch to Moyale from Marsabit a minimum standing herd of fifty camels was kept. As one reads through the yellowing pages of reports written by officers in remote frontier stations, it becomes more and more apparent how vital it was for them to have a

*Safari porters ferrying loads across the Uaso Ngiro river by Archer's Post.*

smoothly running camel transport system as a lifeline, and why it became one of their main preoccupations.

With the growing army of Protectorate employees and K.A.R. soldiers in the Northern Frontier, the fundamental matter of providing sufficient food for them was of increasing concern to their senior officers. At Meru, Horne continued to hold the position of District Commissioner. Under his benign rule great advances had been made, and although the buildings in the compound were still, in 1913, log houses, other aspects of life showed encouraging improvements. A new road between Meru and Archer's Post was ready, and a runner system carried mail once a week between the two places—42 miles (68 kilometres) each way—for one rupee and a ration of posho (maize meal). An Indian trader had opened a flour mill, and Horne wrote with satisfaction in his annual report that 'many hundreds of loads of flour have been supplied to the Northern Frontier District'. The Meru people's country was a rich agricultural land, as both Chanler and Neumann had separately discovered to their advantage almost twenty years before, and under Horne's guidance it became a substantial provider of government needs in the north. Only one thing prevented a steady and sufficient flow of foodstuffs—the hard-pressed transport. In the days when all the traffic was carried by erratic camel and donkey caravan, the remote station at Moyale often had to rely on grain brought from Abyssinians. Exorbitant prices and political uncertainties on occasion made the supply precarious, but somehow the lonely post survived.

The fateful year of 1914 arrived full of promise for the administrators in the Northern Frontier, as many policy changes were being arranged for the district by the Protectorate government, and some eager new faces arrived before the year was over. Then in his last few months of frontier duties, Hope wrote on New Year's Day that: 'I propose closing Marsabit as a station and leave only a police post at Delamere's Water'*. Marsabit by then was hardly more than a staging post on the route to more important Moyale, and although the first Indian trader in the district, Mohamed Moti†, had set up shop there in 1910, and Hope had used the mountain camp as his base since that same year, by 1914 he was doubtful of the station's continued value. Another change he suggested, prompted by his long experience of camel transport frustrations, was the use of vehicles powered by internal combustion engines. He propounded the idea in his handing over report, saying: 'I have strongly recommended that the question of motor transport should be carefully considered'. With that in view, Kittermaster had already done a road survey down the banks of the Uaso Ngiro river from Archer's Post to Melka Galla hill. With Neave's appointment, more such work was soon under way, as efforts to improve the district's communications increased.

On the future of the Constabulary, Hope was confident the tiny force would continue to prove its worth, but at the same time he expressed his reservations. The arms it had been issued with were completely outdated Martinis firing black-powder cartridges, and there were hardly sufficient to go round, assuming they were all in working order. Amongst the staff, the Somali members were not altogether trustworthy, and also 'heartily disliked by the majority of our tribes'; moreover, the Abyssinians in the force were too close to home to be reliable. None the less, there were amongst them many who were deeply loyal to their officers, and in time they became a valued body of men.

By April 1914, when Hope took final farewell of the district he had cared for since its inception, sound foundations for its future administration had been laid, with a substantial military presence to back it up. It was gratifying for him to think that the officers who stepped into his position would benefit from his industrious groundwork.

At the beginning of 1914 an announcement in the Protectorate's Official Gazette proclaimed to its readers that a man named Vincent Goncahrs (Goncalves) Glenday had been appointed Assistant District Commissioner to the Northern Frontier District on 14 January. No one noticing his name would have had the slightest suspicion that the rugged young man of twenty-three would in time become the most renowned, and the longest serving officer ever to work in the Northern Frontier's administration.

Vincent Goncalves Glenday's father, a stockbroker by profession, died suddenly when the boy was only nine. He left an orphaned family of six children, a situation identical to the Chanlers' two decades before. Fortunately for the Glenday orphans, a kindly bachelor uncle—Uncle Ted—took the family into his charge and cared for them in his commodious vicarage at Bury in Lancashire until they had finished their schooling. Vincent Glenday's forebears, like Ralph Hornyold's, were a mixed lot. His grandfather, John, came from Ulster, where he married a girl called Vincent. From her Glenday received his first name. Serving in India as a Colour Sergeant with the 61st Regiment, John Glenday made a name for himself as a fine soldier, and for his displays of courage in many of the Indian Mutiny battles he earned an impressive chestful of

---

*This was the spring Delamere found on the north side of the mountain in 1897, sometimes called Delamere's Njoro.

†Mohamed Moti was the enterprising Indian trader whose pioneering spirit carried his business from Mombasa to Nairobi, and from there to Embu, Meru, Archer's Post and Marsabit.

medals. In time he rose to the rank of General, and eventually, on completion of his service, retired to Scotland. Meanwhile, one of his sons had married a Portuguese lady by the name of Goncalves. She became Vincent Glenday's mother, and it was from her he acquired his second name.

Most of Glenday's schooling was completed at St Bees in Cumberland, where he, like Kittermaster, soon proved a ready ability on the playing fields, developing top class skills at rugby and cricket, in both of which he was chosen for the school's 1st teams. In 1909 he went up to Wadham College, Oxford. The paths of two other young men—John Llewellin and Denys Finch Hatton—who were also studying contemporaneously at Oxford, but at different colleges, would shortly meet up with Glenday's in the Northern Frontier of East Africa. It appeared Glenday must have applied himself equally diligently to both classwork and sport, for he achieved a second class honours in Geology for his Master of Arts degree, complemented by a diploma in Forestry, and a place in his college cricket, football and rugby teams. Rugby in particular was his passion, but, although he played several matches for the University team, he failed, only just, to be selected to play against Cambridge in the traditional game that would have distinguished him with a Blue. Dropped from the team at the last moment on account of his light weight—hooker was his position— Glenday forever after regarded the rejection as one of the greatest disappointments of his life. While at Oxford, the powerfully built, thick-set young man had one other entertainment—boxing. Not only did he box for the University as a middle weight, he also dabbled for amusement in bouts with itinerant fairground pugilists, a practice of which his coach heartily disapproved.

From childhood Glenday had suffered from impaired hearing, caused by an unsuccessful mastoid operation, and the failing may have contributed to his somewhat withdrawn and reserved nature, traits that helped to brand him as a taciturn and charmless individual by men who worked with him in later life. As a boy he had, despite the gregariousness of his sporting pastimes, developed a meditative, inward-looking personality. A quotation from Margaret Kennedy's *Together and Apart*, taken out of a private notebook he kept many years later, reveals the effects of his orphanhood: 'he had grown up alone with no family life, never taking anything or anybody for granted. He knew very little about love and affection. His mind had ripened early, but his heart had been undernourished'. When he left Oxford he had not the slightest inkling that his reticence and avoidance of public display would serve him well in the lonely years ahead, or that he would eventually become that rarity, a senior administrator who had been hero worshipped by many of his subordinates.

In late 1913, the well-qualified Glenday reported to the Colonial Office and was told of his posting to, of all places, the troublesome and primitive Northern Frontier of East Africa. A few months later he arrived in the Protectorate and was allocated his duties as officer in charge of Moyale. There, green as he was in the artifices of frontier squabbles, he soon became well known for his fearlessness in battle—of which there were many—and his flair for handling perfidious Abyssinian and Somali behaviour. Much later, after twenty-five years of hard, unremitting and often intensely lonely service in the wastes of the Northern Frontier District, for which he received many testimonies, Glenday could acknowledge the inspiration of three quotations which had guided him in his career. One by Ester Mermon ran thus: 'In the world of everyday material work nothing much counts but the power to leave it better for your

*Vincent Goncalves Glenday ('Faras Ad') on his white horse. Taken at Moyale, 1915.*

having been born'. The second, and equally indicative of Glenday's philosophy, came from Lord Hardene of Cloan, who wrote: 'When you have come to a deliberate decision then go ahead, and go ahead with grim unshaken resolution to persist'. Lastly, from the Koran: 'God is with those who persevere'.

Glenday finally left the Northern Frontier in 1939 to take up a more exalted post.

Very briefly, before the Italians invaded the country in 1940, he was Governor of British Somaliland. From there he returned to England, and for two years he worked in the dreary monotony, for him, of a Whitehall job. In 1942 he was knighted by King George VI, and then, as Sir Vincent Glenday, he travelled to the Hadhramout in southern Arabia, where for two years he gave his able skills to the country's government in its uphill struggle against anarchists, drought and a sick economy. In appreciation of his strenuous efforts the Sultan honoured him with the title of Pasha. The following year found Glenday working in Zanzibar as the British Resident, and there he stayed for five contented years, the last in his long service for the Colonial Administration. His retirement years commenced in Kenya, the country in which he had spent so much of his earlier working life, and where, for six years he acted as Speaker in the Central Legislative Assembly before finally leaving for his last home, in South Africa. In 1970, at the age of seventy-nine, he died. So passed an extraordinary man. With his tough physical characteristics, his unusual academic qualifications—he was also a Fellow of the Geological Society—and his sternly fierce disciplines, both to himself and to others, he was well equipped to lead; the list of honours bestowed on him were proof of that alone. The clerihew written by one of his subordinates in the 1930s sum up the image he had created for himself:

> Vincent Glenday
> Said 'Bring life what it may,
> I'm the King of the N.F.D.,
> The Grand Seigneur sans merci.'

On Hope's final departure from the Northern Frontier, its burdens fell on the shoulders of a diminutive man, Samuel Frederick Deck. A dwarf among giants, he was, none the less, capable and experienced as an administrator, quite able to hold the district together for the year he held office. Although a holocaust had started in Europe, in contrast the year was a peaceful one on the Frontier, and Glenday, from his fortress at Moyale reported back that most disputes with the Abyssinians had been settled amicably, despite continuing failure to fulfil their promises to the British officials, and worse, their outright defiance of higher orders from Addis Ababa.

The staff of Protectorate officers had increased, notwithstanding the pressing demands from men clamouring to volunteer for service in France. Glenday, amongst others, had tried in vain to enter the army, so as to join two of his brothers who were already engaged in the fight against Germany. To his great disappointment his request was turned down flat; his presence on the border was then of far more importance to the authorities, so there he had to stay.

Neave, in his capacity as Transport Officer, was provided with a budget of £14,000 that critical year, and with those funds he was expected to build rudimentary trunk roads, and generally improve his struggling transport system. By early 1915 his staff was made up of one assistant, a geologist named John Parkinson, whose job it was to survey water supplies along the new district roads, and five waggon conductors. By the end of the year Neave could report that his labour gangs had cut 100 miles (160 kilometres) of good waggon road to Merti, over half way down the path to Wajir. His Merti track, and the well-used highway to Merille on the Marsabit route, were at the time the only stretches of man-made road in the district. Using the money carefully, some claimed too tightly for the comfort of his labourers, Neave also managed to establish an excellent depot on top of Lgirrgirr Hill, a short distance from the buildings of Archer's Post. There he built a small workshop, complete with a cement floor—a feature unique on the busy hilltop. But even with those improvements to the transport facilities, Glenday still had grounds to complain of food shortages during the year, and in his annual reports stated that 'I experienced great anxiety during this period'.

In the middle of all those activities another giant arrived on the scene to join the growing staff of young administrators—John Lionel Bretherton Llywelyn-Llewellin. A contemporary of Glenday's and a history graduate from Lincoln College, Oxford, Llewellin had set his sights on joining the Inner Temple as a student, with an eye to a profession in the diplomatic corps. He never made it: a friend who was on leave from Jubaland 'painted such a glowing picture of life among the nomadic Somali tribes that my imagination was stirred'. An aunt of his soon arranged a lunch date for him with none other than her good friend the Colonial Secretary, the elegantly modish Lewis ('Lulu') Harcourt. From that simple manoeuvre Llewellin procured a job. After completion of the statutory three month training for all recruits to the colonial service, he eagerly boarded a decrepit old steamship at Marseilles, bound for East Africa. His fellow passengers included, in addition to a veteran, Lord Delamere, eight other young government officers, like him all new recruits for service in Africa. At Mombasa he was fortunate in meeting Kittermaster—the man with whom he was to work closely for the next five years—who regaled him with tales of the desert, and gave him useful tips on the modes of behaviour in the heat-ridden desolation of the Frontier. The two immensely tall men must have been an impressive sight to bystanders—Llewellin, just four inches shorter than his senior, still stood six feet, four and three-quarter inches (1.95 metres), deservedly earning his nick-name, Long Lew.

Within his family circle it is claimed that John Llewellin tried to model himself on his uncle, the late Major Bretherton who was the man Kitchener selected as supply and transport officer for the ill-famed Lhasa Expedition which invaded Tibet in 1904. A fine soldier, an enthusiastic sportsman, a competent organiser of great stamina and a remarkable walker, Bretherton was drowned crossing a flooding river in Tibet. A revered family member, he had been highly decorated by the military, and was in his time an active Fellow of the Royal Geographical Society, to whose journal he subscribed several articles on his travels in the east.

On 15 May 1914 Llewellin was appointed to the Northern Frontier as an Assistant District Commissioner, so following Glenday's five-month-old footsteps. In early June the exciting moment he had been anticipating arrived, when he met up with Neave at Thika, left behind the last motor car he would see for another three years, and joined the dusty procession of ox waggons headed for distant Archer's Post. Tramping along at the rate of 12 miles (19 kilometres) a day, their route took them by way of Fort Hall, Nyeri and Meru, before rumbling into the isolated station on the Uaso Ngiro river one month later. There he found that his 'living quarters were a large tent, and my office a rather rickety building of wattle and daub with a grass roof'. His only company, until Neave arrived shortly after, was an Anglo-Indian clerk called Stevens. He was there for only one month before being ordered to move on to Wajir and a long almost unbroken spell of six years among the Somali people—the sole break was a visit to the dentist in Nairobi in 1917 which took two months. To them he became known, quite appropriately, as 'Wellin dera' (Long Llewellin). The house he moved into at Wajir had been planned and built by Deck to match his own short frame, and the only possible way Llewellin could stand up in it was either to raise the roof, or dig down and lower the floor level by two feet. He chose the easier, and least expensive, and dug down.

The year came to an end in a confused state as the frontier's administrators grappled with their tasks, sharpened by the advent of war in Europe, and the increasing difficulties in obtaining supplies. Border raiding continued, Tigre poachers battered away at the elephants, and a few wandering white men trudged round the district in their search for livestock to drive down to the waiting Protectorate centres. Glenday in Moyale persisted in his shaky relationship of friendly distrust with Fitaurari Waldi, his Abyssinian counterpart, who he suspected was tampering with the Protectorate's official mail to Addis Ababa. To help ease his way, Captain Barrett proposed that it might be good politics to present Waldi with a .500 double-barrelled cordite rifle and 100 rounds of ammunition. One does not read that the gift was ever approved. Neave, with his immaculate book-keeper's mind, estimated the cost of running the Northern Frontier District would come to £45,000, out of which £6,470 was needed to provide salaries for everyone, from Deck, the officer in charge, down to the humblest of clerks. One tiny improvement came with the increase of mails from Meru to Archer's Post. The runner service had been doubled, and it was delivering twice weekly. Deck had one serious grouse though, and he concluded his summing up of the year's activities with the sombre note that there were still no hospital facilities of any sort in the huge district.

Early in January 1915 a letter written in elegant manuscript, in French, reached the British Legation in Addis Ababa. Signed by two Greeks, it requested permission to carry trade in flour and coffee from Abyssinia, through Moyale, and into the Protectorate. The two men, Cardovillis and Catrivanos, who were partners of a trader in the Borana country by the name of Salavrakos, also wished to construct a house and store at Moyale as a base for their operations. Their hopes were knocked on the head when Glenday wrote to the legation some months later stating: 'I consider it extremely inadvisable to allow any white trader to settle here under the existing conditions, and especially one who is not conversant with our law, customs or language'. The remark displayed Glenday's youthful sternness, for George Cardovillis, who had lived longer in Africa, could well claim to have a greater experience in dealing with the deviousness of Abyssinian intrigue; and as his future life proved, he was undoubtedly more than capable of handling the intricacies of a trader's life on the border. In any event, the Greeks were not allowed to have their base at Moyale. Undeterred by the obstruction, they later went on to build up a flourishing business as cattle dealers, moving great numbers down to the Protectorate for sale to the white settlers.

Not only the Greeks came under Glenday's severe discipline. By the time he left Moyale at the end of 1915 for the even more remote Garre country on the Daua river, he had drawn up a set of regulations for behaviour in his little township. In their very stiffness they forewarned of the course his command would take in the years to come. For outsiders it was mandatory to have passes for here, passes for there, and most certainly no movement at night was allowed; there were also tight restrictions on the use of certain roads, the carrying of arms, and entry into British territory. Even the townspeople came under his thumb, with a set of no-nonsense rules for them to adhere to; irritatingly for them, Glenday went as far as insisting they keep their yards and streets swept clean of refuse and grime. To cap it all he ordered most of Zaphiro's old huts to be burnt down, 'as they were infested with bugs'. Shortly after, when Kittermaster took over the station, Moyale must have been the showpiece of the district. Glenday had done his job thoroughly, and was then well prepared to face the next and far more testing assignment, when he would require every vestige of his austere self-discipline.

As 1915 wore on two more key points down the line from Moyale were closed: at Marsabit, Hope's forecast came about with the translocation of the Crater Lake camp to a new locale close by Delamere's spring—the site of the present-day town; and further west, the lonely post at Loiengalani on Lake Rudolf was finally abandoned to the desert winds, marking the end of its five years of costly life.

Archer's Post still stood firm. The administration camp had moved over to join the transport depot, and new houses, offices and stores were constructed, 'all admirable buildings of dom palm logs roofed with iron and a grass thatch added above'. In 1915 the post was a hub of activity. There at the centre, Neave waited for the vital loads of flour to come from Meru, and other materials from Nairobi. Four thousand loads of flour alone were needed that year to meet the full requirements of the army and the administration. It still arrived on porters' heads down the 40 miles (64 kilometres) of road from Meru. The rest of the supplies came from Nairobi, lumbering up by way of Nyeri on heavy creaking ox waggons, led by a stalwart band of Afrikaner conductors— Bothma, Klopper, Klynsmith, Prinsloo and Steyn were among their names—to the accompaniment of stentorian shouts, cracking whips, groaning wheels, ever straining oxen and clouds of cloying dust. At Archer's Post the loads were piled onto fresh wagons—more ox waggons to Marsabit, donkey carts to Merti—and sent trundling on their way to the anxiously awaiting outposts.

When he had completed his stint as head of the district, Deck, in collaboration with Neave, put together a comprehensive analysis of the transport situation. The mound of statistics he produced is hardly dull reading. They clearly outline one of the major problems of the Protectorate's largest, most remote and wildest districts. One basic fact emerged: to keep the whole show going 165 tons of food and supplies a year were needed. To lift that bulk to Moyale, Wajir and elsewhere required a brigade of nearly 300 bullocks, 174 donkeys and 150 camels. Because of the rising cost and heavy mortality of the camels, increasing reliance had to be placed on wheeled traffic, and in ever increasing numbers Neave's men sweated in the desert heat to hack roads across the bush lands, rolling aside multitudes of massive lava boulders in their efforts to push through waggon trails. How important the transport system's efficacy was for the administration is clear from the regularity with which the subject arises in official reports. Neave, his white conductors, the Meru porters, the oxen, the donkeys, and the grumbling camels were all part of a team, striving desperately to keep the frontier guards' bellies full, and their weapons supplied with the requisites for battle.

In Europe and German East Africa the war was slogging on into its second year, and manpower was being devoured at an alarming rate. Despite the high demands for men on the foreign battlefields, the need for a tight control in the Northern Frontier assured it a full complement of staff, and so the old hands soldiered on. In 1916 Kittermaster became the officer in charge, and for the next three years lorded it (he was known to the Gabbra as Aba Gudha—Big Father) over the great expanse, and in the far eastern corner of the district, Glenday lived with the Garre people for three lonely years, as Dutton described: 'Glenday became a wanderer with the Gurre [sic] . . . now

*On the road to Marsabit. Afrikaner conductors and their waggons, 1910.*

moving to an oasis, now to water pans, now to the river, always with his nomad people . . . subsisting on their meagre and unpalatable foods, living among them and moving with them from camping-ground to camping-ground in the desert'. During that lonesome time he became well known to the Somali as Faras Ad (white horse), from the white stallion he rode on his rounds.

One of the newer arrivals, Frederick Trevor Bamber, reached the district in 1915, after several months of apprenticeship elsewhere in the Protectorate. He arrived in Moyale during tense times, and promptly left his brand on the land when he dug the defensive lines of trenches round Fort Rose. The wandering ditches were never needed in his day, and were still there a quarter of a century later, when they were quickly restored in readiness for a possible Italian invasion.

Bamber had one thing in common with Kittermaster and Glenday: he shared the taste of an upbringing in the shelter of a vicarage—his father was rector of Long Melford in Suffolk. Young Frederick enjoyed a private education, part of it in Germany, before he went up to Cambridge in 1910. A born linguist, he graduated from Jesus College with second classes in the Modern and Medieval Language Triposes—French and German—in 1913. Just under average height at five feet, seven inches (1.7 metres), Bamber none the less proved an able and enthusiastic cricketer and hockey player while at Jesus, and later in East Africa. However, his intellectual disposition, evident in his ornate and accomplished prose, soon showed itself in his written reports. Many years later his agile mind needed only six months to master the Italian language, secured him an F.R.C.A. in accountancy and an LL.B. in Law. All his life he was superstitious of one thing—the number 13. Ambushed on two separate occasions by Tigre bandits on the 13th of the month, he was also mauled by a lioness on the same date, and finally died on a day with the fateful number.

Bamber was not the only newcomer to the district. Another, and more than welcome addition was Dr G.R.H. Chell, the first fully qualified doctor to be posted to

*Government transport fording the Uaso Ngiro river below Archer's Post, 1915. Kittermaster on horseback.*

the pitiless region. He arrived to take up his duties in November 1915, and soon found much to disturb him. For one thing, he declared that the standard tents for white officers were quite inadequate for frontier conditions, and in his opinion they were one of the main reasons for the low state of health among the staff. He recommended a lining be built into them to minimise the men's discomfort. The observant doctor also wasted no time in pointing out the appalling lack of medical facilities in the district, and warned that immediate action should be taken to rectify the deficiency.

Although Chell proved to be a great asset to the district in his field of medicine, on one occasion he also did a spell as a stand-in administrator at Moyale for a few months. His spirit showed itself only a month after he had arrived in the district, while leading a strong government caravan to Moyale. The party, on taking their camels to the waterhole lying at the foot of Turbi Hill, were fired on by a bunch of Tigre crouched among the rocks above. After losing one man, Chell broke off the aimless engagement, and retired only to find next morning that the ambushers had disappeared during the night. It was just as well he was able to cope with the vagaries of frontier life, for on that particular journey he was acting as guard for a precious government cargo of 20,000 dollars in cash for the station at Moyale, a fact the enemy was suspected of knowing.

In May 1916, when Deck handed the district over to Kittermaster, the huge region

was approaching a period of upheaval and disturbance, and it certainly needed a giant to cope with the unrest. Kittermaster had under him a team of resolute young men, inured to hardship, and prepared at all times for battle. One month after taking office he wrote his annual report. Politically, he noted, affairs were not as satisfactory as in the two previous years: the Tigre raids were on the upsurge; infringements by Abyssinians had increased—one senior official, Gabra Takle, had actually been insolent enough to conduct a hunting party of soldiers 10 miles (16 kilometres) into Protectorate territory; the lonely station at Wajir had had to be evacuated briefly for fear of Somali attack; the transport system was poor, and he admitted that generally: 'The net result of the year's work is disheartening. It may be said that the whole of the N.F.D. has gone out of Administration with the exception of a narrow strip from Archer's Post to Moyale via Marsabit and from Marsabit to Bulesa via Buna'. To add to his woes, the all important mail system showed no signs of improvement, and it still took five weeks from the time of posting a letter at Archer's Post to receipt of a reply from Moyale, a distance of 600 miles (965 kilometres). To speed things up someone suggested heliograph communications might help.

Kittermaster then wrote in detail about the transport—his eternal headache. From Deck he had inherited eleven waggons, all American built and capable of carrying only six loads each. Of those only six were working. There was also a collection of small carts, but of these he gloomily noted: 'Again tho' there are 13 Scotch carts on the books 10 of these cannot be used firstly because the woolwich wheels from England with which they are fitted are too high for the local oxen and secondly because the wood of which the wheels are made tho' perhaps sufficiently seasoned for the English climate does not seem to be able to withstand the intense dry heat of the N.F.D.' Just to worsen the predicament there was still a shortage of trained oxen to pull the carts along the wandering, rut-infested tracks. It took a full team—a span of sixteen bullocks—to pull one loaded waggon, but significantly it took the beasts a full month to recover their strength after each thirsty journey from Archer's Post to Marsabit and back, across the desert stretch where pasture was virtually non-existent for the greater part of the year.

In his hefty farewell memorandum Deck had included his views on how the future administration should function. His was not the first of such documents, and like earlier ones it covered all the most important subjects, but one thing he felt strongly about was the streamlining of the armed forces in the district; at that time they comprised a hotch-potch of K.A.R., a Police Service Battalion, armed Constabulary and the Arab Rifles. Deck recommended the Constabulary be kept as it was, and because of its peculiar value in the district, it should be increased substantially. Wisely, the others were shortly amalgamated into a completely new battalion of K.A.R., known as the Fifth Battalion King's African Rifles (Northern Frontier Force), under the command of the experienced Captain Barrett, who had for the purpose been promoted to a Lieutenant Colonel.

The month before Kittermaster took over his vast province, the Northern Frontier's headquarters had been moved from Moyale down to Archer's post, where a sizeable community had grown up on top of, and around the hill. The post included at the time a newly built hospital and dispensary built of logs and iron, a ferryboat pulled by ropes for use in times of flood, three shops at the bottom of the hill (two Indian* and

---

*Mohamed Moti and Habib Khan.

*Andre Dugand, Head Conductor, Northern Frontier
Transport Corps, 1917.*

one Somali), sundry residents and a cattle pen capable of impounding one thousand beasts. A welcome addition to the amenities was the new telegraph line connecting the post to the administration centre at Meru.

In early 1917 Neave was allocated a new assistant, a most able individual by the name of Dugand, or 'Dugie' to his three Afrikaner conductors. Dugand had first reached South Africa on a French ship as a teenager. There he worked for some years before making his way up to East Africa, learning the art of handling waggon transport as he travelled. A quiet, agreeable man, he could speak Afrikaans, English and French fluently, making him an ideal person for the position under Neave.

Late in 1916 a disrupting event in Abyssinia's trouble-plagued political life resulted in further chaos along the unruly border zone. On Menelik's death in 1913, his grandson, Lij Yasu, mounted the throne. In no way could he match his grandfather's strength as a leader: weak-willed and with inclinations towards the pleasures of Bacchus and Venus, he soon proved ineffective as a ruler. Inevitably, in September 1916, he was ousted, and Zauditu, Menelik's daughter, was made Empress, with Ras Tafari (the future Emperor Haile Selassie) declared heir to the throne.

The internal confusion caused by these jugglings once again had a deleterious effect on border affairs. The Protectorate soon enough felt the repercussions as official grip on Abyssinian discipline slackened. One disquieting result was the upsurge in 1917 and 1918 of the increasingly powerful Tigre influence. Taking advantage of the confusion, it asserted itself to such a degree that its marauding gangs virtually took command of the border region on the Abyssinian side. Only vigorous patrolling by Barrett's newly formed 5 K.A.R. and the armed Constabulary managed to restrain them from attacking deep into Protectorate territory. Somehow, the British forces, scattered as they were along the boundary line, succeeded in coming to terms with their enemy, and Kittermaster could report by 1918 that 'the political situation on the whole at the end of the year was satisfactory ... but it is thoroughly unsound'.

In far away Garre country Glenday continued his lonely life, broken occasionally by a visit from a passing white officer with his contingent of K.A.R. On one such occasion, in February 1917, the patrol, plus the ancient Maxim machine-gun Glenday had been sent from Moyale, engaged the Degodia Somalis in a ferocious battle that raged for several hours in the thick bush by the Daua river. There, as Dutton put it: 'After a dour and bloody fight, the main body were successfully engaged, and the battle won by the slenderest margins ... The losses to Glenday were forty killed, and the Degodia left two hundred on the field'.

Tucked away in the archives of his old college in distant Oxford is a little pile of letters written by him in those years of exile among the Garre, years that Glenday himself never talked much about in his later life. The letters, written in pencil to his former college warden, Joseph Wells, confessed some of his innermost apprehensions and feelings, and admitted that even his iron will was at times tried almost to its limits.

Writing in late 1916 he conceded: 'the dreadful loneliness of the job ... I don't want to go until the War is over when I shall probably resign from the Colonial Office'. It took him, in fact, another thirty-five years to do so. Later, in early 1917, he wrote again: 'It would not be so bad if the work here did not seem so despairing. We seem to be working for no purpose, we lead a hard strenuous life without the ordinary comforts and we stand the heat of the day, seemingly purposelessly'. After the ferocity of the Degodia attack another letter ended with pangs of nostalgia: 'To sit in College gardens would be a delightful pleasure and a great tonic'. At the end of the year he could write: 'This makes my fourth Christmas in exile ... in this land. It never has been anything but a cockpit and blood is very cheap amongst its inhabitants'. In December 1918, after almost five years without a break of decent length, Glenday concluded, 'I fear one takes a pessimistic attitude owing to the effects of the last four years. I must confess ... that I am mentally tired and weary'.

Kittermaster, caught up as he was with the disturbing military confrontations on the northern border, became even more preoccupied with the vital lifelines in his district. The road through to Marsabit, which at long last had been opened to ox-waggon traffic in 1917, was further improved later in the years so that the flimsy new motor cars could be used to hurry things up. Speed and efficiency were becoming ever more vital, especially as the district's annual needs had increased to 350 tons of goods. Despite many of the same old problems, by the middle of 1918 he could look back with satisfaction on the year's advances. In addition to the car road through to Marsabit, a fully equipped garage had been built at Meru, and two little Ford box-body cars had been acquired complete with white drivers seconded from the military. Early in 1918 the road to Marsabit had been improved even more by the industrious Dugand, who spent a month with a gang of sixty men levelling up the bumpy

Magala.
9.4.19.

Dear Glenday.

You mail of the 30th got in yesterday. most excellent news too. I was afraid that you would not have time after your report of the 23rd to do much more as I suspected that the rains with you were much the same as here. You did get a proper move on in ten days. At last these blighters at Wajir have been taught the penalty of disobedience or even delay. I must say I rather grudge it to you after having waited these weary years for it myself. Still its all in the family and I probably should not have got so cleane a success if I had been doing it myself.

You can indeed go home with a quiet mind, feeling something accomplished, something done to earn a night's repose. [If this writing is indistinct know that I'm in the mess & a real lowering sky overhead & I can hardly see.] Still I suppose I can't complain of missing Wajir as I have come in for a first class comedy up here with an off chance of its turning into a tragedy. You will be able to appreciate it. Mescyn has bustled the Abyssinian got into consent to a joint campaign of ourselves & Abyssinia against the Tigre.

First and last pages of a letter from Kittermaster, then officer in charge of the frontier, to Glenday.

Such was the opening fight of the Anglo-Abyssinian Campaign"
I have opened a Subspace Op under this head & am trying to
make out (what I think Hodson really believes) that it is going
to be a big thing, in the hope that thereby we may get
attention to our transport & Frontier. Personally I expect the
whole thing to be a wash out except only perhaps our
occupation of Gudda dumma.

I wish I had had the pluck to take a flying patrol to
Gof to try to recover those cattle. It would have been a crazy
thing to do really as there was every possibility of bumping into
300 or 400 Tigre but there was a chance.

There is also quite a chance that the Tigre may try revenge.
They can put up about one thousand men here & they have their
tails well up from knowing how frightened the Abyssinians
are of them. I wish they would try an attack on the boma.

I am afraid that peace with the Degodi is a fait accompli.
I have however told Plowman that if he can catch Alim Nur
anywhere he is to arrest him at once if he cannot contrive to
shoot him. Let me have a full report on the disarmament as soon as you
can so that I may submit mine to Nairobi. Remember that you did not
burn villages, only camel mats etc. It really is a gratifying note on which to
end the year.

Yrs ever H. B. Kittermaster.

ox-waggon road from the bottom of the mountain to the new station. Dugand by then was a proven man, as was noted in a report from Archer's Post: 'Mr. Dugand was in charge of ox transport and the smooth manner in which it worked is attributable to the skill and care with which he managed his personnel and animals'.

Meanwhile the situation along the border by Moyale had become even more complex as the result of an incident in January 1919, when a band of Abyssinian soldiers tried to apprehend a herd of cattle belonging to a Borana living in the Protectorate who claimed British asylum. Immediate intervention by the K.A.R. saved the day, but only after a short sharp exchange of shots drove the Abyssinians away. That event, insignificant as it may seem now, was in fact the first occasion on which fire had been officially exchanged between British and Abyssinian government forces. Just to compound the tricky state of affairs, the Tigre then saw fit to attack the Abyssinians, who in turn blamed the British, then subsequently fled northwards to Mega in disarray. There they sulked, regarded the British as enemies, and broke off diplomatic relations. A curious triangular impasse then existed for a few months: the Abyssinians severed links with the British and feared the Tigre; the Tigre feared the British and dominated the Abyssinians, and the British in the middle, although ready for peace, were quite prepared to attack anyone who interfered with their rights.

While the K.A.R. was skirmishing with Abyssinians and Tigre, Bamber, based at Moyale, was also embroiled in scuffles with the Tigre. They, in their contrary way, were again in conflict with the British. On one of those occasions, while Bamber was making a visit to Waye in the company of his Somali orderly, he was greeted by a fusilade of shots from the neighbourhood of the wells. Diving to cover, the two men

*Ford box-body car,
circa 1917.*

replied as best they could, but early in the fray a well-directed bullet despatched the orderly, spattering his blood over Bamber's face. For several hours, alone, he sheltered in the same position, firing back whenever he had the chance, and by good fortune managed to escape from his solitary predicament with the arrival of darkness.

Bamber's frays were not always of that small calibre. On 5 April 1919 a strong band of Tigre attempted to drive off a large herd of cattle from the vicinity of Moyale. Turning out his men, Bamber pursued them and drove them off with a hail of bullets, proving that, as with the Abyssinians, the Protectorate forces were willing to meet force with force. Those, and other, incidents proved Bamber to be a spirited defender of British territory, and Kittermaster, his senior, noted with satisfaction that: 'Had Mr. Bamber handled the situation less diplomatically there was nothing to prevent the Tigre sweeping the whole border clean of cattle'.

An about-turn in the affairs of the border zone came with appeals from the Abyssinians for peace, and a call for British military assistance to deal with the region's plague—the insubordinate Tigre. Encouraging for the Protectorate authorities, the change in Abyssinian attitude marked the start of the Anglo-Abyssinian campaign against the Tigre outlaws. Although it ran for most of 1919, the offensive did not prove an overwhelming success from the Abyssinian point of view. Certainly, the Abyssinian army eventually arrived on the border, but the British entertained a lurking suspicion that an ulterior motive lay at the root of their co-operation—the recovery of runaway Borana and their stock. The campaign pursued a haphazard course, achieving little apart from a substantial increase in military forces along the border. In fact it was the K.A.R.* who did most of the work, based at two strategic places: Moyale and Gaddaduma wells. Persistent political intrigue in Addis Ababa undermined the efficiency of the Abyssinian army, and eventually, in a state of disorganisation, hunger and boredom with the whole thing, they packed up and left for home, leaving the Protectorate forces alone to handle the Tigre as best they could, with 'the right to penetrate in pursuit as far as we liked across the border'. With enthusiasm and energy they did just that. Within a short space of time the Tigre were beaten into submission. With large numbers of them laying down their arms an official report could declare with pride: 'The year 1919 thus has been one of great progress on the Frontier, and the position is full of promise for the future. We have shown the Abyssinians and the Tigre that were are perfectly able and willing to hold our own against them'.

As 1919 came to an end, so did Kittermaster's term as chief of the Northern Frontier District. Before handing over to Clifford Plowman he was able to write with satisfaction that 'at last there appears a prospect of real development' and the Constabulary 'have proved their worth time and again'. But there still remained one serious ailment: 'The medical provision for the District continues to be a scandal'. Bamber was more powerful in his views when he opened his grumble: 'If you will pardon my strong language I will say that I think the state of affairs is a scandal and a crying disgrace to the Medical Department of the Government'. He concluded by saying that: 'with the nearest doctor at Wajir, where it may take three weeks to call him, is a state of affairs which I think needs no further comment'. And so, Bamber, the

---

*The K.A.R. detachments were considerably reinforced at that stage by a new unit, the 6 K.A.R. battalion, which was made up of ex-German askaris (soldiers).

junior officer, at a salary of 437 rupees a month, expressed his eloquent opinion. The very next year two doctors, Captain Pick and Dr Boon, arrived to salve the indignant officers' hurts.

Kittermaster had more to say before departing. On one of his favourite subjects, transport, he put forward the proposal that as the army was the principal user of the hard-pressed waggons they should take over its management. They had already donated three stoutly built Napier 30 hundredweight (1,530 kilogram) trucks from their stores, although one broke down on the road from Nairobi and never reached Meru. They, however, proved too heavy for the soft surfaces of the flimsy roads, so were replaced by four Autocar trucks, also ex-military*. These were more successful, although they later had to be fitted with solid rubber tyres on account of the punishing roads and piercing acacia thorns. The solid wheels had another worthwhile advantage: with them the trucks could be loaded up with far heavier loads. The little Ford box-body cars, increased to four in number, each covered over 4,000 miles in 1918. Speeding along in one of them, the Transport Officer could comfortably complete the 42 mile (68 kilometre) stretch of road between Meru and Archer's Post in the breath-taking time of three and a half hours. Serviced at Meru garage by a European mechanic called Waugh, they gave little engine trouble, although the jarring roads regularly cracked their puny frames. Despite the arrival of motors, the bulk of the district's goods still had to be moved by ox waggon, and the conscientious Dugand carried on caring for the treasured bullocks in his customary way, earning more approving words from Kittermaster: 'He has done excellent work and looks after his cattle well . . . I rely largely on Mr. Dugand's advice in all matters of gear etc., for the wagons'. Although the mechanical transport was still at an experimental stage, it was obvious that it would be the ultimate answer to Kittermaster's prayers, and he could foresee an end to the toiling columns of ox waggons and their base on Lgirrgirr Hill. The process took several more years, but by 1919 he clearly envisioned that 'Archer's Post would shortly die'.

In his terminal report Kittermaster included compliments and exhortations. The former declared appreciatively that: 'For the past four years the officers of the Northern Frontier District (and I wish to mention by name Mr. Butler, Mr. Glenday, Mr. Llewellin and Mr. Plowman) have been carrying on the district work under most difficult conditions . . . Isolated during four years of war under circumstances of great strain both physical and even more mental, they have patiently laid the foundations on which to build as soon as the war was ended'. Having said that, he implored his successors to defend the uniqueness of their careers in the Northern Frontier. On the independence of the Constabulary he urged their officer, Captain Rice: 'You should fight strenuously any such attempt to handicap us . . . by putting us under the military or police'. To the incoming administrator he said, with a tinge of forlorn hope, that: 'For many years transport will prohibit the Northern Frontier District being overrun by such people (High Court and Audit Department!) but we should work to bring the . . . District into line so far as possible with the rest of the Protectorate'. With those parting words Kittermaster, the true giant of the north, left to take up higher office.

The year 1920 was historically an auspicious one for the Protectorate. Exactly

---

*For details of the Napier and Autocar trucks see Appendix 4.

*Autocar trucks and Ford, at Archer's Post, circa 1917.*

twenty-five years after Hardinge had taken over charge of the country from the Imperial British East Africa Company, another change was made. In July it became the Colony and Protectorate of Kenya. Important as the alteration in status may have appeared to politicians and white settlers, it made not the slightest jot of difference to the turbulent state of affairs in the Northern Frontier. The Abyssinians, so recently allied to the British in their campaign against the Tigre, had reverted to their raiding along the border, turning their avaricious attentions against the vulnerable Borana and their herds. As the year wore on the position gradually worsened, and fears were pronounced that the civil administration would soon be unable to cope with the mounting pressure. In reality, the region was fast becoming a zone stricken by guerilla warfare, and moves were already being put in hand for a transfer to a military administration.

Hope, Kittermaster, Glenday and all the other officers who had given years of their lives to controlling the volatile conditions along the border may have shown a little disappointment that the first ten years of British rule had not produced a more stable atmosphere in the vast region. But there were roads, improved communications from which had come better security, hospitals at Marsabit and Archer's Post, and new government stations, such as the posts by the strategic wells at North Horr and Maikona on the Chalbi Desert. Moreover, the Ford cars, despite a temporary shortage of spare parts, had introduced a new momentum to the north's lethargic pace. Because of them it took only seven days for a letter to reach Moyale from Archer's Post. Despite their efforts Dugand's bulky waggons were still required for the long haul to Marsabit, but they were now under the care of Prinsloo, who was paid the generous wage of 275 shillings a month.

All was not work, though, as a snippet from a Moyale report brightly admitted in November 1920: 'a tennis court is also in course of completion'. One cannot imagine the players being in the slightest bit concerned that while the district's account books were kept at Archer's Post, the rest of the administration files were lodged forty miles away at Meru, a most cumbersome arrangement.

The Northern Frontier District held a unique place in the story of the East Africa Protectorate. Peopled by tough, resilient but fatalistic nomads, for a brief period its turbulence was curbed by a small band of white officers, who in their solitudes, guarded their independence with a fierce loyalty, and looked on themselves as a breed apart. Living and working in the vast emptiness of their district they evolved a distinct individuality, self-sufficiency and *esprit de corps*. Their attitude, which at times from necessity verged on the autocratic, gave rise to the saying that there were two distinct species of government officer in East Africa—the men from the Northern Frontier, and, uttered by them with a hint of condescension, the rest. The air of superiority was understandable, for nowhere else in the Protectorate were there problems of such magnitude rolled into one—harsh climatic conditions, wild and at times refractory tribes, the tenseness of tricky international politics, poor communications and irregular supplies, unpredictable ambuscades, mutiny, and above all, the severe test of solitude on remote frontier stations, in many cases weeks of travel from their nearest colleagues. Most survived the ordeal. A few left gladly, others reluctantly, and some not at all. Characters, invariably, matured rapidly; a few were undermined and weakened, but without any doubt each one took away vivid memories of their pioneering days in a peerless corner of East Africa.

Three vignettes will suffice to end this tale of the British administration's embryonic years in the north. The first tells of a man who coped, in inimitable fashion; the second of one who failed, and left, weakened in mind; the third reminds one that a few, in fact, never went home.

There was once a District Commissioner at Mandera—probably one of the outermost, and surely one of the most unsought after, posts in the Frontier district— who, like many others of his ilk, had an intense distaste of paper work. On completing his annual stores inventory one year he found, disturbingly, there was one barramil (a metal water tank carried by camels) short. He hoped the loss would be overlooked by head office in Nairobi, but a sharp-eyed clerk there quickly noticed the deficiency and wrote back demanding where it was. By going on leave the officer managed to evade the issue for several weeks, and then fortuitously for him, the rainy season arrived. That meant, in those days, no letter could go out for at least another two months. But in the end, and very reluctantly, he was forced to make an explanation. With tongue in cheek he composed these words: 'The barramil died from lack of grazing in the last drought'. Either his glib reply must have satisfied the unknowing city-dwelling powers-that-be, or else the clerk had an unusual sense of humour, for nothing more was heard about the matter.

The second tale, a sad one, but true, also relates to Mandera, one of the Protectorate's cornerstones. A lonely young district officer, one of the unfortunates who didn't adjust to the sequestered frontier life, helped the days to pass by marking off the hours on a daily chart he had made. As the days dragged monotonously by, he sub-divided the hours into ever smaller fractions, until the chart required he strike out every quarter hour. In the end the tedium of empty days and the torture of unbroken solitude became too great, and tragically, the poor man went clean out of his wits.

For the third and last anecdote, the desert wastes—as always—had the final say.

On 11 January 1920, far away towards the Daua river near a place called Ramo, Lieutenant Frank Dawson Smith, a young 5 K.A.R. officer who had but recently fought with skill and gallantry in the German East Africa campaign, lost his life at the hands of his discontented and mutinying Somali soldiers. Buried under a huge spreading tree, his remains lay there in peace for many years, before they were eventually removed to the precincts of the lonely little fort at Wajir. Today, memory of him is kept alive by a simple brass plaque in a corner of Nairobi Cathedral. Alongside those of Aylmer and Hope, it is a poignant but fitting reminder of all the men who gave part, or full measure, of their lives in the service of the distant Northern Frontier.

*Typical scene in the neighbourhood of Neumann's camp 'Away' on the Uaso Ngiro river.*

# TINKER, TAILOR, . . .

*'What wonder if I hear the call*
*Of that far voice that lured them all.*
*I cross the sandy waste again,*
*That great mimosa-tufted plain.'*

Francis William Rhodes

WITH the close of the nineteenth century came a new era in East Africa. The day of the old-time explorer, tramping along at the head of labouring processions of men, camels and donkeys was almost at an end. Latter-day travellers could journey with the maps of their predecessors to guide them to most places. With the arrival of government officers came a new order. They, too, were pioneers, but of another type, and with distinctly differing goals. The explorations of the 1890s had certainly revealed a land of exciting prospects in the northern deserts. At least, it appeared so for those who sought adventure, with the off-chance of some barter on the side.

This last group, falling as it did between the explorers and the administrators, was made up of a hotch-potch of venturesome men, all intent on following their own particular interests. They hunted for sport and for financial gain; they wandered over the land, tidying up the few remaining geographical puzzles, and attempted to trade. They were a very mixed bunch. Amongst them were aristocrats and potentates, honest men and opportunists, scientists, writers, cattle buyers and shopkeepers. Many wrote accounts of their experiences, engrossing chronicles which tell of the land as it was in those long gone days. There is no record left of just how many such people wandered in East Africa's northern frontier in those embryonic years; how many succeeded in their ambitions; how many failed—some, lamentably, remained, buried below insignificant mounds of rocks or in shallow unmarked graves. It is time to take a cursory look at a few of those who arrived to satisfy their curiosity, and try their luck.

*     *     *

One of the earliest drifters to arrive on the scene was Dr Johann George Kolb, a young German who reached East Africa in the middle of 1894 to join the ill-conceived Freeland Expedition. The Freelanders were members of a short-lived organisation that planned to colonise the fertile lands around the base of Mt Kenya. Multinational— there were Austrians, British, Germans and a Dane amongst the group—the scheme lasted only for three months before fierce internal squabbling broke up the incongruous party. In fact, the expedition never even made a serious departure from its base on Lamu. By the time Kolb arrived to join the Freelanders they were already preparing to abandon the project.

No one has established whether Kolb was a doctor of medicine or of science. Neumann mentioned him 'combining sport with scientific research', but did not detail what he was collecting. Judging by the small ragtag bunch of retainers who marched with him, it was probably of little value. Whichever profession he claimed, his late arrival to the Freeland fiasco did not deter him from planning his own trip to the promised land in the Mt Kenya region. He was next found in the company of Neumann, at the time based on 'Laiju'. In those days Kolb was clearly a greenhorn, but over the next two years he learned quickly, and his subsequent wanderings took him over large tracts of Ukambani, and up to the eastern base of Mt Kenya's topmost peak. Kolb's extensive rambles resulted in significant geographical findings, which were later written up in the prestigious German periodical, *Petermanns Mitteilungen*. He was also given a brief notice in the Royal Geographical Society's quarterly journal.

Very little is known of Kolb's background, although he might almost have been a disciple of the infamous German explorer, Dr Carl Peters, if one considers the words of a report in late November 1894 from a British official in Mombasa, who castigated him as 'a quarrelsome person, much addicted to drink—and going about threatening to shoot people'. In Kolb's defence it should be mentioned that he did actually report in person to Hardinge in Zanzibar, and admitted he had on occasions been forced into skirmishes with indigenous peoples, in much the same way as Teleki, Chanler and even Neumann before him. Kolb viewed his first two years in the bush 'merely as an apprenticeship'. They had been more than that, as his achievements proved, but the myopic traveller, who Neumann described as a 'first-rate shot, though somewhat hampered in the bush by the necessity of wearing spectacles', diffidently wrote in an unpublished piece: 'When, after a year and a day, I returned once more to Kitwi [Kitui] in Ukambani, I had occasion to read again the pages of my journal which had reference to this place. The outcome was that I supplied the deficiency in firewood on this treeless spot by burning my notebooks. I then thought myself but an indifferent chronicler'. Kolb may have been humble in his self-analysis, but his arrogant behaviour nearly earned him deportation, and only by disappearing into the wilds of Rendille country did he evade the reach of authority.

Kolb's life in East Africa was a short one. In 1898, while hunting and journeying in Rendille country in the company of a fellow German, he met up with Delamere and Atkinson, on their way down from Marsabit. While with them he met his end. It came during a rhinoceros hunt, when a wounded beast charged and hoisted him bodily into the air. Atkinson arrived half an hour later to find the dying man calmly waiting his demise. As Kolb himself cold-bloodedly forecast, it came about an hour later. Nearly forty years afterwards the ageing Atkinson told Elspeth Huxley that Kolb's men then built a cairn over his body and raised a ragged loin cloth in the tree above to mark the spot. After the event Kolb's German companion declared: 'I've been writing to his old mother to comfort her—"Our dear doctor Kolb was attacked . . . by the grace of Gott an English doctor was travelling with us. We buried him beneath a mimosa tree and the German flag flies over his grave"'. Exit George Kolb!

In a short notice of Kolb's death, which appeared in the *Geographical Journal* in 1899, mention was made of his visit to Lake Rudolf, but with his death no more details of that journey were received, and it is not certain whether he did in fact reach the lake. His name was immortalised when a small glacier under the main peak of Mt Kenya was called after him. That, too, has since disappeared.

*     *     *

A year or so before Kolb was killed, his companion, Arthur Neumann, returned to England where he occupied himself in writing the book that helped to make his name. It has already been mentioned that Neumann's return to East Africa was delayed by his participation in the Boer War, and it was not until 1902 that he reappeared in his old stamping grounds.

In the period while Neumann was absent Delamere's partner, Dr Atkinson, had put the time to profitable use, hunting voraciously for elephants in Somaliland, Borana country and around Lake Rudolf. In the four years between 1896 and 1900 he managed to execute, by his own claim, about one hundred and fifty of the beasts, and had established a reputation in East Africa as an old hand on the ivory trail.

In early 1900 two young Englishmen, Alfred Arkell-Hardwick and George West, arrived in the railway town of Nairobi. While there Hardwick happened to meet Atkinson. It was not long before they were planning a trip together to the little-known Lorian Swamp, a mysterious spot which had not been visited by white men since its discovery by Chanler seven years before. Hardwick described Atkinson, his guide and mentor, as 'by no means a big man—rather the reverse, in fact', but he was a 'dead shot, and a charming companion . . . A very precise speaker, he had a clear and impartial manner of reviewing anything under discussion . . . his opinions on most . . . subjects were listened to with respect . . . He was said to be one of the most unassuming Englishmen in the Protectorate'. These words of approbation were written after their six-month journey to the Lorian, by which time Hardwick had had ample opportunity to size up his accomplice's character.

The small party's journey to the Lorian Swamp was, apart from some serious skirmishing with the Embe people on the Nyambeni Hills, uneventful, and in early September they arrived at the edge of the swamp. Three years of unremitting drought since Chanler's visit had reduced it to a desiccated state. Greatly disappointed at what they found, Atkinson and his partners immediately retraced their steps, and by early December were back in Nairobi. For the doctor in his search for ivory it had turned out to be a profitless trip.

Just over a year later Atkinson was in trouble, bad trouble. It would have turned out much worse for him had the process of law been somewhat less biased. The story went that the doctor, in the company of two more itinerants, Smith and Vincent (both recent immigrants from South Africa), travelled to Marsabit in late 1901 to trade with the Rendille for ivory. Ivory there was, but a satisfactory agreement on the price could not be reached, and in a devilish move, brought on by an intolerant frustration, Atkinson lit a slow fuse to a keg of gunpowder around which the Rendille were gathered. Discreetly, he then moved off. In the thundering explosion that followed several of the waiting Rendille were blown to shreds. It was a cold-blooded and inhuman act, which later brought the wrath of the authorities down on his head. Tate's expedition to collect evidence and witnesses has already been described, but his efforts were to no avail, for the ensuing court case in Nairobi was a travesty of justice, and the principal witnesses, both black and white, were terrified to make accusations against the culprit. One of the witnesses in the infamous Atkinson trial was Neumann. It is not certain what he was called for as he was only recently returned from the war in South Africa, and he could hardly have had time to reach his hunting fields in the north. The case closed with Atkinson's acquittal, but the other two were promptly deported from the Protectorate. The whole thing dampened Atkinson's ardour for ivory trading, so he retired to his farm outside Nairobi, where for a while he lay low.

\* \* \*

On his return to East Africa in 1902 after five years' absence Neumann found many changes that disturbed him. None the less, he set to and did his best to continue with his former way of life. Returning to his old haunts by the Nyambeni Hills and along the Uaso Ngiro river, he spent the next four years wandering over the northern parts of the Protectorate. Atkinson had left the field open to him, but others were by then arriving to sample the country's rapidly growing popularity for sport. Disgruntled entries in Neumann's last hunting diary regularly complain about the presence of

*A photograph taken of George Kolb in Ukambani, 1894.*

these 'pompommers'—the name he coined for visitors' shooting parties—in his territory. Despite them, his years were profitable, and from his humble base on the Uaso Ngiro river, which, appropriately, he named 'Away'*, he journeyed far and wide in his search for elephants. Trips to the Lorian Swamp alternated with expeditions to Turkana country, the Turkwel river, his old shooting grounds on the Seya river and the Mathews Mountains and in the forests of Marsabit. Everywhere he encountered the depressing evidence of other elephant hunters. The Abyssinians were depleting the beasts on Marsabit Mountain and in the Lake Rudolf region; and Wakamba hunters were killing any they could find in the Mathews range and the vicinity of the Seya and Uaso Ngiro rivers. To crown it all, the Protectorate administration was tightening its stringent rules on game preservation.

At that stage in his life chronic ill health was undermining his morale, and with his unhappy state of mind came a reduced tolerance of the native people he had lived

---

*Samburu Lodge, a tourist haven, now occupies the former position of Neumann's camp 'Away'.

amongst for so long. His diary constantly returns to his endless struggle with sickness and grasping people, as was indicated in one desperate entry, which yet another disillusionment must have driven him to write: 'Bass! [Enough!] I go. I am quite out of conceit both with the country and the people and am becoming generally discontented. Feel lonely at last'. It took him a while longer to break away, and in the interim he continued doggedly with his hunting and trading. Latterly neither was as productive as in earlier years, and his age was beginning to tell. The continuous stresses of professional elephant hunting was, in fact, a younger man's work, and by then Neumann was far into his fifties.

More and more during his last years in the Protectorate he seemed to adopt a feeling of responsibility for the welfare of the Wandorobo and Samburu who regarded him as their 'father'. It was a quasi-official situation, and he regularly sent in reports to Frederick Jackson on the state of the territory where he hunted. He was also on good terms with Sir Donald Stewart, the Commissioner, with whom he often dined when in Mombasa. An outward manifestation of his unusual position came about on one occasion when he took the law into his own hands and attacked an encampment of forty Wakamba poachers who had earlier murdered two Wandorobo men. In the sharp engagement that followed, ten of the miscreants were killed and twelve elephant tusks recovered. Neumann lost one of his men from a poisoned arrow wound. Officialdom did not appear to disapprove of his action, and he continued to wander over his domain at will.

Finally, in July 1906, longing for the company of his own kind and worn out from the years of hard life he had led in the wilderness, Neumann returned to Mombasa. Three months later he was in England, and by the middle of the following year he was dead. Undoubtedly he was one of the most interesting of the people who wandered in the Protectorate's northern district, and it might even be argued that his intense absorption with the region contributed in some measure to his tragic death.

\*     \*     \*

In the first days of October 1904 Neumann was ensconced in his thatched hut at 'Away', busily writing letters for despatch to Mombasa. One item that left with his mail runners was 'a parcel brought here by mistake for Baron Rothschild'. The Rothschild expedition was then camped somewhere in the vicinity of the Uaso Ngiro river, on the southern leg of its extended hunting and collecting trip through Abyssinia and East Africa. Members of the party were, in Neumann's parlance, quite definitely 'pompommers', or, as he mentioned in his diary a little later, they 'must be Judd's killionaires'. Their behaviour could only have appeared strange to the Wandorobo, who, on giving them four small elephant tusks and two pots of honey, saw their precious gifts promptly tossed on the fire. The expedition was still in the proximity of the river several months later when Neumann heard complaints from the Rendille that a white man from the group had forcibly 'commandeered many of their best camels for nothing'. More evidence of the affluent company's journey through the district came from Fred Roy in an entry out of his 1907 diary. He recorded that his men had: 'found old camp where cartridges were discovered. In all about 500 of different bores, a few of which are still good. The only trace as to whose camp, was found by stencilling on a box end ... ROTHS ... DJIBO ... evidently one of the Rothschilds coming here

[Marsabit] through Abyssinia and Borana'. Roy's find clearly demonstrated the casual mores of travellers in those unfettered days.

*     *     *

In December 1906, some five months after Neumann had left his base 'Away' for the last time, a motley procession of Abyssinians and Somalis, with two white men in the lead, forded the Uaso Ngiro river at a spot close by his camp. They were on the final leg of a long arduous march. The principal was none other than the inveterate wanderer, John Boyes; his companion was a young Scandinavian named Selland whom he had signed on in Nairobi some nine months before.

Boyes was then thirty-one years old and a seasoned traveller. A true rolling stone, he had worked his way around the globe since he left his Yorkshire home in Hull at the age of thirteen. Arriving in East Africa in 1898, his brash opportunism enabled him to befriend the ever suspicious Kikuyu tribe and earn the title 'King of the Wakikuyu'. He had also fallen foul of the Protectorate's laws, evaded punishment, and eventually established a respectability for himself in the country's growing white community. During the difficult days at the turn of the century he had been supplies transporter to the army in Uganda and food supplier for the railway construction gangs in the vicinity of Nairobi. He had also hunted elephants for their ivory, and in 1902 accompanied Northrup McMillan, the bulky American millionaire, on his lengthy journey through the Sudan and Abyssinia.

Boyes, as has already been told, was distinctly put out by Riddell's refusal to include him on the Boma Trading Company's expeditions to the north. Goaded into action, but with little capital to help him, he determinedly set forth with his companion Selland in March 1906 for Jibouti. Fortunately, through McMillan's good offices, he carried a pass from Menelik which permitted him to travel and trade in Abyssinia. In that respect he was already one jump ahead of Riddell. Landing at Jibouti, he then marched through to Addis Ababa, where he stopped briefly. Whilst there, according to his own account, the British government offered him the job of Frontier Inspector. As Zaphiro had been appointed to the exacting post only the year before, one wonders at the accuracy of Boyes' words. In any case it was not what he wanted. Another stroke of luck came his way when he was officially contracted to transport a load of ivory belonging to the Protectorate from Moyale to Nairobi. He readily agreed. At least with that custom he was certain of a small return on his impetuous speculation.

At the border he was greeted by Zaphiro, who, suffering badly from recurrent attacks of fever, was anxious to return to Addis Ababa for treatment. Forced to stop in the hot fever-ridden lowland camp by the delayed arrival of the government ivory cache, Boyes agreed to hold the fort for a short spell while Zaphiro went on a brief inspection tour of the boundary line. An example of Boyes' characteristically high-handed methods then took place. One day his Abyssinian headman refused to carry out an order. There are two accounts of what happened next. The first, the formal description of the affair, extracted from *Jubaland and the Northern Frontier District*, was tinged with officialdom's misgivings about Boyes' fitness for the task. It stated, baldly, that on being rebuffed: 'Mr. Boyes proceeded to hang his Abyssinian headman, but before life was extinct Mr. Zaphiro's headman succeeded in cutting him down'. The saved man then fled to Addis Ababa, where he condemned his master's drastic act. Boyes, needless to say, hotly denied the accusation on his return to Nairobi, and declared that he merely tied the man up and warned him to give no further trouble. As Boyes, a small man in size, claimed he roped the Abyssinian up single-handed, there is an element of doubt in the truth of his statement. However, in his defence it should be mentioned that he had ten of his men swear affidavits in Nairobi repudiating the headman's accusation.

Towards the end of October, with a caravan of 32 camels carrying 3,000 pounds (1,365 kilograms) weight of ivory, and a pack of 76 horses and mules, Boyes and Selland at long last departed from their dreary camp. Travelling over the Hurri Hills and by way of Marsabit, the journey to Nairobi took three months. On the way they passed Neumann's old camp on the Uaso Ngiro river, where they found a small supply of beans left in one of his huts. Most likely they were the remains of his stores, abandoned by him a few months before—yet another example of the carelessness of the time.

In the middle of January 1907 a pedestrian in Nairobi's Government Road would have been astonished, even in those days of extraordinary behaviour, by the sight of Boyes riding down the street at the head of his entourage of ivory-laden camels, horses and mules. As he passed on his way he gleefully called out to onlookers to meet him at the Norfolk Hotel for a drink. For those who did, it must have been a riotous occasion as Boyes regaled the crowd with highly coloured tales of his journey down from Abyssinia—all done simply to discomfit Riddell in the first instance. He had every right to boast, for he could claim to be the first white trader to complete the route with success. And success it had been, with a £1,000 profit to show for his efforts.

*     *     *

Laconic comments in Neumann's diary during the years 1905 and 1906 mourn the arrival of increasing numbers of 'pompommer' parties to intrude on his solitary existence. By 1907 Hayes Sadler had become well aware of the need to exert a closer control on what was going on, and with this in view he fully encouraged the young men of the Boma Trading Company in their endeavours. With the upsurge of interest being shown in the north by hunting parties came a growing concern in government circles that the game preservation rules should be enforced. It was a daunting undertaking in such a vast unadministered region. Somali trading caravans from the coast were busily purchasing all the ivory they could, and shooting elephants as well. Abyssinian poachers, too, were encroaching ever southwards into the Protectorate in their search for elephants and rhinoceros. There were ample grounds for complaint by men like Neumann and Roy, irritated by the authorities' apparent laxness in their policy towards these depredations, while at the same time presenting an officious stance towards the activities of legitimate hunters. Theirs was a real grievance, and to counter the marauders some action was urgently needed.

As a first step towards resolving the matter an official expedition to delineate the eastern boundary of the newly formed Northern Game Reserve was mounted, led by Lieutenant Colonel J.H. Patterson, the man who had made a brave name for himself as the slayer of the man-eating lions that caused such havoc during the construction of the railway bridge at Tsavo river in 1898.

Patterson was not a popular man. In physique he was tall, rangy and rather gaunt. Of pedantic nature, he was fastidious in dress and manner. To his subordinates he was somewhat bleak, a pernickety taskmaster and a rigid martinet. The sum total of these characteristics made up a self-satisfied man. His remote and overbearing personality was the result, partly, of years of service in India at the height of the British Raj. A high-ranking soldier, well decorated, and a true product of the regimental tradition, he was a also an enthusiastic sportsman. East Africa, as it turned out, proved a most satisfactory posting for him.

His appointment was not approved of by many, and one who definitely contested it was Frederick Jackson, then acting Commissioner of the Protectorate. His feeling was candidly expressed in a telegram he sent to the Colonial Office in April 1907, which pleaded: 'It is rumoured locally Colonel Patterson is to be appointed Chief of the Game Department. If true, earnestly request that matter be reconsidered as person named considered unsuitable'.

Despite the cries of protest Patterson arrived in the Protectorate in 1907 with an official brief to head the survey of the eastern boundary of the Northern Game Reserve. To start with he was the only white man on the staff, but just as he was about to leave Nairobi two friends arrived from England and begged to join his trek. Mr and Mrs Bligh were the pair, and they were unwittingly on the eve of playing their parts in a sinister mystery that has never been satisfactorily explained. As Patterson himself later wrote, the trio 'set out on what proved to be an eventful and disastrous expedition'. The date of their departure from Nairobi was 21 January 1908.

The caravan marched north to the Uaso Ngiro river by way of Nyeri and Rumuruti, the Blighs shooting to their heart's content as they travelled. On reaching Neumann's old camp on the river they halted. From there Patterson scrambled to the summit of a large hill in the neighbourhood (Koitogor), where he put his men to work on the construction of a large cairn. The task was never completed, for he had observed more giant hills far to the east, and those he considered would make more suitable boundary beacons*.

At that stage Bligh was starting to suffer from a series of fever attacks that never left him. So weak did he become that on occasions he had to be borne in a hammock, and by the time they reached the remote waterholes at Laisaimis he was far from well. While the party was camped there Patterson volunteered to take the burden of nursing him from the exhausted woman, a wearisome chore that entailed sitting by the ailing man's tent through the night hours. Early one morning a single shot broke the quiet of the darkness, and Patterson rushed to Bligh's tent to find him 'lying in bed with a bullet through his head'. In his version of the story, which seemed loaded with alibis, he claimed that he had left Bligh's tent only a short time before to issue instructions to his headman for the day's work. Next, he said, he had been asked to treat a sick servant. At the break of day Patterson acted quickly and poor Bligh was dispensed with. Like Kolb, he was buried under a mound of large stones, and after the men had left Patterson 'remained for a little while by the graveside, thinking over the sad calamity which had so suddenly overtaken us'. Mrs Bligh was reportedly too stunned to attend the interment.

Wasting no time the caravan resumed its march at two o'clock in the afternoon.

---

*Koitogor was eventually used for the south-east corner beacon of the Northern Game Reserve.

With duty foremost in his mind, Patterson struck out for Marsabit as 'it was clearly incumbent on me to carry through my work'. The widow tagged along—she had no option with a man like him—and on arrival at Crater Lake was ensconced in Patterson's tent, although he was careful to record that with Victorian correctness he had a 'partition put up along the centre of it which made it into two tents'. Having done this he in turn was struck down with fever and dysentery, so the good lady had to resume her Nightingale role once again.

On recovering Patterson dutifully completed his survey, and his caravan then retraced its footsteps homewards, but by a road that circumvented the unhappy spot at Laisaimis. Coincidentally, Fred Roy happened to be resting at the waterholes with his caravan, while on his return to the Company's depot at Marsabit. He had been told about Bligh's death by the local Rendille, as his terse diary entry declared: 'Heard that Bligh had shot himself at Laisamis. Evidently some misunderstanding between him and his wife, she preferring Col Patterson. The Rendille say she was a bad woman. May have been touch of the sun'. A few days later Roy visited Bligh's grave and matter-of-factly noted that 'the hyenas had had a good try to disinter the body'.

Whatever the truth of the matter, rumours spread fast, and there were many told-you-so cynics who doubted the veracity of Patterson's account. Later, he married the widow, a deed his self-righteous nature doubtless felt was the correct thing to do. With that, more accusing fingers were raised.

Patterson lasted a year in his post before being ousted, a move Jackson must have looked on with great favour. Bligh, tragically, had played his last part and so became yet another victim of the desert north.

*   *   *

On 23 April 1909 a 'pompommer' of exceptional political stature arrived at Mombasa. He was greeted with a personal telegram from King Edward VII, which read: 'I bid you heartily welcome on your arrival in British East Africa. I trust that your expedition may prove enjoyable and may be attended with every success'. The visitor was none other than the late President of the United States of America, Theodore Roosevelt.

Roosevelt had proved himself an able president, in a rugged outdoor style, and prior to his retirement had served his country for seven years. A champion of fair dealing and honest living, he had run up against considerable opposition in his attacks on certain aspects of American commercialism. It was purported that one senior member of the financial world in New York, on hearing of Roosevelt's imminent departure for the wilds of Africa, muttered: 'America hopes every lion will do its duty'. The Nelsonian sentiment was not shared by the masses, who admired Roosevelt's sympathetic leadership.

But the ex-President was not only a man of action; his intellectual ability was immense. In his teenage years he had developed a passion for hunting and everything to do with nature. By the time he entered Harvard his sole ambition was to become a natural history scientist. However, his involvement in politics disrupted his plans. Despite that he never lost touch with the world of nature, and later came to be recognised as one of the world's most able lay naturalists. In this achievement he had undoubtedly been assisted by his phenomenal memory. Everything he read he absorbed. Moreover, he counted in his circle of friends many of the great hunters,

*The ex-President of the United States of America, Theodore Roosevelt.*

wildlife artists and nature lovers of the day. Among their number were Chanler, a fellow-countryman and friend in social life, but across the floor in politics; Millais, the brilliant artist-hunter; and Selous, the renowned big-game hunter and naturalist. Although Roosevelt had never visited Africa before, through extensive reading he made a close study of the wild creatures of the continent, with the result that his knowledge of its animal and bird life was prodigious. So, it was quite understandable that he should plan an extended trip to East Africa for the day of his retirement from office. With that aim in view he asked an expert on Africa, his old friend Selous, to give him advice. In due course a route was mapped out for him, which included East Africa and the Sudan.

When Roosevelt arrived in the country he was accompanied by a powerful team of three naturalists from the Smithsonian Institution in Washington. To guide them on their long journey he had employed two expert hunters: R.J. Cunninghame, a Scotsman; and Leslie Tarlton, an Australian. For company he took his twenty-year-old son with him. The expedition had been Roosevelt's conception, and his intention was to provide the renowned museum with a comprehensive collection of animal and bird specimens from East Africa. Finance for the ambitious scheme came from two main sources: $67,000 was raised from private donors, and $50,000 was produced by Roosevelt's publishers.

The expedition has always been considered the largest ever to leave Nairobi. Nearly three hundred men were reported to have lined up to carry the immense pile of loads required to keep the busy collecting party in the field. Four months after their arrival at Mombasa, Roosevelt and his men reached the country bordering the Uaso Ngiro river. There they found several new species to add to their growing list of specimens—Grevy zebra, reticulated giraffe and gerenuk amongst them—and in that country Roosevelt spent a contented month gathering material. On its way upstream the caravan passed the remains of Neumann's old camp 'Away'. Roosevelt's comments on the late hunter were frank. He wrote that the man lived 'in this far-off region exactly like a native, and all alone amongst the natives; living in some respects too much like a native'. True words indeed. Neumann's female Ndorobo mate produced two daughters by him, one of whom lived until 1987.

At the conclusion of his 1,200-mile (1,930 kilometres) journey Roosevelt had every reason to be satisfied with his efforts. The Smithsonian benefited by a monumental collection of large and small mammals, birds, reptiles and to top it all, five thousand plant specimens. When the full bag of animals, which included a total of twenty rhinoceros, black and white, was made public, he was immediately censured by indignant conservationists. To this day their cries are repeated on occasion by kindred spirits. The value of Roosevelt's work was, however, strongly defended by those who recognised it as the most comprehensive single collection ever made of East African fauna and flora. It is still used extensively by researchers.

*     *     *

Roosevelt's enormous expedition was not the only one of its kind to leave America with the intention of collecting for the natural history museums of that great country. As he left Africa his place was taken almost immediately by another group of scientists from the United States. Led by an enthusiastic young paleontologist named Henry

Clay Frick, their journey took them through Abyssinia, down the shore of Lake Rudolf, and on through to the Protectorate's capital, Nairobi.

When Frick organised his expedition he was already a veteran of travel in East Africa. Two years before, in 1908, he had done a scientific trip round the base of Mt Kenya. He was well qualified to do so, being a trained geologist preoccupied with fossils of the Pliocene period. Fortunately for him, his business involvements in the steel industry with the powerful Carnegie family of Pittsburgh enabled him to follow his interest in paleontology on an independent basis. Today, many of his fossil specimens are housed in the Natural History Museum in New York.

Frick's journey through East Africa in 1910 was made primarily to collect bird specimens. To aid him in his task he took along the famous American ornithologist Colonel Mearns, who, having only just completed his work with the Roosevelt expedition, could also claim to be experienced in Africa's ways. Their collections on the Frick undertaking were extensive, and were, like Roosevelt's, duly deposited in the Smithsonian.

Shortly after, the First World War came to prevent another visit to Africa, but Frick put the time to good use. Before the war he had been taught to fly by the famous pioneer aviators, the Wright brothers. On the start of conflict with Germany he felt bound to enter the battle, but on volunteering to join the renowned American flying group, the Lafayette Escadrilles, he was rejected for combat duties on account of his near-sightedness. However, he was accepted by them for other duties, and it was while attached to them that his able brain was put to good use with the group which developed the synchronisation of the machine-gun firing through aircraft propellers.

After the war Frick made one more expedition to east Africa, in 1923. But this time he restricted his efforts to Abyssinia. An American of unusual qualities, he was, however, not the last one who would ramble in the Protectorate's north.

*     *     *

Not all Neumann's 'pompommers' were run-of-the-mill sportsmen out to satisfy their appetites in the chase of big African game. Roosevelt's pursuit of specimens for a world-famous museum had a specific function; Frick's journey had likewise enhanced zoologists' knowledge of wild creatures; and in 1910 another exceptional American arrived in East Africa to see for himself whether there was reality in the tales he had heard. Stewart Edward White was the searcher, and journeyed with his spirited wife, Elizabeth. An adventurous creature by nature, she had the distinction of joining Mrs Bligh in the ranks of early lady visitors to the Protectorate's hostile north.

By 1910 White was a well-established writer. His speciality was the rip-roaring story of outdoor life and adventure in America's West. Growing up in the world of lumbermen in Michigan—his father became prosperous through the timber business—young Stewart ran wild until the age of sixteen, when he was eventually sent to school. His exceptional brain soon put him ahead of his fellow students, and by the time he was twenty-two he had graduated from Michigan University with a Bachelor of Philosophy degree. Between times he continued with his diligent study of woodland birdlife, wrote numerous articles on the topic, and a substantial monograph that was later published by the Ornithologist's Union.

The greater part of White's early life was spent outdoors, where his enjoyment of nature and adventure provided him with abundant material for his books. Hunting was another of his pastimes. In his travels around East Africa he found ample opportunity to exercise his skill with the gun. His first expedition to the Protectorate lasted for twenty months, during which he marched for many miles over its rich gamefields, exercising his interests in the animal and bird life, exploration of new country, and ethnic studies of the different tribes he encountered along the way. On his return he was elected a Fellow of the Royal Geographical Society. One of the members who recommended him was no less than Sir Clements Markham. White also wrote a gem of literature describing his escapades in East Africa, and vowed he would return, which he did.

On one leg of his wide-ranging travels White dropped away from the highlands to the hot low-lying valley of the Uaso Ngiro river, then followed it down to its

*Stewart Edward White – author, naturalist, hunter – and 1912 trophy.*

confluence with the Isiolo stream. On the bank of the tiny brook, with its shady acacia and palm trees as shelter, they set up a camp of thatched huts and settled down for a spell. The party hunted lions, rhinoceros and whatever else they could find, at the same time revelling in the harshness of the countryside Neumann and Kolb had known so well in wilder days. White later wrote words of great charm illustrating the beauties of the land. Unlike most of the other 'pompommers' who paid their brief visits there, looked, shot and departed, he left a brilliant account of his days in the scorched country along the banks of the well-known river. His story must have helped to entice many others to follow in his footsteps.

\*      \*      \*

In the few years immediately before the First World War broke out, ever-increasing numbers of newcomers arrived to try their luck in the Protectorate's northern district. The enterprising Indian trader, Mohamed Moti, who installed his remote shops at Archer's Post and Marsabit in 1910, has already been mentioned. The Boma Trading Company had retired from the field in that same year, but representatives of another European concern, the Meru Trading Company, came in 1912 to view the prospects. Owned by three young men, Dunman, Claydon and Nicholas, their business first opened a shop on the south bank of the Uaso Ngiro river, just opposite Archer's Post. From their modest base they endeavoured to break into the growing livestock trade. A more certain line of business they tried was providing vital stores of flour to the rising number of itinerant caravans and hunting parties. Ambitiously they next set up a branch post at Melka Galla, far down the river towards the Lorian Swamp, tended by a young man named Gordon. The luckless youth was doomed to share the fate of Bligh and Kolb, and so become another victim of the merciless desert land. Sometime in 1913, while tending his lonely store, his Meru sheep herders were panicked into flight by a report that a Somali raiding party was approaching. Gordon, left entirely on his own, must have been terrified out of his wits, judging by his subsequent actions. That night, aiming blindly into the dark, he fired off countless rounds from his stock of precious ammunition. By morning, with no cartridges left, and with several of his flock dead from his randomly directed bullets, he abandoned the fearful place. All alone, and unarmed, he set out for Archer's Post. He never arrived. Sometime later all that remained of him was found on the road, 60 miles (96 kilometres) away—a few scraps of crunched bone and a tuft of his red hair. Abandoned in his camp were found his rifle, leaning against a tree, and his diary. The tragedy was heightened when it was learnt that the Somalis were in reality a party of peaceful Borana coming to visit him. Poor Gordon, he didn't even need a cairn to cover his pathetic remains.

\*      \*      \*

The same year Gordon was devoured by lions, the Maharajah of Datia was touring the neighbourhood on a grandiose hunting spree. His party, as it happened, was just one of the many that passed through Meru to shoot in the countryside bordering the Uaso Ngiro river. A dry comment in an official report records that Datia and his accomplices bagged seventeen lions while there. Maybe Gordon's killers were amongst them. Even if they weren't, a conservation-minded official in Meru, aware of the heavy inroads

*Mrs Adele Bailey on safari in Marsabit forest, 1910.*

being made on the lion population by sportsmen, suggested that a measure of lion protection would be a sound step.

\*     \*     \*

Sportsmen there were in numbers, and some, as White had done, took along their wives. One such man, a Mr Arthur Bailey from Nairobi, was good friends with Geoffrey Archer. While Archer was stationed at Marsabit, Bailey and his wife Adele paid him a visit. In written words of outspoken admiration Archer compared her to a pretty piece of Dresden china. Outwardly that is how her trim frame may have appeared to his entranced eyes, but inwardly she was sprightly in spirit and courageous. She begged him to let her shoot a buffalo, but in the ensuing hunt it was she who nearly met her end. A well-aimed bullet from Archer's rifle collapsed the charging beast almost at her feet.

\*     \*     \*

Another chance visitor arrived at Marsabit while Archer was busy constructing his station by the Crater Lake. Max Fleischman, a rich American businessman, but an

*Ignazio Nicolo Dracopoli.*

out-and-out novice at big-game hunting wandered out early one morning through the dense mists to the great crater of Gof Bongole. There, to his amazement, he found a gigantic bull elephant clambering out of the crater on its way back to the shelter of the forest. Quite unconcerned, he ambushed it from behind a large rock and laid it low. His delight can only be imagined when he learned that its huge tusks, each well over 100 pounds (45 kilograms) in weight, were the largest yet procured on the mountain by a foreign hunter.

\*     \*     \*

In October 1912 an ardent young traveller by the name of Ignazio Nicolo Dracopoli arrived in Mombasa. Although born in France, his family's ancient origins could be traced back to the Greek Archipelago. When he arrived in East Africa he was barely twenty-four years old. He had been schooled in England, first at Malvern College, and then for a year at University College, Oxford. But a driving desire to travel took him away prematurely from the world of academics, and for the next three years he wandered, first in Arizona and then in East Africa, where he hunted big game with his younger brother. His experiences served only to increase his appetite for further exploration, so, to prepare himself for future work of geographical value, he completed a course in surveying at the Royal Geographical Society's offices. Armed with his new skill he travelled extensively in Mexico, making maps, and collecting more animal specimens for the British Museum.

East Africa lured him back in 1912, but this time he had decided on a definite objective. By then few parts of the Protectorate's northern district had escaped the investigations of travellers, hunters or administrators, but there was one desperate stretch that remained unknown: the country between the Indian Ocean and the Lorian Swamp. Dracopoli's account of his journey across the arid wasteland between the port of Kismayu and the swamp is a fascinating story of latter-day exploration. On its successful conclusion many questions were answered, maps were drawn, zoological specimens were donated to the museum and articles published. The journey across the harsh Somali quarter won him words of praise from the Vice President of the Royal Geographical Society: 'I think we must all feel that he is an ideal specimen of the modern traveller'. Rewardingly, his achievement earned him the Society's Back Grant bronze medal, membership of the American Geographical Society, and a Fellowship of the Royal Astronomical Society.

Dracopoli returned once more to East Africa, for a hunting trip in 1914. Shortly after, war broke out, whereupon he immediately volunteered his services. By then he had become a British subject. Declared unfit for frontline fighting he served on the staff of the Royal Flying Corps for the duration of the war, and was decorated with an O.B.E. (Order of the British Empire). He was, however, not destined to live long, for the severity of his Jubaland expedition in 1912 had played havoc with his health. In 1923, at the early age of thirty-six, he died, another victim of the malevolent influence exerted by the Protectorate's northern badlands.

\*     \*     \*

The red-headed Gordon was not the only one trading in livestock along the Uaso Ngiro river in those early days. One morning in 1914 John Llewellin, while trekking down the river on his way to Wajir, came round a clump of bushes and saw a lone white man approaching him. Quite the opposite of the petrified Gordon, this person was nonchalantly at ease as he ambled along. To Llewellin's surprise it was none other than Denys Finch Hatton, whom he had last seen in Oxford three years before. In the course of conversation it transpired that he was on his way back from a cattle-buying expedition to Italian Somaliland. His purchases, he said, were following along a few days behind in the care of his partner, Baron Blanco. Having exchanged pleasantries and news, the two Oxford men went their solitary ways. Although of such divergent interests they shared a common bond—their love of lonely unspoilt places.

\*     \*     \*

The war brought a temporary halt to the 'pompommers' and their ramblings. The traders, too, disappeared to serve their country's interests in other ways. But as soon as the conflict ended, they reappeared in numbers. The very month fighting stopped, Berkeley Cole, the aristocratic pioneer settler, reached Moyale with his band of Maasai to buy cattle. For some reason his journey was a failure. Almost a year later, Marcos Salavrakos passed through the town with a large herd of beasts for sale in the

Protectorate. In his efforts he was more successful, but, as has been told already, very shortly afterwards he, too, was killed by a lion.

The days of aristocratic shooting parties also resumed, as is evidenced when the Meru District Commissioner reported with satisfaction that one hundred porters were signed on without difficulty for Baron Franchetti's trip to the Lorian Swamp.

As the years went by the Northern Frontier District continued to attract those who could not resist its call. It is a call that is clear to this very day. A few words, written by Dracopoli in 1913, sum up everything, whether in the context of the sentiments of yesteryear's travellers, or the feelings of present-day explorers, who move speedily and in comfort through those fascinating parts. He said: 'Now that the highlands are so over-crowded with tourist-sportsmen and amateur travellers, it is pleasing to remember that there are still large areas in East Africa where it is possible for a brief space to pass out of the limits of civilisation and enter a land as yet untouched . . . It is devoutly to be hoped that this state of things may continue'.

# EPILOGUE

THE finish of the second decade of the twentieth century marked the end of a long chapter in East Africa's northern desert land. The remote frontier country had metamorphosed from a raw, hardly known and largely untended wilderness, into a territory regulated by white man's rules—alien, but fundamentally well intentioned.

The preceding pages have flitted over a cornucopia of events as they were experienced by both black men and white. Reverses went hand-in-hand with successes, tragedy in company with elation. The only common denominator was hardship, prevalent in its many forms throughout the Protectorate's starkly beautiful badlands. It was certainly never an easy country in which to live and work, as many could stand witness. For the original dwellers there, the wandering explorers, the duty-bound administrators and soldiers and the itinerant traders, there were no comfortable short cuts, and every inch gained was won by punishing effort. The cost of progress was often severe, but inexorably, headway was made, and transition came about. The internal combustion engine and other alien effects arrived, in their arrogance, to speed up the lonely tract's gentle pace, spreading the tentacles of civilisation deep into the remotest parts, where formerly the leisurely tread of the camel had capably controlled the tempo of life from ancient times.

Many decades have passed since those stirring times. Even now, despite the encroachments of present-day conveniences, Kenya's desert north can still claim to have retained much of its aloofness, its unpredictability, its dangers and its mystery. Dutton, in recalling the concluding words of an appraisal by Glenday of the vast savage district he had ruled for so many years, succeeded in putting the final and appropriate touch on the matter: 'Yet the fact remains that the only people who know the Northern Frontier are those who have lived in it in the days gone by ... To the newcomers ... the real, the essential North is a closed book. A firmly closed book'.

# APPENDIX 1

## *Portion of a letter from Count Teleki to Prince Rudolf*

THE extract below comes from the translation of a private letter written by Teleki while he was arranging his expedition in Zanzibar. It was printed in the weekly newspaper *Marosvidek* on 7 May 1887, and gives some idea of Teleki's witty and flamboyant style of writing. Had he written a personal account of the journey there is little doubt that it would have been articulate, perceptive and of excellent literary value, compared with von Höhnel's rather prosaic version.

For two months now I have been inhaling the garlic-scented sweat of the blacks who pack, move, lift and weigh our goods in my store, day after day, amid infernal noise. Such 'mesigos' [loads], some 450 of them, are needed to satisfy the greed of the Masai and Kikuyu and the demands of my porters' bellies. A happy land is this, everything grows here, except mokka, and that is hard to come by. It is full of the worst type of European swindlers, fraudulent big merchants, missionaries turned into head-waiters, French black nuns given to coquetry, scientific researchers who cannot count! A European hotel with a black poison-monger and, I may add, nourishment to which one truly needs to become acclimatised, as I have. My hotel is very good—it is four weeks since the window broke, and in pours the rain! The chair is mine and it is my Somali and negro servants who serve the whole hotel. Incidentally, everyone is cheerful here. If you talk to someone, he promptly runs off to do you a favour, never extends his hand and is amazed if he is given something. The virgins hail you with loud 'Jambos' and open their mouths wide enough for a coconut. My good friend, the Sultan, is original in his outlook. The Germans try to skin him, the English won't allow it so that they in turn may skin him quietly later. The one is rude to him, infinitely tactless and bullying, the other protects him, spoils him, fills him with money but has the same aim—to take the skin off him. You may well guess who manages better; and indeed the poor Germans are being killed wherever they are caught.

# APPENDIX 2

## *Emperor Menelik's letter to Heads of State*

THE text of a letter written in the Amharic language, sent by Emperor Menelik II in 1891 to the Heads of State of Britain, France, Germany, Italy and Russia. Five paragraphs which do not relate to the boundary discussed in this work have not been included.

Being desirous to make known to our friends the Powers (Sovereigns) of Europe the boundaries of Ethiopia, we have addressed also to you (your Majesty) the present letter.

These are the boundaries of Ethiopia:
[Three paragraphs of line limits]
Toward the east are included within the frontier the country of Borana Gallas and the Arussi country up to the limit of the Somali's, including also the province of Ogaden.
[Two more paragraphs of line limits]
While tracing today the actual boundaries of my Empire, I shall endeavour, if God gives me life and strength, to re-establish the ancient frontiers of Ethiopia up to Khartoum, and as far as Lake Nyanza with all the Gallas.

Ethiopia has been for fourteen centuries a Christian land in a sea of Pagans. If Powers at a distance come forward to partition Africa between them, I do not intend to be an indifferent spectator.

As the Almighty has protected Ethiopia up to this day, I have confidence that He will continue to protect her, and increase her borders in the future. I am certain He will not suffer her to be divided among other Powers.

Formerly the boundary of Ethiopia was the sea. Having lacked sufficient strength, and having received no help from Christian powers, our frontier on the sea fell into the power of Mussulman.

At present we do not intend to regain our sea frontier by force, but we trust that the Christian Power, guided by our Saviour will restore to us our sea-coast line, at any rate, certain points on the coast.

Written at Addis Ababa, the 14th Mazir, 1883 EC (April 10, 1891).

# APPENDIX 3

## *Instructions from Sir Percy Girouard for the Northern Frontier District*

CONFIDENTIAL                                                      GOVERNMENT HOUSE

Secretary,

The following instructions should be conveyed to Mr. Hope as to the administration of what is presently intended to be called 'The Northern Frontier District'.

JURISDICTION. Mr Hope will for the present work in conjunction with the Provincial Commissioner, Kenia, until such time as he can definitely report to me that this independent unit can be established.

BOUNDARIES. The Northern Frontier District will comprise the present Meru District of the Kenia Province on the South; its western boundary will be the Baringo District of the Naivasha Province; on the north the still undefined Abyssinian Boundary; on the east a boundary to be fixed at a later period when Mr. Hope with the fresh knowledge which he may get and his present knowledge of Jubaland may be able to recommend a boundary line.

GARRISON. It is intended for the present to maintain a military force both at Marsabit and at Moyale. The O.C. Troops at these two stations should do everything in their power to assist in the administration until such time as more definite civil arrangements can be made for police protection &c. I would impress on Mr. Hope the desirability of building up his Police as tribal police somewhat on the method adopted by Mr. Horne at Meru. Protectorate policy will only be made available for headquarter work and for dealing with any non-natives of the frontier district who may have committed offences within the area.

NATIVE COURTS. The establishment of Native Courts should be considered.

POLICY. I would impress upon Mr. Hope and all officers the importance of the work which is to be carried out on the frontier. The present situation in Abyssinia demands very careful handling in the northern district. Every care must be taken to avoid anything in the nature of hostilities and great discretion used with regard to illicit ivory hunting &c. I should hope to see as a result of the administration slow work for the next 6/9 months but the eventual gathering of much useful information which would then justify us in dealing with a situation thoroughly appreciated. The Secretary of State would decide when the services of Mr. Zaphiro are to be utilized, and this could be done and reported on. I am not in favour of the employment of Abyssinian mercenaries at Moyale; the military forces ought to be sufficient for our purposes.

After Mr. Hope has obtained a thorough knowledge of the conditions obtaining at his base, Meru, he should proceed to Marsabit and Moyale. I must request however that no movement should be made to any great distance from these posts without my special sanction.

S/d. E.P.C. Girouard.
Feb. 16th 1910.

# APPENDIX 4

## *Specification of N.F.D. Trucks*

T HE 2 ton Autocar was built in America at the Autocar factory in Philadelphia. Its short 8 feet long chassis was extremely sturdy, made from channel-section pressed steel, with a reinforcing of hard wood. The large 36 × 6 inch pneumatic tyres originally fitted were later replaced by solid rubber tyres for trouble-free running in the frontier district. The power unit was most unusual in that there were only two large opposed cylinders of 4¾ inch bore, which produced 18–20 horsepower, and had the advantage of easy accessibility: big ends could be adjusted by simply undoing a top cover and replacing shims; decarbonising could be done in a few minutes by removing the spark-plug and a lower plug, and scratching around with a screwdriver. The back axle was massive, with Timken roller bearings used throughout. All in all this compact and simple truck was in many ways eminently suitable for the pioneering work it had to do in the Northern Frontier District.

The Napier truck was built in Britain by D. Napier and Son Limited. The model used in East Africa was most probably the 45 hundredweight version, which first came off the assembly line in early 1915. A more orthodox-looking vehicle than the Autocar, the Napier had a four-cylinder engine producing 20 horsepower, and was used extensively by the military in the First World War.

# TEXT NOTES

TO avoid the distraction of endnote indicators in the text I have resorted to the system of writing explanatory notes for each section. Included in these notes are most of my acknowledgements. By using this means I hope I have made the background to the construction of the work more digestible. Full details of the books, papers and official documents from which quotes were extracted appear in the Bibliography.

## PROLOGUE

FOR permission to include the passage from *Black Laughter* I am grateful to Redcliffe Press.

## IN THE BEGINNING

## *One*  The Mythical Giants

IN my attempt to translate an anthropologist's problem into lay language I was greatly assisted by three able students of the subject: Dr Harry Merrick, at one time on the staff of the National Museum in Nairobi; James de Vere Allen, a well-known East African historian; and Dr Paul Robinson, a world authority on the Gabbra people. The latter two gave me invaluable assistance with their wholly constructive criticism of the early drafts. The final stamp of approval came from James Allen, although I must take full blame for any deficiencies in the construction and writing of the text. Book references to the wells and cairns came from Donaldson Smith's *Through Unknown African Countries*, Dracopoli's *Through Jubaland to the Lorian Swamp*, Hodson's *Seven Years in Southern Ethiopia*, and Huxley's *White Man's Country*. Gabbra comments on the Wardai came from Paul Robinson's erudite thesis on the Gabbra tribe, and the early postulations by Curle and Watson were extracted from *MAN*, the Royal Anthropological Institute's publication. The remarks by Aylmer and Maud came from their writings in the *Geographical Journal*, the quarterly magazine published by the Royal Geographical Society. John Llewellin's note came from private papers of his in my possession. I am also grateful to Dr Daniel Stiles for his ready willingness to provide me with information on his cairn excavations at Kalacha. I have not tried to prove anything in this chapter; I am not qualified to do so, and one can only hope that in the near future adequate funds and suitable persons may continue the fascinating research work started by Stiles. In my own superficial examination of cairns, wells and hidden troves of rock art, many miles were covered, and some remote and hardly touched places were visited.

## *Two*   The Nomads

RESEARCHING material for this subject meant dabbling in the specialised field of ethnography and introduced me, an amateur in the topic, to the study of tribal traditions and history. Two of the most up-to-date works on the peoples of the region were consulted while writing about them. Dr Neal Sobania's scholarly dissertation was invaluable for a broad view of the tribes who live in the Lake Rudolf region, and Dr Paul Robinson's recent thesis was used in describing the Gabbra race's travails. Two other useful references were read: Dr Spencer's explicit account of the curious Samburu/Rendille relationship, and Paul Goto's paper on his fellow-tribesmen, the Borana. The early European comments came from the works of von Höhnel, *Discovery by Count Teleki of Lakes Rudolf and Stefanie*, Neumann, *Elephant Hunting in East Equatorial Africa*, Thomson, *Through Masai Land*, and Stigand, *To Abyssinia through an Unknown Land*.

While there is an element of repetition in the accounts of the various tribes' activities, due mainly to the events common to them all in the 1890s, in fact each group ran its individual course, and in these, anyway, there were clear differences.

For helpful comments and valuable guidance I am indebted to Dr Robinson, whose authoritative advice kept me from veering too far off course.

## THE REVELATION

## *Three*   Those Intrepid Souls

GATHERING material for this part, the heart of the book, involved extensive travel, to England, France, Italy, Scotland and the United States of America. Moreover, research by correspondence reached to Austria, Australia, Hungary, South Africa and Roumania. Local investigation in Kenya necessitated more journeys to the northern parts of the country to supplement my already considerable knowledge of the region.

The line drawing of Menelik in the preamble came from a paper written by Prince Henri d'Orleans in 1898, 'Une visite à l'Empereur Ménélick'.

## Teleki expedition

In my search for information on the main characters, Teleki and von Höhnel, I was afforded the most generous assistance by Dr Christl Unterrainer of the Salzburg University Library. She applied great diligence in answering my many questions, and I am very appreciative of all she did to make the task easier. Her guidance led me towards Budapest and into contact with Dr Pésci of the Hungarian Geographical Society, and Dr Gyula Gábris of the Geography Department of Eötvös University. Both kindly provided me with material on Teleki and also recommended other sources. This in turn led me, in correspondence, to Bucharest, where the Biblioteca Centrala de Stat helpfully sent me a copy of Lajos Erdeyli's booklet on Teleki's journey to Lake Rudolf. I am also most grateful to Lady Judith Listowel, a historian in her own right, who found me accurate details of Teleki's family background. Two Hungarian friends gave me sterling help by translating long passages of Erdeyli's work: I owe George Balazs and Sándor Liptay Wagner gratitude for this chore well done. Iris Hunt ably assisted me in translating (from the German) biographical material on Teleki and von Höhnel.

The section's foundation was based on von Höhnel's classic two-volume account of the pair's long journey, *Discovery by Count Teleki of Lakes Rudolf and Stefanie*. References to Teleki's nature were taken from Sir Frederick Jackson's *Early Days in East Africa* and Sir John Willoughby's *East Africa and its Big Game*. An extract from the Royal Geographical Society's obituary of von Höhnel is quoted, and a page from a fascinating manuscript written by von Höhnel for Sir Vivian Fuchs has been reproduced. This paper divulged the reason why relations between the two explorers were somewhat strained to start with. The suggestive remark by Xantus came from the Hungarian publication *ACTA*.

The National Library of Austria in Vienna produced the photographs of Prince Rudolf, Princess Stefanie and Teleki. The picture of von Höhnel came from the Chanler archive in Rokeby, while the line drawings came from his account of the journey.

## Chanler expedition

For access to the Chanler home, Rokeby, some seventy miles up the Hudson river from New York City, I am first of all indebted to Mrs Maddie De Mott, a niece of the irascible American explorer. She introduced me to her nephew, Winthrop Aldrich, who as the family historian extended kind hospitality and a ready willingness to assist in my search. Two days were spent contentedly browsing through the contents of a small tin chest full of papers, correspondence between Chanler and von Höhnel, letters to his sisters written during his disastrous expedition in 1892, and a pile of the original photographs taken by him. Yellowed with age, and of poor quality, they represent the only surviving pictorial record of the journey. Working in the history-laden atmosphere of the old library, surrounded by Chanler family memorabilia, was an experience not to be forgotten.

Source material used in this section came mainly from Chanler's own account of his expeditions, *Through Jungle and Desert*. Some brief passages from letters to his sisters helped to illustrate his mentality, and a descriptive piece of von Höhnel writing was found in the New York Historical Society's archives. The latter was of great value in describing in detail von Höhnel's first meeting with Chanler and the events that followed as a consequence.

The portraits of Chanler and Galvin came by courtesy of the Chanler and Galvin families respectively.

### Neumann expedition

Locating material on Neumann was eased by the fact that for many years collecting information on the tragic man has been a hobby of mine. Supplementary details came from Mrs Patsy Heckterman, who trustingly loaned me a selection of documents, including Neumann's own annotated maps, a few of his photographs and sundry minor papers. From Miss Iris Plinston came more family background and a rare photograph of him, probably the last ever taken. Raoul Millais, the son of Neumann's great artist friend, and possibly the only white man alive who remembers him in person, told me what he could recall of him in 1907. Graham Sacker, the owner of Neumann's two war medals, did his best to assist me in my search for his burial place, but to no avail. Involved in this difficult project, too, was Colonel Lionel Leach, whose industry turned up a curious little news cutting from the *Daily Mirror* about Neumann's death by suicide. Tony Dyer generously loaned me a typewritten transcript of Neumann's last diary. Finally, the enthusiasm of Dr George Yerbury resulted in much useful information, from which Neumann's will, the greatest prize of all, was run to ground.

While the principal publication used in composing the section was Neumann's own book, *Elephant Hunting in East Equatorial Africa*, others consulted included Margery Perham's *Lugard's Diaries*, J.G. Millais's *Wanderings and Memories*, and R. Meinertzhagen's *Kenya Diary*. Some interesting papers on Neumann were turned up in the Public Records Office in Kew. My thanks are also due to Mr Charles Gore, Keeper of Relics at Dunvegan Castle, for his assistance in research. Permission to quote Meinertzhagen came from Eland Books.

### Donaldson Smith expedition I

The meticulous American doctor is well known in the annals of exploration in east Africa. He was the second noteworthy American to visit the region, but despite this he proved most elusive in research. By good fortune a friend, Dr Pascal Imperato of New York, produced a comprehensive document on the explorer just as I was coming to the end of my text. The culmination of twenty-five years of careful fact-finding, the fascinating life story proved of particular value to me when composing Donaldson Smith's biographical vignette. I am indebted to Dr Imperato for a copy of his perceptive paper, a variety of useful photographs, and for being a willing and generous research ally.

In describing Donaldson Smith's journey, the only reference work used was his own volume, *Through Unknown African Countries*. Brief extracts from the President of the Royal Geographical Society's vote of thanks to the explorer's report on his second expedition came from the December 1900 issue of the *Geographical Journal*.

## Bottego expedition

The redoubtable Italian explorer was a rewarding subject. A special journey was made to his home town of Parma in northern Italy, where, thanks to the efforts of a good friend who lives there, Dr Michele Vitali, not only were visits made to places of particular interest in the Bottego story, but of even more importance I was introduced to two persons who proved of invaluable assistance. Professor Vittorio Parisi of the Natural History Department in Parma University, and the keyholder of the renowned Bottego Museum, showed me round that amazing repository of nature specimens, all collected by the industrious soldier-explorer. Furthermore, he generously supplied me with copies of material I needed for my work. The second, and the most important link with the Bottego research, was Manlio Bonati, who is considered a world authority on the subject. For two years he, in an able and generous manner, answered my questions, researched for me and found rare photographs. In the end he edited the biographic text and corrected the inevitable mistakes. A historian by hobby, his advice was highly valued.

The classic volume written by the two survivors, Citerni and Vanutelli, *L'Omo*, was the main source of information on which the Bottego saga was based. For some useful background I consulted Campioni's *I Giam Giam*, and the little magazine *Historia*. A few extracts from biographical dictionaries helped to fill in the gaps. Much of the labour of translation was done with the assistance of Mrs Juliana Moretti and Dr Vitali.

## Cavendish expedition

Finding material on the subject proved difficult. Only two sources of any substance were located. To describe his expedition, the account of his talk to the Royal Geographical Society, as reported in the April 1898 number of the *Geographical Journal*, was used exclusively. A contemporary photograph of him was found in the German geographical publication *Globus*. Efforts to find some shred of information on his companion, Lieutenant Andrew, met with no success. Even the British Museum of Natural History had difficulty in coming up with anything, despite Cavendish's generous donations of specimens to their stores. Contacts with the Waterpark family also failed to produce results, so Cavendish remains a shadowy figure.

## Delamere expedition

The account of Lord Delamere's journey relied on sparse background material for its construction: principally his biography by Elspeth Huxley, *White Man's Country*. A photograph album held in Rhodes House Library, Oxford, contained a series of photographs taken by Delamere during his long trek. The annotations are his only written records. Using these two documents the story of Delamere's extraordinary meandering course was assembled. As with Cavendish it was minimal material on which to base the account.

## Wellby expedition

To start with material on Wellby, apart from his book, proved hard to find. However, the able sleuthing of Mrs Christine Kelly, the Royal Geographical Society's Archivist, helped to run the explorer's nephew to ground in County Kerry, Eire. After that all went easily, and a meeting in London gathered Guy Wellby and two of his sisters, Barbara and Nancy, to meet me and show what material they had on their uncle. It was of great interest, one volume being packed with cuttings collected by Wellby's mother from British newpapers describing the explorer's progress and ultimate success. A quick visit to the historic village of Westham in Sussex took me to the Norman church in which the Wellby memorial window stands. The regimental museum of the 13/18 Hussars provided information on Wellby's army life.

Armed with Wellby's own publication, *'Twixt Sirdar and Menelik*, two quotes from his obituary in the *Geographical Journal* of September 1900 and one from the *Army Quarterly* magazine, there was ample substance from which to describe his epic journey. An extract out of a letter from the Librarian of Rugby School pointedly described Wellby's 'lack of scholarliness'.

### Donaldson Smith expedition II

This section was compiled entirely from his paper to the Royal Geographical Society.

### Harrison expedition

It was not, in my opinion, a true journey of exploration—certainly not with the spirit and dedication of the Donaldson Smith and Wellby efforts. Essentially geared to the sporting interest of the various members, it did nevertheless survey fragments of new country, and of importance for the present purpose it skirted along Lake Rudolf's shores. Harrison did not prove an easy person to research, but a visit to the handsome home he once owned, Brandesburton Hall, now a hospital, proved he must have been a man of means and local influence. All photographs of him exhibit a rather surly expression, and one is left wondering what sort of person he really was. On perusing correspondence it becomes quite understandable why Powell-Cotton fell out with him early on in the trip. Because there were four members, research took me to far parts. For the scant material on Harrison, the Hull Central Library was most helpful. On Powell-Cotton there was much, and I am grateful to his son, Christopher, in his own right an old Africa (Uganda) hand, who allowed me access to his father's papers in the Quex House Museum. The Scottish member, Butter, will be met again, and is given fuller treatment on p. 416. Whitehouse proved the hardest person to run to ground, but a stroke of good fortune gave me his son's address in Florida. I am indebted to William Whitehouse for kindly providing me with anything I asked for on his father, and for sending me a copy of his elusive extract, *To Lake Rudolph and Beyond*. Armed with this conglomeration of family backgrounds I was enabled to write briefly on the mixed little group.

The expedition's route was described from Harrison's paper in the September 1901 *Geographical Journal*. This was augmented by Powell-Cotton's comments in the early pages of his book, *A Sporting Trip through Abyssinia*, and brief remarks in his personal diary. The discussion about Royal Geographical Society sponsorship was found in a series of letters between Harrison and Dr Keltie which provided a titbit pertinent to the former's attitude to his venture.

### Austin expedition

In view of the horrendous human mortality, Austin's journey was by far the most disastrous of the fourteen expeditions to Lake Rudolf described. The Royal Engineer officer was an exceptional man, as was confirmed by his son in an interview. Despite his formidable experience of railway surveying in India and Africa, endless months caravaning in the wilds, and later a variety of postings and activities, the dynamic man never learnt to drive a motor vehicle. An early attempt ended up with the car bent round a tree. That decided him never to take the wheel again! I was provided with every facility to research Austin by his grandson Simon, who keeps the family archive. It was at a lunch kindly arranged by Simon that I met Austin's son and daughter, discussed their father, saw pertinent papers, and most rewarding of all had a sight of the beautifully inscribed gold watch presented to him by the Royal Geographical Society. The family, in allowing me to borrow two precious photographs of Austin showed great trust, and I am grateful for their generosity. I am also indebted to Miss E.D. Norris of the Royal Engineer's Library at Chatham, who answered my questions in correspondence, and assisted me on the day I spent in the library researching Austin, Gwynn and Maud.

Books used for descriptive extracts included Austin's own *Rambles of a Sapper* and *With Macdonald in Uganda*. Others used were Sir Frederick Jackson's *Early Days in East Africa*, and a paper describing the rules laid down by the Royal Geographical Society for their Cuthbert Peek award. The account of his troubled march was written with the aid of two documents: papers Austin wrote for the June 1902 issue of the *Geographical Journal* and Volume XVIII of the *Royal Scottish Geographical Society Magazine*.

### Wickenburg expedition

Describing this unusual man and his journey in 1901 was probably one of the most absorbing tasks in the series. The Austrian count has never before been extensively written about in the English language, and I was privileged in being allowed to make the first modest attempt. It came about through a request by an Austrian lady who asked whether I could take her up to remote Mt Foroli on the Kenya–Ethiopia border. As it turned out she was none other than Wickenburg's daughter, Baroness Marietheres Waldbott Bassenheim. Following that first pilgrimage we made two more trips, tracing her father's trail from Lake Stefanie to Marsabit and down to Laisamis. With his exquisite maps to guide us, we plotted many of his campsites and visited scenes he had described over eighty years before. I owe much to Marietheres for her generous provision of papers describing his journey, copies of his photographs, and last but not least, her company on those safaris. With all that to build on I was able to compile a short account of the amazing man's lonely trek. To Hanns Windhager I am grateful for the translation of many pages of German text.

### De Bozas expedition

While the young Frenchman shared the same fate as Bottego, in his case the diaries kept, the maps made and the specimens collected all reached France in safety. Paris proved the focal point for gathering material on the ill-fated man. I owe gratitude to old family friends there, the de Longevialles, for their help in my research. Guy, a man who spent forty years of his adult life in Kenya, and an amateur historian himself, was my kind host. Corinne, his daughter, found me a beautiful copy of the expedition's published account, and Hugue, his son, translated several documents I found in the Bibliothèque Nationale in Paris. In that institution I was given able assistance by Alfred Fierro. Professor Marcel-M. Chartier of La Société de Géographie kindly provided papers on the subject and directed me to other sources.

With the expedition account in hand, the de Bozas section was written. A rusty ability at French was stretched to the limit, but with the assistance of two friends, Bruce Baum and Dr Marie Pierre Stefan, this obstacle was overcome and quoted passages ably checked. The well-illustrated volume, *De la Mer Rouge a L'Atlantique*, was the sound base on which the story was told.

### Stigand expedition

A man with an exceptional variety of interests, all of which he pursued with energy and studious diligence, Stigand was a renowned figure on the East African scene of pre-World War I days. He appeared to have been a dynamo of industry, and this is clear from the versatility and volume of his writings. Numerous books and articles were produced, many to be published, others to lie sleeping in the dark corners of archives. Some of these were used in the preparation of this text. Good fortune smiled on me when I located his granddaughter, Lady Juliet Chilston. In her hands are safely lodged an entertaining manuscript autobiography he wrote not long before he met his end in the Sudan. Moreover, she also holds intimate letters from Stigand to his wife written during the last months of his life. These very personal records containing his latter-day feelings towards his profession were most illuminating, and I am most grateful to her for allowing me access to such precious family records.

Papers used in putting together Stigand's story were his books, *To Abyssinia through an Unknown Land* and the posthumously published *Equatoria* (the latter contains the valuable Wingate memoir), his manuscript autobiography, and sundry family letters. In addition a letter and a long resume of his life written by a distant relative came from the Oriental Library in Durham University. Within the Royal Geographical Society's archives lie a sizeable collection of his unpublished typescripts and his last diary, which were also consulted.

## STRIDING ONWARDS

## *Four* The Theodolite Brigade

IN constructing this piece I was confronted with the jugglings of international politics, which involved searching through a wide variety of material. The description of what could have been a very dry affair was brightened by the discovery of the private diaries written by the two principals on the 1903 survey expedition—Butter and Maud. I am indebted to John Butter's kind hospitality, and for the loan of his father's diaries (six notebooks) and private letters relating to the trip. I was also allowed to photograph Butter's portrait, and copy pictures from the voluminous album of Harrison expedition photos. All these, except for the portrait, were found buried in a cupboard in the Butter's Scottish home. Finding Maud's papers proved more difficult, and Christine Kelly once again did her bit successfully. A son, Colonel David Maud, was finally tracked down in a far corner of Somerset, and he too turned up trumps, producing his father's diary and other papers, plus a superb photograph of the stern man. To the late David Maud goes my gratitude for entrusting me with those precious things. Both these sets of diaries were used extensively to humanise an otherwise mundane subject. Obtaining information on Count Colli was a matter Manlio Bonati in Parma succeeded in doing. He came up with a photograph of the man, together with some literature. One of the papers had been written by Professor G. Vedovato of La Società Geografica Italiana. For the comments on Zaphiro I relied on the words of John Cardovillis. A fellow Greek, he knew Zaphiro well in the days they both lived in Addis Ababa. This background was supported by the article Chenevix Trench wrote for *History Today*.

The writing of the chapter was accomplished with the aid of the following books and papers. First of all, the subject of the opening paragraph came from the historic first volume of *Icecap*. Other material used came from three books: Donaldson Smith's *Through Unknown African Countries*, McEwen's *International Boundaries of East Africa* and Wellby's *'Twixt Sirdar and Menelik*. An interesting analysis of the boundary problem came from Marcus's paper. It proved of great value in that it described the sequence of events and so gave me a skeleton on which to build. Brief quotations came from Gwynn's article in the *Geographical Journal*. Extracts from documents (C.O. 533, F.O. 1, F.O. 401, F.O. 403) in the Public Records Office illustrated several points.

# *Five*  Pax Britannica

PROBABLY the most outstanding figure in this chapter was Glenday. Very early in my search I found his youngest son, Richard, who fortunately holds all that remains of the family papers and pictures. This was a substantial enough store of material, and I appreciated the generosity with which I, a complete stranger, was entrusted with much of it for study and copying. It formed a base on which to construct a picture of the man's forthright character. For a personal recollection of Glenday I have letters from William Hale, who served under him as a District Commissioner in the late 1930s. For the clerihew on him I am grateful to Sir Richard Turnbull, who originally composed the lines. Early on in my research I was most fortunate in meeting Lady Winifred Kittermaster, who, although ninety years of age, arranged for all the papers available in family hands on her late husband to be at my disposal. I am very grateful to her for the loan of precious photographs, a diary, and her permission to copy pictures. Later, her daughter Helen allowed me to have the evocative photograph of the oxwaggon crossing the Uaso Ngiro river reproduced. Carey Keates, John Llewellin's nephew, kindly showed me what he had on his uncle, and John Bamber likewise told me what he remembered of his father. Information on Archer was scant, but brief comments in sundry letters in Rhodes House Library, Oxford, and correspondence with Kenneth Henderson, late of the Sudan Civil Service, all aided in making a picture of the man. Lesley Forbes of Durham University Oriental Library was helpful in researching material and photographs from the Archer collection. On the important part the Boma Trading Company played I relied heavily on private papers. Elizabeth ('Diggy') Spyratos, Riddell's daughter, most generously went out of her way to bring papers, photographs and sundry documents all the way from California and Greece for my perusal. For her considerate act I am very grateful, as it enabled me to give a description of her father and the activities of his unfortunate company. John Ward likewise willingly supplied material on his father. This was supplemented by some military research by a friend interested in army history, Sir Torquil Matheson, who clarified Ward's career in the Irish Guards. Through the Riddell family I was put in touch with Antony Hornyold. He assisted as much as he could, providing me with background history on his father and the family. I owe Mrs Yvonne Bell a debt of gratitude for allowing me to spend several days going through her father's diaries, papers, letters and photographs. Fred Roy's records in diaries and letters are brilliant descriptions of his day, enhanced by his exquisite handwriting which made reading the more pleasurable. The accounts gave a close look at the events of far-off days, and sharply clear photographs—amazingly all developed by himself in the wilds—depict scenes and people vividly. This was a treasure trove of Kenya history. Two historic photographs—the group of administration officers and the picture of the Northern Frontier car—came respectively from friends, Tom Bower and Brian Boulton. To various schools in England I must express my thanks for information on former pupils: Eton, Harrow, Shrewsbury and St Bees. Oxford colleges that assisted were Christ Church, Lincoln and Wadham. Dr Mason of the first and Dr Clifford Davies of the last were always willing to answer my questions and send me useful material. The Royal Greenjackets Museum in Winchester produced a background on Aylmer, and the Imperial War Museum and the National Army Museum in London also found snippets of information. The War Graves Commission helpfully sent me the drawing of the King's African Rifles badge of the period. The National Motor Museum came up with literature on the Autocar and Napier trucks. Writing about Neave was aided by Mrs Venetia Halstead who provided me with information on her grandfather. Dugand was a grey shadow until Mr Ronald Nelson showed me a photograph from a wartime album, and explained they had campaigned together in 1941 against the Italians in Abyssinia.

A formidable mound of literature was used in compiling this account. Undoubtedly the most valuable staff I leant on was Dr Gordon Mungeam's highly readable *British Rule in Kenya 1895–1912*. For a perceptive appraisal of that period in Kenya's history it is hard to beat, and for my special task it proved a good friend. Other books consulted included Archer's *Personal and Historic Memoirs of an East African Administrator*, Dutton's well-coloured *Lillibulero*, Sir Charles Eliot's *The East Africa Protectorate*, Lloyd Jones's two soldiering tales *Havash!* and *K. A. R.*, McDermott's famous explanation in *I.B.E.A.*, and Moyse Bartlett's military account *History of the King's African Rifles*. Not to be forgotten on the list is the little handbook *Jubaland and the Northern Frontier District.* In addition many official documents in the Public Records Office were consulted, and pertinent passages have been quoted. After considerable research in the Kenya National Archives in Nairobi extracts were taken from its fascinating files. The documents from these two sources from which quotations were taken appear in the Bibliography.

# *Six*  Tinker, Tailor . . .

THESE anecdotes were all along planned as a lightweight ending to the book, despite the rather macabre mishaps to some of those concerned. They prove it was not a country to treat lightly, although several tried.

A fascinating mixture of papers and books were used in its preparation. For instance, an original manuscript of Kolb's produced the candid self-criticism of his writing ability; the last field diary kept by the manic-depressive Neumann sadly views the changes in the district he preferred above others; the itinerant Arkell Hardwick's book *An Ivory Trader in North Kenia* described a somewhat profitless trip, but has interesting reflections on Dr Atkinson's make-up, substantiated by remarks in Errol Trzebinski's *The Kenya Pioneers*; Patterson's rather pompous and self-righteous tale *In the Grip of the Nyika*, still provokes thought—it did in fact prompt the late Ernest Hemingway to write a novel based on the incident of Bligh's death; the tragic tale of young Gordon's demise came from a short account written by John Llewellin of his early days in the Northern Frontier titled 'My sole claim to fame'; and last but certainly not least, the bit about John Boyes came partly from his own book, *The Company of Adventurers*, partly from Hunter's compendium, *Bush Adventures*, and partly from the Northern Frontier bible, *Jubaland and the Northern Frontier District*. To add padding here and there, bits were used from Roy's diaries, Colonial Office documents and out of Kenya National Archives files.

The American influence was extracted from Roosevelt's well-known volume, *African Game Trails*, and White's little gem of descriptive writing *The Land of Footprints*. The photographs of Roosevelt and White were kindly provided by the Smithsonian News Agency and Dr Harwood White respectively. Brief mention of an early tourist hunting elephants came from Archer's autobiography, *Personal and Historical Memoirs* . . . while from Dr Henry Clay Frick II came the information on his versatile father.

Probably one of the last persons to make a solid contribution to geography in the district was Dracopoli. I am grateful to his relations in Italy for giving details on him, plus a perfect portrait.

At the very last, ladies made an appearance. It was not really their kind of country, but there are alway adventurous ones, and Adele Bailey undoubtedly won the prize. A photograph from the collection of the admiring Archer clearly shows why.

# BIBLIOGRAPHY

Archer, Sir Geoffrey, *Personal and Historical Memoirs of an East African Administrator*. London: Oliver and Boyd, 1963.

Arkell-Hardwick, A., *An Ivory Trader in North Kenia*. London: Longmans, Green, 1903.

Austin, H.H., *Among Swamps and Giants in Equatorial Africa*. London: Edward Arnold, 1902.

——, *Some Rambles of a Sapper*. London: Edward Arnold, 1928.

——, *With Macdonald in Uganda*. London: Edward Arnold, 1903; reprinted by Dawsons of Pall Mall, London, 1973.

Barclay, Edgar N., *Big Game Shooting Records*. London: Witherby, 1932.

Boyes, John, *The Company of Adventurers*. London: 'East Africa', 1927.

Campioni, Silvio, *I Giam Giam*. Parma: Casa Editrice Luigi Battei, 1960.

Chanler, William Astor, *Through Jungle and Desert*. London: Macmillan, 1896.

Churchill, Winston S., *My African Journey*. London: Hodder and Stoughton, 1908.

De Bozas, Vicomte Robert du Bourg (Editor F.R. de Rudeval), *De la Mer Rouge a L'Atlantique*. Paris: Rudeval, 1906.

Donaldson Smith, Dr A., *Through Unknown African Countries*. London: Edward Arnold, 1897; reprinted by Greenwood Publishers, New York, 1969.

Dracopoli, I.N., *Through Jubaland to the Lorian Swamp*. London: Seeley, Service, 1914.

Dutton, E.A.T., *Lillibulero or the Golden Road*. Zanzibar: Private Printing, 1947.

Eliot, Sir Charles, *The East Africa Protectorate*. London: Edward Arnold, 1905.

Erdelyi, Lajos, *Teleki Samu Afrikaban*. Bucharest: Kriterion Konyukiado, 1977.

Foran, W. Robert, *The Kenya Police, 1887–1960*. London: Hale, 1962.

Greenfield, R., *Ethiopia*. London: Pall Mall Press, 1965.

Hardy, Ronald, *The Iron Snake*. London: Collins, 1965; New York, Putnam, 1965.

Hindlip, Lord, *Sport and Travel—Abyssinia and British East Africa*. London: Fisher Unwin, 1906.

Hodson, Arnold Weinholt, *Seven Years in Southern Abyssinia*. London: Fisher Unwin, 1927.

Höhnel, Ludwig von, *Discovery by Count Teleki of Lakes Rudolf and Stefanie*. London: Longmans, Green, 1894.

Hollis, A.C., *The Masai, Their Language and Folklore*. Oxford: Clarendon Press, 1905.

Hunter, J.A. and Mannix, Daniel P., *African Bush Adventures*. London: Hamish Hamilton, 1954.

Huxley, Elspeth, *White Man's Country*. London: Chatto and Windus, 1935; reprinted by Praeger, New York, 1968.

Jackson, Sir Frederick, *Early Days in East Africa*. London: Edward Arnold, 1930; reprinted by Dawsons of Pall Mall, London, 1969.

Letcher, O., *The Bonds of Africa*. London: John Long, 1913.

Lloyd Jones, W., *Havash!* London: Arrowsmith, 1925.

——, *K.A.R.* London: Arrowsmith, 1926.

Meinertzhagen, R., *Kenya Diary 1902–1906*. London: Oliver and Boyd, 1957.

Millais, J. G., *Wanderings and Memories*. London: Longmans, Green, 1919.

Millar, Charles, *The Lunatic Express*. London: Macdonald, 1927.

Monod, Théodore, *Pastoralism in Tropical Africa*. London: Oxford University Press, 1975.

Moorehead, Alan, *The White Nile*. New York: Harper and Bros, 1960.

Moyse-Bartlett, H., *The King's African Rifles*. Aldershot: Gale and Polden, 1956.

McDermott, P.L., *British East Africa or IBEA*. London: Chapman and Hall, 1893; reprinted by Frank Cass, London, 1971.

McEwen, A.C., *International Boundaries of East Africa*. Oxford: Clarendon Press, 1971.

Mungeam, Dr G.H., *British Rule in Kenya 1895–1912*. Oxford: Clarendon Press, 1966.

Neumann, A.H., *Elephant Hunting in East Equatorial Africa*. London: Rowland Ward, 1898; reprinted by Abercrombie and Fitch, New York, 1966.

Patterson, J.H., *In the Grip of the Nyika*. London: Macmillan, 1909.

Perham, Margery, *Lugard's Diaries*. London: Faber and Faber, 1959.

Powell-Cotton, P.G., *A Sporting Trip through Abyssinia*. London: Rowland Ward, 1902.

Powys, Llewellyn, *Black Laughter*. New York: Harcourt, Brace, 1924; reprinted by Redcliffe Press, Bristol, 1983.

Pratt, D.J. and Gwynne, M.D., *Rangeland Management and Ecology in East Africa*. London: Hodder and Stoughton, 1977.

Rey, C.F., *The Real Abyssinia*. London: Seeley Service, 1935.

Roosevelt, Theodore, *African Game Trails*. New York: Syndicate Publishing, 1910.

Spencer, Paul, *Nomads in Alliance*. London: Oxford University Press, 1973.

Stigand, C.H., *To Abyssinia through an Unknown Land*. London: Seeley, 1910.

——, *Equatoria: The Lado Enclave*. London: Constable, 1923.

Stirling, John, *The Colonials in South Africa 1899–1902*. Edinburgh: William Blackwood, 1909.

Thomas, Lately, *A Pride of Lions*. New York: William Morrow, 1971.

Thomson, Joseph, *Through Masai Land*. Boston: Houghton Mifflin, 1885; reprinted by Frank Cass, London, 1968.

Trzebinski, Errol, *The Kenya Pioneers*. London: Heinemann, 1985.

Weisbord, Robert, *African Zion*. Philadelphia: Jewish Publication Society of America, 1968.

Wellby, M.S., *'Twixt Sirdar and Menelik*. London: Harper, 1901; reprinted by Negro Universities Press, New York, 1969.

White, Stewart Edward, *The Land of Footprints*. London: Thomas Nelson, 1912.

Wickenburg, Count E., *Wanderungen in Ost-Afrika*. Vienna: Gerold, 1899.

Willoughby, Sir John C., *East Africa and its Big Game*. London: Longmans Green, 1889.

Vanutelli, L. and Citerni, C., *L'Omo*. Milan: Ulrico Hoepli, 1899.

# OFFICIAL RECORDS

1. Kenya National Archives, Nairobi.

Documents used for reference, and for quotations in the text, came from the following files:

| a. | PC/NFD1/1/2 | Annual Reports (1913–1921) |
|----|-------------|---------------------------|
| b. | PC/NFD1/4/1 | Annual Reports—Uaso Nyiro Post (Archer's Post) |
| c. | PC/NFD1/6/1 | Annual Reports—Moyale |
| d. | PC/NFD2/1/1 | Handing over reports |
| e. | PC/NFD2/6/1 | Handing over reports—Moyale (1915–31) |
| f. | PC/NFD4/1/2 | |
| g. | PC/NFD4/1/3 | Northern Frontier Political Documents (1910–43) |
| h. | PC/NFD4/3/1 | Abyssinian Affairs—Raids and Claims (1913–19) |
| i. | PC/NFD4/3/2 | Abyssinian Affairs (1913–23) |
| k. | DC/MBT 5/1 | Marsabit reports |
| l. | DC/MBT 7/1/2 | Marsabit Political Records |
| m. | DC/MRU 1/1 | Meru District Annual Reports (1912–24) |

2. Public Records Office, Kew, England.

Material was used from the series CO 533 (volumes 1–115), and CO 534 (King's African Rifles). Extracts also came from FO 1, FO 401, and FO 403.

# SOCIETY RECORDS

1. Royal African Society.

Fuchs, V.E., Foreword to Admiral von Höhnel's manuscript. *R.A.S. Journal* 37 (1938).
Gwynn, C., 'The Frontiers of Abyssinia'. *R.A.S. Journal* 36 (1937).
Höhnel, L. von, 'The Lake Rudolf Region. Its discovery and subsequent exploration 1888–1909'. *R.A.S. Journal* 37 (1938).


2. Royal Geographical Society.

Archer, G., 'Recent Exploration and Survey in the north of British East Africa'. *Geographical Journal* XLII (1913).
Austin, H.H., 'Journeys to the North of Uganda, II Lake Rudolf'. *Geographical Journal* XIV (1899).
——, 'A journey from Omdurman to Mombasa via Lake Rudolf'. *Geographical Journal* XIX (1902).
Aylmer, L., 'The Country between the Juba River and Lake Rudolf'. *Geographical Journal* XXXVIII (1911).
Cavendish, H.S.H., 'Through Somaliland and around and south of Lake Rudolf'. *Geographical Journal* XI (1898).
Donaldson Smith, A., 'An expedition between Lake Rudolf and the Nile'. *Geographical Journal* XVI (1900).
French, C.N., 'A Journey from the River Juba by Dolo, Moyale and Mt. Marsabit to the Uaso Nyiro'. *Geographical Journal* XLII (1913).
Gwynn, C., 'A journey in Southern Abyssinia'. *Geographical Journal* XXXVIII (1911).
Harrison, J.J., 'A journey from Zeila to Lake Rudolf'. *Geographical Journal* XVIII (1901).
Maud, P., 'Exploration of the Southern Borderland of Abyssinia'. *Geographical Journal* XXIII (1904).
Tate, H.R., 'Journey to the Rendille Country, British East Africa'. *Geographical Journal* XXIII (1904).
Wellby, M.S., 'King Menelik's dominion and the country between Lake Gallop (Rudolf) and the Nile Valley'. *Geographical Journal* XVI (1900).
Editor, 'A record of exploration in North-East Africa'. *Geographical Journal* XV (1900).


3. Royal Scottish Geographical Society.

Austin, H.H., 'Through the Sudan to Mombasa via Lake Rudolf'. *Scottish Geographical Magazine* XVIII (1902).
Capenny, H.S.F., 'The Proposed Anglo-Abyssinian Boundary in East Africa'. *Scottish Geographical Magazine* XXI (1905).

4. Sundry Papers.

Allen, J., 'The Freelanders at Lamu, 1894: Whites as Drop-outs'. (British) African Studies Association Annual Conference, Oxford, 1978.

Bulatovich, A.K., 'Dall'Abissinia al Lago Rudolfo per il Caffa'. *Bulletino della Società Geografica Italiana*. Serie IV 1900.

Casada, J., 'The motivational underpinnings of the British exploration of East Africa'. Proceedings of the South Carolina Historical Association, 1973.

Chenevix Trench, C., 'Why a Greek?' *History Today*, vol.15, no.1, 1965.

Curle, A.T., 'Prehistoric Graves in the Northern Frontier Province of Kenya Colony'. *MAN*, 1933.

Imperato, Dr Pascal, 'Arthur Donaldson Smith and the Exploration of Lake Rudolf'. *New York State Journal of Medicine*, 1987.

Kádár, Dr Laszlo, 'The man whose name the African Teleki volcano bears'. *Acta*. Tomus XII–XIII, 1967.

Leontieff, N., 'Explorations des Provinces équatoriales d'Abyssinie'. *La Géographie*, 1900.

Malcolm, G.I., 'Two soldiers in Tibet'. *Army Quarterly*. Vols. 73–74, 1956.

Mountain Club of Kenya, *Icecap*. No.1, 1932.

Parkinson, John, 'The Stone Cairns of Northern Kenya'. *MAN*, 1935.

Riddell, G.H., 'The Boma Trading Company'. *Blackwoods Magazine*, April 1943.

Sobania, Dr N.W., 'Background history of the Mt Kulal Region of Kenya'. IPAL report A-2, 1979.

Stiles, Daniel and Munro-Hay, S.C., 'Stone cairn burials at Kokurmatakore, northern Kenya'. *Azania*, vol. XVI, 1981.

Tate, H.R., 'A journey to Rendille'. *The East African Annual*, 1951–1952.

Troughear, A., 'The lone man who carved Kenya's northern border'. *Sunday Nation*, 24 April 1983.

Watson, C.B.G., 'Wells, Cairns, and Rainpools in Kenya Colony'. *MAN*, 1927.

Whitehouse, W.F., 'To Lake Rudolph and Beyond'.


5. Unpublished Papers and Theses.

Goto, Paul, 'The Boran of Northern Kenya: Origins, Migrations and Settlements in the Nineteenth Century'. B.A. Thesis, University of Nairobi, 1972.

Marcus, H.G., 'Ethio-British Negotiations concerning the Southern Border with British East Africa, 1897–1912'. Haile Selassie University.

Robinson, Dr P.W., 'Gabbra Nomadic Pastoralism in Nineteenth and Twentieth Century Northern Kenya'. D.Phil. Thesis, Northwestern University, Illinois, 1985.

Sobania, Dr N.W., 'The Historical Tradition of the Peoples of the Eastern Lake Turkana Basin c. 1840–1925'. D.Phil. Thesis, University of London, 1980.

# PICTURE SOURCES

# INDEX